ACCOUNTING FOR REAL ESTATE TRANSACTIONS

DEAR PHIL,

THANK YOU FOR REVIEWING
CHAPTER TWO OF THE
MANUSCRIPT!
I APPRECIATE YOUR INPUT!!!
SINCERELY,

Maria

APRIL 2008

Update Service

BECOME A SUBSCRIBER!
Did you purchase this product from a bookstore?

If you did, it's important for you to become a subscriber. John Wiley & Sons, Inc. may publish, on a periodic basis, supplements and new editions to reflect the latest changes in the subject matter that you *need to know* in order to stay competitive in this ever-changing industry. By contacting the Wiley office nearest you, you'll receive any current update at no additional charge. In addition, you'll receive future updates and revised or related volumes on a 30-day examination review.

If you purchased this product directly from John Wiley & Sons, Inc., we have already recorded your subscription for this update service.

To become a subscriber, please call **1-877-762-2974** or send your name, company name (if applicable), address, and the title of the product to:

mailing address: **Supplement Department**
                              John Wiley & Sons, Inc.
                              One Wiley Drive
                              Somerset, NJ 08875

e-mail: **subscriber@wiley.com**
fax: **1-732-302-2300**
online: **www.wiley.com**

For customers outside the United States, please contact the Wiley office nearest you:

Professional & Reference Division
John Wiley & Sons Canada, Ltd.
22 Worcester Road
Etobicoke, Ontario M9W 1L1
CANADA
Phone: 416-236-4433
Phone: 1-800-567-4797
Fax: 416-236-4447
Email: canada@wiley.com

John Wiley & Sons Australia, Ltd.
33 Park Road
P.O. Box 1226
Milton, Queensland 4064
AUSTRALIA
Phone: 61-7-3859-9755
Fax: 61-7-3859-9715
Email: brisbane@johnwiley.com.au

John Wiley & Sons, Ltd.
The Atrium
Southern Gate, Chichester
West Sussex PO 19 8SQ
ENGLAND
Phone: 44-1243-779777
Fax: 44-1243-775878
Email: customer@wiley.co.uk

John Wiley & Sons (Asia) Pte., Ltd.
2 Clementi Loop #02-01
SINGAPORE 129809
Phone: 65-64632400
Fax: 65-64634604/5/6
Customer Service: 65-64604280
Email: enquiry@wiley.com.sg

ACCOUNTING FOR REAL ESTATE TRANSACTIONS

A GUIDE FOR PUBLIC ACCOUNTANTS
AND
CORPORATE FINANCIAL PROFESSIONALS

MARIA K. DAVIS

WILEY

JOHN WILEY & SONS, INC.

For general information on our other products and services, or technical support, please contact our Customer Care Department within the United States at 800-762-2974, outside the United States at 317-572-3993 or fax 317-572-4002.

Wiley also publishes its books in a variety of electronic formats. Some content that appears in print may not be available in electronic books.

For more information about Wiley products, visit our Web site at http://www.wiley.com.

Library of Congress Cataloging-in-Publication Data:

Davis, Maria K.
   Accounting for real estate transactions: a guide for public accountants and corporate financial professionals / Maria K. Davis.
      p. cm.
   Includes index.
      ISBN 978-0-470-19852-0 (cloth)
      1. Real property—Accounting.   2. Real estate investment—Accounting.   I. Title.
   HF5686.R3D38   2008
   657'.8335—dc22
                                                                                2007043222

Printed in the United States of America

10 9 8 7 6 5 4 3 2 1

To Leon Mayshak
who taught me the ins and outs of real estate accounting.

CONTENTS

PREFACE

What is real estate? Land and structures, brick and mortar to some, a bundle of rights and obligations to others. Real estate can be sold outright or it can be securitized. Investors can buy real estate properties or invest in Real Estate Investment Trusts. The many facets of real estate and the size of the real estate market—trillions of U.S. dollars in the United States alone—make it so intriguing. ACCOUNTING FOR REAL ESTATE TRANSACTIONS focuses on historical cost accounting under U.S. Generally Accepted Accounting Principles (U.S. GAAP). It is a comprehensive reference guide that provides financial professionals with a tool to evaluate the accounting consequences of specific deals, enabling them to structure transactions with the accounting consequences in mind and to account for them in accordance with U.S. GAAP. It helps members of audit committees and oversight boards better understand the applicable accounting literature, assess the proper application of the accounting rules, and evaluate the conclusions reached by their companies' management.

The book is divided into two parts:

- Part I of ACCOUNTING FOR REAL ESTATE TRANSACTIONS explains the rules governing a variety of real estate transactions applicable to companies of all industries, the acquisition and development of real estate properties, real estate sales and exchanges, and lease and sale-leaseback transactions.
- Part II of the guide covers accounting for interests in real estate ventures, time-sharing transactions, and retail land sales, which are specific to companies operating in the real estate industry.

Each chapter of ACCOUNTING FOR REAL ESTATE TRANSACTIONS includes a synopsis of authoritative literature related to the type of transaction under discussion, including Financial Accounting Standards Board (FASB) Statements and Interpretations, FASB Staff Positions, FASB Technical Bulletins, consensus positions of the FASB Emerging Issues Task Force, and American Institute of Certified Public Accountants Statements of Position.

Accounting theory is not static and, particularly with U.S. standard-setters focusing on convergence with International Accounting Standards, new concepts are being introduced into U.S. GAAP. Areas for which the question is not whether, but when change will occur include the accounting for real estate leases, for which a major overhaul is expected when the "Lease Project" gets finalized, and fair value accounting for certain assets and liabilities as a result of new standards on the horizon.

This guide will be updated periodically to reflect new authoritative guidance and address emerging issues faced by practitioners.

Readers are welcome to provide feedback and input on accounting issues they believe are prevalent and should be addressed in this guide; these issues will be considered for inclusion in future editions.

ACKNOWLEDGEMENTS

I wish to sincerely thank my husband Richard and my family for their continual encouragement, and all of the friends and professionals who provided comments and suggestions during the research, writing, and production process.

Above all, I would like to extend my special thanks to Bill Platt for his support, and to my colleagues from Deloitte for their input, contributions, and diligent technical review of the manuscript.

TECHNICAL REVIEWERS

Val Bitton	Peter Pruitt
Phil Callif	Dustin Schultz
Chris Dubrowski	Wyn Smith
Michael Harding	Randall Sogoloff
Michael Morrissey	Bob Uhl
Ignacio Perez	Lou Weller

Maria Davis
Norwalk, CT
April 2008

ABOUT THE AUTHOR

Maria K. Davis is a partner in the Accounting Consultation Group at Deloitte & Touche LLP's National Office in Wilton, Connecticut. In her current position, she provides accounting guidance on technical accounting issues, primarily in the subject matters of *Real Estate and Leases* and *Joint Ventures and Consolidation*, both under U.S. GAAP and IFRS. Before joining Deloitte's National Office, she worked directly with Leon Mayshak, who was then Deloitte's Real Estate Industry Professional Practice Director. In that role, Ms. Davis participated actively in the standard-setting process by contributing to the AICPA Statement of Position 04-2, *Accounting for Time-Sharing Transactions*, and the proposed Statement of Position, *Accounting for Certain Costs and Activities Related to Property, Plant, and Equipment*. A native German, Ms. Davis has published on U.S. accounting standards in the pre-eminent German accounting journal *Der Betrieb*. She also contributes to Deloitte's interpretations of accounting standards in Deloitte's Technical Library.

Over the course of her career with Deloitte, Ms. Davis has provided attest and advisory services to Deloitte's clients in a variety of industries in both the United States and Germany.

Ms. Davis received a Master's Degree in Accounting from the University of North Florida, as well as a Degree in Finance from the Hochschule München, Germany. In addition to her CPA qualification, she also holds professional qualifications as a German certified public accountant and a German certified tax advisor. Ms. Davis is a member of several professional organizations, including the American Institute of Certified Public Accountants, the Florida Institute of CPAs, and the German Institute of Certified Public Accountants.

LIST OF ABBREVIATIONS

AcSEC	AICPA Accounting Standards Executive Committee
ADC	Acquisition, Development, Construction
AICPA	American Institute of Certified Public Accountants
AIN	FASB Accounting Interpretation
APB	Accounting Principles Board
ARB	Accounting Research Bulletin
ARDA	American Resort Development Association
CON	FASB Statements of Financial Accounting Concepts
CPI	Consumer Price Index
EITF	Emerging Issues Task Force
FAS	FASB Statement
FASB	Financial Accounting Standards Board
FHA	Federal Housing Administration
FIN	FASB Interpretation
FFO	Funds from Operations
FSP	FASB Staff Position
FTB	FASB Technical Bulletin
FV	Fair Value
GAAP	Generally Accepted Accounting Principles
HLBV	Hypothetical Liquidation at Book Value
HVAC	Heat, Ventilation, and Air-Conditioning
II	Interval International
IAS	International Accounting Standard
IASB	International Accounting Standards Board
IASCF	International Accounting Standards Committee Foundation
IFRIC	International Financial Reporting Interpretations Committee
IFRS	International Financial Reporting Standards
IRC	Internal Revenue Code
LLC	Limited Liability Company
IRS	Internal Revenue Service
MLP	Master Limited Partnership
MLP	Minimum Lease Payments
NAREIT	National Association of Real Estate Investment Trusts
OA	Owners Association

PB	Primary Beneficiary
PP&E	Property, Plant, and Equipment
PRP	Potentially Responsible Party
PV	Present Value
RCI	Resort Condominium International
REIT	Real Estate Investment Trust
SAB	SEC Staff Accounting Bulletin
SEC	Securities and Exchange Commission
SIC	Standing Interpretations Committee
SOP	AICPA Statement of Position
SPE	Special Purpose Entity
TB	FASB Technical Bulletin
TPA	AICPA Technical Practice Aid
UPREIT	Umbrella Partnership Real Estate Investment Trust
U.S. GAAP	U.S. Generally Accepted Accounting Principles
VA	Veterans Administration
VIE	Variable Interest Entity

ACCOUNTING FOR REAL ESTATE TRANSACTIONS

PART 1

ACCOUNTING FOR REAL ESTATE TRANSACTIONS—GENERAL

CHAPTER 1

ACQUISITION, DEVELOPMENT, AND CONSTRUCTION OF REAL ESTATE

1.1   OVERVIEW

Investments in real estate projects require significant amounts of capital. For real estate properties that are developed and constructed, rather than purchased, project costs include the costs of tangible assets, such as land and other hard costs (sometimes referred to as "bricks and mortar"); intangible assets and other soft costs, such as architectural planning and design; and interest and taxes. Costs are often incurred before the actual acquisition of the project, which raises certain questions—for example, from what point in time should costs be capitalized? What types of costs are capitalizable?

Determining what types of costs to capitalize in the preacquisition, acquisition, development, and construction stages of a real estate project has been an issue for many years. Several decades ago, the American Institute of Certified Public Accountants (AICPA) issued the following accounting guidance relating to cost capitalization, reacting to significant diversity in practice:

- Industry Accounting Guide, *Accounting for Retail Land Sales*, issued in 1973
- Statement of Position (SOP) 78-3, *Accounting for Costs to Sell and Rent, and Initial Rental Operations of, Real Estate Projects*, issued in 1978
- SOP 80-3, *Accounting for Real Estate Acquisition, Development, and Construction Costs*, issued in 1980

In 1982, the Financial Accounting Standards Board (FASB) issued FASB Statement No. 67, *Accounting for Costs and Initial Operations of Real Estate Projects*, extracting the accounting principles provided by these AICPA pronouncements. Nevertheless, diversity in practice has continued to exist in some areas, including the capitalization of indirect costs during the development and construction period and the treatment of repair and major maintenance costs incurred subsequent to the completion of real estate projects.

The AICPA undertook another project to develop a comprehensive framework for cost capitalization and, in 2003, issued for public comment the proposed Statement of Position, *Accounting for Certain Costs and Activities Related to Property, Plant, and Equipment*. That proposed SOP was approved by the AICPA Accounting Standards Executive Committee (AcSEC), in September 2003; however, a final SOP was never issued. In April 2004, the FASB decided not to clear that proposed SOP, mainly for the following stated reasons:

- Lack of convergence with International Accounting Standards
- The concept of componentization, particularly the amount of judgment allowed, which could potentially result in lack of comparability
- Implications for the capitalization of major overhaul expenses

1.2 ACQUISITION, DEVELOPMENT, AND CONSTRUCTION COSTS

FASB Statement No. 67 provides the primary authoritative guidance for the cost capitalization of real estate project costs. That Statement divides the costs incurred to acquire, develop, and construct a real estate project into preacquisition and project costs. Preacquisition costs encompass costs incurred in connection with, but prior to the acquisition of, real estate. Project costs include costs incurred at the time of the real estate acquisition, as well as costs incurred during the subsequent development and construction phase (see Exhibit 1.1).

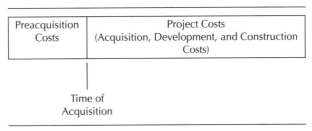

Exhibit 1.1   Illustration of Cost Classification

Real estate developed by a company for use in its own operations other than for sale or rental is not within the scope of Statement 67.[1] Because—aside from the proposed SOP, *Accounting for Certain Costs and Activities Related to Property, Plant, and Equipment*—there is no authoritative literature relating to the capitalization of costs for properties used by an enterprise in its own operations, the guidelines in Statement 67 are generally also applied to properties used by an enterprise in its own operations.

---

1   FAS 67, paragraph 2(a)

1.2.1 PREACQUISITION COSTS   Preacquisition costs are costs related to a real estate property that are incurred for the express purpose of, but prior to, obtaining that property.[2] They may include a variety of costs, such as:

- Payments to obtain an option
- Legal fees
- Architectural fees
- Other professional fees
- Costs of environmental studies
- Costs of feasibility studies
- Costs of appraisals
- Costs of surveys
- Planning and design costs
- Costs for zoning and traffic studies

1.2.1.1 Principles for the Capitalization of Preacquisition Costs
OPTIONS TO ACQUIRE REAL PROPERTY
Payments for options to acquire real property are capitalized.[3]

PREACQUISITION COSTS OTHER THAN OPTIONS TO ACQUIRE REAL PROPERTY
Preacquisition costs other than the cost of options can only be capitalized if the acquisition of the property (or an option to acquire the property) is probable,[4] and if the costs meet the following two criteria:

- The costs must be directly identifiable with the property.
- The costs would be capitalized if the property were already acquired.[5]

FASB Statement No. 67 has established a high threshold for the capitalization of preacquisition costs with the requirement that the acquisition of real property be *probable*. If the purchaser is not actively seeking to acquire the real estate property or does not have the ability to finance or obtain financing for the property, or if there is an indication that the real estate property the purchaser seeks to acquire will not be available for sale, the project is not considered probable.[6] Any costs (other than costs relating to an option to acquire real estate) incurred before a project is considered probable have to be expensed as incurred. If the project becomes probable at a later point in time, costs incurred prior to the project becoming probable cannot subsequently be capitalized.

---

2   FAS 67, Appendix A, paragraph 28
3   Land option deals may pose special accounting issues, as discussed in Section 1.7.3 of this chapter.
4   Footnote 3 of FASB Statement No. 67 states that "probable" in this context means "likely to occur," referring to the use of "probable" in FASB Statement No. 5. Paragraph 13 of the proposed SOP, *Accounting for Certain Costs and Activities Related to Property, Plant, and Equipment*, uses that same threshold for the capitalization of preacquisition costs.
5   FAS 67, paragraph 4
6   FAS 67, paragraph 4(c)

EXAMPLE—PREACQUISITION COSTS

BetterStore Inc. (B) plans to build five storage centers in various cities throughout the United States. Ten suitable land parcels have been identified. The land parcels upon which B is considering building the storage centers are for sale, and B has the ability to obtain financing. The final decision as to which locations to use for the storage centers will be made after certain feasibility studies have been completed. To date, B has paid advisors $1 million for feasibility studies.

Can B capitalize the costs incurred for these feasibility studies?

No. Since B has not identified the specific locations for the storage centers, the costs incurred should be expensed.

Preacquisition costs that meet the requirements for capitalization outlined above are capitalized. Once the real estate property is acquired, any capitalized preacquisition costs are included in project costs. If, on the other hand, a company determines that the acquisition of the property is no longer probable, capitalized preacquisition costs are charged to expense to the extent they are not recoverable through the sale of plans, options, etc.[7]

The proposed SOP, *Accounting for Certain Costs and Activities Related to Property, Plant, and Equipment*, states with respect to preacquisition costs when it becomes probable that the property will not be acquired:[8]

> If it becomes no longer probable that specific PP&E [property, plant, and equipment] will be acquired or constructed, previously capitalized preacquisition stage costs related to the specific PP&E should be reduced to the lower of cost or fair value. A rebuttable presumption exists that the fair value of the asset consisting of those preacquisition stage costs (excluding option costs) is zero (that is, the costs of the asset would be charged to expense), unless management, having the authority to approve the action, has committed to a plan to either (a) sell the asset and the proceeds can be reasonably estimated or (b) redeploy the asset in other specific PP&E of the entity and the redeployed asset meets the criteria for capitalization under the project stage framework in this SOP. If an entity subsequently acquires or constructs PP&E previously considered no longer probable to acquire or construct, preacquisition stage costs charged to expense under this paragraph should not be reversed.

AcSEC establishes a rebuttable presumption that the fair value of any capitalized preacquisition costs is zero once a project is abandoned, because the majority of the costs incurred in this stage would be "soft" costs that would generate only limited value for other projects.[9]

---

7   FAS 67, paragraph 5
8   Proposed SOP, *Accounting for Certain Costs and Activities Related to Property, Plant, and Equipment*, paragraph 24
9   Proposed SOP, *Accounting for Certain Costs and Activities Related to Property, Plant, and Equipment*, paragraph A29

1.2.1.2 Capitalization of Internal Preacquisition Costs   Activities in the preacquisition stage may be carried out by a company's in-house departments, which raises the question of (1) whether and (2) to what extent such internal preacquisition costs should be capitalized.

Emerging Issues Task Force (EITF) Issue No. 97-11, *Accounting for Costs Relating to Real Estate Property Acquisitions*, provides that internal preacquisition costs[10] are only capitalizable if the property is expected to be nonoperating at the date of acquisition. They are not capitalizable if the property is expected to be operating at the date of acquisition, such as internal preacquisition costs relating to the purchase of an existing shopping mall.[11]

A prerequisite for the capitalization of internal preacquisition costs is that they be directly identifiable with the specific property.[12] While "directly identifiable" is not further defined in Statement 67, the term has been interpreted narrowly in practice.

One may look to the proposed SOP, *Accounting for Certain Costs and Activities Related to Property, Plant, and Equipment*, for implementation guidance:[13]

> . . . [d]irectly identifiable costs include only:
>
> a. Incremental direct costs of PP&E preacquisition activities incurred for the specific PP&E.
> b. Certain costs directly related to preacquisition activities performed by the entity (or by parties not independent of the entity) for the specific PP&E. Those costs include only payroll and payroll benefit–related costs (for example, costs of health insurance) of employees who devote time to a PP&E preacquisition stage activity, to the extent of time the employees spent directly on that activity and in proportion to the total hours employed.
> c. Payments to obtain an option . . . to acquire PP&E.

Notwithstanding the foregoing, an option to acquire property, plant, and equipment that meets the definition of a derivative instrument within the scope of FASB Statement No. 133, *Accounting for Derivative Instruments and Hedging Activities*, is accounted for following the guidance in Statement 133.[14]

Further, that proposed SOP states that costs of facilities, such as rent and depreciation, as well as general and administrative costs, should be expensed as incurred, as should all costs of executive management, corporate accounting,

---

10   EITF Issue No. 97-11 does not address the accounting for costs incurred for acquisitions of real estate properties that will be used in a company's own operations, other than for sale or rental.
11   EITF Issue No. 97-11
12   FAS 67, paragraph 4(a)
13   Proposed SOP, *Accounting for Certain Costs and Activities Related to Property, Plant, and Equipment*, paragraph 19
14   Proposed SOP, *Accounting for Certain Costs and Activities Related to Property, Plant, and Equipment*, footnote 4

acquisitions, office management and administration, marketing, human resources, and similar costs or functions.[15]

While that proposed SOP has never been issued in final form, the guidance provided by that proposed SOP nevertheless proves helpful when interpreting the provisions in Statement 67.

1.2.2 PROJECT COSTS   Project costs are defined as "[c]osts clearly associated with the acquisition, development, and construction of a real estate project."[16] In certain real estate projects, land is developed and structures are being built or refurbished. In addition to the costs of acquiring land, development and construction costs are incurred to complete the project. Other real estate projects involve property acquisition only, such as the acquisition of shopping centers that are already in operation.

Paragraph 7 of Statement 67 states the general concept for the accounting for project costs:

> Project costs clearly associated with the acquisition, development, and construction of a real estate project shall be capitalized as a cost of that project.

While this concept may appear straightforward, determining which costs are clearly associated with a real estate project can require significant judgment.

1.2.2.1 Direct Costs   Direct project costs are incremental costs that are directly related to the acquisition, development, and construction of the property. They may include the same types of costs as preacquisition costs, because certain activities can be performed before or after the acquisition. In addition to the types of costs listed in Section 1.2.1 of this chapter, project costs typically include:

- Purchase price[17]
- Commissions due to third parties
- Brokerage fees due to third parties
- Fees for title guarantee and title searches
- Recording fees
- Property taxes incurred during construction
- Insurance costs incurred during construction
- Costs of permits
- Engineering costs

---

15   Proposed SOP, *Accounting for Certain Costs and Activities Related to Property, Plant, and Equipment*, paragraphs 20 and 21

16   FAS 67, paragraph 28

17   Special issues may arise if seller and buyer of a real estate property enter into an arrangement, under which the seller agrees to lease (or lease up) the property. EITF Issue No. 85-27 addresses the accounting for such arrangements, which may, in substance, be adjustments to the purchase price of the property.

- Environmental remediation costs
- Demolition costs
- Construction costs (materials, labor)
- Costs of amenities[18]
- Donated land

All costs incurred need to be carefully evaluated to determine whether they qualify for capitalization. For example, the costs of real estate donated to governmental agencies that benefit a certain project are part of that project's costs.[19] However, if donated land does not benefit (and was not made in conjunction with) a real estate project, the costs should be expensed, rather than capitalized. Similarly, demolition costs incurred within a reasonable period after the acquisition of property are generally capitalized when they are incurred, if demolition is probable at the time of acquisition.[20] Industry practice is diverse with respect to the capitalization of demolition costs that are not incurred within a reasonable period after acquisition. The proposed SOP, if it had been issued in final form as proposed, would have required that demolition costs not incurred within a reasonable period of time after acquisition be expensed.[21] Questions also arise with respect to the capitalization of environmental remediation costs. While environmental remediation costs incurred within a reasonable period of time after the acquisition of property are generally capitalized as part of the project costs, determining whether environmental remediation costs incurred at a later point in time are capitalizable is more complex and involves significant judgment.[22]

1.2.2.2 Indirect Costs   Indirect project costs are capitalized to the extent they clearly relate to the acquisition, development, or construction of a real estate project. The following are examples of indirect internal project costs:

- Costs of planning department
- Costs of construction administration (for example, the costs associated with a field office at a project site)
- Internal costs incurred for cost accounting or project design[23]
- Depreciation of machinery and equipment used directly in construction[24]
- Payroll costs and employee benefits for employees working on the project

---

18   See Section 1.7.1 of this chapter.
19   FAS 67, paragraph 14
20   Proposed SOP, *Accounting for Certain Costs and Activities Related to Property, Plant, and Equipment*, paragraph 34
21   Id.
22   See also Section 1.7.5 for further discussion regarding environmental remediation costs.
23   FAS 67, Appendix A, paragraph 28
24   Proposed SOP, *Accounting for Certain Costs and Activities Related to Property, Plant, and Equipment*, paragraph 26

For internally incurred indirect costs to be capitalizable, a cost accounting system needs to be in place and adequate documentation needs to be maintained to support cost capitalization. For example, time may be recorded by the in-house designers to determine the percentage of their salaries to be allocated to a certain project. Indirect costs for which sufficient support cannot be provided, or that do not clearly relate to a project under development or construction, including general and administrative expenses, are expensed as incurred.[25]

Statement 67 does not provide any further guidance on how to determine what costs are clearly associated with the acquisition, development, and construction of a real estate project. As a result, considerable diversity in practice exists with respect to the types of indirect project costs that are capitalized.

The proposed SOP, *Accounting for Certain Costs and Activities Related to Property, Plant, and Equipment,* limits the capitalization of indirect costs to:

- Costs that are directly identifiable with the specific property
- Costs incurred for property taxes and insurance for the portion of the property under construction[26]
- Demolition costs incurred in conjunction with the acquisition of PP&E, if demolition is probable at the time of acquisition and is expected to occur within a reasonable period after acquisition[27]

The proposed SOP, *Accounting for Certain Costs and Activities Related to Property, Plant, and Equipment,* provides that the capitalization of directly identifiable indirect project costs should be limited to:

- Incremental direct costs of acquiring, constructing, or installing the property
- Payroll and payroll benefit–related costs of employees who devote time to the project
- Depreciation of machinery and equipment used in construction or installation
- The cost of inventory used in construction or installation[28]

The proposed SOP does not provide for the capitalization of other indirect costs, such as occupancy costs (including rent, depreciation, and other costs associated with facilities); these costs should be charged to expense as incurred.[29] While the proposed SOP may prove helpful in interpreting Statement 67, one has

---

25   FAS 67, paragraph 7
26   Proposed SOP, *Accounting for Certain Costs and Activities Related to Property, Plant, and Equipment,* paragraph 31
27   Proposed SOP, *Accounting for Certain Costs and Activities Related to Property, Plant, and Equipment,* paragraph 34
28   Proposed SOP, *Accounting for Certain Costs and Activities Related to Property, Plant, and Equipment,* paragraph 26
29   Proposed SOP, *Accounting for Certain Costs and Activities Related to Property, Plant, and Equipment,* paragraph 27

to keep in mind that the FASB has not cleared that proposed SOP, and therefore, it is low-level GAAP.

1.2.2.3 General and Administrative Expenses FASB Statement No. 67 provides that "[i]ndirect costs that do not clearly relate to projects under development or construction, including general and administrative expenses . . . be charged to expense as incurred"[30] without providing further guidance as to which expenses should be considered general and administrative expenses. The proposed SOP, *Accounting for Certain Costs and Activities Related to Property, Plant, and Equipment,* is more specific: "All costs (including payroll and payroll benefit–related costs) of executive management, corporate accounting, acquisitions, office management and administration, marketing, human resources, and similar costs and functions should be charged to expense as incurred."[31]

1.2.2.4 Property Taxes and Insurance Property taxes, insurance, and interest are commonly referred to as holding costs. Taxes and insurance are capitalized as part of the property's cost during the period in which activities necessary to get the property ready for its intended use are in progress.[32] The capitalization period for property taxes and insurance (beginning, end, and suspension) coincides with the capitalization period for interest set forth in FASB Statement No. 34, *Capitalization of Interest Cost,*[33] outlined in Section 1.2.2.5 of this chapter. After the real estate property is ready for its intended use, property taxes and insurance are charged to expense as incurred. Special considerations are necessary when development activities occur only on a portion of a real estate property. For example, a company may own a 50-acre parcel of land and is constructing a building on 5 of these 50 acres. The capitalization of property taxes and insurance would only be appropriate for interest and taxes relating to the five acres under construction.[34]

Insurance and taxes are capitalized during the construction period irrespective of whether the real estate is newly acquired or whether it has been used subsequent to its acquisition, with construction activities starting at a later point in time. For example, a hotel building may be redeveloped (refurbished) after it has been operating for many years. The proposed SOP, *Accounting for Certain Costs and Activities Related to Property, Plant, and Equipment,* uses the "avoidable cost concept" to determine whether property taxes and insurance should be capitalized.[35] If the property has been used in the past as an operating asset,

---

30   FAS 67, paragraph 7
31   Proposed SOP, *Accounting for Certain Costs and Activities Related to Property, Plant, and Equipment,* paragraph 28
32   FAS 67, paragraph 6; depending on the real estate property: The term "ready for its intended use" encompasses both "ready for use" and "ready for sale." [FAS 34, paragraph 6, footnote 3]
33   FAS 67, paragraph 6, footnote 4
34   Proposed SOP, *Accounting for Certain Costs and Activities Related to Property, Plant, and Equipment,* paragraph 31
35   Proposed SOP, *Accounting for Certain Costs and Activities Related to Property, Plant, and Equipment,* paragraph A37

but is removed from operations for purposes of construction, property taxes and insurance are avoidable costs of construction, even though they are not incremental to the entity, since the entity could avoid the property taxes and insurance by choosing to dispose of the property. However, for properties under construction that remain in operation while construction takes place, the proposed SOP suggests that costs incurred for property taxes and insurance should be capitalized only if they are incremental and directly attributable to the construction activities.[36]

1.2.2.5 Interest   Undertaking real estate projects requires significant capital, and financing cost is a major cost factor. If real estate is acquired that is not ready for its intended use, interest expense incurred during the development and construction period is part of a project's costs that is capitalized.[37] FASB believes that through interest capitalization, a measure of acquisition cost is obtained that reflects the company's investment in the real estate asset.[38] Accordingly, interest capitalization is not discontinued when a real estate project is impaired; any write-down is increased by interest expected to be capitalized in future accounting periods.[39]

There may be a period of time in which a company generates interest income from the investment of unused funds on project financing obtained. Generally, such interest income is recognized as income when earned. It is not offset against interest cost when determining the amount of interest cost to be capitalized, except in the case of certain tax-exempt borrowings.[40]

The determination of the amount of interest to be capitalized in a real estate project is a four-step process:

Step 1. Determine whether the real estate project qualifies for interest capitalization.

Step 2. Determine the types of expenditures that qualify for interest capitalization.

Step 3. Determine the capitalization period.

Step 4. Determine the amount of interest cost to be capitalized.

STEP 1. DETERMINE WHETHER THE REAL ESTATE PROJECT QUALIFIES FOR
INTEREST CAPITALIZATION
The following assets qualify for interest capitalization:[41]

1. Assets that are constructed or otherwise produced for a company's own use
2. Assets intended for sale or lease that are constructed or otherwise produced as discrete projects, such as real estate developments

---

36   Proposed SOP, *Accounting for Certain Costs and Activities Related to Property, Plant, and Equipment,*
      paragraph 31
37   FAS 34, paragraph 6
38   FAS 34, paragraph 7
39   FAS 34, paragraph 19; FAS 144, paragraph 20
40   FAS 62, paragraph 3
41   FAS 34, paragraph 9

Additionally, investments in equity method investees may be qualifying assets, as explained in Section 1.7.6 of this chapter.

FASB Statement No. 34, *Capitalization of Interest Cost,* precludes interest capitalization for certain types of assets, including (1) assets that are in use or ready for their intended use, and (2) assets that, although not in use, are not undergoing activities to get them ready for their use.[42]

Land that is not undergoing activities necessary to get it ready for its intended use is not an asset qualifying for interest capitalization. Once activities are undertaken for the purpose of developing land for a particular use, the acquisition and development expenditures qualify for interest capitalization while those activities are in progress. If a structure is built on the land, such as a plant or an office building, interest capitalized on the land expenditures is part of the cost of the structure. If a tract of land is developed and subdivided to be sold as developed lots, interest capitalized on the land expenditures becomes part of the cost of the land.[43]

STEP 2. DETERMINE THE TYPES OF EXPENDITURES THAT QUALIFY FOR
INTEREST CAPITALIZATION

After it has been determined that a project qualifies for interest capitalization, the expenditures incurred for that project have to be evaluated to determine whether they qualify for interest capitalization. As a general rule, expenditures that do not require the transfer of cash or other assets or the incurrence of liabilities on which interest is accrued do not qualify for interest capitalization. As such, capitalized amounts financed through trade payables, retainages, or progress payment collections from customers may lead to differences between capitalized project costs and the amount of expenditures that qualify for interest capitalization. Paragraph 16 of FASB Statement No. 34 provides, however, that capitalized expenditures for an asset may be used as a reasonable approximation of expenditures on which interest is capitalized, unless the difference is material.

STEP 3. DETERMINE THE CAPITALIZATION PERIOD

Interest is capitalized when the following three conditions are present:[44]

- Expenditures for the asset (that qualify for interest capitalization) have been made.
- Activities that are necessary to get the asset ready for its intended use are in progress.
- Interest cost is being incurred.

The term "activities that are necessary to get the asset ready for its intended use" is interpreted broadly in practice. Such activities include administrative and

---

42   FAS 34, paragraph 10
43   FAS 34, paragraph 11
44   FAS 34, paragraph 17

technical activities before ground is broken, such as the development of plans or the process of obtaining permits from governmental authorities. If a company suspends substantially all activities related to the development of the property, the company has to evaluate the reason and duration of the suspension and determine whether interest capitalization during such period of suspension is appropriate. An interruption that is brief or inherent in the asset development process, such as labor strikes or weather conditions, would not lead to a cessation of interest capitalization, whereas a company-induced suspension in construction activities due to a decline in the real estate market would preclude interest capitalization.[45]

The capitalization period ends when the asset is substantially complete and ready for its intended use. By requiring that the capitalization period end when the asset is "substantially complete," the FASB intended to prohibit the continuation of interest capitalization in situations in which the final completion of assets is intentionally delayed. For example, a developer may choose to defer installing fixtures and fittings until condominium units are being sold to give buyers a choice of styles and colors.[46]

Paragraph 22 of FASB Statement No. 67 allows for a maximum period of one year after cessation of major construction activities, over which a developer may assert that the project is not substantially completed, by requiring that "[a] real estate project shall be considered substantially completed and held available for occupancy upon completion of tenant improvements by the developer but no later than one year from cessation of major construction activity . . ."

Real estate projects may need to be divided into separate assets or parts for purposes of determining whether they are ready for their intended use. For example, a condominium building is comprised of individual condominiums, which can be used independently from each other.[47] Each such condominium constitutes a separate asset, and interest ceases to be capitalized on condominiums that have been completed and are ready for use. Other real estate assets must be completed in their entirety before any part of the asset can be used, such as the construction of a manufacturing facility.

Judgment must be exercised when determining whether a real estate project should be divided into separate parts for purposes of interest capitalization.

STEP 4. DETERMINE THE AMOUNT OF INTEREST COST TO BE CAPITALIZED
The amount of interest cost to be capitalized is intended to be that portion of the interest cost incurred during the asset's acquisition and construction period that theoretically could have been avoided if expenditures for the asset had not been made.[48]

---

45   FAS 34, paragraph 58
46   FAS 34, paragraph 58
47   FAS 34, paragraph 18
48   FAS 34, paragraph 12

The total amount of interest cost that may be capitalized in an accounting period is limited to the total amount of interest cost incurred by the company in that period.[49]

For purposes of FASB Statement No. 34,[50] interest cost incurred by a company includes:

- Interest recognized on obligations with explicitly stated interest rates (including the amortization of discount or premium and debt issue costs)
- Interest imputed on certain types of payables, in accordance with Accounting Principles Board (APB) Opinion No. 21, *Interest on Receivables and Payables*
- Interest on capital leases determined in accordance with FASB Statement No. 13, *Accounting for Leases*

The amount of interest cost to be capitalized in an accounting period is determined by applying an interest rate to the average amount of accumulated expenditures for the asset during the period. In determining what interest rate to use, the objective is to determine a reasonable measure of the cost of financing the acquisition and development of the asset. The interest rate or interest rates used should be based on the rates applicable to borrowings outstanding during the period. If a company has obtained a specific loan for a qualifying asset, the company may use the rate on that borrowing as the capitalization rate for the expenditures for the asset. If the average accumulated expenditures for the asset exceed the amounts of that loan, the capitalization rate applied to any excess is a weighted average of the rates applicable to other borrowings of the company.[51] Paragraph 14 of Statement 34 provides with respect to the weighted average interest rate to be used: "In identifying the borrowings to be included in the weighted average rate, the objective is a reasonable measure of the cost of financing the acquisition of the asset in terms of the interest cost incurred that otherwise could have been avoided. Accordingly, judgment will be required to make a selection of borrowings that best accomplishes that objective in the circumstances."

Section 1.7.6 of this chapter discusses special considerations if financing is provided by related parties. It also discusses interest capitalization by a company on investments in an equity method investee.

1.2.3 COST ALLOCATION   As real estate projects often span long time periods until their completion, it is of critical importance to evaluate at the outset of a real estate project whether—for cost allocation purposes—a project should be divided into two or more phases. For example, a real estate development company may purchase a large tract of land to be developed over several years; portions of the land will be developed and sold before the project as a whole is completed.

---

49   FAS 34, paragraph 15
50   FAS 34, paragraph 1
51   FAS 34, paragraph 13

If that real estate development project is not divided into phases, the appropriate allocation and monitoring of costs is difficult, and project costs relating to the earlier stages of the development may inappropriately be allocated to a later stage, thereby overstating profits in the earlier years. Certain project costs may benefit one individual unit (such as a lot, home, or condominium unit) or a group of units within one phase; other costs may benefit one or more phases of a project or more than one project, such as utilities or access roads. As such, the allocation of costs to individual units, between different phases of one project, or to different projects generally involves several cost pools and multiple steps.

When allocating project costs, one needs to consider costs already incurred, as well as costs to be incurred in current and future periods. For example, in a master-planned community, individual homes are often sold before amenities (for example, golf courses, swimming pools, or parks) have been completed. To appropriately reflect the cost of sales that relates to one individual home sold, a portion of the costs expected to be incurred in future periods for the construction of the amenities must be allocated to that home.[52]

Selecting an appropriate cost allocation method requires judgment. As a general rule, costs should be allocated to the portions of a project that benefit from the costs. The intent is to achieve a constant gross margin on sales for the project, irrespective of the point in time sales occur. FASB Statement No. 67 outlines three different ways to allocate costs:[53]

1. Specific identification method
2. Relative value method
3. Area methods or other value methods

SPECIFIC IDENTIFICATION METHOD
Where practicable, the costs of a real estate project are assigned to individual components of a project based on specific identification. The specific identification method is most frequently used for the allocation of acquisition costs and direct construction costs in small projects. For example, costs charged by a contractor to install a staircase in a new home directly relate to that home. The amount invoiced by the contractor should be included in the cost basis of that home.

RELATIVE VALUE METHOD
If specific identification is not feasible or is impracticable, as is the case for indirect costs or common costs, costs should be allocated based on the relative value of the components, if possible.[54] Under this method, costs are allocated based on the relative fair values of the individual components of a project, based on either (1) the fair value before construction or (2) the relative sales value of the units.

---

52   The accounting for costs of amenities is further discussed in Section 1.7.1.
53   FAS 67, paragraph 11
54   FAS 67, paragraph 11

Allocation Based on Relative Fair Value before Construction.   Land costs and all other common costs incurred before construction occurs (including the costs of any amenities) are allocated to the land parcels benefited, with cost allocation based on the relative fair value before construction. For example, a developer that purchases a tract of land on which to build a master-planned community, a shopping center, and an office building would allocate the cost of the land based on estimates of the relative fair value of the land parcels of (1) the master-planned community, (2) the shopping center, and (3) the office building, prior to the construction of the structures. A cost allocation based on the size of the parcels would not reflect any differences in values and is generally not considered appropriate. Unusable land and land that is donated to municipalities or other governmental agencies that will benefit the project are allocated as common costs of the project.[55]

Allocation Based on the Relative Sales Value of the Units.   Under the relative value method, construction costs for a project, such as a condominium complex, are allocated to the individual units (for example, homes, condominium units) based on the relative sales value of the units.[56] When allocating costs based on the relative value method, the sales values of the units must be comparable. This is achieved by assuming that all of the units will be completed and ready for sale at the same point in time; any expected price increases for units that will be completed in future periods are not taken into consideration.

   The relative sales value method results in allocating greater costs to more valuable components of a project. In practice, the relative value method is often implemented through the application of a gross profit method. Under the gross profit method, a cost-of-sales percentage is calculated by dividing the sum of capitalized project costs and project costs to be incurred in the current and future periods by the estimated sales value of the unsold units. When a unit is sold, the cost-of-sales amount attributable to that sale is determined by multiplying the sales value of that unit by the cost-of-sales percentage.

Area Methods or Other Value Methods
If the relative value method cannot be applied, as would be the case if a real estate development company has not determined the ultimate use of the land, another method for cost allocation has to be used. FASB Statement No. 67 suggests the use of the area method, such as the allocation of costs to parcels based on square footage, or "another reasonable value method."[57]

   Under the area method, costs are allocated based on lot sizes, the square footage of a structure, or the number of units in a development. The use of the area method is appropriate only if the allocation is not materially different from

---

55   FAS 67, paragraph 14
56   FAS 67, paragraph 11
57   FAS 67, paragraph 11

an allocation that is based on relative value methods, or if the application of the relative value method is impracticable.

EXAMPLE—COST ALLOCATION
Developers-R-Us (D) purchases land for $10 million, which it intends to divide into three parcels. On Parcel 1, which is along the highway, it plans to construct a shopping center. On Parcel 2, which is behind the shopping center, D plans on building a row of 40 townhouses. Parcel 3 will be developed into a master-planned community. The fair value of the land before construction has been determined to be $4 million, $1 million and $5 million for parcels 1, 2, and 3, respectively. The sales prices for the shopping center, the town houses, and the master-planned community are estimated to amount to $40 million, $12 million, and $100 million.   How much land cost should be allocated to Townhouse Unit 1 (TH 1), which has an estimated sales price of $500,000?   The first step is to allocate the cost of the land to the individual parcels based on the relative fair value before construction; accordingly, an amount of $1 million is allocated to Parcel 2. The land value allocated to the parcel on which townhouses are to be constructed then becomes part of the common cost pool for the townhouse, which is allocated to each townhouse based on its relative sales value. As such, TH 1 will be allocated land costs of $41,667. That amount is calculated as follows: The sales value of TH 1 divided by the sales value of all THs, multiplied by the cost of land allocated to the townhouse development: $0.5 million/$12 million multiplied by $1 million

The allocation of costs needs to be reviewed every reporting period to ensure that changes in circumstances, such as a change in estimate of project costs or sales prices or in the design of the project, are taken into consideration.[58] Cost reallocations within or between phases of a project are not uncommon, as the design of a project may evolve.

1.2.4 CHANGE IN ESTIMATES OR PROJECT PLANS AND ABANDONMENTS OF PROJECTS
Due to the length of time involved in the development and construction of real estate properties, a project's plans, cost estimates, and expected sales prices may change over the course of the project.

CHANGE IN ESTIMATES

Paragraph 12 of FASB Statement No. 67 requires that estimates and cost allocations be reviewed at the end of each financial reporting period until a project is substantially completed and available for sale. Generally, any changes in cost estimates are accounted for prospectively as changes in estimate, in accordance with paragraphs 19 through 22 of FASB Statement No. 154, *Accounting Changes and Error Corrections.*

---

58   FAS 67, paragraph 12

The accounting for any cost revisions may be reflected in the current period or in current or future periods, depending on the facts and circumstances:

- If the difference in cost estimates relates to direct costs for units already sold, such as additional sales commissions, they are charged to expense at the time the information becomes available to the developer.
- If the difference in cost estimates arises from an increase or decrease in common costs—streets, utilities, etc.—any cost increases or decreases are accounted for prospectively.

The prospective accounting for changes in common cost estimates can lead to different margins over the time of project development and construction. If cost estimates for common costs increase, common costs attributable to units already sold will be allocated to the costs of unsold units.[59] Consequently, the profit margin of units sold in future periods would be lower than the profit margin of units already sold.

Changes in estimates in sales values, which impact cost allocation under the relative value methods, are also accounted for as a change in estimate pursuant to paragraphs 19 through 22 of FASB Statement No. 154.

CHANGE IN DEVELOPMENT PLANS

Changes in market demand or other factors may arise after significant development and construction costs have already been incurred (such as the change in the housing market in the summer of 2007). If a developer decides to change its development plans, development and construction costs need to be charged to expense to the extent that the capitalized costs incurred and to be incurred for the redesigned project exceed the estimated value of the redesigned project when it is substantially complete and ready for its intended use.[60] This charge to expense based on the fair value upon completion is required irrespective of whether an impairment loss needs to be recognized pursuant to the provisions of FASB Statement No. 144, *Accounting for the Impairment or Disposal of Long-Lived Assets.*

When determining the amount to be charged to expense upon such change in plans, any future interest capitalization has to be taken into consideration pursuant to paragraph 19 of FASB Statement No. 34, *Capitalization of Interest Cost,* which provides, in part:

> Interest capitalization shall not cease when present accounting principles require recognition of a lower value for the asset than acquisition cost; the provision required to reduce acquisition cost to such lower value shall be increased appropriately.

---

59   The prospective accounting for changes in estimated project costs required by paragraph 12 of FASB Statement No. 67 differs from the accounting for a change in estimated costs for construction contracts. Paragraph 83 of SOP 81-1, *Accounting for Performance of Construction-Type and Certain Production-Type Contracts,* requires the use of the cumulative catch-up method when accounting for any revisions to revenue, cost, and profit estimates for long-term construction contracts. Under the cumulative catch-up method, a change in estimate is accounted for in the period of change so that the balance sheet at the end of the period of change and the accounting in subsequent periods are as they would have been if the revised estimate had been the original estimate.

60   FAS 67, paragraph 15

ABANDONMENT OF A REAL ESTATE PROJECT
If a real estate project is abandoned, the capitalized costs of that project need to be expensed to the extent they are not recoverable. Any capitalized expenses for which a future use cannot be clearly established should not be allocated to other phases or other projects.[61]

1.3 COSTS INCURRED TO SELL OR RENT A REAL ESTATE PROJECT

In real estate properties that are intended for rent or sale after development is completed, leasing and selling activities generally occur throughout the acquisition, development, and construction phases of a project. Successful preleasing and preselling efforts are evidence of a project's viability, and funds received from buyers are often used to finance a project's development. Commissions; legal fees; closing costs; advertising costs; and costs for grand openings are examples of costs to sell or rent; however, based on the type of real estate property, leasing and sales activities—and related costs incurred—may vary.

1.3.1 COSTS INCURRED TO SELL A REAL ESTATE PROJECT   Costs incurred to sell a real estate project are generally substantial. Depending on the type of selling costs incurred, they are accounted for in one of three ways:

- Included in project costs
- Deferred
- Expensed

SELLING COSTS TO BE INCLUDED IN PROJECT COSTS[62]
Selling costs are included in project costs if all of the following criteria are met:

- They are reasonably expected to be recovered from the sale of the project or from incidental operations
- They are incurred for:
  - Tangible assets that are used directly throughout the selling period to aid in the sale of the project, or
  - Services that have been performed to obtain regulatory approval of sales

Examples of costs that generally qualify as project costs are:[63]

- Costs of model units and their furnishings
- Costs of sales facilities
- Legal fees for the preparation of prospectuses
- Costs of semipermanent signs.

Selling costs that qualify for inclusion in project costs become part of a common cost pool that is allocated to individual units. Model units and their furnishings are

---

61   FAS 67, paragraph 13
62   FAS 67, paragraph 17
63   FAS 67, paragraph 17

generally sold at the end of the sales period; the amount allocated to common costs is the excess of the costs of the model units over their estimated sales proceeds.

SELLING COSTS TO BE DEFERRED[64]

FASB Statement No. 67 provides for the deferral of certain selling costs. It is important to note that deferred selling costs are not part of project costs. If the percentage-of-completion method were applied, the incurrence of selling costs would not increase a project's percentage of completion. Additionally, deferred selling costs are not part of qualifying expenditures for interest capitalization.

Selling costs are accounted for as prepaid costs; that is, they are deferred if they meet the following criteria: They must be directly associated with successful sales efforts, and their recovery must be reasonably expected from sales. FASB Statement No. 67 provides for the deferral of such selling costs until the related profit is recognized. If profit is recorded under the accrual method of accounting, a deferral of selling costs is generally not necessary, as the selling costs are incurred in the period of sale. For example, a seller may incur brokerage commissions at the time of closing. If profit from a real estate sale is recognized under a method of accounting other than the accrual method, such as the deposit or installment method, paragraph 18 of Statement 67 provides for cost deferral until the related profit is recognized.

If a sales contract is canceled or if the receivable from a real estate sale is written off as uncollectible, any related unrecoverable deferred selling costs are charged to expense.[65]

ADVERTISING COSTS

Costs of advertising, which include the costs of producing advertisements (such as the costs of idea development, artwork, printing, and audio and video production) and communicating advertisements that have been produced (such as the costs of magazine space, television airtime, billboard space, and distribution costs) are accounted for based on the provisions of SOP 93-7, *Reporting on Advertising Costs.*

Costs of advertising are expensed, either as incurred or the first time the advertising takes place (e.g., the first public showing of a television commercial or the first appearance of a magazine advertisement) with the following two exceptions provided for in paragraphs 26 and 27 of that SOP.

1. Direct-response advertising whose primary purpose is to elicit sales to customers who could be shown to have responded specifically to the advertising and that results in probable future economic benefits. Costs of direct response advertising that are capitalized should be amortized over the period during which the future benefits are expected to be received.[66]

---

64   FAS 67, paragraph 18
65   FAS 67, paragraph 19
66   SOP 93-7, paragraph 46

2. Expenditures for advertising costs that are made subsequent to recognizing revenues related to those costs. For example, a company may assume an obligation to reimburse its customers for some or all of the customers' advertising costs (cooperative advertising). In that scenario, revenues related to the transactions creating those obligations are earned and recognized before the expenditures are made. For purposes of applying SOP 93-7, those obligations should be accrued and the advertising costs should be expensed when the related revenues are recognized.

SELLING COSTS TO BE EXPENSED[67]

Costs that do not meet the criteria for capitalization as project costs or for cost deferral are expensed as incurred.

EXAMPLE—SELLING COSTS

Developers-R-Us (D) sells developed lots. The buyers of the lots have made only nominal down payments, and D has determined that the application of the deposit method of accounting is appropriate. D intends to defer the following five types of costs incurred in connection with D's efforts to sell the lots:

1. Wages and commissions paid to sales personnel, and related insurance, taxes, and benefits for sales personnel
2. Costs for the corporate sales department
3. Radio and newspaper advertising expenses
4. Telephone, hospitality, meals, and travel costs for customers and prospective customers
5. Title insurance and professional fees incurred in the sale

D intends to defer these costs, as they are incurred in connection with D's efforts to sell the lots. Is a deferral of these costs appropriate?

1. To the extent the costs for wages and commissions to sales personnel relate directly to successful sales efforts, their deferral (together with the deferral of any related insurance, taxes and benefits) is appropriate.
2. Costs of the corporate sales department are not directly associated with successful sales and should not be deferred.
3. For advertising costs, the guidance in SOP 93-7 should be followed.
4. To the extent that telephone, hospitality, meals, and travel costs for customers and prospective customers are incurred directly for successful sales efforts, their deferral is appropriate.
5. Title insurance and professional fees are incurred directly in connection with the sales; their deferral is appropriate.

The AICPA has issued SOP 04-2, *Accounting for Real Estate Time-Sharing Transactions*, which includes guidance relating to the deferral of costs for the sale of time-sharing intervals. That guidance may provide additional insights when considering what types of selling costs to defer.

---

67   FAS 67, paragraph 19

1.3.2 COSTS INCURRED TO RENT A REAL ESTATE PROJECT[68]   Costs to rent a real estate project under operating leases fall in one of two categories: (1) initial direct costs and (2) other than initial direct costs. Costs to rent projects under direct financing or sales-type leases are treated like costs to sell.

FASB Statement No. 67 does not apply to initial direct costs.[69] Initial direct costs are incremental direct costs incurred by the lessor in negotiating and consummating leasing transactions, and certain costs directly related to specified activities performed by the lessor.[70] The accounting for such costs is provided in FASB Statement No. 13, *Accounting for Leases,* and further discussed in Section 4.5.2 of Chapter 4.

Costs other than initial direct costs to rent real estate projects under operating leases that are related to and are expected to be recovered from future rental operations are deferred (capitalized). Examples of such costs are costs of:[71]

- Model units and their furnishings
- Rental facilities
- Semipermanent signs
- Grand openings, and
- Unused rental brochures

Deferred rental costs that are directly related to a specific operating lease are amortized over the lease term. Deferred rental costs not directly related to revenue from a specific operating lease are amortized over the period of expected benefit. The amortization period of capitalized rental costs begins when the project is substantially complete and held available for occupancy. Any amounts of unamortized capitalized rental costs associated with a lease or group of leases that are estimated not to be recoverable are charged to expense when it becomes probable that the lease or group of leases will be terminated.[72]

Costs of advertising are accounted for based on the provisions of SOP 93-7, *Reporting on Advertising Costs.*

Costs that do not meet the criteria for capitalization and are not advertising costs—for example, general and administrative costs—are expensed as incurred.[73]

1.4 INCIDENTAL OPERATIONS

Incidental operations are revenue-producing activities, such as rentals, that are undertaken during the holding or development period to reduce the cost of holding or developing the property for its intended purpose. For example, a developer

---

68   Paragraphs 20 through 23 of FASB Statement No. 67 do not apply to real estate rental activity, in which the predominant rental period is less than one month. [FAS 67, paragraph 2]
69   FAS 67, paragraph 2(b)
70   FAS 13, paragraph 5(m)
71   FAS 67, paragraph 20
72   FAS 67, paragraph 21
73   FAS 67, paragraph 20

may engage in the following incidental operations to reduce the cost of project development:

- Operation of temporary parking facility on the future site of an office building before construction of the building commences
- Lease of undeveloped land for farming or for a golf driving range while the project is in the planning phase of development
- Lease of apartment building while it is converted into a condominium building

Incremental revenue from incidental operations in excess of incremental costs of incidental operations is accounted for as a reduction of development costs, whereas incremental costs from incidental operations in excess of incremental revenue from incidental operations are charged to current operations. The different accounting treatment reflects the intent for undertaking incidental operations; incidental operations are entered into to reduce the cost of developing the property for its intended use, rather than to generate revenues.[74] Accordingly, if the objective of reducing costs has not been achieved, any excess operating expenses from incidental operations are charged to expense.[75]

A real estate company may construct an office building that it intends to lease. Some offices may be leased before the office building is substantially complete and ready for occupancy. Until the building in its entirety is substantially complete and ready for occupancy, it is not depreciated, and any rental income and expense is accounted for as incidental operations.[76]

1.5 ACCOUNTING FOR COSTS INCURRED SUBSEQUENT TO PROJECT COMPLETION

1.5.1 DETERMINING THE DATE OF PROJECT COMPLETION   A real estate project is considered substantially completed and held available for occupancy upon completion of tenant improvements by the developer, but no later than one year from cessation of major construction activity.[77] Once a real estate project is substantially completed and held available for occupancy, a rental project changes from nonoperating to operating, with the following consequences:

- Rental revenues and operating costs are recognized as they accrue
- Carrying costs (such as taxes and insurance) are expensed when incurred

---

74   FAS 67, paragraph 10
75   The accounting treatment of incidental operations under IFRS differs from the accounting treatment under U.S. GAAP. Paragraph 21 of IAS 16 provides, in part: "Because incidental operations are not necessary to bring an item to the location and condition necessary for it to be capable of operating in the manner intended by management, the income and related expenses of incidental operations are recognized in profit or loss and included in their respective classifications of income and expense."
76   See also discussion under Section 1.5.1 of this chapter.
77   FAS 67, paragraph 22

- Interest capitalization ceases
- Depreciation commences
- Amortization of deferred rental costs commences

Paragraph 23 of Statement 67 states:

> If portions of a rental project are substantially completed and occupied by tenants or held available for occupancy, and other portions have not yet reached that stage, the substantially completed portions should be accounted for as a separate project. Costs incurred shall be allocated between the portions under construction and the portions substantially completed and held available for occupancy.

Judgment must be used to determine what constitutes a project and, once identified, when that project is substantially completed and ready for its intended use. For example, a company may identify separate buildings in an office complex as separate projects. However, an individual rental project, such as an office building, is considered one real estate project in its entirety, and that rental project is evaluated in its entirety of whether it is substantially complete. The FASB considered and rejected a phase-in of depreciation and other operating costs based on a percentage-of-occupancy method over the period of lease-up of a building.[78] As such, depreciation commences for an office building held for rental in its entirety, rather than on a floor-by-floor basis. Similarly, costs incurred for property taxes and insurance relate to the building and land as a whole and, therefore, capitalization of those costs should cease when the building is substantially complete and ready for its intended use, rather than being phased in over time.

1.5.2 COSTS INCURRED SUBSEQUENT TO PROJECT COMPLETION   For properties that are developed for a company's own use or rental operations, costs will be incurred subsequent to the completion of the project. Questions of how to account for costs incurred subsequent to a property's completion are encountered not only by real estate companies, but by all companies owning real estate.

The accounting treatment of such costs will depend on the type of costs incurred and the reason for their incurrence. Costs incurred may be start-up costs within the scope of SOP 98-5, *Reporting on the Costs of Start-Up Activities*;[79] they may constitute normal maintenance expenses; or they may stem from renovations, remodeling, or refurbishing activities.

Normal repair and maintenance costs are commonly expensed as incurred. Questions remain, however, with respect to other costs incurred. If a company replaces the roof of a building, for example, should that new roof be capitalized?

---

78   FAS 67, paragraph 38
79   Section 1.7.2 discusses the accounting for start-up costs.

If so, is it appropriate or necessary to write off the estimated net book value of the existing roof?

Aside from a general rule that expenditures that extend the life of the property or increase its value are capitalized and that normal recurring repair and maintenance expenditures are expensed, very little guidance exists with respect to the accounting treatment of costs incurred subsequent to project completion. The proposed SOP, *Accounting for Certain Costs and Activities Relating to Property, Plant, and Equipment*, offers guidance with respect to costs incurred during the "in service stage;" however, that proposed SOP was not cleared by the FASB. Additionally, the proposed SOP introduces the concept of components, which is generally not followed in U.S. Generally Accepted Accounting Principles (GAAP).

1.6 PURCHASE OF INCOME PRODUCING PROPERTY

A transaction to acquire real estate held for rental, commonly referred to as income-producing property, may constitute the purchase of a business or the purchase of an asset/asset group. The determination of whether an acquisition constitutes the acquisition of a business or of an asset/asset group is essential for the appropriate allocation of the purchase price.

1.6.1 PURCHASE OF A BUSINESS   The main guidance for the determination of whether a business or an asset/asset group is being purchased is provided by EITF Issue No. 98-3, *Determining Whether a Nonmonetary Transaction Involves Receipt of Productive Assets or of a Business*.[80] That Issue states:[81]

> A business is a self-sustaining integrated set of activities and assets conducted and managed for the purpose of providing a return to investors. A business consists of (a) inputs, (b) processes applied to those inputs, and (c) resulting

---

80   In December 2007, the FASB issued FASB Statement No. 141(R), *Business Combinations*, which will replace FASB Statement No. 141 and nullify EIT Issue No. 98-3. FASB Statement No. 141(R) defines a business as follows: "A *business* is an integrated set of activities and assets that is capable of being conducted and managed for the purpose of providing a return in the form of dividends, lower costs, or other economic benefits directly to investors or other owners, members, or participants." [FAS 141(R), paragraph 3(d)]. That Statement applies prospectively to business combinations for which the acquisition date is on or after the beginning of the first annual reporting period beginning on or after December 15, 2008.

81   Unlike EITF Issue No. 98-3, FASB Statement No. 141(R) does not require outputs for an integrated set of activities and assets to qualify as a business. Paragraph A5 of FASB Statement No. 141(R) explains: "To be capable of being conducted and managed for the purposes defined, an integrated set of activities and assets requires two essential elements—inputs and processes applied to those inputs, which together are or will be used to create outputs. However, a business need not include all of the inputs or processes that the seller used in operating that business if market participants are capable of acquiring the business and continuing to produce outputs, for example, by integrating the business with their own inputs and processes."

outputs that are used to generate revenues. For a transferred set of activities and assets to be a business, it must contain all of the inputs and processes necessary for it to continue to conduct normal operations after the transferred set is separated from the transferor, which includes the ability to sustain a revenue stream by providing its outputs to customers.[82]

EITF Issue No. 98-3 outlines a three-step process to determine whether a transferred set of assets and activities is a business:[83]

Step 1: Identify the elements included in the transferred set.

Step 2: Identify any missing elements through a comparison of the elements identified in Step 1 with the complete set of elements necessary to conduct normal operations.

Step 3: If any elements are missing, assess whether these missing elements are minor. If the missing elements are minor, their absence would not lead to the conclusion that the transferred set of assets is not a business. When assessing whether missing elements are minor, factors such as the uniqueness or scarcity of the missing element, the time frame, level of effort and cost required to obtain the missing element should be considered.

Often, the evaluation of whether or not a set of activities and assets acquired constitutes a business requires significant judgment.

If all but a *de minimis* amount of the fair value of the transferred set of activities and assets is represented by a single tangible or identifiable intangible asset, the concentration of value in the single asset is an indicator that an asset rather than a business is being received in the transfer.[84] On the other hand, if goodwill is present in a transferred set of activities and assets, it should be presumed that the excluded items are minor and that the transferred set is a business.[85]

The purchase of individual income-producing properties, such as office buildings or warehouses, does often not constitute the acquisition of a business, whereas the purchase of a hotel or restaurant may very well constitute the acquisition of a business, depending on the components included in the transfer.[86] It is important to note that the manner in which the purchaser intends to operate the purchased set of activities and assets is not relevant to the determination of whether a business or an asset group is being purchased.

---

82   EITF Issue No. 98-3, paragraph 6
83   EITF Issue No. 98-3, paragraph 6; FASB Statement No. 141(R) does not include a process similar to the three-step process outlined in EITF Issue No. 98-3.
84   EITF Issue No. 98-3, paragraph 6; the guidance in FASB Statement No. 141(R) does not include a similar indicator.
85   EITF Issue No. 98-3, paragraph 6; like EITF Issue No. 98-3, FASB Statement No. 141(R) provides that the presence of goodwill creates the presumption that a set of assets and activities is a business. [FAS 141(R), paragraph A9]
86   EITF Issue No. 98-3 provides examples relating to the determination of whether a transfer of hotels and restaurants constitutes a business. [EITF Issue No. 98-3, Exhibit 98-3A, Examples 2 and 3]

1.6.2 PURCHASE OF AN ASSET/ASSET GROUP   If the purchase of real estate does not meet the criteria of a business as established in EITF Issue No. 98-3,[87] it constitutes the purchase of an asset/asset group.[88]

One key accounting difference between the acquisition of an asset/asset group and the acquisition of a business is that in the acquisition of a business, the assets acquired and liabilities assumed are recorded at their fair values, with any excess of acquisition cost over the amounts assigned to the assets acquired and liabilities assumed being recognized as goodwill.[89] In an asset acquisition, on the other hand, the allocation of the purchase price is based on the *relative* fair values of the individual assets and liabilities of the purchased set.[90] The *relative* fair values of the assets purchased and liabilities assumed may differ from their fair values. Section 1.6.5 in this chapter includes an example that illustrates the purchase price allocation in the acquisition of a business versus the acquisition of an asset group.

1.6.3 RECOGNITION OF INTANGIBLE ASSETS ACQUIRED   Before the issuance of FASB Statements No. 141, *Business Combinations* and No. 142, *Goodwill and Other Intangible Assets*, the purchase price for income-producing real estate was generally allocated to land and buildings. Any intangibles acquired, such as lease agreements, were considered part of the value of the land or buildings and not separately accounted for. Statements 141 and 142 have changed the way acquisitions of income-producing real estate properties are being accounted for. In both pronouncements, the FASB mandates that intangible assets be identified and recognized separately from land and buildings.[91] This has resulted in a change to previous accounting practice.

RECOGNITION CRITERIA IN BUSINESS ACQUISITIONS VS. ASSET ACQUISITIONS
In the acquisition of a business, an intangible asset is recognized as a separate asset only if one of the following two criteria is met:[92]

1. The asset arises from contractual or other legal rights.
2. The asset is separable, that is, capable of being separated or divided from the acquired entity and sold, transferred, licensed, rented, or exchanged (regardless of whether there is an intent to do so).[93]

---

87   For business combinations with an acquisition date on or after the beginning of the first annual reporting period beginning on or after December 15, 2008, FASB Statement No. 141(R) applies.
88   Similar guidance is provided in FASB Statement No. 141(R): If the assets acquired and liabilities assumed are not a business, a purchase transaction is accounted for as an asset acquisition. [FAS 141(R), paragraph 4]
89   FAS 141, paragraphs 35 and 43
90   FAS 141, paragraph 9
91   FAS 141, paragraph 7; FAS 142, paragraph 9
92   Under FASB Statement No. 141(R), the acquirer recognizes, separately from goodwill, the identifiable assets acquired, the liabilities assumed, and any noncontrolling interest in the acquiree. [FAS 141(R), paragraph 12] Paragraph 3(k) of FASB Statement No. 141(R) provides that an "asset is *identifiable* if it either: (1) Is separable, that is, capable of being separated or divided from the entity and sold, transferred, licensed, rented, or exchanged, either individually or together with a related contract, identifiable asset, or liability, regardless of whether the entity intends to do so; or (2) Arises from contractual or other legal rights, regardless of whether those rights are transferable or separable from the entity or from other rights and obligations."
93   FAS 141, paragraph 39

In a purchase of income-producing property that does not meet the definition of a business, however, all intangible assets that meet the asset recognition criteria in Concepts Statement No. 5, *Recognition and Measurement in Financial Statements of Business Enterprises*, must be recognized in the financial statements, even though they may not meet either of these two asset recognition criteria.[94]

INTANGIBLES IN THE ACQUISITION OF INCOME-PRODUCING PROPERTIES

Intangibles commonly encountered in the acquisition of income producing real estate properties[95] are:

- In-place leases
  - at-market component
  - above- and below-market component
- Tenant (customer) relationships

Other intangible assets, such as tenant (customer) lists or trade names, may also be present, depending on the individual facts and circumstances.

In-Place Leases. Companies acquiring income-producing properties segregate leases that are in place at the date of acquisition ("in-place leases") into (1) an at-market component and (2) an above- and below-market component.

The at-market component of in-place leases represents the value of having lease contracts in place at terms that are market. The above- and below-market component of in-place leases represents the present value of the difference in cash flows between the contractually agreed-upon rentals and current prevailing rental rates for the in-place leases. If in-place leases are above-market, they represent assets from the acquiring company's perspective, because the acquiring company will receive rentals that are above market in future periods. If in-place leases are below-market, they represent liabilities (balance sheet credits). The above- and below-market components of acquired leases are determined on a lease-by-lease basis. As such, the acquisition of one income-producing property may result in both above-market leases (assets) and below-market leases (liabilities [balance sheet credits]); the amounts of above- and below-market leases are not presented "net" on the balance sheet.

Tenant Relationships. A tenant relationship is a relationship between the lessor of the property and its tenants, akin to a customer relationship.[96]

FASB Statement No. 141 states with respect to customer relationships:[97]

> For purposes of this Statement, a customer relationship exists between an entity and its customer if (a) the entity has information about the customer and has regular contact with the customer and (b) the customer has the ability to make

---

94   FAS 142, paragraphs 9 (footnote 7) and B37
95   In both business acquisition and asset acquisition
96   FAS 141, paragraph F1; EITF Issue No. 02-17
97   FAS 141, paragraph F1

direct contact with the entity. Relationships may arise from contracts (such as supplier contracts and service contracts). However, customer relationships may arise through means other than contracts, such as through regular contact by sales or service representatives.

A tenant relationship may provide the landlord with the ability to generate a future income stream besides rentals from in-place leases; for example, a landlord may be able to attract an anchor tenant of one shopping mall to its other shopping malls. Or a well-known anchor tenant, such as a high-end retailer, may act as a magnet for other tenants.[98]

1.6.4 VALUATION OF LAND, BUILDINGS, AND INTANGIBLES   Fair value is defined as the price that would be received to sell an asset or paid to transfer a liability in an orderly transaction between market participants at the measurement date.[99]

The FASB provides the following general guidance regarding the valuation of individual assets acquired in a business combination:

- Land at appraised values[100]
- Plant and equipment
  - Plant and equipment to be used at the current replacement cost, unless the expected future use of the assets indicates a lower value to the acquiring entity[101] (replacement cost can be estimated from the replacement cost new less estimated accumulated depreciation[102])
- Plant and equipment to be sold at fair value less cost to sell[103]
- Intangible assets at their estimated fair values[104]

An intangible asset arising from a contractual or other legal right represents the future cash flows that are expected to result from the ownership of that contractual or legal right.[105] The FASB observed that "a contract may have value for reasons other than terms that are favorable relative to market prices. The Board therefore concluded that the amount by which the terms of a contract are favorable relative to market prices would not always represent the fair value of that contract."[106]

---

98   Views differ as to whether to include the fair value arising from expected future lease renewals in the intangible asset *in-place leases*, or whether to consider that fair value in the intangible asset *tenant relationships*.

99   FAS 157, paragraph 5; prior to changes effected by FASB Statement No. 157, fair value is defined as the amount at which an asset (or liability) could be bought (or incurred) or sold (or settled) in a current transaction between willing parties, that is, other than in a forced or liquidation sale. [FAS 142, Appendix F, paragraph F1]

100   FAS 141, paragraph 37(f)

101   FAS 141, paragraph 37(d)(1)

102   The SEC has indicated in comment letters to SEC registrants that the fair value of buildings acquired in an asset purchase should be determined on an as if-vacant basis.

103   FAS 141, paragraph 37(d)(2)

104   FAS 141, paragraph 37(e)

105   FAS 141, paragraph B172

106   FAS 141, paragraph B41

Since the issuance of Statements 141 and 142, industry practice, largely driven by Securities and Exchange Commission (SEC) comment letters, has developed with respect to identifying and measuring the individual assets and liabilities (balance sheet credits) that are recorded upon the acquisition of real estate properties. Changes to prior industry practice relate primarily to the valuation of buildings—to be valued on an as if-vacant basis—and the separate recognition and valuation of in-place leases.

The requirement to measure intangibles at fair value necessitates a consideration of future contract renewals, consistent with FASB's view that estimates used should incorporate assumptions that market participants would use in making estimates of fair value.[107] In a lease with renewal options granted to the lessee, it appears appropriate to assume that a lessee would likely not renew a lease at above-market terms, and that a lessee would renew the lease if it could renew at below-market terms (or if the lessee were to incur a contractual or economic penalty if it decided not to exercise its renewal option).[108]

IN-PLACE LEASES AT MARKET

With respect to the valuation of in-place leases at market, one possible valuation approach may be to calculate—from an investor's perspective—the present value of the cash flow difference of acquiring the property with the in-place leases (at current market rates) versus acquiring the property without leases in place and having to lease up the property. That cash flow differential is an approximation of the difference a seller would expect to receive when selling a building already leased up versus selling a building without leases in place. The following elements are often significant when evaluating that cash flow differential in the purchase of income-producing properties:

- Lost rental revenue over the expected lease-up period
- Additional operating costs incurred as a result of not receiving tenant reimbursements
- Expenses relating to leasing commissions and legal fees to be incurred
- Reduced maintenance expenses for property not leased

As the accounting literature does not prescribe any particular valuation method, other methods may be used if they are consistent with the general

---

107   FAS 141, paragraph B174; FAS 142, paragraph B42
108   Views differ as to whether or not to include the fair value of expected future lease renewals in the intangible asset *in-place leases*, or whether to consider that fair value in the intangible asset *tenant relationships*.

guidance provided by Statements 141 and 142 that intangibles be measured at their fair values.[109]

IN-PLACE LEASES ABOVE- AND BELOW-MARKET
The fair value of the above- and below-market component of in-place leases is generally determined by calculating the present value of the difference in cash flows between the contractually agreed-upon rentals and current prevailing rental rates for the leases in place in the same geographic area at the time of acquisition.

1.6.5 ALLOCATION OF ACQUISITION COST   In the purchase of real estate property that meets the definition of a business, the acquisition cost is allocated to the assets acquired and liabilities assumed based on their fair values. Any excess of cost over the amounts assigned to assets acquired and liabilities assumed is recognized as goodwill.[110]

If the purchase of real estate does not constitute a business, the acquisition cost is allocated to the individual assets and liabilities acquired based on their *relative* fair values.[111] The allocation of the acquisition cost based on the fair values of individual assets and liabilities, with a residual being allocated to one of the elements, is not an acceptable method. The SEC staff has expressed the following view with respect to the use of a residual method in business combinations, the concept of which applies—by analogy—to asset acquisitions also:[112]

> Some have asserted that the residual method provides an acceptable approach for determining the fair value of the intangible asset to which the residual is assigned, either because it approximates the value that would be attained from a direct value method or because they believe that other methods of valuation are not practicable under the circumstances. Others have indicated that the residual method should be used as a proxy for fair value of the intangible asset in these situations, since the fair value of the intangible asset in question is not determinable. . .

---

109   FAS 141, paragraph 37(e); paragraph 36 of FASB Statement No. 141 provides that the following may be useful in determining the estimated fair values of assets acquired and liabilities assumed: "Among other sources of relevant information, independent appraisals and actuarial or other valuations may be used as an aid in determining the estimated fair values of assets acquired and liabilities assumed . . ."

110   If the fair value of the assets acquired and liabilities assumed were to exceed the cost, such excess would be allocated as *pro rata* reduction of long-lived assets. [FAS 141, paragraph 44] Under FASB Statement No. 141(R), any excess of the fair value of the identifiable net assets acquired and liabilities assumed over the fair value of the consideration transferred (and the fair value of any noncontrolling interest in the transferee) would be recognized in earnings as a gain attributable to the acquirer. [FAS 141(R), paragraphs 34 and 36]

111   FAS 142, paragraph 9

112   EITF Topic No. D-108, *Use of the Residual Method to Value Acquired Assets Other Than Goodwill*

The SEC staff believes that the residual method does not comply with the requirements of Statement 141. . . . The SEC staff notes that a fundamental distinction between other recognized intangible assets and goodwill is that goodwill is both defined and measured as an excess or residual asset, while other recognized intangible assets are required to be measured at fair value. The SEC staff does not believe that the application of the residual method to the valuation of intangible assets can be assumed to produce amounts representing the fair values of those assets.

The requirement in FASB Statement No. 142 to allocate the purchase price in an asset acquisition based on the *relative* fair values of the assets acquired and liabilities assumed is frequently implemented as follows:

ACQUISITION COST EXCEEDS FAIR VALUE OF NET ASSETS ACQUIRED

Any difference between the acquisition cost and the fair value of the net assets acquired is allocated to the assets acquired based on their relative fair values, except for financial assets (other than investments accounted for by the equity method), assets that are subject to a fair value impairment test, such as inventories, and any indefinite-lived assets. Allocating cost to these assets in an amount above their fair values would frequently require the recognition of an impairment loss subsequent to the acquisition of the asset group.

FAIR VALUE OF NET ASSETS ACQUIRED EXCEEDS ACQUISITION COST

Any difference is generally allocated consistent with the allocation method for negative goodwill, as described in paragraph 44 of FASB Statement No. 141:

> That excess shall be allocated as a pro rata reduction of the amounts that otherwise would have been assigned to all of the acquired assets . . . except (a) financial assets other than investments accounted for by the equity method, (b) assets to be disposed of by sale, (c) deferred tax assets, (d) prepaid assets relating to pension or other postretirement benefit plans, and (e) any other current assets.
>
> The acquired assets include research and development assets acquired and charged to expense in accordance with paragraph 5 of Interpretation 4 (refer to paragraph 42).

Although in most asset acquisitions, the relative fair values of the assets and liabilities will not exactly match the acquisition cost, a relatively large discrepancy between the acquisition cost and the fair value of the assets acquired and liabilities assumed may be an indication that either (1) not all intangibles have been identified, or (2) certain fair value determinations are not appropriate.

EXAMPLE—ACQUISITION OF INCOME-PRODUCING REAL ESTATE

This example illustrates the difference in the initial recording of the tangible and intangible assets acquired based on the assessment, whether the purchase of real estate property is the acquisition of a business or the acquisition of an asset/asset group.

Company B purchases a hotel for a purchase price of $10m. The fair values of the individual components amount to:

Land:	$4 million
Hotel building:	$3 million
Tenant improvements:	$0.2 million
In-place leases, at market:	$0.6 million
In-place leases, above market:	$1 million
Tenant relationships:[113]	$0.2 million
Total:	$9 million

Scenario 1: The purchase of the hotel is the purchase of a business.
Scenario 2: The purchase of the hotel does not constitute the purchase of a business.
How would Company B record the acquisition under Scenarios 1 and 2?

SCENARIO 1: Company B would record the purchase of the hotel as follows:

Land:	$4 million
Hotel building:	$3 million
Tenant improvements:	$0.2 million
In-place leases, at market:	$0.6 million
In-place leases, above market:	$1 million
Tenant relationships:	$0.2 million
Goodwill:	$1.0 million
Total:	$10 million

The fair values of the identifiable tangible and intangible assets amount to $9 million. The residual amount of $1 million represents goodwill.

SCENARIO 2: Company B would record the purchase of the hotel as follows:

Land:	$4.45 million (*)
Hotel building:	$3.33 million
Tenant improvements:	$0.22 million
In-place leases, at market:	$0.67 million
In-place leases, above market:	$1.11 million
Tenant relationships:	$0.22 million
Total:	$10 million

The tangible and intangible assets are recorded at their relative fair values. The difference between the acquisition cost ($10 million) and the fair values of the tangible and intangible assets ($9 million) is allocated to the identified tangible and intangible assets based on their fair values.

(*) Rounding difference

---

113 Tenant relationships in a hotel or resort may result from relationships with the owners of gift stores or the operators of amenities, from relationships with recurring customers established through frequent stay programs, conventions, and conferences, for example.

1.6.6 ACCOUNTING SUBSEQUENT TO ACQUISITION   FASB Statement No. 142 provides that the accounting for recognized intangible assets is based on their useful lives to the reporting entity.[114] The useful life of an intangible asset to a company is the period over which the asset is expected to contribute directly or indirectly to the future cash flows of the company. An intangible asset is amortized over its expected useful life to the company using a method of amortization that reflects the pattern in which the economic benefits of the intangible asset are consumed or used up. A straight-line amortization method is deemed appropriate if that pattern cannot be reliably determined.[115] The amount of an intangible asset to be amortized is the amount assigned to that asset at the time of acquisition less any residual value.[116]

The above- or below-market value of in-place leases is amortized over the remaining term of the leases (including any expected renewals if renewal assumptions were used to determine the fair value of the in-place leases[117]) and presented either as a reduction of or an addition to rental revenue. The theory behind that presentation in the income statement is that the acquirer paid a premium for above-market leases or received a discount for leases with contractual terms that are below-market. When including the amortization of the above- or below-market component of in-place leases in rental revenue, the revenue in the income statement more closely reflects rental revenue that represents market terms.

1.7 SPECIAL ACCOUNTING ISSUES

1.7.1 COSTS OF AMENITIES   Amenities are facilities that benefit or enhance a real estate project; they are often used by a developer as a marketing tool, particularly in a soft real estate market. They include golf courses, swimming pools, lakes, parks, and marinas to make a development more desirable, as well as sewage treatment plants or other utilities required by regulatory authorities. Amenities may or may not be revenue-producing.

The costs to be capitalized for the construction of amenities are determined in accordance with the criteria for cost capitalization discussed in Section 1.2 of this chapter. As a general rule, FASB Statement No. 67 provides that costs of amenities be allocated among the land parcels that benefit from the amenities, to the extent that the development of the parcels is probable.[118] The term "land parcel" is to be interpreted broadly: It may be an individual lot, unit, or phase of a real estate project.

The accounting treatment of amenities depends on whether the developer intends to (1) sell or transfer the amenities in connection with the sale of individual

---

114   Goodwill and intangible assets with indefinite useful lives are not amortized. [FAS 142, paragraphs 16 and 18]
115   FAS 142, paragraph 12
116   FAS 142, paragraph 13
117   EITF Issue No. 03-9, paragraph 5: " . . . The Task Force noted that the useful life—the period over which an intangible asset is expected to contribute to an entity's cash flows—for amortization purposes should be consistent with the estimated useful life considerations used in the determination of the fair value of that asset."
118   FAS 67, paragraph 8

units, or (2) sell the amenities separately to a third party or retain and operate the amenities. For example, clubhouses may be transferred to a homeowners association upon completion or sell-out of a development, whereas golf courses may be retained and operated by a developer.

FASB Statement No. 67 provides the following guidance for the treatment of costs incurred in connection with the construction and operation of amenities:

AMENITIES THAT ARE TO BE SOLD OR TRANSFERRED IN CONNECTION WITH THE SALE OF INDIVIDUAL UNITS[119]

Amenities that are to be sold or transferred in connection with the sale of individual units are clearly associated with the development and sale of the units in a project. To the extent that the costs of amenities and any expected future operating costs to be borne by the developer—until they are assumed by the buyers of the individual units—are not recoverable through proceeds from a future sale of these amenities, they are considered common costs of the project. Any changes in estimates relating to construction costs, to the operating results of the amenities before they are assumed by the buyers of the individual units, or to the amenities' sales proceeds (if any) are treated as changes in estimates and accounted for prospectively in accordance with FASB Statement No. 154, *Accounting Changes and Error Corrections*.

AMENITIES THAT ARE TO BE SOLD SEPARATELY TO A THIRD PARTY OR RETAINED BY THE DEVELOPER[120]

If a developer plans to sell amenities to a third party or retain them, capitalizable costs in excess of the estimated fair value of the amenities as of the date of substantial completion are allocated as common project costs. If a change in cost or fair value estimate of the amenities occurs prior to the amenities being substantially completed, the allocation of the amenities' costs to common costs of the project is revisited. After the amenities are substantially completed, no cost reallocations are made; accordingly, a subsequent sale may result in a gain or loss, which is included in the period of sale.

Operating results for amenities that are sold separately to a third party or operated by the developer are treated as follows:[121]

- Operating income (or loss) from the amenities before they are substantially completed and available for use is included as a reduction of (or an addition to) common costs.
- Operating income (or loss) from the amenities after they are substantially completed is included in the current operating results of the developer.

See Exhibit 1.2 for a graphic depiction of the accounting for costs of amenities.

---

119   FAS 67, paragraph 8(a)
120   FAS 67, paragraphs 8(b) and 9
121   FAS 67, paragraph 9

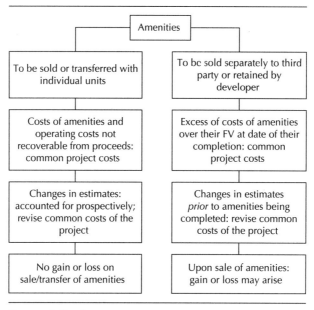

EXHIBIT 1.2   AMENITIES

1.7.2 START-UP COSTS   Start-up activities are one-time activities relating to opening a new facility, introducing a new product or service, conducting business in a new territory or with a new class of customer, initiating a new process, organizing a new entity, or commencing some new operation.[122] Start-up costs are costs incurred in connection with start-up activities; they are expensed as incurred.[123]

A retailer may construct a facility in which it plans to operate a new store. Between the time of completion of the facility and the store opening, there is typically a period of time during which start-up activities take place—for example, inventory may be stocked, employees may be trained, and registers may be tested. Costs incurred in connection with these activities are not part of the acquisition, development, and construction costs of the facility; they are start-up costs. Determining whether costs constitute start-up costs is based on the nature of the activities and not necessarily on the time period in which they occur; that is, start-up costs may be incurred before operations begin or after operations have begun, but before the normal productive capacity is reached.[124]

The following are some examples of start-up costs within the scope of SOP 98-5, *Reporting on the Costs of Start-Up Activities:*[125]

- Organization costs
- Training costs of employees

---

122   SOP 98-5, paragraph 5
123   SOP 98-5, paragraph 12
124   SOP 98-5, paragraphs 30 and 31
125   SOP 98-5, paragraphs 44 and 45

- Consultant fees
- Salaries and salary-related expenses for new employees
- Costs of recruiting
- Nonrecurring operating losses
- Amortization and depreciation of leasehold improvements and fixed assets that are used in the start-up activities

Examples for costs incurred in conjunction with start-up activities that are outside the scope of SOP 98-5 are:[126]

- Costs of acquiring or constructing long-lived assets[127]
- Costs of acquiring intangible assets[128]
- Internal-use computer software systems development costs
- Costs of acquiring or producing inventory
- Financing costs and costs of raising capital
- Advertising costs
- Security, property taxes, insurance, and utilities costs related to construction activities
- Costs incurred in connection with existing construction contracts[129]

EXAMPLE—START-UP COSTS[130]

ToyCo. (T), a retail chain, is opening a new store. T rents the store, which it will build out and furnish. T incurs capital expenditures for leasehold improvements and furniture. T expects that it will require three months to set up the store. Among the costs incurred during the three-month period are costs for security, property taxes, insurance, and utilities.

Can T capitalize these costs?

No. The building, although requiring some set-up costs (leasehold improvements, furniture) is substantially ready for its intended use upon entering into the lease, and no construction activities need to be performed in connection with the store. The costs for security, property taxes, insurance, and utilities are start-up costs within the scope of SOP 98-5 that should be expensed.

1.7.3 LAND OPTIONS   Obtaining land options is a common means for land developers and homebuilders to secure land for future development without having to finance the land, incur carrying costs and bear the risk of a decline in

---

126   SOP 98-5, paragraphs 8, 44
127   The costs of using long-lived assets that are allocated to start-up activities (for example, depreciation of computers) are within the scope of SOP 98-5. [SOP 98-5, paragraph 8]
128   The costs of using intangible assets that are allocated to start-up activities are within the scope of SOP 98-5. [SOP 98-5, paragraph 8]
129   AcSEC believes that start-up costs incurred in connection with existing contracts (whether or nor incurred in anticipation of follow-on contracts) are contract costs related to a specific source of revenue subject to the accounting prescribed in SOP 81-1, *Accounting for Performance of Construction-Type and Certain Production-Type Contracts*. [SOP 98-5, paragraph 39]
130   Adapted from SOP 98-5, paragraph 44 (Illustration 3).

land value. In exchange for the payment of an option premium, the option holder obtains the right to purchase the land under option at a fixed price over a certain period or at some future point in time. As discussed in Section 1.2.1, option premiums are preacquisition costs that qualify for cost capitalization.

The option holder may be required to consolidate the entity owning the land under option pursuant to the provisions of FASB Interpretation No. (FIN) 46(R), *Consolidation of Variable Interest Entities*, rather than merely capitalizing the option premium. Whether the consolidation guidance in FIN 46(R) has to be evaluated depends on the counterparty to the transaction. If the land under option is owned by an individual, such as a farmer, no further considerations are necessary. If, however, the land under option is being held by a legal entity, the provisions of FIN 46(R) may apply. More often than not, land under option is held by a legal entity, because it provides the option holder with better control over the land under option; it also isolates the land from any liabilities of the owner. As such, holders of land options will likely have to consider FIN 46(R). When performing a FIN 46(R) analysis, holders of land options need to consider any other arrangements with the entity; they may have agreements in place to develop the land, to provide financing, or to guarantee certain obligations of the entity. Contractual arrangements between the entity owning the land and the option holder (or any related party) may constitute variable interests that impact the evaluation of whether the option holder has to consolidate the entity owning the land.

FIN 46(R) analyses are very complex; the following discussion intends to highlight some aspects that need to be considered when evaluating land options. It is not intended to cover all aspects that need to be considered.

LAND UNDER OPTION IS MAJORITY OF ENTITY'S ASSETS
A legal entity owns land and has granted to a homebuilder the option to purchase the land at a fixed price within a specified period of time. If the land under option represents the entity's only asset or a majority of the entity's assets when measured at fair value, the option is deemed a variable interest in the entity. In that case, the entity generally meets the definition of a variable interest entity (VIE) for the following reason: As a result of the option, the option holder has the ability to participate in the future appreciation of the land. In FIN 46(R)-speak, the entity's holders of equity investment at risk do not have the right to receive the entity's expected residual returns.[131] Whenever the holders of an entity's equity investment at risk do not have the right to receive the entity's expected residual returns, the entity meets the definition of a VIE.[132] The entity may also be considered a VIE for reasons other than the one cited, such as insufficient equity investment at risk.

---

131   If the deposit is nonrefundable, the option holder would also absorb expected losses of the entity.
132   FIN 46(R), paragraph 5(b)(3)

LAND UNDER OPTION IS NOT MAJORITY OF ENTITY'S ASSETS

Variable interests in assets that comprise 50% or less of the fair value of an entity's assets are not variable interests in the entity and do not pose any FIN 46(R) consolidation issues, with the following two exceptions:

- The option holder holds another variable interest in the entity.
- A silo has been created.

Option Holder Holds Another Variable Interest in the Entity.   Paragraph 12 of FIN 46(R) provides that a variable interest in specified assets of an entity that comprise 50% or less of the entity's assets is considered a variable interest in the entity if the variable interest holder holds another variable interest,[133] for example, an equity interest, in the entity itself. In that case, the entity would generally meet the definition of a variable interest entity for the reason outlined above.

A Silo Has Been Created.[134]   Silos exist if the variability arising from specified assets inures to the benefit or detriment of variable interest holders in these assets, rather than to the benefit or detriment of variable interest holders in the entity. In other words, essentially none of the variability generated by these specified assets affects the expected losses or expected residual returns of the variable interest holders of the entity.

If such a silo exists, it has to be evaluated whether the entity meets the criteria of a variable interest entity. If the entity does not meet the criteria of a variable interest entity, no further FIN 46(R) considerations are necessary.

The FIN 46(R) considerations relating to land options are illustrated in Exhibit 1.3.

CONSOLIDATION CONSIDERATIONS

Once it has been determined that the option holder holds a variable interest in a VIE or in any siloed assets of a VIE, the option holder has to evaluate whether it is the primary beneficiary (PB), that is, whether it has to consolidate the entity or silo.[135] The option holder may be the entity's primary beneficiary if the option holder and its related parties[136] absorb a majority of the entity's expected losses, receive a majority of the entity's expected residual returns, or both.[137]

---

133   Except for interests that are insignificant or have little or no variability. [FIN 46(R), paragraph 12]

134   FIN 46(R), paragraph 13; FSP FIN 46(R)-1

135   A silo in a VIE is treated as a separate variable interest entity. Therefore, in the following discussion, no distinction has been made between an option holder that has an interest in a VIE and an option holder that has an interest in a silo of a VIE.

136   FIN 46(R), paragraph 16; for purposes of FIN 46(R), the term "related parties" includes the parties identified in FASB Statement No. 57, *Related Party Disclosures*, and certain other parties that are acting as de facto agents or de facto principals of the variable interest holder.

137   FIN 46(R), paragraph 14

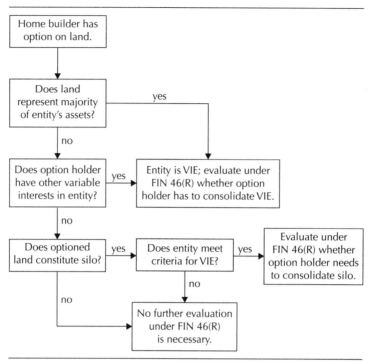

EXHIBIT 1.3   FIN 46(R) DECISION TREE—LAND OPTIONS

EXAMPLE—SILO

Palm West LLC (LLC) is a newly created entity. Its only assets are three parcels of land, which have been contributed by its members. The LLC has obtained a mortgage loan on each of the three parcels of land approximating each parcel's fair value, and has distributed the amounts received under the loans to the members of the LLC. The mortgage loans are nonrecourse to the LLC or its members. The LLC writes a call option to a third-party homebuilder on one of the parcels, the exercise price of which approximates the parcel's fair value. If the land parcel increases in value, the option holder will benefit from the appreciation. If the land decreases in value, the option holder will likely not exercise the option, and the lender will have to absorb the losses, since the loan is nonrecourse to the LLC.

Does a silo exist with respect to the land under option?

Yes. The land is isolated from the remainder of the LLC. The members of the LLC do not participate in any appreciation of the land due to the option. They also have virtually no downside risk, as the LLC has obtained a loan approximating the fair value of the land. The entity meets the criteria of a VIE pursuant to paragraph 5(a)(1) of FIN 46(R), because it does not have any equity investment at risk. The option holder will have to perform a FIN 46(R) analysis to determine whether it has to consolidate the silo (consisting of the land and the mortgage on the land).

However, if the members of the LLC were subject to absorbing variability created by the land under option, a silo would not have been created. That would be the case, for example, if the borrowings on the land were substantially lower than the fair value of the land.

The features of the option, particularly refundability and amount of option premium relative to the fair value of the optioned land, play a major role when determining which variable interest holder is the primary beneficiary.

Certain option premiums may be *refundable* for a certain period of time, for example, to allow the option holder time to perform feasibility studies on the optioned land. As long as the option premium is refundable, the option holder does not have an obligation to absorb any of the entity's expected losses. If no other party absorbs a majority of the entity's expected losses, a FIN 46(R) analysis would nevertheless have to be performed to determine whether the option holder receives the majority of an entity's expected residual returns.

If option premiums are *nonrefundable*, the option holder's downside is limited to the option premium: If the fair value of the land under option were to decline by more than the option premium, the option holder would either not exercise the option or renegotiate the purchase price. As such, the size of the option premium is an important factor in the evaluation of which party absorbs the majority of the entity's expected losses. The larger the size of the option premium in relation to the fair value of the land, the more likely it is that the option holder will have to consolidate the entity.

1.7.4 FINANCING AS PART OF A PURCHASE TRANSACTION

In real estate acquisitions, financing is often an integral part of the purchase transaction. The seller may provide financing to the buyer, or the buyer may assume a mortgage on the property. When financing is provided in an arm's-length transaction, there is a presumption that the stated interest rate is fair and adequate. This presumption is not appropriate when (1) the note does not have a stated interest rate, (2) the stated interest rate is unreasonable, (3) the stated face amount of the note (together with any down payment) is materially different from the current cash sales price for similar property, or (4) the stated face amount of the note is materially different from the market value of the note at the date of the transaction.[138]

If, in a purchase transaction, financing is provided at unreasonable rates, the property acquired should be recorded at (1) the fair value of the property or (2) an amount that approximates the market value of the note plus the fair value of any other consideration provided to the seller, whichever is more clearly determinable.[139] If such determination cannot be made due to a lack of established exchange prices or market value of the note, the present value of the note should be determined by discounting all future payments on the note using an imputed rate of interest. The rate used to determine the present value of the note is normally at least equal to the rate at which the debtor can obtain financing from other sources at the date

---

138   APB 21, paragraph 12
139   APB 21, paragraph 12

of the transaction. "The objective is to approximate the rate which would have resulted if an independent borrower and lender had negotiated a similar transaction under comparable terms and conditions with the option to pay the cash price upon purchase or to give a note for the amount of the purchase which bears the prevailing rate of interest to maturity."[140] Accordingly, the facts and circumstances of the individual transaction need to be considered. This includes an evaluation of the terms of the financing, any collateral and security provided to the lender, the down payment the purchaser has made, the credit rating of the purchaser, and tax consequences to the buyer and seller.[141]

If it has been determined that financing has been provided at an unreasonable rate and that the imputation of interest is required, the difference between the present value and the face amount of the note is treated as discount or premium and amortized as interest expense. The discount or premium is eligible for inclusion in the amount of interest cost capitalized in accordance with FASB Statement No. 34.[142]

Paragraph 16 of APB Opinion No. 21 provides with respect to the presentation of such premium or discount in the financial statements:

> The discount or premium resulting from the determination of present value in cash or non-cash transactions is not an asset or liability separable from the note which gives rise to it. Therefore, the discount or premium should be reported in the balance sheet as a direct deduction from or addition to the face amount of the note. It should not be classified as a deferred charge or deferred credit. The description of the note should include the effective interest rate; the face amount should also be disclosed in the financial statements or in the notes to the statements.

1.7.5 ENVIRONMENTAL COSTS AND LIABILITIES Property owners are required to comply with federal, state, and local laws that govern the removal and containment of environmental contamination in land and buildings. Being subject not only to current but also to future legislation, property owners may incur significant costs for known or yet undiscovered conditions or events.

Real estate acquisition and development is affected by accounting issues relating to environmental cleanup, particularly by issues relating to the recognition and measurement of liabilities, the accounting for environmental cleanup costs (that is, capitalization vs. expensing of costs), as well as financial statement presentation and disclosures. Depending on the type of contamination, different guidance applies to the accounting for costs incurred in connection with environmental cleanup.

---

140   APB 21, paragraph 13
141   APB 21, paragraph 13
142   APB 21, paragraph 15

1.7.5.1 Asset Retirement Obligations   FASB Statement No. 143, *Accounting for Asset Retirement Obligations*, provides guidance relating to legal obligations associated with the retirement[143] of a tangible long-lived asset that result from the acquisition, development construction, or the normal operation of the long-lived asset. "Retirement" is defined as the other-than-temporary removal of a long-lived asset from service, which includes its sale, abandonment, or disposal in some other manner.[144] Although not addressed further in this section, asset retirement obligations are not necessarily tied to environmental contamination or clean-up. For example, a landowner that grants a company the right to cut down timber may impose an obligation on that company to reforest the land at the end of the agreement.[145] Obligations may also be imposed on lessees, such as the obligation to remove leasehold improvements at the end of a lease. If the lessee is obligated to make or can be required to make such payments in connection with the leased property, the payments meet the definition of minimum lease payments;[146] FASB Statement No. 13, *Accounting for Leases*, rather than FASB Statement No. 143 applies to the obligations of a lessee that meet the definition of minimum lease payments or contingent rentals.[147] Determining whether an obligation to retire a leased asset should be accounted for as a minimum lease payment or as an asset retirement obligation is facts- and circumstances-based. As a general rule, if the obligation is directly related to the leased asset (or a component thereof), the lessee should account for the obligation in accordance with Statement 13. Conversely, if the asset retirement obligation relates to lessee-owned assets placed into service by the lessee at the leased premises, or if the asset retirement obligation relates to improvements made to the leased property by the lessee during the lease term, the lessee would generally account for them as asset retirement obligations following the provisions of Statement 143.

Legal obligations associated with the retirement of tangible long-lived assets, which give rise to asset retirement obligations, can result from (1) a government action, such as a law or statute, (2) an agreement between entities, or (3) a promise conveyed to a third party that imposes a reasonable expectation of performance.[148]

RECOGNITION AND MEASUREMENT

An asset retirement obligation should be recognized at fair value in the period in which it is incurred, if a reasonable estimate of fair value can be made; otherwise, at a later point in time, when such reasonable estimate of fair value can be made.

---

143   The term *asset retirement obligation* refers to an obligation associated with the retirement of a tangible long-lived asset. The term *asset retirement cost* refers to the amount capitalized that increases the carrying amount of the long-lived asset when a liability for an asset retirement obligation is recognized. [FAS 143, footnote 1]
144   FAS 143, footnote 2; FAS 143, paragraph A6
145   FAS 143, Appendix C, Example 4; the "lease of land" for the exploitation of timber is not within the scope of FASB Statement No. 13. [FAS 13, paragraph 1]
146   FAS 13, paragraph 5(j)(i)
147   FAS 143, paragraph 17
148   FAS 143, paragraph A2

Instances in which asset retirement obligations are not reasonably estimable are expected to be rare. If a tangible long-lived asset with an existing asset retirement obligation is acquired, a liability for that obligation needs to be recognized at the asset's acquisition date as if that obligation were incurred on that date.[149]

The fair value of an asset retirement obligation is reasonably estimable if at least one of the following criteria is met:[150]

- It is evident that the fair value of the obligation is embodied in the acquisition price of the asset
- An active market exists for the transfer of the obligation
- Sufficient information exists to apply an expected present value technique

Upon recognition of an asset retirement obligation, a company capitalizes a corresponding asset retirement cost by increasing the carrying amount of the related long-lived asset by the same amount as the liability. That asset retirement cost is charged to expense over the asset's useful life, using a systematic and rational method.[151]

Subsequent to initial measurement, the fair value of the liability is adjusted to reflect changes resulting from:

- The passage of time, using the credit-adjusted risk-free rate that existed when the liability was initially measured
- Revisions to either the timing or the amount of the original estimate of undiscounted cash flows; upward revisions in the amount of undiscounted estimated cash flows are discounted using the current credit-adjusted risk-free rate, whereas downward revisions are discounted using the credit-adjusted risk-free rate that existed when the liability was originally recognized[152]

The increase in the fair value of an asset retirement obligation due to the passage of time constitutes operating expense; changes as a result of revisions to either the timing or the amount of the original estimate of cash flows that do not only affect the current period increase or decrease the carrying amount of the related long-lived asset.[153]

CONDITIONAL ASSET RETIREMENT OBLIGATIONS
Conditional asset retirement obligations are not conditional obligations. Rather, they are legal obligations to perform an asset retirement activity, with the timing and (or) method of settlement being conditional on a future event that may or may not be

---

149   FAS 143, footnote 4
150   FIN 47, paragraph 4
151   FAS 143, paragraph 11
152   FAS 143, paragraph 15
153   FAS 143, paragraphs 14 and 15

within the control of the entity.[154] As such, a liability needs to be recognized in the financial statements if the fair value can be reasonably estimated. When FIN 47, *Accounting for Conditional Asset Retirement Obligations,* became effective in 2005, many real estate companies recorded asset retirement obligations to reflect their legal obligations in connection with the removal of asbestos in their buildings.

EXAMPLE—ASSET RETIREMENT OBLIGATION[155]

Store-4-U, Inc. (S) has acquired a fuel storage facility. A certain amount of spillage is inherent in the normal operations of the fuel storage facility. In the current period, improper operation resulted in a catastrophic accident that caused an unusual amount of spillage.

Is the environmental remediation liability that results from (1) the normal operations and/ or (2) from the accident within the scope of Statement 143?

The environmental remediation liability that results from the normal operations of the fuel storage facility is within the scope of Statement 143. Any obligation to remediate the spillage from the accident is not within the scope of Statement 143. However, S has to evaluate whether the recognition of an obligation to remediate the spillage is required by other authoritative guidance, such as SOP 96-1, *Environmental Remediation Liabilities.*

DISCLOSURES

FASB Statement No. 143 requires the following disclosures:[156]

- A general description of the asset retirement obligations and the associated long-lived assets
- The fair value of assets that are legally restricted for purposes of settling asset retirement obligations
- A reconciliation of the beginning and ending aggregate carrying amount of asset retirement obligations, showing separately the changes attributable to (1) liabilities incurred in the current period, (2) liabilities settled in the current period, (3) accretion expense, and (4) revisions in estimated cash flows whenever there is a significant change

Additionally, in certain rare instances in which a company is not able to estimate the fair value of an asset retirement obligation, financial statement disclosures are required describing that circumstance and the company's reason for its inability to determine fair value.

1.7.5.2 Environmental Remediation Liabilities   For contamination that is outside of the scope of Statement 143, a company may nevertheless be required to recognize a liability under SOP 96-1, *Environmental Remediation Liabilities.* SOP

---

154   FIN 47, paragraph 3
155   Adapted from FASB Statement No. 143, paragraph A13
156   FAS 143, paragraph 22

96-1 provides accounting guidance for "environmental remediation liabilities that relate to pollution arising from some past act."[157]

A company's association with the site through past or present ownership or operation of a site, or the contribution or transportation of waste to a site, at which remedial actions (at a minimum, investigation) must take place may give rise to the recognition of an environmental remediation liability.[158]

Following the accounting guidance provided by FASB Statement No. 5, *Accounting for Contingencies*, a liability needs to be accrued if (1) information available prior to the issuance of the financial statements indicates that it is probable that an asset has been impaired or a liability has been incurred at the date of the financial statements ("probability criterion") and (2) the amount of the loss can be reasonably estimated.[159]

PROBABILITY CRITERION

Paragraph 108 of SOP 96-1 provides that in the context of environmental remediation liabilities, FASB Statement No. 5's probability criterion is met if both of the following elements are present on or before the date the financial statements are issued:

- It has been asserted (or it is probable that it will be asserted) that the entity is responsible for participating in a remediation process because of a past event.
- Based on available information, it is probable that the entity will be held responsible for participating in a remediation process because of that past event.

If litigation has commenced, a claim or an assessment has been asserted, or commencement of litigation or assertion of a claim or assessment is probable, and the company is associated with the site, there is a presumption that the outcome of the claim or assessment will be unfavorable.[160]

ABILITY TO REASONABLY ESTIMATE THE LIABILITY

Once a company has determined that it is probable that an environmental remediation liability has been incurred, the company should estimate that liability based on available information. The estimate of the liability includes the company's (1) allocable share of the liability for a specific site, as well as its (2) share of amounts related to the site that will not be paid by other potentially responsible parties (PRPs) or the government.[161]

Due to the fact that environmental remediation is a complex process involving many steps, estimating the amount required to effect such remediation may

---

157   SOP 96-1, paragraph 99
158   SOP 96-1, paragraphs 107 and 109
159   SOP 96-1, paragraph 105
160   SOP 96-1, paragraph 109
161   SOP 96-1, paragraph 121

prove difficult. This is particularly true in the beginning stages of remediation.[162] The ability to reasonably estimate a *range of loss* is sufficient to meet the requirement for the recognition of an accrual in FASB Statement No. 5, assuming it is probable that an environmental remediation liability has been incurred.[163]

MEASUREMENT

SOP 96-1 provides that ". . . the overall liability that is recorded may be based on amounts representing the lower end of a range of costs for some components of the liability and best estimates within ranges of costs of other components of the liability."[164] If various potentially responsible parties are involved, the amount to be recorded as a liability is based on the company's estimate of the share of the joint and several remediation liability that will ultimately be allocated to the company.[165]

Costs that should be included in determining the amount of liability are:[166]

1. Incremental direct costs of the remediation effort, such as:
   - Legal, engineering, and consulting fees
   - Costs related to completing the remedial investigation/feasibility study
   - Costs of contractors performing remedial actions
   - Government oversight costs
   - The cost of machinery and equipment dedicated to the remedial actions that do not have alternative uses
2. Costs of compensation and benefits for those employees who are expected to devote a significant amount of time directly to the remediation effort, to the extent of the time expected to be spent directly on the remediation effort. This may include technical employees who are involved with the remediation effort or internal legal staff dealing with remedial action.

The Accounting Standards Executive Committee (AcSEC) concluded that for purposes of measuring environmental remediation liabilities, the measurement should be based on enacted laws and adopted regulations and policies, rather than laws that are expected to be in force at a future point in time. The impact of changes in laws, regulations, and policies should be recognized when such changes are enacted or adopted.[167]

SOP 96-1 is more restrictive than Statement 143 as far as the discounting of the liability is concerned; it allows for discounting of the liability only, if

---

162   SOP 96-1, paragraph 110
163   SOP 96-1, paragraph 111; FIN 14, paragraph 3
164   SOP 96-1, paragraph 113
165   SOP 96-1, paragraph 133
166   SOP 96-1, paragraphs 124–127
167   SOP 96-1, paragraph 129

the aggregate amount of the liability or component and the amount and timing of cash payments for the liability or component are fixed or reliably determinable.[168] Entities that file with the SEC should follow the guidance in SEC Staff Accounting Bulletin (SAB) Topic 5Y.[169] That Staff Accounting Bulletin discusses the appropriate discount rate to be used: The rate used to discount the cash payments should be the rate that will produce an amount at which the environmental liability could be settled in an arm's-length transaction with a third party.

POTENTIAL RECOVERIES

A company may expect to recover certain amounts expended for environmental remediation; for example, amounts may be recoverable from other potentially responsible parties, from the government, or from insurance companies. The amount of an environmental remediation liability should be determined independent from any potential claim for recovery, and an asset relating to any recovery should be recognized only when realization of the claim for recovery is deemed probable. If the claim is the subject of litigation, a rebuttable presumption exists that realization of the claim is not probable.[170]

PRESENTATION AND DISCLOSURE

Generally, environmental remediation–related expenses are included in operating expenses, because the events underlying the incurrence of the obligation relate to the operations of a company. Paragraph 149 of SOP 96-1 explains:

> Although charging the costs of remediating past environmental impacts against current operations may appear debatable because of the time between the contribution or transportation of waste materials containing hazardous substances to a site and the subsequent incurrence of remediation costs, environmental remediation–related expenses have become a regular cost of conducting economic activity. Accordingly, environmental remediation–related expenses should be reported as a component of operating income in income statements that classify items as operating or nonoperating. Credits arising from recoveries of environmental losses from other parties should be reflected in the same income statement line. Any earnings on assets that are reflected on the entity's financial statements and are earmarked for funding its environmental liabilities should be reported as investment income.

Depending on the facts and circumstances, environmental remediation liabilities may be recorded on a discounted or undiscounted basis. APB Opinion No. 22, *Disclosure of Accounting Policies,* requires the disclosure of accounting

---

168   SOP 96-1, paragraph 132
169   SAB Topic 5Y, Question 1
170   SOP 96-1, paragraph 140

principles that materially affect the determination of financial position or results of operations, particularly where accounting alternatives exist. With respect to environmental remediation obligations, financial statements should disclose whether the accrual for environmental remediation liabilities is measured on a discounted or undiscounted basis.[171] SAB Topic 5Y also discusses disclosure requirements relating to liabilities for environmental remediation that are discounted and gives detailed examples of disclosures that may be necessary to prevent the financial statements from being misleading.[172]

Additionally, FASB Statement No. 5 requires certain disclosures for loss contingencies, including disclosures relating to the nature of accruals. If no accrual is recognized for environmental remediation because the criteria for recording a liability have not been met, the contingency needs to be disclosed when there is at least a reasonable possibility that a loss may have been incurred.[173] SOP 96-1 provides additional guidance relating to disclosures for environmental remediation loss contingencies.[174]

1.7.5.3 Capitalizing versus Expensing of Environmental Remediation Costs

Recording an environmental remediation liability usually results in a corresponding charge to income.[175] In certain limited situations, such as those listed below, it is appropriate to capitalize environmental remediation costs:

- Environmental treatment costs may be capitalized if one of the following criteria is met, assuming the costs are recoverable:[176]
  - The costs extend the life, increase the capacity, or improve the safety or efficiency of the property owned. For purposes of this criterion, the condition of the property after the costs are incurred must be improved as compared with the condition of the property when originally constructed or acquired.
  - The costs mitigate or prevent environmental contamination that has yet to occur and that otherwise may result from future operations or activities. In addition, the costs improve the property compared with its condition when constructed or acquired, if later.
  - The costs are incurred in preparing for sale property that is currently held for sale.
  - The costs are incurred for the removal of asbestos.[177]

---

171   SOP 96-1, paragraphs 151 and 152
172   SAB Topic 5Y, Question 1
173   FAS 5, paragraph 10; SOP 96-1, paragraph 155
174   SOP 96-1, paragraphs 155–169
175   SOP 96-1, paragraph 147
176   EITF Issue No. 90-8
177   EITF Issue No. 89-13

- In conjunction with the initial recording of a purchase business combination or the final estimate of a preacquisition contingency at the end of the allocation period following the guidance in FASB Statement No. 141, *Business Combinations,* an environmental liability is considered in the determination and allocation of the purchase price.[178]
- When recording the receipt of property received as a contribution, any environmental remediation liability associated with the contribution should be taken into consideration.[179]

EITF Issue No. 90-8 includes explicit examples with respect to the question of when it is appropriate to capitalize vs. expense costs to treat environmental contamination.

EXAMPLE—COSTS TO TREAT ENVIRONMENTAL CONTAMINATION[180]

Lead pipes in an office building owned by EnCo. contaminate the drinking water in the building. EnCo. removes the lead pipes and replaces them with copper pipes. Removing the lead pipes has improved the safety of the building's water system compared with its condition when the water system was built or acquired.

  May EnCo. capitalize the replacement pipes?

  Yes. EnCo. may capitalize the costs to remove the lead pipes and install copper pipes, because EnCo., as the owner of the water system, incurs costs to treat environmental contamination that improve the safety of the water system as compared with its condition when the building was acquired. The estimated book value of the lead pipes should be charged to expense at the time they are removed.

1.7.6 TRANSACTIONS WITH RELATED PARTIES   This section discusses three aspects of related party relationships:

- Financing provided by related parties
- Interest capitalization on investments accounted for under the equity method of accounting
- Purchase of real estate from a party that is under common control with the buyer

1.7.6.1 Financing Provided by Related Parties   As outlined in Section 1.2.2.5 of this chapter, interest cost incurred during the development and construction period of a real estate project is capitalized and becomes part of project costs. That includes interest cost incurred on financing provided by a parent company or affiliate. The related interest income to the parent or affiliate is deferred to the

---

178   SOP 96-1, paragraph 147
179   SOP 96-1, paragraph 147
180   Adapted from EITF Issue No. 90-8, Exhibit 90-8A, Example 4.

extent of any ownership interest in the project or in the company; in subsequent periods, such deferred interest income is amortized to offset the company's amortization of capitalized interest cost, if the building is used in the company's operations, or recognized into income upon sale of the real estate property.

If a real estate project is financed by a parent company that does not charge interest, no interest cost may be capitalized at the subsidiary level, since the subsidiary does not incur any interest cost.[181] The capitalization of interest is nevertheless appropriate at the *consolidated* level; the amount to be capitalized at the consolidated level is determined by following the four-step approach outlined in Section 1.2.2.5 of this chapter.

1.7.6.2 Interest Capitalization on Investments Accounted for by the Equity Method   Paragraph 9(c) of FASB Statement No. 34, *Capitalization of Interest Cost*, provides that assets qualifying for interest capitalization include investments (equity investments, loans, and advances) accounted for by the equity method while the investee has activities in progress necessary to commence its planned operations, provided that the investee's activities include the use of funds to acquire qualifying assets for its operations. Interest capitalization on investments in equity method investees is illustrated in more detail in Chapter 6 (Section 6.4.8).

1.7.6.3 Purchase of Real Estate from Party under Common Control   In real estate purchase transactions between unrelated parties, the purchaser of real estate generally records the real estate acquired at its purchase price. The purchase price represents the culmination of an arm's-length bargaining and presumably is reflective of the fair value of the real estate property. An exception to this general rule is the acquisition of property from a party that is under common control with the buyer; parties under common control do not bargain at arm's length, because the shareholders are essentially self-dealing. If companies under common control enter into transactions that are in the ordinary course of business, the agreed-upon purchase price is readily comparable to the price negotiated in similar transaction with unrelated parties. In these types of transactions, the purchaser would ordinarily not be precluded from recording property acquired at its purchase price, if it is reflective of the market price. However, because of the special characteristics of real estate, the purchase of real estate from a party under common control is generally not comparable to similar transactions with unrelated parties. A step-up in basis by the acquirer is therefore not considered appropriate;[182] rather, real estate purchased from an entity under common control is recorded at the transferor's

---

181   FAS 34, paragraph 15
182   Similarly, a seller is precluded by paragraph 34 of FASB Statement No. 66 to recognize profit from the sale of real estate to parties that are controlled by the seller.

carrying value, after write-down for impairment.[183] Any excess of consideration given over the transferor's carrying value is accounted for as a reduction in equity, often referred to as "dangling debit."[184] Authoritative literature does not address the accounting for "dangling debits." Companies account for a "dangling debit" in one of two ways. They:

1. Account for the dangling debit as a separate component of equity and reduce the "dangling debit" through depreciation charges over the life of the real estate (if the real estate is held for use in operations) or include the "dangling debit" in the cost of sale (when the property is sold to a third party).

2. Account for the "dangling debit" as capital distribution (disproportionate dividend to the controlling shareholder) with no further entries required in periods subsequent to property acquisition.

1.8 FINANCIAL STATEMENT PRESENTATION AND DISCLOSURE

1.8.1 CASH FLOW STATEMENT PRESENTATION   Pursuant to paragraph 15 of FASB Statement No. 95, *Statement of Cash Flows*, investing activities include "acquiring and disposing of . . . property, plant, and equipment and other productive assets, that is, assets held for or used in the production of goods or services by the enterprise . . ." Operating activities include all transactions and other events that are not defined as investing or financing activities, which generally involve producing and delivering goods and providing services.[185]

The classification of cash payments for real estate acquired or constructed depends on the intended use for the property. Cash paid to acquire or construct real estate that will be used as "productive asset," such as rental property, is classified as investing cash outflows. However, if land were acquired by a real estate developer to be subdivided and sold, any cash payments to purchase that real estate would be classified as operating cash flows; the real estate acquired is akin to inventory in other businesses.[186]

The three categories of operating, investing, and financing are not necessarily mutually exclusive, that is, alternative classifications are acceptable in certain situations.[187] For example, if an office building is being constructed that is intended for sale after it has been leased up, a question may arise whether that property

183   This is consistent with the guidance provided in paragraph D12 of FASB Statement No. 141, which states: "When accounting for a transfer of assets or exchange of shares between entities under common control, the entity that receives the net assets or the equity interests shall initially recognize the assets and liabilities transferred at their carrying amounts in the accounts of the transferring entity at the date of transfer."
184   This may not be the case in situations, in which equity instruments are issued as consideration for the real estate transferred.
185   FAS 95, paragraph 21
186   FAS 102, paragraph 24
187   FAS 95, paragraph 86

should be treated like inventory, with any cash payments to acquire and construct the asset being classified as operating cash flows, or whether it should be viewed as a productive asset, with any cash flows being classified as investing cash flow.

Paragraph 24 of Statement 95 provides that in instances in which a cash payment pertains to an item that could be considered either inventory or a productive asset, the appropriate classification should depend on the activity that is likely to be the predominant source of cash flows for the item.

1.8.2 SEGMENT DISCLOSURES FOR PUBLIC COMPANIES FASB Statement No. 131, *Disclosures about Segments of an Enterprise and Related Information*, requires that public companies report in their financial statements certain information about their reportable operating segments. Operating segments are "components of an enterprise about which separate financial information is available that is evaluated regularly by the chief operating decision maker in deciding how to allocate resources and in assessing performance."[188] Public real estate companies have to carefully evaluate whether they operate in different segments that have to be reported separately. For example, a homebuilder may segregate its business based on geographic region for internal reporting purposes. If information relating to geographic regions is regularly provided to the chief operating decision maker of the homebuilder, the homebuilder would likely be considered to have different operating segments.[189] In situations in which these operating segments do not have similar economic characteristics (e.g., they have dissimilar operating margin percentages or trends), they do not meet the criteria for segment aggregation in paragraph 17 of FASB Statement No. 131. In the year 2006, the SEC challenged the segment disclosures of public homebuilders and several companies restated their financial statements to report segment information based on regions of the country.

1.8.3 OTHER PRESENTATION AND DISCLOSURE REQUIREMENTS Presentation and disclosure requirements relating to real estate acquisition, development, and construction activities are included in FASB Statement No. 34, *Capitalization of Interest Cost*, with respect to the capitalization of interest cost, and FASB Statement No. 142, *Goodwill and Other Intangible Assets*, relating to intangible assets acquired in connection with the purchase of income producing properties.

---

188 FAS 131, Summary
189 Paragraph 13 of FASB Statement No. 131 describes a scenario in which an enterprise produces reports in which its business activities are presented in different ways. "If the chief operating decision maker uses more than one set of segment information, other factors may identify a single set of components as constituting an enterprise's operating segments, including the nature of the business activities of each component, the existence of managers responsible for them, and information presented to the board of directors."

DISCLOSURES RELATING TO THE CAPITALIZATION OF INTEREST

Paragraph 21 of FASB Statement No. 34 requires the following disclosures relating to interest cost, either in the income statement or in the notes to the financial statements:

- For an accounting period in which no interest cost is capitalized, the amount of interest cost incurred and charged to expense
- For an accounting period in which interest cost is capitalized, the total amount of interest cost incurred during the period and the amount that has been capitalized

PRESENTATION AND DISCLOSURES RELATING TO THE ACQUISITION OF INTANGIBLES

A company acquiring intangible assets (such as in-place leases in connection with the acquisition of income-producing properties) is subject to the financial statement presentation and disclosure requirements outlined in paragraphs 42 through 47 of Statement 142. Intangible assets need to be presented as a separate line item (or separate line items) in the balance sheet. Similarly, the aggregate amount of goodwill also needs to be presented as a separate line item in the balance sheet.[190]

Paragraph 44 of Statement 142 includes the following disclosure requirements in the period of acquisition:

- For intangible assets subject to amortization:
  - The total amount assigned and the amount assigned to any major intangible asset class
  - The amount of any significant residual value, in total and by major intangible asset class
  - The weighted-average amortization period, in total and by major intangible asset class
- For intangible assets not subject to amortization, the total amount assigned and the amount assigned to any major intangible asset class

Paragraph 45 of Statement 142 includes the following disclosure requirements for each period for which a balance sheet is presented:

- For intangible assets subject to amortization:
  - The gross carrying amount and accumulated amortization, in total and by major intangible asset class
  - The aggregate amortization expense for the period
  - The estimated aggregate amortization expense for each of the five succeeding fiscal years

---

190   FAS 142, paragraphs 42 and 43

- For intangible assets not subject to amortization, the total carrying amount and the carrying amount for each major intangible asset class
- The changes in the carrying amount of goodwill during the period, including:
  - The aggregate amount of goodwill acquired
  - The aggregate amount of impairment losses recognized
  - The amount of goodwill included in the gain or loss on disposal of all or a portion of a reporting unit

Companies that report segment information in accordance with FASB Statement No. 131 are required to provide the information about goodwill in total and for each reportable segment, as well as any significant changes in the allocation of goodwill by reportable segment. Additional disclosure requirements exist if a portion of the goodwill has not been allocated to a reporting unit.[191]

Additionally, FASB Statement No. 142 has specific disclosure requirements if a company recognizes an impairment loss related to intangible assets or goodwill.[192]

1.9 INTERNATIONAL FINANCIAL REPORTING STANDARDS

Two international accounting standards deal with property, plant, and equipment: International Accounting Standard (IAS) 40, *Investment Property*, which applies to real estate held for investment purposes, and IAS 16, *Property, Plant and Equipment*, which applies to all other types of tangible, long-lived assets.

1.9.1 IAS 16   IAS 16 provides a comprehensive model that deals with the acquisition, development, and construction costs of property, plant and equipment, as well as with costs incurred subsequent to a property's acquisition or construction.

RECOGNITION CRITERIA FOR PROPERTY, PLANT, AND EQUIPMENT[193]
An item of property, plant, and equipment is recognized as an asset only if the following criteria are met:

- It is probable that future economic benefits associated with the item will flow to the entity
- The cost of the item can be measured reliably

INITIAL MEASUREMENT OF PROPERTY, PLANT, AND EQUIPMENT
Property, plant, and equipment that qualifies for recognition as an asset is measured at its cost, which is the amount of cash or cash equivalents paid and/or the

191   FAS 131, paragraph 45
192   FAS 142, paragraph 47
193   IAS 16, paragraph 7

fair value of other consideration given to acquire the asset at the time of acquisition or construction.[194] The recognition of costs ceases when the item is in the location and condition necessary for it to be capable of operating in the manner intended by management.

The cost of property, plant, and equipment is comprised of:[195]

- Purchase price
- Any costs directly attributable to bringing the asset to its location and condition necessary for it to be capable of operating in the manner intended by management, such as:
  · Costs of employee benefits arising directly from construction or acquisition
  · Costs of site preparation
  · Initial delivery and handling costs
  · Installation and assembly costs
  · Costs of testing
  · Professional fees
- Estimated costs of dismantling and removing the item and restoring the site on which it is located[196]

Examples of costs that are not capitalizable as part of the cost of the asset:[197]

- Costs of opening a new facility
- Costs of introducing a new product or service
- Costs of conducting business in a new location with a new class of customer
- Administrative and other general overhead costs
- Costs incurred while an item capable of operating in the manner intended by management has yet to be brought into use or is operated at less than full capacity
- Initial operating losses
- Costs of relocating or reorganizing part or all of an entity's operations

The cost of a *self-constructed asset* is determined by applying the same principles as for an acquired asset. If an entity produces similar assets for sale in the normal course of business, the cost of the asset is usually the same as the cost of constructing an asset for sale, which is addressed in IAS 2, *Inventories*.[198]

---

194   IAS 16, paragraph 6
195   IAS 16, paragraph 16
196   This is similar to the requirement under FASB Statement No. 143 to capitalize asset retirement cost.
197   IAS 16, paragraphs 19 and 20
198   IAS 16, paragraph 22

Measurement Subsequent to Initial Recognition

Two models exist for measuring property, plant, and equipment subsequent to initial recognition: (1) the cost model and (2) the revaluation model. The accounting policy a company selects—cost model or revaluation model—has to be applied to an entire asset class of property, plant, and equipment;[199] a company's assets of similar nature and use in its operations form an asset class. Land; land and buildings; furniture and fixtures; and office equipment are examples of separate classes.[200]

Use of the Cost Model.   When using the cost model, property, plant, and equipment is carried at its cost less accumulated depreciation and any accumulated impairment losses.[201]

Use of the Revaluation Model.   Assets whose fair value can be measured reliably may be accounted for using the revaluation model. Paragraph 31 of IAS 16 provides that under the revaluation model, property, plant, and equipment is carried at a revalued amount, which is its fair value at the date of revaluation less subsequent depreciation and impairment losses. To ensure that the carrying amount does not materially differ from that which would be determined using fair value at balance sheet date, revaluations have to be made with sufficient regularity. For items of property, plant, and equipment that experience significant changes in fair value, annual revaluations may be necessary; for other items that experience only insignificant changes in fair value, a revaluation every three to five years may be sufficient.[202] However, to avoid a selective revaluation of assets, a simultaneous revaluation of all of the assets of one class is required (or a revaluation of all of the items within a class on a rolling basis provided that the revaluation for the entire class is completed within a short period of time).[203]

If an asset's carrying amount is increased as a result of a revaluation, the increase is credited directly to equity (revaluation surplus), unless it reverses a revaluation decrease of the same asset previously recognized in profit or loss; in that case, any increase is recognized in profit or loss.[204] If an asset's carrying amount is decreased as a result of a revaluation, the decrease is recognized in profit or loss, unless a credit balance exists in revaluation surplus with respect to that asset. In the case of a credit balance, the decrease is debited to equity (revaluation surplus).[205] Revaluation surplus relating to an asset is transferred to

---

199   IAS 16, paragraph 29
200   IAS 16, paragraph 37
201   IAS 16, paragraph 30
202   IAS 16, paragraph 34
203   IAS 16, paragraphs 36 and 38
204   IAS 16, paragraph 39
205   IAS 16, paragraph 40

retained earnings. The revaluation surplus can either be transferred to retained earnings when the asset is retired or disposed of or the revaluation surplus can be amortized to retained earnings as the asset is being depreciated. Paragraph 41 of IAS 16 explains: "In such a case, the amount of the surplus transferred would be the difference between depreciation based on the revalued carrying amount of the asset and depreciation based on the asset's original cost. Transfers from revaluation surplus to retained earnings are not made through profit or loss."

COSTS INCURRED SUBSEQUENT TO INITIAL RECOGNITION

IAS 16 also provides accounting guidance for costs incurred after the property has been placed in service. IAS 16 differentiates between day-to-day servicing and costs for the replacement of (other than small) parts of an asset. The costs of day-to-day servicing, which may include labor, consumables, and small parts, are expensed as incurred. The costs of a replacement of parts of an item of property, plant, and equipment are capitalized, assuming the recognition criteria outlined above are met. Any remaining carrying amount of the part replaced is derecognized.[206] Similarly, costs of major inspections, such as inspections for aircrafts, are capitalized as part of the asset as a replacement, if the recognition criteria for property, plant, and equipment are met. Any remaining carrying amount of a previous inspection is derecognized at that time.[207]

DISCLOSURES

IAS 16 requires extensive disclosures for property, plant, and equipment, including the measurement bases used for determining the gross carrying amount; depreciation methods used; useful lives or depreciated rates used; and gross carrying amount and accumulated depreciation at the beginning and the end of the period together with a reconciliation.[208]

Additionally, paragraph 74 of IAS 16 requires the following disclosures:

- The existence and amounts of restrictions on title, and property, plant, and equipment pledged as security for liabilities
- The amount of expenditures recognized in the carrying amount of an item of property, plant, and equipment in the course of its construction
- The amount of contractual commitments for the acquisition of property, plant, and equipment
- If it is not disclosed separately on the face of the income statement, the amount of compensation from third parties for items of property, plant, and equipment that were impaired, lost, or given up that is included in profit or loss

---

206   IAS 16, paragraphs 12 and 13
207   IAS 16, paragraph 14
208   IAS 16, paragraph 73

For items of property, plant, and equipment that are stated at revalued amounts, the following disclosures are required:[209]

- The effective date of the revaluation
- Whether an independent valuer was involved
- The methods and significant assumptions applied in estimating the items' fair values
- The extent to which the items' fair values were determined directly by reference to observable prices in an active market or recent market transactions on arm's-length terms or were estimated using other valuation techniques
- For each revalued class of property, plant, and equipment, the carrying amount that would have been recognized had the assets been carried under the cost model
- The revaluation surplus, indicating the change for the period and any restrictions on the distribution of the balance to shareholders

1.9.2 IAS 40
SCOPE OF IAS 40
IAS 40 provides accounting guidance for investment property. Investment property, which may be land, building, part of a building, or land and building, is defined as property held (by the owner or by the lessee under a finance lease) to earn rentals or for capital appreciation or both, rather than for (1) use in the production or supply of goods or services or for administrative purposes or (2) sale in the ordinary course of business.[210]

Additionally, a lessee may classify and account for property leased under an operating lease as investment property, if the property otherwise meets the definition of investment property, and the lessee uses the fair value model (described below) for all other investment property it holds.[211]

Real estate property may by comprised of a portion that is held to earn rentals or for capital appreciation and another portion that is held for use in the production or supply of goods or services or for administrative purposes. Portions of "mixed-use" property are accounted for separately, if they could be sold or leased separately under finance leases; otherwise, "mixed-use" property is considered investment property only if an insignificant portion is held for use in the production or supply of goods or services or for administrative purposes.[212]

A property owner may provide ancillary services to occupants of a property. That property is classified as investment property if the ancillary services are

---

209   IAS 16, paragraph 77
210   IAS 40, paragraph 5
211   IAS 40, paragraph 6
212   IAS 40, paragraph 10

insignificant to the arrangement (for example, security and maintenance for office buildings). The property is not considered investment property if the ancillary services provided are significant to the arrangement, such as guest services in an owner-managed hotel.[213]

Recognition Criteria for Investment Property[214]

The recognition criteria for investment property are the same as the recognition criteria for property, plant, and equipment under IAS 16. Investment property is recognized as an asset only if the following criteria are met:

- It is probable that the future economic benefits that are associated with the property will flow to the entity
- The cost of the investment property can be measured reliably

IAS 40 does not address the separate recognition of intangible assets—such as in-place leases and customer relationships—acquired in connection with the acquisition of investment property, which is required under U.S. GAAP;[215] The IASB is concerned about the "double-recognition" of assets, however. Paragraph 50 of IAS 40 provides, in part:

> In determining the fair value of investment property, an entity does not double-count assets or liabilities that are recognised as separate assets or liabilities. For example:
>
> **(a)** Equipment such as lifts or air-conditioning is often an integral part of a building and is generally included in the fair value of the investment property, rather than recognized separately as property, plant, and equipment.
> **(b)** If an office is leased on a furnished basis, the fair value of the office generally includes the fair value of the furniture, because the rental income relates to the furnished office. When furniture is included in the fair value of investment property, an entity does not recognize that furniture as a separate asset.

Initial Measurement of Investment Property

Initially, investment property is measured at its cost. The types of costs that are capitalizable are the same as those for property, plant, and equipment, discussed in Section 1.9.1 of this chapter. During the development and construction of property, IAS 16 applies. At the date of completion, the property becomes investment property, and IAS 40 becomes applicable.[216]

---

213   IAS 40, paragraphs 11 and 12
214   IAS 40, paragraph 16
215   Discussed in Section 1.6 of this chapter.
216   IAS 40, paragraph 22

Any interest in property held by a lessee that is classified as investment property is initially recognized at the lower of the fair value of the property or the present value of minimum lease payments.[217]

MEASUREMENT AFTER INITIAL RECOGNITION

After initial recognition, IAS 40 provides a choice between two accounting models, the fair value model and the cost model. As a general rule, the accounting policy selected has to be applied to all of a company's investment properties.[218] There are three exceptions to this general rule:

1. A company may choose the fair value model or the cost model for "investment property backing liabilities that pay a return linked directly to the fair value of, or returns from, specified assets including that investment property."[219]
2. When a property interest held by a lessee under an operating lease is classified as investment property, the company has to apply the fair value model to all of its other investment property.[220]
3. If there is clear evidence at the time of acquisition that the fair value of the investment property will not be reliably determinable on a continuing basis, the company has to use the cost model.[221]

Under the fair value model, investment property is valued at fair value, with changes in fair value recognized in profit or loss.[222] The cost model follows the guidelines established in IAS 16 for measurement subsequent to initial recognition.[223] If the cost model is used, the fair value of investment property needs to be disclosed if it can be determined reliably, which is a rebuttable presumption pursuant to paragraph 53 of IAS 40.[224] Accordingly, companies that hold investment properties are generally required to determine the fair value of these properties, regardless of the accounting policy adopted.

IAS 40 allows for a change in accounting policy only if it leads to a more appropriate presentation; a change from the fair value model to the cost model will generally not satisfy that requirement.[225]

---

217 IAS 40, paragraph 25
218 IAS 40, paragraph 30
219 IAS 40, paragraph 32A
220 IAS 40, paragraph 34
221 IAS 40, paragraph 53
222 IAS 40, paragraph 35
223 IAS 40, paragraph 56
224 IAS 40, paragraph 79(e); additional disclosures are required if a company cannot determine the fair value of the investment property reliably.
225 IAS 40, paragraph 31

Costs Incurred Subsequent to Initial Recognition

Costs of day-to-day servicing are expensed as incurred.[226] Costs of replacing parts of an existing investment property, such as interior walls, are capitalized at the time of replacement. The parts that are being replaced are derecognized at that time.[227] Under the fair value model, the fair value of the investment property may already reflect that the parts that are being replaced have lost their value, or it may be difficult to determine by what amount to reduce the fair value of the property as a result of the derecognition of the replaced parts. When it is not practical to determine the amount by which the fair value of the property should be decreased, a company may include the cost of the replacement in the carrying amount of the asset and then reassess the fair value, as would be required for additions not involving replacements.[228]

Change in Use

When a company uses the cost model, a transfer between investment property, owner-occupied property, and inventory does not impact the carrying amount of the property transferred.[229] A company that uses the fair value model accounts for a transfer between investment property, owner-occupied property, and inventory as follows:

- If a property carried at fair value is transferred from investment property to owner-occupied property or inventory, the property's fair value at the date of change in use is deemed to be its cost.[230]
- If owner-occupied property becomes investment property carried at fair value, any difference between the fair value and the carrying amount at the date of change in use is accounted for like a revaluation under IAS 16.[231]
- If inventory is transferred to investment property carried at fair value, any difference between the fair value of the property at the date of transfer and its previous carrying amount is recognized in profit and loss.[232]

Disclosures

IAS 40 includes the following disclosure requirements:[233]

- Which model (the fair value model or the cost model) is applied
- If the fair value model is applied, whether, and in what circumstances, property interests held under operating leases are classified and accounted for as investment property

---

226   IAS 40, paragraph 63
227   IAS 40, paragraph 19
228   IAS 40, paragraph 68
229   IAS 40, paragraph 59
230   IAS 40, paragraph 60
231   IAS 40, paragraph 61
232   IAS 40, paragraph 63
233   IAS 40, paragraph 75

- When classification is difficult, the criteria used to distinguish investment property from owner-occupied property and from property held for sale in the ordinary course of business
- The methods and significant assumptions applied in determining the fair value of investment property, including a statement whether the determination of fair value was supported by market evidence or was more heavily based on other factors because of the nature of the property and lack of comparable market data
- The extent to which the fair value of investment property is based on a valuation by an independent valuer who holds a relevant professional qualification and has requisite recent experience
- The amounts recognized in profit or loss for
  - Rental income from investment property
  - Direct operating expenses arising from investment property that generated rental income during the period
  - Direct operating expenses arising from investment property that did not generate rental income during the period
  - The cumulative change in fair value recognized in profit or loss on a sale of investment property from a pool of assets in which the cost model is used into a pool in which the fair value model is used[234]
- The existence and amounts of restrictions on the realizability of investment property or the remittance of income and proceeds of disposal
- Contractual obligations to purchase, construct, or develop investment property, or for repairs, maintenance, or enhancements

Additional disclosures are required by paragraphs 76 through 79 of IAS 40, depending on whether the cost or the fair value model is used.

1.10 SYNOPSIS OF AUTHORITATIVE LITERATURE

FASB STATEMENT NO. 34, *CAPITALIZATION OF INTEREST COST*

FASB Statement No. 34 establishes standards for capitalizing interest cost as part of the historical cost of acquiring assets. To qualify for interest capitalization, assets must require a period of time to get them ready for their intended use. Interest capitalization on inventories that are routinely manufactured is not permitted.

---

234   Generally, a company either applies the fair value model or the cost model to its investment property. There is an exception to this general rule if a company has investment property backing liabilities that pay a return linked directly to the fair value of, or returns from, specified assets, including that investment property. [IAS 40, paragraphs 30 and 32A]

FASB Statement No. 58, Capitalization of Interest Cost in Financial Statements That Include Investments Accounted for by the Equity Method, an Amendment of FASB Statement No. 34

FASB Statement No. 58 amends FASB Statement No. 34 to limit capitalization of consolidated interest cost to qualifying assets of the parent company and consolidated subsidiaries and to include investments (equity, loans, and advances) accounted for by the equity method as qualifying assets of the investor while the investee has activities in progress necessary to commence its planned principal operations, provided that the investee's activities include the use of funds to acquire qualifying assets for its operations.

FASB Statement No. 62, Capitalization of Interest Cost in Situations Involving Certain Tax-Exempt Borrowings and Certain Gifts and Grants, an amendment of FASB Statement No. 34

FASB Statement No. 62 amends FASB Statement No. 34 to require capitalization of interest cost of restricted tax-exempt borrowings less any interest earned on temporary investment of the proceeds of those borrowings from the date of borrowing until the specified qualifying assets acquired with those borrowings are ready for their intended use and to proscribe capitalization of interest cost on qualifying assets acquired using gifts or grants that are restricted by the donor or grantor to the acquisition of those assets.

FASB Statement No. 67, Accounting for Costs and Initial Rental Operations of Real Estate Projects

FASB Statement No. 67 provides accounting guidance for the capitalization of costs associated with the acquisition, development, and construction of real estate projects and with the allocation of costs to individual components of a project. It also addresses the accounting for costs to sell or rent real estate projects.

FASB Statement No. 141, Business Combinations

FASB Statement No. 141 addresses the financial accounting and reporting for business combinations. All business combinations within the scope of FASB Statement No. 141 must be accounted for using the purchase method.

FASB Statement No. 141(revised 2007), Business Combinations

FASB Statement No. 141(R) replaces FASB Statement No. 141. FASB Statement No. 141(R) retains the requirement in FASB Statement No. 141, that the acquisition method of accounting (referred to as purchase method in FASB Statement No. 141) be used when accounting for business combinations. Significant changes to the provisions in FASB Statement No. 141 include the separate recognition of acquisition-related costs, measurement of the noncontrolling interest in the acquiree at fair value, recognition of assets acquired and liabilities assumed arising from contractual contingencies, and recognition of gain from a bargain purchase.

FASB STATEMENT NO. 142, *GOODWILL AND OTHER INTANGIBLE ASSETS*
FASB Statement No. 142 addresses the financial accounting and reporting for acquired goodwill and other intangible assets. It provides guidance for the accounting of intangible assets that are acquired individually or with a group of other assets upon their acquisition. The Statement also addresses how goodwill and other intangible assets should be accounted for subsequent to their recognition in the financial statements.

FASB STATEMENT NO. 143, *ACCOUNTING FOR ASSET RETIREMENT OBLIGATIONS*
FASB Statement No. 143 provides accounting guidance for legal obligations associated with the retirement of tangible long-lived assets that result from the acquisition, development, construction, and/or normal operation of long-lived assets, and for the associated asset retirement costs. FASB Statement No. 143 does not provide guidance for obligations of lessees in connection with leased property that meet the definition of either minimum lease payments or contingent rentals.

FASB INTERPRETATION NO. 47, *ACCOUNTING FOR CONDITIONAL ASSET RETIREMENT OBLIGATIONS*
FIN 47 clarifies that the term "conditional asset retirement obligation" as used in FASB Statement No. 143 refers to a legal obligation to perform an asset retirement activity in which the timing and/ or method of settlement are conditional on a future event that may or may not be within the control of the company. FIN 47 also clarifies when a company would have sufficient information to reasonably estimate the fair value of an asset retirement obligation.

EITF ISSUE NO. 85-27, *RECOGNITION OF RECEIPTS FROM MADE-UP RENTAL SHORTFALLS*
Issue. A real estate developer sells a recently constructed office building to a syndication. For the payment of a fee, the developer enters into a master-leaseback arrangement with the seller, under which it leases the vacant space at a market rate for a two-year period. How should the syndication account for the fee it pays to the seller and the rent it receives from the seller?

Consensus/Status. The Task Force reached a consensus that payments to and receipts from the seller should be treated by the syndication as adjustments to the basis of the property. This consensus also applies to a property that is fully rented at the time of sale if the seller agrees to make up any decrease in rentals resulting from lease terminations during a specified period after the sale.

EITF ISSUE NO. 89-13, *ACCOUNTING FOR THE COST OF ASBESTOS REMOVAL*
A property owner may incur costs to remove or contain asbestos in compliance with federal, state, or local laws.

Issues

1. Should the costs incurred to treat asbestos when a property with a known asbestos problem is acquired be capitalized or charged to expense?
2. Should the costs incurred to treat asbestos in an existing property be capitalized or charged to expense?
3. If it is deemed appropriate to charge asbestos treatment costs to expense, should they be reported as an extraordinary item?

Consensuses/Status.   The Task Force reached the following consensuses:

1. Costs incurred to treat asbestos within a reasonable time period after a property with a known asbestos problem is acquired should be capitalized as part of the cost of the acquired property, subject to an impairment test.
2. Costs incurred to treat asbestos may be capitalized as a betterment subject to an impairment test for that property. When costs are incurred in anticipation of a sale, they should be deferred and recognized in the period of sale to the extent that the costs can be recovered from the estimated sales price.
3. Asbestos treatment costs that are charged to expense are not extraordinary items under Opinion 30.

The consensuses do not apply to asset retirement obligations that are within the scope of FASB Statement No. 143.

EITF Issue No. 90-8, Capitalization of Costs to Treat Environmental Contamination

Issue.   A company incurs costs to remove, contain, neutralize, or prevent existing or future environmental contamination. Should environmental contamination treatment costs be capitalized or expensed?

Consensus/Status.   The Task Force reached a consensus that in general, environmental contamination treatment costs should be charged to expense. They may be capitalized if recoverable, but only if one of the following criteria is met:

1. The costs extend the life, increase the capacity, or improve the safety or efficiency of property owned by the company. The condition of the property after the costs are incurred must be improved as compared to the condition of the property when originally constructed or acquired.
2. The costs mitigate or prevent environmental contamination that has yet to occur and that otherwise may result from future operations or activities. In addition, the costs must improve the property compared with its condition when constructed or acquired.
3. The costs are incurred in preparing for sale property currently held for sale.

The consensus does not apply to obligations for environmental contamination treatment costs that are within the scope of FASB Statement No. 143.

EITF Issue No. 93-5, Accounting for Environmental Liabilities

Incorporated in and effectively nullified by SOP 96-1.

EITF Issue No. 95-23, The Treatment of Certain Site Restoration/ Environmental Exit Costs When Testing a Long-Lived Asset for Impairment

Issue. Should cash flows associated with environmental exit costs that may be incurred if a long-lived asset is sold, is abandoned, or ceases operations be included in the undiscounted expected future cash flows used to test a long-lived asset for recoverability under FASB Statement No. 144?

Consensus/Status. The Task Force reached a consensus that whether environmental exit costs should be included in the undiscounted expected future cash flows used to test a long-lived asset for recoverability under FASB Statement No. 144 depends on management's intent with respect to the asset. EITF Issue No. 95-23 provides examples for situations in which cash flows for environmental exit costs should be excluded from the FASB Statement No. 144 recoverability test.

EITF Issue No. 97-11, Accounting for Internal Costs Relating to Real Estate Property Acquisitions

Issue. Many companies incur internal costs related to a real estate property that are incurred for the purpose of, but prior to, obtaining that property. Can internal preacquisition costs be capitalized as part of the cost of a real estate property acquisition?

Consensus/Status. The Task Force reached a consensus that internal costs of preacquisition activities incurred in connection with the acquisition of a property that will be classified as nonoperating at the date of acquisition, that are directly identifiable with the acquired property, and that were incurred subsequent to the time that acquisition of that specific property was considered probable (that is, likely to occur) should be capitalized as part of the cost of that acquisition. If the entity subsequently determines that the property will be classified as operating at the date of acquisition, such costs should be charged to expense and any additional costs should be expensed as incurred.

Internal costs of preacquisition activities incurred in connection with the acquisition of a property that will be classified as operating at the date of acquisition should be expensed as incurred. If the entity subsequently determines that the property will be classified as nonoperating at the date of acquisition, previously expensed costs should not be capitalized as part of the cost of that acquisition.

EITF Issue No. 98-3, Determining Whether a Nonmonetary Transaction Involves Receipt of Productive Assets or of a Business

Issue.   The EITF addresses how to determine whether an asset/asset group or a business has been acquired in a nonmonetary exchange. The guidance is equally applicable to the evaluation of whether productive assets or a business have been acquired in exchange for monetary consideration. How should a business be defined?

Consensus/Status.   The EITF describes a business as a self-sustaining integrated set of activities and assets conducted and managed for the purpose of providing a return to investors. A business consists of (1) inputs, (2) processes applied to those inputs, and (3) resulting outputs that are used to generate revenues. For a transferred set of activities and assets to be a business, it must contain all of the inputs and processes necessary for it to conduct normal operations after the transferred set is separated from the transferor, which includes the ability to sustain a revenue stream by providing its outputs to customers.

The EITF includes a three-step process that should be followed in the evaluation of whether a business has been acquired.

FASB Statement No. 141(R), which is effective for annual reporting periods beginning on or after December 15, 2008, nullifies EITF Issue No. 98-3.

EITF Issue No. 99-9, Effect of Derivative Gains and Losses on the Capitalization of Interest

Issue.   Should the interest rate used in capitalizing interest pursuant to the provisions of FASB Statement No. 34 be the effective yield after gains and losses on the effective portion of a derivative instrument that qualifies as a fair-value hedge of the fixed interest rate date, or should it be the original effective rate of the fixed-rate debt?

Consensus/Status.   The Task Force reached a consensus that amounts recorded in an entity's income statement as interest costs should be reflected in the capitalization rate under FASB Statement No. 34. Those amounts could include amortization of the adjustments of the carrying amount of the hedged liability if an entity elects to begin amortization of those adjustments during the period in which interest is eligible for capitalization. The ineffective portion of the fair-value hedge should not be reflected in the capitalization rate.

FASB Statement No. 133 prohibits the capitalization of the gain or loss on the hedging instrument in a cash-flow hedge. The FASB Staff believes that, when the variable-rate interest on a specific borrowing is associated with an asset under construction and capitalized as a cost of that asset, the amounts in accumulated comprehensive income related to a cash-flow hedge of the variability of that interest should be reclassified into earnings over the depreciable life of the constructed asset, since that depreciable life coincides with the amortization period for the capitalized interest cost on the debt.

EITF Issue No. 02-17, *Recognition of Customer Relationship Intangible Assets Acquired in a Business Combination*

Issues.   FASB Statement No. 141 requires that intangible assets be recorded apart from goodwill, if they arise from contractual or legal rights (the contractual-legal criterion), or if they are capable of being separated or divided from the acquired entity (the separability criterion). The EITF addresses three issues relating to the application of FASB Statement No. 141.

Consensus/Status.   The Task Force reached consensuses, and the EITF Abstract includes examples of the application of these consensuses.

EITF Issue No. 03-9, *Determination of the Useful Life of Renewable Intangible Assets under FASB Statement No. 142, Goodwill and Other Intangible Assets*

Issues.   Four issues are addressed in that EITF Abstract, relating to the determination of the useful life of intangible assets (Issues 1 through 3) and to the recognition of an intangible asset apart from goodwill (Issue 4).

Consensuses/Status.   No consensuses were reached. EITF Issue No. 03-9 was removed from the EITF agenda. At the recommendation of the Task Force, the FASB added this issue to the FASB agenda and has issued proposed FSP FAS 142F.

EITF Issue No. 03-17, *Subsequent Accounting for Executory Contracts That Have Been Recognized on an Entity's Balance Sheet*

Issues.   The issues are:

1. What is the appropriate amortization of an asset arising from an executory contract?
2. What is the appropriate method of derecognition for a balance sheet credit arising from an executory contract?

Consensuses/Status.   The issue has been removed from the EITF agenda.

EITF Issue No. 04-1, *Accounting for Preexisting Relationships between the Parties to a Business Combination*

Issues.   The EITF addresses the accounting for pre-existing relationships between the parties to a business combination. The issues are:

1. Should a business combination between two parties that have a pre-existing relationship be evaluated to determine if a settlement of a pre-existing relationship exists, thus requiring accounting separate from the business combination?
2. How should the effective settlement of an executory contract in a business combination be measured?
3. Should the acquisition of a right that the acquirer had previously granted to the acquired entity to use the acquirer's recognized or unrecognized

intangible assets be included in the measurement of the settlement amount or included as part of the business combination?

4. Should the acquirer recognize, apart from goodwill, an acquired entity's intangible asset(s) that, before the business combination, arose solely from the acquired entity's right to use the acquirer's intangible asset(s)?

5. Is it appropriate for an acquirer to recognize a settlement gain in conjunction with the effective settlement of a lawsuit or an executory contract in a business combination?

Consensuses/Status.   The Task Force reached the following consensuses:

1. Consummation of a business combination between parties with a pre-existing relationship should be evaluated to determine if a settlement of a pre-existing relationship exists. A business combination between two parties that have a pre-existing relationship is a multiple-element transaction, with one element being the business combination and the other element being the settlement of the pre-existing relationship.

2. The effective settlement of an executory contract in a business combination as a result of a pre-existing relationship should be measured at the lesser of:

   a. The amount by which the contract is favorable or unfavorable from the perspective of the acquirer when compared to pricing for current market transactions for the same or similar items

   b. Any stated settlement provisions in the contract available to the counterparty to which the contract is unfavorable

3. The acquisition of a right that the acquirer had previously granted to the acquired entity to use the acquirer's recognized or unrecognized intangible assets should be included as part of the business combination. If the contract granting such right is favorable or unfavorable when compared to current market transactions, a settlement gain or loss should be recognized, measured based on the consensus reached in Issue 2.

4. A reacquired right should be recognized as an intangible asset apart from goodwill.

5. A settlement gain or loss should be recognized in conjunction with the effective settlement of a lawsuit or executory contract in a business combination.

EITF ISSUE NO. 04-2, *WHETHER MINERAL RIGHTS ARE TANGIBLE OR INTANGIBLE ASSETS*

Issues.   The issues are:

1. Are mineral rights tangible or intangible assets?

2. If mineral rights are intangible assets, are mineral rights finite-lived or indefinite-lived intangible assets?

Consensuses/Status

1. The Task Force reached a consensus that mineral rights are tangible assets, the aggregate carrying amount of which should be reported as separate component of property, plant, and equipment either on the face of the financial statements or in the notes to the financial statements.

2. As a result of the consensus reached on Issue 1, the Task Force did not discuss Issue 2.

EITF TOPIC NO. D-108, *USE OF THE RESIDUAL METHOD TO VALUE ACQUIRED ASSETS OTHER THAN GOODWILL*

FASB Statement No. 141 requires that intangible assets that meet the recognition criteria be recorded at fair value. The SEC staff does not believe that the application of the residual method to the valuation of intangible assets can be assumed to produce amounts representing the fair values of those assets. Accordingly, the SEC staff believes that a direct value method, rather than the residual method, should be used to determine the fair value of all intangible assets other than goodwill.

AICPA STATEMENT OF POSITION 93-7, *REPORTING ON ADVERTISING COSTS*

SOP 93-7 provides guidance on the accounting, reporting, and disclosure of advertising costs in financial statements. It requires that the costs of advertising be expensed either as incurred or at the first time the advertising takes place, except for direct-response advertising (1) whose primary purpose is to elicit sales to customers who could be shown to have responded specifically to the advertising and (2) that results in probable future economic benefits. For direct-response advertising that may result in reported assets, the SOP addresses how such assets should be measured initially, how the amounts ascribed to such assets should be amortized, and how the realizability of such assets should be assessed.

AICPA STATEMENT OF POSITION 96-1, *ENVIRONMENTAL REMEDIATION LIABILITIES*

SOP 96-1 is divided into two parts. Part 1 provides an overview of key environmental laws and regulations. Part 2 provides guidance on the accounting, presentation and disclosure of environmental remediation liabilities that relate to pollution arising from some past act, generally as a result of the provisions of Superfund, the corrective-action provisions of the Resource Conservation and Recovery Act, or analogous state and non-U.S. laws and regulations. Following the general guidance of FASB Statement No. 5, SOP 96-1 provides that a liability be accrued if (1) it is probable that an asset has been impaired or a liability has been incurred and (2) the amount of the loss can be reasonably estimated. For purposes of measuring environmental remediation liabilities, the measurement should be based on enacted laws and adopted regulations and policies. Discounting the liability to reflect the time value of money is considered appropriate only if certain conditions are met.

If there is more than one party involved, SOP 96-1 provides that the environmental remediation liability recorded by a company should be based on an estimate of the company's allocable share of the joint and several remediation liability. The amount of an environmental remediation liability should be determined independently from any potential claim for recovery, and an asset relating to the recovery should be recognized only when realization of the claim for recovery is deemed probable.

AICPA STATEMENT OF POSITION 98-5, *REPORTING ON THE COSTS OF START-UP ACTIVITIES*

SOP 98-5 provides guidance on the financial reporting of start-up costs and organization costs; the costs of start-up activities and organization costs are to be expensed as incurred. The SOP defines start-up activities as one-time activities relating to opening a new facility, introducing a new product or service, conducting business in a new territory, conducting business with a new class of customer or beneficiary, initiating a new process in an existing facility, or commencing some new operation. Start-up activities include activities related to organizing a new entity (organization costs).

AICPA PROPOSED STATEMENT OF POSITION, *ACCOUNTING FOR CERTAIN COSTS AND ACTIVITIES RELATED TO PROPERTY, PLANT, AND EQUIPMENT*

The proposed SOP provides guidance on accounting for property, plant, and equipment, which is based on the following principles:

- Property, plant, and equipment consists of one or more components, which should be recorded at cost.
- A component of property, plant, and equipment should be depreciated over its expected useful life.
- The costs of a replacement property, plant, and equipment component replaced should not concurrently be recorded as assets.

SEC STAFF ACCOUNTING BULLETIN TOPIC 5Y[235], *ACCOUNTING AND DISCLOSURES RELATING TO LOSS CONTINGENCIES*

SAB Topic 5Y addresses the following questions:

1. What discount rate should be used to determine the present value of an environmental remediation or product liability that meets the conditions for recognition on a discounted basis in SOP 96-1, and what special disclosures are required in the notes to the financial statements?
2. What financial statement disclosures should be furnished with respect to recorded and unrecorded product or environmental remediation liabilities?

---

235   SAB 92

3. What disclosures regarding loss contingencies may be necessary outside the financial statements?
4. What disclosures should be furnished with respect to site restoration costs or other environmental remediation costs?

Interpretive Responses:

1. The rate used to discount the cash payments should be the rate that will produce an amount at which the environmental or product liability could be settled in an arm's-length transaction with a third party.
2. Typically, product and environmental remediation liabilities are of such significance that detailed disclosures regarding the judgments and assumptions underlying the recognition and measurement of the liabilities are necessary to prevent the financial statements from being misleading and to inform readers fully regarding the range of reasonably possible outcomes that could have a material effect on the registrant's financial condition, results of operations, or liquidity.
3. Registrants should consider Items 101 (Description of Business), 103 (Legal Proceedings), and 303 (MD&A) of Regulations S-K and S-B. The Commission has issued interpretive releases that provide additional guidance with respect to these items.
4. Material liabilities for site restoration, post-closure, and monitoring commitments, or other exit costs that may occur on the sale, disposal, or abandonment of a property as a result of unanticipated contamination of the asset should be disclosed in the notes to the financial statements.

SEC Staff Accounting Bulletin Topic 10F, Presentation of Liabilities for Environmental Costs
SAB Topic 10F addresses questions relating to rate-regulated enterprises' recognition and presentation of liabilities for environmental costs.

International Accounting Standard 16, Property, Plant, and Equipment
IAS 16 prescribes the accounting for property, plant, and equipment, including their recognition, measurement, and derecognition; it provides guidance with respect to depreciation charges and impairment losses, and disclosures relating to property, plant, and equipment. The Standard allows for the use of the cost model or the revaluation model.

International Accounting Standard 40, Investment Property
IAS 40 prescribes the accounting—and related disclosures—for investment property, that is, real estate property held by the owner or by the lessee under a finance lease to earn rentals or for capital appreciation or both, rather than for (1) use in the production or supply of goods or services or for administrative purposes; or (2) sale in the ordinary course of business.

CHAPTER 2

NONMONETARY EXCHANGES OF REAL ESTATE

2.1 OVERVIEW

Typically, the acquisition and disposition of real property is effected through use of cash or other monetary assets and liabilities, such as mortgage loans or notes. Monetary assets and liabilities represent contractual claims to specified amounts of cash.[1]

---

[1] Paragraph 3(a) of APB Opinion No. 29 describes monetary assets and liabilities as "assets and liabilities whose amounts are fixed in terms of units of currency by contract or otherwise. Examples are cash, short- or long-term accounts and notes receivable in cash, and short- or long-term accounts and notes payable in cash."

The amount of monetary assets and liabilities exchanged generally provides an objective basis for measuring the cost of the real estate acquired, as well as for measuring gain or loss on the real estate transferred.[2]

Real estate exchange transactions involve the exchange of real estate for other real estate, that is, the exchange of nonmonetary assets for other nonmonetary assets. Two of the issues that have been debated are: Should real estate properties acquired in nonmonetary exchange transactions be recorded at their fair values? And: Should gain be recognized when appreciated real property is exchanged for other real property, such as an office building being exchanged for another office building by a real estate investment trust (REIT)?

The disposition of real estate in real estate exchange transactions is not governed by the provisions of Financial Accounting Standards Board (FASB) Statement No. 66, *Accounting for Sales of Real Estate*; rather, Accounting Principles Board (APB) Opinion No. 29, *Accounting for Nonmonetary Transactions*, is the guidance applicable to such exchange transactions. Exchanges of real estate assets for nonmonetary assets other than real estate are also governed by APB Opinion No. 29.[3]

In 2002, the Financial Accounting Standards Board (FASB) and the International Accounting Standards Board (IASB) issued a Memorandum of Understanding, the so-called "Norwalk Agreement," documenting their commitment to the convergence of U.S. and international accounting standards. As one of several initiatives to further the convergence between the international accounting standards and U.S. Generally Accepted Accounting Principles (GAAP), a short-term convergence project was initiated. That project is limited to certain areas of accounting in which the standard-setters believe convergence can be achieved in a relatively short time frame, generally by selecting between existing international accounting standards and U.S. GAAP.

In December 2004, as part of that short-term convergence project, the FASB amended the accounting guidance for nonmonetary transactions with the issuance of FASB Statement No. 153, *Exchanges of Nonmonetary Assets*. The general principle of fair value underlying the accounting for nonmonetary transactions was not changed by Statement 153. However, the requirement previously in place, which stated that the "earning process must be culminated"[4] as prerequisite for recording a nonmonetary exchange at fair value, precluded the use of fair value for almost all real estate exchange transactions. Statement 153, effective for nonmonetary asset exchanges occurring in fiscal periods beginning after June 15, 2005, introduced the concept of "commercial substance." Following that concept, many real estate properties acquired in exchange transactions qualify for being recorded at fair value, rather than at carryover basis. The new accounting rules are expected to enable companies that

---

2   APB 29, paragraph 1
3   FASB Action Alert 07-30, July 26, 2007
4   See section 2.4.2 of this chapter for further discussion.

effect Internal Revenue Code (IRC) Section 1031 Exchanges to accomplish a deferral of gain for income tax purposes, while at the same time being able to recognize a gain for financial accounting purposes.

2.2 SECTION 1031 EXCHANGE

Nonmonetary exchanges of real estate properties are often income tax–driven: Section 1031 of the IRC provides an exception to the general rule that realized gain or loss upon disposition of property be recognized. Section 1031 acknowledges the fact that property exchanges may not change the substance of the taxpayer's relative economic position. The replacement property received in the exchange is viewed as a continuation of the old investment.[5] The recognition of gain or loss on the exchange is postponed until the property received in the nontaxable exchange is subsequently disposed of in a taxable transaction. Nonrecognition of gain or loss is mandatory if the properties exchanged are (1) qualifying properties and (2) of like kind.

Due to the importance of IRC Section 1031 for exchanges of real estate properties, this chapter provides a basic overview of the tax rules relating to real estate exchanges before addressing the accounting implications of nonmonetary exchanges of real estate properties.

Many different forms of Section 1031 exchanges have been developed, such as exchanges involving multiple properties, deferred exchanges, and reverse exchanges. Irrespective of their structure, they have to satisfy the requirements of Section 1031: To qualify as a Section 1031 exchange, the form of the transaction must be considered an exchange and both the property transferred and the property acquired (1) must be held for productive use in a trade or business, or for investment (referred to as "qualifying properties") and (2) must be of like kind. Property held for productive use in a trade or business may be exchanged for property held for investment, and *vice versa*, as long as the properties are of like kind.

Qualifying Property
The four primary categories of qualifying property are:

1. Real property
2. Depreciable tangible property, such as business equipment[6]
3. Intangible nondepreciable personal property, such as patents, copyrights, and trademarks[7]
4. Nondepreciable personal property, such as art, antiques, and coin collections[8]

---

5   Reg. Section 1.1002-1(c)
6   Reg. Section 1.1031(a)(2)(b)
7   Reg. Section 1.1031(a)(2)(c)
8   Reg. Section 1.1031(a)(2)(c)

Section 1031 specifically excludes from qualifying property properties held for sale, such as land held in inventory, as well as financial instruments, such as stocks, bonds, notes, or other securities, and interests in partnerships.[9] Real estate used as a primary residence does also not qualify for Section 1031 exchange treatment, since it is not used in a trade or business. There is some controversy about the status of vacation homes as qualifying property, but unless an owner can demonstrate at least some rental use of a vacation home, it is unlikely that it will be considered a qualifying property.[10]

LIKE-KIND PROPERTIES

The term "like kind" refers to the nature or character of the property. For example, real property may not be exchanged for personal property, since their nature and character are not considered to be of like kind. In an exchange of two real estate properties, it is inconsequential, for purposes of applying Section 1031, if one property is improved (that is, with roads or buildings) and the other is unimproved; the properties are considered like-kind. However, real property in the United States and real property outside the United States are not considered like-kind properties.[11]

Exchanges such as the following qualify for like-kind exchanges:

- Exchange of apartment building for farm
- Exchange of office building for hotel
- Exchange of raw land for retail space

HOLDING PERIOD

Section 1031 provides that the property to be exchanged must *be held* for productive use in a business or for investment, such as for future appreciation or rental income, before it can be exchanged in a Section 1031 exchange. There are no statutory requirements mandating a certain minimum holding period for a property to qualify for a Section 1031 exchange; however, the Internal Revenue Service (IRS) has ruled that property exchanged shortly after acquisition is not considered *held* for investment or production of income.

EXCHANGE INVOLVING BOOT OR MORTGAGE RELIEF

Consideration received or given in an exchange other than qualifying like-kind property is considered boot. Thus, boot includes cash, nonqualifying property, or property that is qualifying but not of like kind to the property exchanged. When boot is received in addition to the real property acquired in the exchange, Section 1031(b) requires that gain be recognized to the extent of the boot received, unless the boot received can be

---

9   IRC Section 1031(a)(2); also excluded are certain other assets
10   See Moore vs. Commissioner, Tax Court Memo 2007-134.
11   IRC Section 1031(h)(1)

offset by the boot given. The unrecognized gain is deferred until the property acquired in the exchange is disposed of in a taxable transaction.

EXAMPLE—EXCHANGE INVOLVING BOOT

BreezeCo. (BR) exchanges a real estate property with a fair value of $10 million for a real estate property with a fair value of $4 million and $6 million cash. BR's property is not encumbered by a mortgage. BR's basis in the real estate property is $4.5 million. Both properties are qualifying properties and are of like kind.

How much gain will BR have to recognize for tax purposes at the time of the transaction?

The gain realized from the exchange amounts to $5.5 million. Since the cash received by BR ($6 million) exceeds the gain from the sale ($5.5 million), all of the gain is recognized and thus is taxable.

If the property is encumbered by mortgages, the relief of liabilities either through repayment or due to an assumption of the mortgages by the acquirer creates so-called "mortgage relief" or "mortgage boot." Mortgage relief is treated like cash received; that is, it is considered boot. To avoid taxable gains, new liabilities must be created or assumed that equal or exceed the liabilities from which the taxpayer is relieved, or the taxpayer must add cash toward the acquisition of replacement property in the exchange.

EXAMPLE—EXCHANGE INVOLVING MORTGAGE RELIEF

BreezeCo. (BR) exchanges a real estate property with a fair value of $10 million that is encumbered by a mortgage of $6 million for a real estate property with a fair value of $4 million. BR's basis in the property is $4.5 million. Both properties are qualifying properties and are of like kind.

How much gain will BR have to recognize for tax purposes?

BR realizes a gain of $5.5 million on the exchange transaction. The mortgage relief on the transaction amounts to $6 million. BR will have to recognize the $5.5 million gain for tax purposes, since the mortgage relief exceeds the gain on the exchange.

EXAMPLE—NETTING OF MORTGAGE BOOT

BreezeCo. (BR) and ExCo. enter into an exchange transaction for real estate properties. BR exchanges real estate property with a fair value of $25 million, a basis of $15 million and an outstanding mortgage of $12 million for replacement property with a fair value of $26 million and an outstanding mortgage of $13 million. ExCo. assumes the mortgage of $12 million, and BR assumes the mortgage of $13 million. Both properties are qualifying properties and are of like kind. ExCo's basis in the property relinquished is $10 million.

Questions:

1. How much gain will BR have to recognize for tax purposes?
2. How much gain will ExCo. have to recognize for tax purposes?

Answers:

1. The amounts of mortgage relief received and given are netted. BR is treated as having paid boot of $1 million. BR, as the payer of boot, will not have to recognize any gain.
2. ExCo. is treated as having received $1 million of net boot, resulting in recognition of $1 million gain.

USE OF QUALIFIED INTERMEDIARY

To qualify for tax deferral under Section 1031, a transaction must be structured as an exchange, with the taxpayer relinquishing and receiving property, rather than the taxpayer receiving sales proceeds or having control of the sales proceeds. A "qualified intermediary" is typically used as a middleman between the parties to the exchange to facilitate the exchange transaction. A qualified intermediary is an entity that enters into an exchange agreement with the owner of the property to be relinquished (exchanged), agreeing to receive and transfer (sell) the relinquished property and to acquire and transfer to that owner (exchanger) one or more replacement properties.[12] To be considered a qualified intermediary, the intermediary must not be a relative or agent of the exchanging party, or have common ownership of more than 10%.

In any Section 1031 exchange, if the seller receives the sales proceeds from the sale of the real estate relinquished, the transaction becomes taxable. Similarly, boot received directly by the seller as part of an exchange transaction will result in taxable gains, even if the boot is used in the acquisition of replacement property.[13] However, receipt of sales proceeds on relinquished property by a qualified intermediary and a qualified intermediary's expenditure of funds to purchase replacement property is not treated as receipt or expenditure by the taxpayer.

The use of a qualified intermediary is particularly important in a deferred exchange transaction. In a deferred exchange, the exchange of property to be relinquished is effected in two (or more) steps: (1) the sale of the property to be relinquished, and (2) the subsequent purchase of replacement property. The deferred exchange will almost always involve a three-party or multi-party exchange, rather than a literal property "swap" between two owners of qualifying real estate properties. In a deferred exchange, replacement property must be "identified" within 45 days of the transfer (closing) of the relinquished property. Additionally, the exchange must be completed within the earlier of 180 days of the transfer of the relinquished property or the due date of the tax return for the taxpayer's tax reporting.[14]

---

12   Reg. Section 1.1031(k)-1(g)(4)
13   Reg. Section 1.1031(k)-1
14   IRC Section 1031(a)(3)

The above overview over Section 1031 exchanges focuses on the underlying principles and covers only the basics of like-kind exchanges. There are many intricacies and different forms that have not been considered in this section.

2.3 NONMONETARY EXCHANGES NOT GOVERNED BY APB OPINION NO. 29

Paragraph 3(c) of APB Opinion No. 29 defines an exchange as:

> . . . a reciprocal transfer between an enterprise and another entity that results in the enterprise's acquiring assets or services or satisfying liabilities by surrendering other assets or services or incurring other obligations. A reciprocal transfer of a nonmonetary asset shall be deemed an exchange only if the transferor has no substantial continuing involvement in the transferred asset such that the usual risks and rewards of ownership of the asset are transferred.[15]

Transactions that do not meet this definition of an exchange are not within the scope of APB Opinion No. 29, even though they may qualify as like-kind exchanges (IRC Section 1031 exchanges) for tax purposes.

The following sections address some exchanges that are not within the scope of APB Opinion No. 29.[16]

2.3.1 EXCHANGE WITH CONTINUING INVOLVEMENT OF THE TRANSFEROR

If the transferor retains substantial continuing involvement in a real estate property transferred in an exchange transaction, so that the usual risks and rewards of ownership in the property are not transferred, the transaction is not a nonmonetary exchange of real estate properties for purposes of APB Opinion No. 29.[17]

As discussed in Chapter 3, the transferor of real estate often retains some form of continuing involvement with the real estate property transferred, even after title has passed. FASB Statement No. 66, *Accounting for Sales of Real Estate*, specifically addresses the following scenarios in which the risks and rewards of ownership are not considered transferred—the real estate property sold remains on the books of the transferor:

- Option or obligation to repurchase the property[18]
- Seller is general partner in a limited partnership that acquires an interest in the property sold and holds a receivable from the buyer for a significant part of sales price[19]

---

15   FAS 153, paragraph 2(a), APB 29, paragraph 3(c)
16   Other exchange transactions not governed by APB Opinion No. 29 include:
      - A transfer of nonmonetary assets between companies (or persons) under common control
      - A transfer of nonmonetary assets between a corporate joint venture and its owners
      - A transfer of assets to an entity in exchange for an equity interest in the entity
      - A transfer of a financial asset within the scope of FASB Statement No. 140 [APB 29, paragraph 4]
17   APB 29, paragraph 3(c)
18   FAS 66, paragraph 26
19   FAS 66, paragraph 27

- Seller guarantees the return of the buyer's investment or a return on that investment for extended period[20]
- Seller is required to initiate or support operations or continue to operate the property at its own risk for an extended period[21]

Additionally, any conditions that preclude gain recognition in a real estate sale transaction due to continuing involvement would also preclude gain recognition in an exchange transaction: The standards for gain recognition in exchange transactions are not less restrictive than the standards for gain recognition on sales transactions.[22]

Questions have arisen as to what forms of continuing involvement are deemed substantial continuing involvement in the transferred asset such that the usual risks and rewards of ownership of the asset are not transferred, resulting in the transfer not being within the scope of APB Opinion No. 29.[23] The FASB may address this issue in a FASB Staff Position (FSP) and provide clarification. The author believes that the FASB's intent was to not establish a higher threshold for nonmonetary exchanges than for exchanges involving monetary considera-tion;[24] that is, if derecognition of a real estate asset is not precluded under FASB Statement No. 66 for certain forms of continuing involvement, nonmonetary exchanges involving these forms of continuing involvement would be governed by APB Opinion No. 29.

2.3.2 IN-SUBSTANCE SALE AND PURCHASE TRANSACTION   A like-kind exchange of property under Section 1031 of the IRC often involves three or more unrelated parties that exchange monetary and nonmonetary assets, using escrow accounts or an intermediary to satisfy the requirements of Section 1031. In sub-stance, such exchange transactions may be comprised of a monetary transaction, the sale of an asset, followed by another monetary transaction, the purchase of a replacement asset. The use of an escrow account or an intermediary to execute monetary transactions does not turn such monetary exchanges into nonmonetary transactions for accounting purposes.

---

20   FAS 66, paragraph 28
21   FAS 66, paragraph 29
22   Paragraph A15 of FASB Statement No. 153 provides, in part: "The Board noted that certain transactions that appear to be nonmonetary exchanges are, in fact, not exchanges at all because the transferor does not relinquish control of a transferred asset such that derecognition is appropriate. The Board did not want this Statement to establish a less restrictive standard for gain recognition than the standard for gain recognition that is applicable to similar transactions involving monetary consideration."
23   APB 29, paragraph 3(c)
24   FAS 153, paragraph A15

EXAMPLE—THREE PARTY EXCHANGE

Company SunSellers (S) is contemplating a transaction in which S would sell a parcel of land to XchangeCo., which would place the cash purchase price in an escrow account. Cash in that escrow account would then be used to purchase a parcel of land from LandCo. at the direction of S.

This transaction structure may qualify as a "like-kind" exchange under Section 1031 of the IRC. Assuming the exchange meets the criteria established in Section 1031, S's tax basis in the new parcel would be the same as in the old parcel, and S would achieve tax deferral on any gains from the exchange.

For accounting purposes, this transaction does not qualify as a nonmonetary exchange, since S does not exchange its real property for real property held by LandCo. The use of XchangeCo. merely enables S to avoid the actual receipt of cash, but it does not turn this transaction into a nonmonetary exchange. Rather, this transaction is comprised of two monetary transactions, the sale of the parcel of land followed by the purchase of another parcel of land.

2.3.3 NONMONETARY EXCHANGE INVOLVING BUSINESS   Certain exchanges of real estate may constitute nonmonetary exchanges. Nevertheless, they may not be considered nonmonetary exchanges of *assets* governed by the provisions of APB Opinion No. 29 if the real estate properties exchanged are businesses, rather than assets. The exchange of businesses is accounted for following the provisions of FASB Statement No. 141, *Business Combinations*. Statement 141 requires that an exchange of a business for another business be accounted for at fair value.

The determination of whether real estate property is considered an asset or a business is based on the guidance provided in Emerging Issues Task Force (EITF) Issue No. 98-3, *Determining Whether a Nonmonetary Transaction Involves Receipt of Productive Assets or of a Business*,[25] which provides:

> A business is a self-sustaining integrated set of activities and assets conducted and managed for the purpose of providing a return to investors. A business consists of (a) inputs, (b) processes applied to those inputs, and (c) resulting outputs that are used to generate revenues. For a transferred set of activities and assets to be a business, it must contain all of the inputs and processes necessary for it to continue to conduct normal operations after the transferred set is separated from the transferor, which includes the ability to sustain a revenue stream by providing its outputs to customers.[26]

The transfer of an individual real estate property may or may not be the transfer of a self-sustaining integrated set of activities and assets that meets the definition of

---

25   FASB Statement No. 141(R) nullifies EITF Issue No. 98-3; see Section 1.6.1 of Chapter 1 for further discussion
26   EITF Issue No. 98-3, paragraph 6

a business.[27] The determination of whether an exchange transaction involves businesses or assets is based on the individual facts and circumstances of the transaction and requires significant judgment.

2.3.4 INVOLUNTARY CONVERSION   Events and transactions in which nonmonetary assets that are involuntarily converted to monetary assets (as a result of total or partial destruction, theft, seizure, or condemnation) are reinvested in other nonmonetary assets are considered monetary transactions, rather than nonmonetary transactions. FASB Interpretation (FIN) No. 30, *Accounting for Involuntary Conversions of Nonmonetary Assets to Monetary Assets*, provides guidance on how to account for involuntary conversions. If an involuntary conversion occurs, FIN 30 requires that a gain or loss be recognized in the period of conversion, calculated as the difference between the carrying amount of the nonmonetary asset and the proceeds from the conversion. In some cases, a nonmonetary asset is destroyed or damaged in one accounting period, and the amount of monetary assets to be received is not determinable until a subsequent accounting period. In those cases, gain or loss is recognized in accordance with FASB Statement No. 5, *Accounting for Contingencies*.[28]

2.4 ACCOUNTING FOR NONMONETARY EXCHANGES

APB Opinion No. 29 provides the primary accounting guidance for exchanges of nonmonetary assets, such as real estate properties.

2.4.1 GENERAL PRINCIPLE—FAIR VALUE   In general, the accounting for nonmonetary transactions is based on the fair values of the assets or services exchanged. Fair value is defined as the price that would be received to sell an asset or paid to transfer a liability in an orderly transaction between market participants at the measurement date.[29]

Paragraph 18 of APB Opinion No. 29 provides that:

> . . . the cost of a nonmonetary asset acquired in exchange for another nonmonetary asset is the fair value of the asset surrendered to obtain it, and a gain or loss should be recognized on the exchange. The fair value of the asset received should be used to measure the cost if it is more clearly evident than the fair value of the asset surrendered. . . . If one of the parties in a nonmonetary transaction could have elected to receive cash instead of the nonmonetary asset, the amount of cash that could have been received may be evidence of the fair value of the nonmonetary assets exchanged.[30]

---

27   See Section 1.6.1 of Chapter 1 for further discussion
28   FIN 30, paragraph 3
29   FAS 157, paragraph 5; prior to the changes effected by FASB Statement No. 157, paragraph 25 of APB Opinion No. 29 provides guidance for the determination of fair value in nonmonetary transactions
30   APB 29, paragraph 18

This fair value principle has been in place since the issuance of APB Opinion No. 29 in 1973, yet most real estate exchanges were recorded at carryover basis before the amendment of APB Opinion No. 29 by FASB Statement No. 153 in 2004. Why? Paragraph 21 of APB Opinion No. 29 provided that the accounting for an exchange of a nonmonetary asset should be based on the recorded amount, if the exchange did not constitute the culmination of an earning process: An exchange (1) of a productive asset not held for sale in the ordinary course of business for a similar productive asset or an equivalent interest in the same or similar productive asset, and (2) of a property held for sale in the ordinary course of business for a property to be sold in the same line of business to facilitate sales to customers other than the parties to the exchange were considered not to culminate an earning process. APB Opinion No. 29[31] specifically mentioned the exchange of real estate for real estate as an example of exchanges of productive assets that would not qualify for being recorded at fair value.

The provisions in paragraph 21 of APB No. 29 were interpreted very narrowly. Only transactions in which real estate held for productive use (such as an office building held for rental) was exchanged for real estate held for sale in the ordinary course of business (such as land inventory) were considered to "culminate an earning process." That is, the fair value principle applied only to these transactions. For most real estate exchanges, the real estate acquired was not recorded at fair value and gain on the exchange was not recognized.

With the issuance of FASB Statement No. 153 in December 2004, this exception to the use of fair value was eliminated. However, FASB Statement No. 153 also includes certain exceptions to the use of fair value in nonmonetary exchanges, as outlined below.

2.4.2 EXCEPTIONS TO THE FAIR VALUE PRINCIPLE[32]   If the conditions specified in APB Opinion No. 29 for the recording of real estate acquired in exchange transactions at their fair value have not been met, the real estate acquired is measured based on the recorded amount of the real estate asset relinquished, rather than at fair value.

A long-lived asset to be disposed of in an exchange that is measured based on the recorded amount of the nonmonetary asset relinquished continues to be classified as held and used until it is disposed of in the exchange.[33] Correspondingly, that asset is subject to the provisions of recognition and measurement of an impairment loss that are applicable to other long-lived assets classified as held and used.

---

31   APB 29, paragraph 7
32   FAS 153, paragraph 2(c); APB 29, paragraph 20
33   FAS 144, paragraph 27

Paragraph 29 of FASB Statement No. 144, *Accounting for the Impairment or Disposal of Long-Lived Assets*, provides, in part:

> If the asset . . . is tested for recoverability while it is classified as held and used, the estimates of future cash flows used in that test shall be based on the use of the asset for its remaining useful life, assuming that the disposal transaction will not occur. In addition to any impairment losses required to be recognized while the asset is classified as held and used, an impairment loss, if any, shall be recognized when the asset is disposed of if the carrying amount of the asset . . . exceeds its fair value.

CONDITIONS PRECLUDING THE USE OF FAIR VALUE

Paragraph 20 of APB Opinion No. 29 provides that a nonmonetary exchange of assets is measured based on the recorded amount of the asset relinquished (after reduction, if appropriate, for an indicated impairment of value), and not based on the fair value of the properties exchanged, if any of the following three conditions are present:

1. *Fair Value Not Determinable.* The fair value of neither the asset received nor the asset relinquished in the exchange is determinable within reasonable limits.[34]

    An example of a real estate transaction for which the fair value may be difficult to determine could be the exchange of parcels of raw land, if there are no comparable land sales. Raw land, different from income-producing properties, does not produce any cash flows or income that can be used for the determination of fair value through discounted cash flow analyses or multipliers.

2. *Exchange Transaction to Facilitate Sales to Customers.* The exchange is an exchange of an asset held for sale in the ordinary course of business for another asset to be sold in the same line of business. The transaction is entered into to facilitate sales to customers other than the parties to the exchange.[35]

    Typically, the exception provided for in paragraph 20(b) of APB No. 29 is not an issue for real estate exchange transactions.

3. *Exchange Transaction Lacks Commercial Substance.*[36] As discussed above, before the amendment of APB Opinion No. 29 by FASB Statement No. 153, exchanges that were not the culmination of an earning process were based on recorded amounts, rather than on the fair value of the assets

---

34 The FASB noted that the exception in APB Opinion No. 29 for exchanges in which the fair value is not determinable within reasonable limits has the same intent as the IASB's exception for nonmonetary asset exchanges in which the fair value of the assets exchanged is not reliably measurable, which is addressed in paragraph 24 of IAS 16. [APB 29, paragraphs 20(a); FAS. 153, paragraph A22]

35 APB 29, paragraph 20(b)

36 APB 29, paragraph 20(c)

exchanged. FASB Statement No. 153 replaced the concept of "culmination of an earning process" with the concept of "commercial substance." When does a nonmonetary exchange have commercial substance?[37] Paragraph 21 of APB Opinion No. 29 explains:

A nonmonetary exchange has commercial substance if the entity's future cash flows are expected to significantly change as a result of the exchange. The entity's future cash flows are expected to significantly change if either of the following criteria is met:

a. The configuration (risk, timing, and amount) of the future cash flows of the assets received differs significantly from the configuration of the future cash flows of the assets transferred.[38]

b. The entity-specific value of the assets received differs from the entity-specific value of the assets transferred, and the difference is significant in relation to the fair values of the assets exchanged.

Essentially, APB Opinion No. 29 requires a quantitative, cash flow–based analysis to determine whether a transaction has commercial substance, albeit acknowledging that in some instances a qualitative assessment may be "conclusive."[39]

The entity-specific value[40] of an asset attempts to capture the value of an asset or liability to a particular entity. An entity computing the entity-specific value of an asset uses its expectations about its use of that asset, rather than the use assumed by marketplace participants.[41]

As real estate properties are generally different from each other as far as risk, timing, and/or amount of the future cash flows are concerned, many exchanges of real estate properties have commercial substance.

2.5 NONMONETARY EXCHANGE OF REAL ESTATE INVOLVING MONETARY CONSIDERATION

Exchanges of real estate often involve some monetary consideration, in addition to a nonmonetary portion, to equalize the fair value of the real estate exchanged. APB Opinion No. 29 also applies to those transactions.[42]

---

37   APB 29, paragraph 21; FAS 153, paragraph 2(d)
38   A change in *any* of the elements—risk, timing, or amount—would be a change in configuration of future cash flows. [FAS 153, paragraph 21(a), footnote 5c] Whether a transaction has commercial substance is evaluated from the reporting entity's perspective. [FAS 153, paragraph A7]
39   APB 29, paragraph 21, FAS 153, paragraph 2
40   Concepts Statement No. 7, *Using Cash Flow Information and Present Value in Accounting Measurements,* states with respect to entity-specific value: "The entity-specific value (resulting from entity-specific measurement) can be characterized as the amount at which independent willing parties that share the same information and ability to generate the entity's estimated cash flows would agree to a transaction that exchanges the estimated future cash flows for a current amount." [CON 7, footnote 4]
41   FAS 153, paragraph 2(d); APB 29, paragraph 21(b), footnote 5(d)
42   FAS 153, paragraph 2(b); APB 29, paragraph 4

Real estate exchange transactions that include some monetary consideration are divided into a portion constituting a monetary exchange, which is treated as a sale, and a portion constituting a nonmonetary exchange, which is accounted for in accordance with the provisions of APB Opinion No. 29.[43] The determination of the percentage to be allocated to the monetary versus the nonmonetary portion is based on the relative fair values at the date of the exchange.

EXAMPLE—DETERMINATION OF MONETARY PORTION OF EXCHANGE[44]

BreezeCo. (BR) transfers real estate with a fair value of $2 million and a book value of $1.5 million to ExCo. In return, BR receives $400,000 cash, a $400,000 note, and real estate with a fair value of $1.2 million. (The net book value of the real estate transferred to BR is $800,000 on ExCo.'s books.)

What are the monetary and nonmonetary portions of the transaction?

The monetary portion of the transaction is 40%, determined as the total monetary consideration ($400,000 cash and $400,000 note) divided by the total fair value of the exchange ($2 million). The nonmonetary portion of the transaction is 60%, determined as the fair value of the real estate exchanged ($1.2 million) divided by the total fair value of the exchange.

2.5.1 ACCOUNTING BY RECEIVER OF MONETARY CONSIDERATION   For the receiver of monetary consideration, the monetary portion is accounted for as the sale of an interest in the underlying real estate following the guidance in FASB Statement No. 66, and the nonmonetary portion is accounted for pursuant to the guidance in APB Opinion No. 29. The real estate acquired in the exchange is recorded at fair value, unless a condition is present, which would preclude the use of fair value.[45]

2.5.2 ACCOUNTING BY PAYER OF MONETARY CONSIDERATION   If the exchange transaction meets the criteria for being recorded at fair value, the payer of monetary consideration records the real estate acquired at fair value. Fair value is measured as the sum of cash paid plus the fair value of the real estate transferred in the exchange, or the fair value of the real estate received, if the fair value of the real estate received is more clearly evident. Additionally, if one of

---

43   For exchanges other than real estate, exchange transactions involving boot of more than 25% are treated as monetary transactions in their entirety; they are not divided into a monetary and a nonmonetary portion. [EITF Issue No. 01-2, Issue No. 8(a); Issue 10(a)]

44   Adapted from EITF Issue No. 01-2, Issue 10(b)

45   Discussed in section 2.4.2

EXAMPLE—ACCOUNTING BY RECEIVER OF MONETARY CONSIDERATION[46]

The example continues the example above—Determination of Monetary Portion of Exchange.

For purposes of this example, it is assumed that the nonmonetary exchange transaction does not meet the conditions for being recorded at fair value, and that the criteria for the accrual method of accounting (for the monetary portion) have been met.

QUESTIONS

1. How much gain will BreezeCo. (BR) recognize at the time of the transaction?

2. What is the accounting basis of the property acquired by BR?

ANSWERS

1. Gain to be recognized

MONETARY PORTION

The gain on sale is computed as the monetary consideration received less the proportionate book value of the real estate transferred in the exchange. BR will recognize $200,000 gain on the sale of real estate, computed as follows: $800,000 monetary consideration received ($400,000 cash and $400,000 note) less $600,000 book value of real estate ($1.5 million total book value of real estate transferred × 40%).

NONMONETARY PORTION

As the nonmonetary portion of the transaction does not meet the criteria for being recorded at fair value, BR will not recognize any gain on the sale of the nonmonetary portion.

2. Accounting Basis of Property Acquired

BR acquires real estate with a fair value of $1.2 million through the nonmonetary exchange. The portion of the book value of the real estate transferred in the exchange that is allocated to the nonmonetary exchange amounts to $900,000 ($1.5 million × 60%). As the property acquired in the nonmonetary exchange does not meet the conditions for being recorded at fair value, the real estate acquired in the nonmonetary exchange is recorded at its carryover basis of $900,000.

---

the parties to the exchange transaction could have elected to receive cash instead of the real estate, the amount of cash that could have been received may provide evidence of the fair value of the real estate.[47] If the exchange transaction does not meet the criteria for being recorded at fair value, the real estate acquired in the exchange transaction is recorded at cash paid plus the carrying amount of the real estate asset transferred in the exchange.

---

46   Adapted from EITF Issue No. 01-2, Issue 10(b)
47   APB 29, paragraph 25

EXAMPLE—ACCOUNTING BY PAYER OF MONETARY CONSIDERATION[48]

The example continues the example above—Determination of Monetary Portion of Exchange.

For purposes of this example, it is assumed that the nonmonetary exchange transaction does not meet the conditions for being recorded at fair value.

How would ExCo. record the exchange transaction?

ExCo. would not recognize any gain. The real property acquired would be recorded at $1.6 million. This amount is calculated as follows:

MONETARY PORTION

The monetary portion of the transaction represents an acquisition of real estate for monetary consideration of $800,000 ($400,000 cash and $400,000 note).

NONMONETARY PORTION

ExCo. records the real estate acquired through the exchange at $800,000, which represents the carrying amount of the real estate transferred in the exchange.

2.6 SPECIAL ACCOUNTING ISSUES

2.6.1 EXCHANGE-LEASEBACK   In a real estate exchange-leaseback transaction, the "seller"-lessee exchanges real estate assets for other real estate assets owned by the "buyer"-lessor and leases back the real estate transferred in the exchange. An exchange-leaseback is within the scope of FASB Statement No. 98, *Accounting for Leases: Sale-Leaseback Transactions Involving Real Estate, Sales-Type Leases of Real Estate, Definition of the Lease Term, Initial Direct Costs of Direct Financing Leases.* When evaluating an exchange-leaseback transaction, one has to determine whether the criteria for sale-leaseback accounting set forth in paragraph 7 of Statement 98 are met:

Sale-leaseback accounting is appropriate only if the exchange-leaseback includes all of the following:[49]

- A normal leaseback (active use of the property)
- Adequate initial and continuing investments in the property
- Payment terms and provisions that transfer all of the other risks and rewards of ownership and the absence of any other continuing involvement by the seller-lessee

Generally, in a real estate exchange, adequate initial and continuing investments in the properties acquired in the exchange do not present any issues, since the real estate received in the exchange takes the place of cash payments made by the buyer.

---

48   Adapted from EITF Issue No. 01-2, Issue 10(b)
49   See chapter 5, section 5.2.1.1, for further discussion.

If the criteria for sale-leaseback accounting in paragraph 7 of Statement 98 are not met, the seller-lessee continues to carry the property exchanged on its books and accounts for it using the deposit method or as a financing transaction, whichever is appropriate under Statement 98.

If the criteria for sale-leaseback accounting are met, the seller removes the property transferred in the exchange from its books. The seller-lessee then applies APB Opinion No. 29 to determine the appropriate accounting for the exchange transaction—that is, to determine whether the real estate acquired through the exchange transaction should be accounted for at fair value or carryover basis. Any gains resulting from the exchange transaction are deferred and amortized over the lease term in the same manner as a gain on a sale-leaseback transaction.[50]

2.6.2 TRANSACTIONS BETWEEN RELATED PARTIES   The scope exceptions in APB Opinion No. 29 include the following exchange transactions between related parties:[51]

- Transfer of nonmonetary assets solely between companies or persons under common control, such as:
  - Between a parent company and its subsidiaries
  - Between two subsidiary corporations of the same parent
  - Between a corporate joint venture and its owners
- Acquisition of nonmonetary assets or services on the issuance of the capital stock of an enterprise
- Stock issued or received in stock dividends and stock splits, which are accounted for in accordance with Accounting Research Bulletin (ARB) No. 43, Chapter 7B
- Transfer of assets to an entity in exchange for an equity interest in that entity

There is a lack of comprehensive authoritative guidance relating to exchange transactions between a company and its owners, between entities under common control, and between related parties in general. Determining the appropriate basis for an asset acquired in a nonmonetary transaction and deciding whether it is appropriate to recognize gain on the exchange are issues frequently encountered in practice.

NONRECIPROCAL TRANSFERS TO OWNERS
In-kind distributions to owners—other than distributions in a spin-off, reorganization, or liquidation, described below—are generally recorded at the fair value of the nonmonetary assets transferred with a gain or loss recognized on the disposition of the asset, assuming the fair value of the nonmonetary assets distributed is objectively measurable and would be realizable to the distributing entity in an outright sale.[52] If a company acquires outstanding stock (for treasury or for

---

50   FAS 13, paragraph 33
51   APB 29, paragraph 4
52   APB 29, paragraphs 18 and 23

retirement) by transferring assets to its shareholders, the fair value of the company's reacquired stock may be a more clearly evident measure of the fair value of the assets distributed and should be used to record the exchange.[53] If the fair value of the nonmonetary assets distributed is not objectively measurable, the transfer is accounted for at the recorded amounts of the assets transferred.

The general rule of recording transfers of assets to owners at the fair value of the assets transferred is not followed, if the assets are transferred in a spin-off, reorganization or liquidation of an entity. Rather, such transfers are accounted for at the recorded amounts of the assets transferred or their fair value, if lower.[54]

TRANSFERS OF ASSETS BETWEEN COMPANIES UNDER COMMON CONTROL

Gain recognition on transfers of real estate—not in the ordinary course of business—between entities under common control, between a controlling shareholder and a corporation, or between subsidiary and parent is generally deferred until the real estate assets leave the controlled group.[55] At the time of the exchange transaction, the real estate transferred in the exchange is measured based on the recorded amount of the asset relinquished, after reduction for an impairment of value. Similarly, the entity that receives the asset would record the asset at the transferor's carrying amount at the date of the transfer.[56]

TRANSFERS OF NONMONETARY ASSETS BY JOINT VENTURE PARTNERS

Venture partners often contribute nonmonetary assets, such as land, to real estate ventures. The appropriate accounting depends on the nature of the transaction and the circumstances surrounding it. In exchanges of real estate for equity interests that occur at the formation of a joint venture, a full or partial step-up in basis is generally not permissible, unless the transfer involves a partial sale.[57] Assets or businesses contributed to a joint venture subsequent to its formation are generally recorded at fair value.

2.7 FINANCIAL STATEMENT PRESENTATION AND DISCLOSURE

APB Opinion No. 29 requires the following disclosures for nonmonetary transactions:[58]

- Nature of the transactions
- Basis of accounting for the assets transferred
- Gains or losses recognized on transfers

---

53   APB 29, paragraph 18
54   APB 29, paragraph 23
55   In the sale of real estate to an entity controlled by the seller, paragraph 34 of FASB Statement No. 66 requires that no profit on the sale be recognized until it is realized from transactions with outside parties through sale or operations of the property.
56   FAS 141, paragraph D12
57   See chapter 6, section 6.3.1.2 for further discussion.
58   APB 29, paragraph 28

Gains or losses resulting from involuntary conversions of nonmonetary assets to monetary assets are classified in accordance with the provisions of APB Opinion No. 30, *Reporting the Results of Operations—Reporting the Effects of Disposal of a Segment of a Business, and Extraordinary, Unusual, and Infrequently Occurring Events and Transactions.*[59]

2.8 INTERNATIONAL FINANCIAL REPORTING STANDARDS

The issue of nonmonetary exchanges of assets was part of the short-term convergence project between the FASB and the IASB. With the amendment of APB Opinion No. 29 by FASB Statement No. 153, the FASB adopted the criteria set forth in International Accounting Standard (IAS) 16 that, if met, require that property, plant, and equipment acquired in a nonmonetary exchange transaction—or in a combination of a nomonetary and a monetary transaction—be measured at fair value. This section does not address the transfer of real estate that is classified as inventory in exchange for nonmonetary assets.

Paragraph 24 of IAS 16 provides: If property, plant, and equipment is acquired in exchange for nonmonetary assets, or a combination of monetary and nonmonetary assets, the cost to the acquiring company is "measured at fair value unless (a) the exchange transaction lacks commercial substance or (b) the fair value of neither the asset received nor the asset given up is reliably measurable." If measurement at fair value is not appropriate based on these criteria, the assets acquired are recorded at the carrying amount of the assets given up.

2.8.1 COMMERCIAL SUBSTANCE OF EXCHANGE TRANSACTION   The determination of whether an exchange transaction has commercial substance involves a consideration of the cash flow effects relating to that transaction. Paragraph 25 of IAS 16 provides that an exchange transaction has commercial substance if:

(a) The configuration (risk, timing, and amount) of the cash flows of the asset received differs from the configuration of the cash flows of the asset transferred; or

(b) The entity-specific value of the portion of the entity's operations affected by the transaction changes as a result of the exchange; and

(c) The difference in (a) or (b) is significant relative to the fair value of the assets exchanged.

In evaluating whether a transaction has commercial substance, an entity should base its calculations on the present value of the post-tax cash flows it expects to derive from operations affected by the transaction. The discount rate

---

59   FIN 30, paragraph 4

should reflect the entity's own assessment of the time value of money and the risks specific to those operations, rather than marketplace participants' assessments.[60]

2.8.2 FAIR VALUE MEASUREMENT   Paragraph 6 of IAS 16 defines fair value as "the amount for which an asset could be exchanged between knowledgeable, willing parties in an arm's length transaction." Like APB Opinion No. 29,[61] IAS 16 provides that the fair value of the asset given up be used to measure the cost of the asset received, unless the fair value of the asset received is more clearly evident.[62]

For some exchange transactions, comparable market transactions may not exist. For such exchange transactions, fair value is nevertheless considered reliably measurable, if

(a) the variability in the range of reasonable fair value estimates is not significant for that asset or

(b) the probabilities of the various estimates within the range can be reasonably assessed and used in estimating fair value.[63]

2.9 SYNOPSIS OF AUTHORITATIVE LITERATURE

APB OPINION NO. 29, *ACCOUNTING FOR NONMONETARY TRANSACTIONS*
APB Opinion No. 29 provides guidance for nonmonetary exchanges of assets or services, or a combination of nonmonetary and monetary exchanges of assets or services. In general, the accounting for nonmonetary transactions is based on the fair values of the assets or services involved. Following this general principle, the cost of a nonmonetary asset acquired in exchange for another nonmonetary asset is the fair value of the asset surrendered to obtain it; a gain or loss is recognized on the exchange.

FASB STATEMENT NO. 153, *EXCHANGES OF NONMONETARY ASSETS, AN AMENDMENT OF APB OPINION NO. 29*
FASB Statement No. 153 amends APB Opinion No. 29; it retains the general principle of APB Opinion No. 29 that nonmonetary exchanges should be based on the fair values of the assets or services exchanged. Before its amendment, APB Opinion No. 29 required as prerequisite for recording a nonmonetary exchange at fair value that the earning process be culminated. FASB Statement No. 153 replaces that prerequisite with the concept of commercial substance.

FASB INTERPRETATION NO. 30, *ACCOUNTING FOR INVOLUNTARY CONVERSIONS OF NONMONETARY ASSETS TO MONETARY ASSETS*
FIN 30 provides accounting guidance for the involuntary conversion of nonmonetary assets (such as property or equipment) to monetary assets (such as insurance

---

60   IAS 16, paragraph BC22
61   APB 29, paragraph 18
62   IAS 16, paragraph 26
63   IAS 16, paragraph 26

proceeds). Any gains or losses from such conversions need to be recognized, irrespective of whether an enterprise reinvests the monetary assets received in replacement assets.

EITF Issue No. 84-39, *Transfers of Monetary and Nonmonetary Assets among Individuals and Entities under Common Control*
Deemed no longer technically helpful.

EITF Issue No. 86-29, *Nonmonetary Transactions: Magnitude of Boot and the Exceptions to the Use of Fair Value*
Codified in EITF Issue No. 01-2.

EITF Issue No. 87-29, *Exchange of Real Estate Involving Boot*
Codified in EITF Issue No. 01-2.

EITF Issue No. 89-7, *Exchange of Assets or Interest in a Subsidiary for a Noncontrolling Equity Interest in a New Entity*
Codified in EITF Issue No. 01-2.

EITF Issue No. 96-2, *Impairment Recognition When a Nonmonetary Asset Is Exchanged or Is Distributed to Owners and Is Accounted for at the Asset's Recorded Amount*
Codified in EITF Issue No. 01-2.

EITF Issue No. 98-3, *Determining Whether a Nonmonetary Transaction Involves Receipt of Productive Assets or of a Business*

Issues

1. Can the exchange of assets or groups of assets involving the receipt of a consolidated business be considered an exchange of similar productive assets accounted for at historical cost pursuant to paragraph 21 of APB Opinion No. 29?
2. How should a "business" be defined?

Consensuses/Status

1. This Issue is resolved with respect to the exchange of similar businesses with the issuance of FASB Statement No. 141. Paragraph 10 of FASB Statement No. 141 states that "the exchange of a business for a business also is a business combination."
2. The Task Force reached a consensus that a business is a self-sustaining integrated set of activities and assets conducted and managed for the purpose of providing a return to investors. For a transferred set of activities and assets to be a business, it must contain all of the inputs and processes necessary for it to continue to conduct normal operations after the transferred set is

separated from the transferor. The assessment of whether a transferred set is a business should be made without regard to how the transferee intends to use the transferred set.

In December 2007, the FASB issued FASB Statement No. 141(R), which applies prospectively to business combinations for which the acquisition date is on or after the beginning of the first annual reporting period beginning on or after December 15, 2008. FASB Statement No. 141(R) nullifies EITF Issue No. 98-3.

EITF ISSUE NO. 98-7, *ACCOUNTING FOR EXCHANGES OF SIMILAR EQUITY METHOD INVESTMENTS*
Codified in EITF Issue No. 01-2.

EITF ISSUE NO. 00-5, *DETERMINING WHETHER A NONMONETARY TRANSACTION IS AN EXCHANGE OF SIMILAR PRODUCTIVE ASSETS*
Codified in EITF Issue No. 01-2.

EITF ISSUE NO. 01-2, *INTERPRETATIONS OF APB OPINION NO. 29, ACCOUNTING FOR NONMONETARY TRANSACTIONS*

Issues[64]

1. What level of monetary consideration in a nonmonetary exchange causes the transaction to be considered monetary in its entirety and, therefore, outside the scope of APB Opinion No. 29?[65]
2. Does FASB Statement No. 66 apply to an exchange of similar real estate that is not subject to APB Opinion No. 29 because the transaction involves enough boot for the exchange to be considered monetary under the consensus for Issue 8(a)?[66]
3. If FASB Statement No. 66 does apply, how should it be applied?[67]
4. An enterprise distributes loans receivable to its owners by forming a subsidiary, transferring those loans receivable to the subsidiary, and then distributing the stock of that subsidiary to shareholders of the parent. Should the enterprise report the distribution at book value as a spinoff or at fair value as a dividend-in-kind if the book value of the loans receivable, which may be either the "recorded investment in the receivable" or the "carrying amount of the receivable," is in excess of their fair value, and how should the recipient record the transaction?[68]

---

64   Several of the issues addressed in EITF Issue No. 01-2 have been nullified by FASB Statement No. 153. Some of the issues that have not been nullified are outlined here.
65   EITF Issue No. 01-2, Issue 8(a)
66   EITF Issue No. 01-2, Issue 10(a)
67   EITF Issue No. 01-2, Issue 10(b)
68   EITF Issue No. 01-2, Issue 11

5. Should a non-*pro rata* split-off of all or a significant segment of a business in a corporate plan of reorganization be accounted for at historical cost or at fair value?[69]

Consensuses/Status

1. The Task Force reached a consensus that a transaction should be considered monetary (rather than nonmonetary) if the boot is significant, and agreed that "significant" should be defined as at least 25% of the fair value of the exchange. For the monetary part of the transaction, both parties record the exchange at fair value. If boot in an exchange transaction is less than 25%, the *pro rata* gain recognition guidance in paragraph 22 of APB Opinion No. 29 should be applied by the receiver of boot, and the payer of boot would not recognize a gain.

2. The Task Force reached a consensus that a transaction involving an exchange of real estate that is considered a monetary transaction because boot is at least 25% of the fair value of the exchange would be allocated between two components: A monetary portion and a nonmonetary portion. The allocation between the monetary and nonmonetary portions of the transaction should be based on their relative fair values at the time of the transaction.

3. For the receiver of boot, the monetary portion is accounted for under FASB Statement No. 66 as the equivalent of a sale of an interest in the underlying real estate, and the nonmonetary portion is accounted for based on the fair value or the recorded amount pursuant to the provisions in APB Opinion No. 29. For the payer of boot, the monetary portion is accounted for as the acquisition of real estate, and the nonmonetary portion is accounted based on fair value or the recorded amount, pursuant to the provisions in APB Opinion No. 29.

4. The Task Force reached a consensus that the distribution should be reported at fair value by the enterprise and the recipient. The transaction is not a spin-off because the subsidiary does not constitute a business. Rather, the transaction should be considered a dividend-in-kind. Under paragraph 23 of APB Opinion No. 29, dividends-in-kind are nonreciprocal transfers of nonmonetary assets to owners that should be accounted for at fair value if the fair value of the nonmonetary asset distributed is objectively measurable and would be clearly realizable to the distributing entity in an outright sale at or near the time of distribution.

5. A non-*pro rata* split-off of a segment of a business in a corporate plan of reorganization should be accounted for at fair value. The Task Force also reached a consensus that a split-off of a targeted business, distributed

---

69   EITF Issue No. 01-2, Issue 12

on a *pro rata* basis to the holders of the related targeted stock, should be accounted for at historical cost. If the targeted stock was created in contemplation of the subsequent split-off, the creation of the targeted stock and the split-off cannot be separated; the split-off should be recorded at fair value.

American Institute of Certified Public Accountants (AICPA) Issues Paper, *Accounting for Grants Received From Governments*

Superseded by IAS 20.

SEC Staff Accounting Bulletin Topic 5G, *Transfers of Nonmonetary Assets By Promoters or Shareholders*[70]

SAB Topic 5G addresses transfers of nonmonetary assets by promoters or shareholders for all or part of a company's common stock just prior to or contemporaneously with a first-time public offering. Normally, such transfers are recorded at the transferor's historical cost. In situations where the fair value of either the stock issued or the assets acquired is objectively measurable and the transferor does not retain a substantial indirect interest in the assets as a result of stock ownership in the company, recording of the assets received at their fair value may be acceptable.

International Accounting Standard 16, *Property, Plant, and Equipment*

IAS 16 provides guidance relating to property, plant, and equipment acquired in exchange transactions. Property, plant, and equipment acquired in exchange for nonmonetary assets or in a combination of monetary and nonmonetary assets are recorded at fair value, unless the exchange transaction lacks commercial substance, or unless the fair value of neither of the assets exchanged can be determined reliably. Before its amendment in 2003 (effective 2005), IAS 16 required that property, plant, and equipment acquired in an exchange transaction be measured at fair value unless the exchanged assets were similar.

International Accounting Standard 20, *Accounting for Government Grants and Disclosure of Government Assistance*

IAS 20 provides guidance regarding the accounting for government grants, including grants of nonmonetary assets. Government grants are not recognized until there is reasonable assurance that the entity will comply with the conditions attached to them, and that the grants will be received. Once they meet the criteria for being recognized, both the grant and the asset may be recorded at fair value. Alternatively, the asset and related grant may be recorded at nominal amounts. The following two methods of presentation are considered acceptable: (1) setting up the grant as deferred income, which is recognized as income on a systematic and rational basis over the useful life of the asset, or (2) deducting the grant in arriving at the carrying amount of the asset. Under this method, the grant is recognized into income over the life of a depreciable asset through a reduced depreciation charge.

---

70   SAB 48

REAL ESTATE SALES

3.1 OVERVIEW

Premature profit recognition on real estate sales transactions had been an issue for many years when, in 1962, the Securities and Exchange Commission (SEC) provided examples of real estate transactions for which it would be inappropriate to recognize profit at the time of sale. In subsequent years, real estate transactions became increasingly innovative and complex, and their legal form frequently did not reflect the substance of the transaction. These developments prompted the American Institute of Certified Public Accountants (AICPA) to establish the Committee on Accounting for Real Estate Transactions in 1971. The Committee was formed to study and evaluate revenue and profit recognition applied in practice and to recommend changes. As a result of the Committee's recommendations, the AICPA Industry Accounting Guide, *Accounting for Profit Recognition on Sales of Real Estate*, was issued in 1979. Financial Accounting Standards Board (FASB) Statement No. 66, *Accounting for Sales of Real Estate*, extracts the principles from that Accounting Guide and from the guidance in the two Statements of Position, SOP No. 75-6, *Questions Concerning Profit Recognition on Sales of Real Estate,* and SOP No. 78-4, *Application of the Deposit, Installment, and Cost Recovery Methods in Accounting for Sales of Real Estate.*

The sales and profit recognition principles in FASB Statement No. 66 contain many bright lines that are intended to be minimum percentages. In many cases, the standard of materiality cannot be applied, and even a minor "violation" of the rules and bright lines may result in a sale transaction that does not qualify for sale recognition or in profit having to be deferred to future periods.

3.2 APPLICABILITY OF FASB STATEMENT NO. 66

FASB Statement No. 66 provides guidance for the recognition of profit on all real estate transactions without regard to the nature of the seller's business. While Statement 66 specifically mentions the sale of hotels, motels, marinas, and mobile home parks as being within its scope, it does not explicitly define the term "real estate" or the transactions that are within its scope.

FASB Interpretation No. (FIN) 43, *Real Estate Sales*, provides clarification of the scope of Statement 66:[1]

---

1   FIN 43, paragraph 2

Statement 66 applies to all sales of real estate, including real estate with property improvements or integral equipment. The terms *property improvements* and *integral equipment* as they are used in this Interpretation refer to any physical structure or equipment attached to the real estate that cannot be removed and used separately without incurring significant cost. Examples include an office building, a manufacturing facility, a power plant, and a refinery.

Equipment is considered integral when the cost of removing the equipment and the resulting decrease in value, which includes the cost of shipping and reinstalling the equipment at a new site, exceeds 10% of the fair value of the equipment.[2]

Whether something is determined to be a business or not is not a factor in determining whether its sale is subject to the provisions of Statement 66. The attributes of the combined assets being sold (that is, the manufacturing facility, the power plant, or the hotel plus the land, receivables, payables, etc.) need to be considered when determining whether the nature of the assets being sold is in substance the sale of real estate.[3]

The sale of timberlands or farms (that is, land with trees or crops attached to it) is viewed as being similar to the sale of land with property improvements or integral equipment and thus also subject to the guidance relating to the sale of real estate. However, natural assets that have been extracted from the land (such as oil, gas, coal, and gold) are not subject to the provisions governing the sale of real estate. Similarly, the sale of timber or harvested crop (that is, anything that will have been detached from the land by the time it reaches the buyer) is not subject to the provisions relating to the sale of real estate.[4]

Also subject to the provisions of FASB Statement No. 66 are the sale of corporate stock of enterprises with substantial real estate and the sale of interests in real estate partnerships.[5] However, a marketable investment in a real estate company, such as an investment in a real estate investment trust (REIT) that is accounted for in accordance with FASB Statement No. 115, *Accounting for Certain Investments in Debt and Equity Securities*, is not considered an investment that is in substance real estate;[6] such sale or transfer of ownership interest accounted for in accordance with Statement 115 is subject to the provisions of FASB Statement No. 140, *Accounting for Transfers and Servicing of Financial Assets and Extinguishments of Liabilities.*[7]

---

2   EITF Issue No. 00-13; Section 5.2 in Chapter 5 includes an example relating to integral equipment.
3   FIN 43, paragraph 24
4   FIN 43, paragraph 14
5   FAS 66, paragraph 101
6   EITF Issue No. 98-8
7   Paragraph 4 of FASB Statement No. 140 provides that transfers of ownership interests that are in substance sales of real estate are outside the scope of FASB Statement No. 140.

EXAMPLE—SALE OF PARTNERSHIP INTERESTS

LandCo. owns limited partnership interests in a real estate partnership. The primary activity of the limited partnership is to invest in low-income housing properties. LandCo. sells the limited partnership interests to a third party.

Is the sale of the limited partnership interests within the scope of FASB Statement No. 66?

Yes. EITF Issue No. 98-8, *Accounting for Transfers of Investments that Are in Substance Real Estate*, clarifies that for purposes of applying the provisions of Statement 66, real estate includes investments that are in substance real estate, such as the investment in the real estate partnership. Accordingly, the sale of the limited partnership interests should be treated as a sale of real estate.

The provisions of FASB Statement No. 66 do not apply to transactions that involve the following:[8]

- The sale of only property improvements or integral equipment without a concurrent (or contemplated) sale of the underlying land, unless the underlying land is leased to the buyer;[9] such lease may be explicit or implicit. An example of a sale of property improvements not subject to the provisions of Statement 66 would be the sale of storage tanks attached to real estate that are not used on the property and are removed subsequent to the sale.
- The sale of the stock or net assets of a subsidiary or a segment of a business containing real estate, unless the transaction is, in substance, the sale of real estate.
- The sale of securities that are accounted for in accordance with FASB Statement No. 115, *Accounting for Certain Investments in Debt and Equity Securities*.

3.3 SALE AND PROFIT RECOGNITION

When evaluating a real estate sale transaction, two separate issues arise:

1. Is it appropriate to record the transaction as a sale? and, if a sale can be recorded,
2. What method should be used to recognize profit on the sale?

A real estate sale transaction cannot be recorded as a sale until the sale has been consummated, which requires that the following four criteria be met:[10]

- The parties are bound by the terms of a contract.
- All consideration has been exchanged.

---

8   FIN 43, paragraph 3
9   FIN 43, footnote 1
10   FAS 66, paragraph 6

- Any permanent financing for which the seller is responsible has been arranged.[11]
- All conditions precedent to closing have been performed.[12]

Paragraph 6 of Statement 66 states that, usually, those four conditions are met at the time of closing or after closing, not when an agreement to sell is signed or at a preclosing. However, in a few limited exceptions, a sale may be consummated before closing has occurred. For example, if the trustee has received all consideration for the sale, as well as title to the property, but the mechanics of the closing process have not been completed, a sale may be recorded at the time title was transferred and consideration was received by the trustee.

SALE OF REAL ESTATE WITH LONG CONSTRUCTION PERIODS
As outlined above, a sale is not recorded until it has been consummated. One criterion for the consummation of a sale is that "all conditions precedent to closing have been performed, including that the building be certified for occupancy."[13] For sales of real estate properties with long construction periods, such as office buildings, condominiums, shopping centers, and similar structures, Statement 66 provides an exception to the requirement that all conditions precedent to closing must have been performed in order for sale recognition to be appropriate. For these types of real estate properties, sale and related profit are recognized during the process of construction using the percentage-of-completion method of accounting, assuming the other criteria for sale and profit recognition are met and the costs of development can be reasonably estimated.[14]

3.4 PROFIT RECOGNITION UNDER THE ACCRUAL METHOD
Under the accrual method of accounting, profit on a real estate sale transaction is recognized in full, rather than deferred and recognized in future periods. A number of requirements must be met for the accrual method to be appropriate.

3.4.1 GENERAL RULE   As a general rule, profit from a real estate sale is recognized in full when the following two conditions are met:[15]

- The profit is determinable; that is, the collectibility of the sales price is reasonably assured or the amount that will not be collectible can be

---

11   The obligation to *arrange* permanent financing is considered to be a sale contingency. This is different from the seller's obligation to *provide* financing, which would not preclude sale recognition.
12   For the sale of a building, this requires that the building is certified for occupancy.
13   FAS 66, paragraph 20
14   FAS 66, paragraph 20; see also Section 3.5.4.7 in this chapter
15   FAS 66, paragraphs 3 and 4

estimated. Collectibility of the sales price is demonstrated by the buyer's commitment to pay, which requires substantial initial and continuing investments that give the buyer a stake in the property sufficient that the risk of loss through default motivates the buyer to honor its obligations to the seller. When considering the collectibility of the sales price, factors such as the credit standing of the buyer, the age and location of the property, the terms of financing provided to the buyer (for example, recourse or nonrecourse), and the adequacy of cash flow from the property are taken into consideration.

- The earnings process is virtually complete; that is, the seller is not obligated to perform significant activities after the sale to earn the profit.

Unless both of these general conditions are met at the time of sale, a portion or all of the profit has to be deferred.

Statement 66 includes specific criteria to make this general rule operational. These criteria are intended to be minimum requirements.

3.4.2 SPECIFIC CRITERIA Profit on a real estate sale transaction is not recognized by the accrual method until a sale has been consummated and all of the following criteria are met:[16]

- The buyer's initial and continuing investments are adequate to demonstrate a commitment to pay for the property.
- The seller's receivable is not subject to future subordination.
- The seller has transferred to the buyer the usual risks and rewards of ownership in a transaction that is in substance a sale and does not have a substantial continuing involvement with the property.

3.4.2.1 Adequate Initial and Continuing Investments The application of the accrual method requires that the profit is determinable; that is, the collectibility of the sales price must be reasonably assured or the amount that will not be collectible must be estimable. Collectibility of the sales price is demonstrated by the buyer's commitment to pay, which in turn is supported by substantial initial and continuing investments that give the buyer a stake in the property sufficient that the risk of loss through default motivates the buyer to honor its obligation to the seller.[17]

Statement 66 establishes certain *minimum* thresholds for initial and continuing investments that must be met in order for profit recognition under the accrual

---

16   FAS 66, paragraph 5
17   FAS 66, paragraphs 3 and 4

method of accounting to be appropriate.[18] These minimum investment requirements are intended to measure the investment of the buyer, not the cash received by the seller. Thus, any payment a buyer makes to pay off existing debt on the property is included in the amount of initial and continuing investments. The adequacy of the buyer's initial and continuing investments is determined by comparing the sales value of the property to the amount of the initial and continuing investments.[19] In addition to this quantitative assessment of collectibility, FASB Statement No. 66 requires a qualitative assessment of collectibility; the seller has to consider factors such as the credit standing of the buyer, the age and location of the property, and the adequacy of cash flows from the property sold.[20]

SALES VALUE

As outlined above, when determining the adequacy of the buyer's initial and continuing investments, the buyer's investments are compared to the sales value of the real estate, rather than to its sales price. The sales value of real estate is determined by adjusting the sales price of the real estate property for any additional proceeds to the seller that are in substance additional sales proceeds, as well as for any amounts included in the sales price that in substance represent payments for future services or interest on a below-market note.[21]

DETERMINATION OF SALES VALUE[22]

Sales Price	
Plus:	Proceeds from the issuance of a real estate option that is exercised
Plus:	Other payments that are in substance additional sales proceeds, such as:
	— Management Fees
	— Points
	— Prepaid Interest
	— Other Fees
Less:	Discount to reduce receivable to present value
Less:	Net present value of services that the seller commits to perform without compensation
Less:	Net present value of services in excess of compensation
Sales Value	

---

18   See also Section 3.7.4 of this chapter, which discusses the effect of nonrecourse financing on profit recognition.

19   When the seller has received all amounts it is entitled to from the sale and is not at risk related to the financing, the buyer's commitment to pay for the property is not a factor in the seller's recognition of profit. [EITF Issue No. 88-24]

20   FAS 66, paragraph 4

21   FAS 66, paragraph 7

22   FAS. 66, paragraph 7

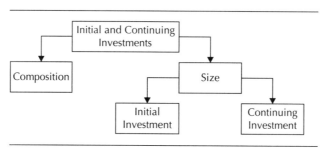

EXHIBIT 3.1   INITIAL AND CONTINUING INVESTMENTS DIAGRAM

INITIAL AND CONTINUING INVESTMENTS

When evaluating the sufficiency of the buyer's initial and continuing investments, one must assess whether the consideration received from the buyer qualifies as initial and continuing investments (its composition) and the sufficiency of the investments (its size), as illustrated in Exhibit 3.1.

COMPOSITION OF INITIAL AND CONTINUING INVESTMENTS

FASB Statement No. 66 is very specific as to what consideration received by the seller qualifies as initial and continuing investments:[23]

- Cash paid as a down payment
- Buyer's notes supported by irrevocable letters of credit from an independent established lending institution[24]
- Payments by the buyer to third parties to reduce existing indebtedness on the property
- Other amounts paid by the buyer that are part of the sales value

All other consideration received by the seller, including other notes of the buyer, are included as part of the buyer's initial investment at the time that the consideration is sold or otherwise converted to cash without recourse to the seller.[25]

---

23   Paragraph 9 of FASB Statement No. 66 specifically addresses only the composition of the buyer's initial investment; the same requirements apply to a buyer's continuing investment. [EITF Issue No. 88-24; EITF Issue No. 06-8, paragraph 5]

24   An irrevocable financial instrument, such as a surety bond, from an established independent insuring institution that conveys to the seller all of the rights and obligations of an irrevocable letter of credit may be considered by the seller to be equivalent to an irrevocable letter of credit and included as part of the buyer's initial and continuing investments in determining whether it is appropriate to recognize profit under the accrual method. [EITF Issue No. 87-9] If a buyer were to provide an irrevocable letter of credit to meet the continuing investment requirements, the amount guaranteed by the letter of credit would have to be sufficient to cover the initial and continuing investment requirements, as well as interest thereon.

25   FAS 66, paragraph 9

EXAMPLE—SALE OF RECEIVABLE WITH RECOURSE[26]

In March 2007, Masterbuilder Inc. (M) sells a home to a buyer and provides financing for 100% of the sales value. The note provides for a one-year period during which the buyer does not have to make any interest or principal payments on the note. On the date of sale, M sells the receivable to a bank, granting the bank the right to put the receivable back to M within the first 30 days of transfer, should customer default occur within that time frame. The transfer of the receivable qualifies for sale recognition under the provisions of FASB Statement No. 140, *Accounting for Transfers and Servicing of Financial Assets and Extinguishments of Liabilities*. M has determined that aside from potential issues with the financing provided to the buyer, all other prerequisites for recognizing profit under the accrual method of accounting have been met.

Should M recognize profit under the accrual method of accounting (1) in March 2007, (2) in April 2007, or (3) at the time the buyer has made sufficient initial and continuing investments?

M should recognize profit under the accrual method of accounting in April 2007. As paragraph 9 of FASB Statement No. 66 specifically provides that consideration cannot be included as part of the buyer's investment, as long as there is recourse to the seller, profit recognition in March 2007 is not appropriate. Although the buyer has not made any investment in April 2007, and thus M would ordinarily not be able to use the accrual method of accounting, EITF Issue No. 88-24, *Effect of Various Forms of Financing under FASB Statement No. 66*, provides an exception to this general rule, as M has received all monies due from the sale and is not at risk related to the financing. As such, the buyer's commitment to pay for the property is not a factor in the seller's recognition of profit.

The following forms of considerations do not qualify as part of a buyer's initial and continuing investments:[27]

- Payments by the buyer to third parties for improvements to the property[28]
- A permanent loan commitment by an independent third party to replace a loan made by the seller
- Any funds that have been or will be loaned, refunded, or directly or indirectly provided to the buyer by the seller
- Loans guaranteed or collateralized by the seller for the buyer

---

26   The FASB's agenda includes the project *Impact of a Transfer of Receivables on Profit Recognition under Statement 66*. The objective of that project is to provide guidance in the form of a FASB Staff Position (FSP) regarding the impact on a company's subsequent evaluation of the initial and continuing investment tests under FASB Statement No. 66 when the entity either (1) transfers a note receivable with recourse in a transaction that qualifies as a sale under FASB Statement No. 140, or (2) transfers a note receivable in a transaction that does not qualify as a sale under FASB Statement No. 140. The author believes that unless the standard-setters provide authoritative guidance to the contrary, the explicit guidance in paragraph 9 of FASB Statement No. 66 should be followed.

27   FAS 66, paragraph 10; paragraph 10 only addresses initial investment, but the same requirements apply to a buyer's continuing investment. [EITF Issue No. 88-24; EITF Issue No. 06-8, paragraph 5]

28   However, if the seller were to make improvements to the property purchased, payments made to the seller for property improvements that increase the sales value and the sales price of the property would be includible in the amount of initial investment.

Generally, funds to be provided directly or indirectly by the seller or by parties related to the seller must be subtracted from the buyer's contractually required payments in determining whether the initial and continuing investments are adequate;[29] otherwise, the seller could effectively circumvent the initial and continuing investment requirements in FASB Statement No. 66. Such funds provided by the seller may include loan guarantees provided to the buyer's lender, funding commitments for future property improvements, and any arrangements in which the seller risks suffering losses as a result of funds borrowed by the buyer. Additionally, "circular transactions" may be devised in which a party related to the seller purchases real estate properties from a party related to the buyer; such transactions should be carefully evaluated to determine whether, in substance, the seller provides funds to the buyer.

SIZE OF INITIAL INVESTMENT

As outlined above, the buyer's initial and continuing investments need to be adequate to demonstrate the buyer's commitment to pay for the property. The adequacy of a buyer's initial investment is measured by comparing it to the sales value of the property. Statement 66[30] establishes minimum percentages based on the type of real estate property sold. That is, for a seller to be able to use the accrual method of accounting for recognizing profit, the buyer must have made a minimum initial investment as compared to the sales value of the property. These minimums, reproduced in Exhibit 3.2, Minimum Initial Investment Percentages Prescribed by FASB Statement No. 66, are based on the lending practices of independent established lending institutions; they reflect the usual loan limits.[31] As these percentages are intended as *minimums*, a failure to meet these minimums even by a minor amount (for example, a down payment of 9.5% versus 10% for secondary residences) will preclude the use of the accrual method of accounting.

For properties that are not listed in Exhibit 3.2, the size of the initial investment requirement is determined by analogy to property types specified in that Exhibit, or by analogy to the risks of a particular property type.

Additionally, if a recently placed permanent loan or firm permanent loan commitment for maximum financing of the property exists, a company cannot merely use these minimum percentages, but *in addition* has to take into consideration the maximum amount of financing that can be obtained in relation to the sales value of the property.

---

29   If a future loan on normal terms from an established lending institution bears a fair market interest rate and the proceeds of the loan are conditional on use for specified development of or construction on the property, the loan need not be subtracted in determining the buyer's investment. [FAS 66, paragraph 12]

30   FAS 66, paragraphs 53–54

31   FAS 66, paragraphs 11 and 53

	MINIMUM INITIAL INVESTMENT EXPRESSED AS A PERCENTAGE OF SALES VALUE
Land	
Held for commercial, industrial, or residential development to commence within two years after sale	20
Held for commercial, industrial, or residential development to commence after two years	25
Commercial and industrial property[32]	
Office and industrial buildings, shopping centers, and so forth:	
Properties subject to lease on a long-term lease basis to parties with satisfactory credit rating; cash flow currently sufficient to service all indebtedness	10
Single-tenancy properties sold to a buyer with a satisfactory credit rating	15
All other	20
Other income-producing properties (hotels, motels, marinas, mobile home parks, and so forth):	
Cash flow currently sufficient to service all indebtedness	15
Start-up situations or current deficiencies in cash flow	25
Multifamily residential property	
Primary residence:	
Cash flow currently sufficient to service all indebtedness	10
Start-up situations or current deficiencies in cash flow	15
Secondary or recreational residence:	
Cash flow currently sufficient to service all indebtedness	15
Start-up situations or current deficiencies in cash flow	25
Single-family residential property (including condominium or cooperative housing)	
Primary residence of the buyer:	5[33]
Secondary or recreational residence:	10[34]

EXHIBIT 3.2   MINIMUM INITIAL INVESTMENT PERCENTAGES PRESCRIBED BY FASB STATEMENT NO. 66[35]

---

32   The term "commercial and industrial property" includes operating facilities such as manufacturing facilities, power plants, and refineries. [FIN 43, paragraph 13]

33   Paragraph 54 of FASB Statement No. 66 provides specific guidance for transactions in which the seller provides financing and independent first mortgage financing is not used.

34   Paragraph 54 of FASB Statement No. 66 provides specific guidance for transactions in which the seller provides financing and independent first mortgage financing is not used.

35   FAS 66, paragraph 54

For owner-occupied single-family residential property financed under an FHA or VA government-insured program, lower down payment requirements may apply due to loan guarantees provided by the governmental agencies.[36]

FORMULA FOR DETERMINING MINIMUM INITIAL INVESTMENT IF COMMITMENT FOR MAXIMUM FINANCING HAS BEEN OBTAINED[37]

The minimum initial investment is the greater of 1. and 2.

1. The minimum percentage of the sales value of the property as prescribed by FASB Statement No. 66 (see Exhibit 3.2)
2. The lesser of:
    a. The amount of the sales value of the property in excess of 115% of the amount of a newly placed permanent loan or firm permanent loan commitment from a primary lender that is an independent established lending institution
    b. 25% of the sales value

EXAMPLE—DETERMINING THE ADEQUACY OF INITIAL INVESTMENT

Skyco (S) sells a single tenant office building to a buyer with a satisfactory credit rating. The property's sales value is $2,000,000. A recently placed firm permanent loan commitment exists for maximum financing of the property in the amount of $1,400,000.

What is the minimum amount of initial investment that is necessary so that S can apply the accrual method of accounting?

Sales value of property	$2,000,000	
Down payment required[38] (15% × $2,000,000)		$300,000 (1)
Maximum permanent loan commitment	$1,400,000	
115% of permanent loan commitment	$1,610,000	
Lesser of excess of sales value over 115% of permanent loan commitment	$390,000[39]	
or 25% of sales value	$500,000	$390,000 (2)
Minimum initial investment:		
Greater of (1) or (2)		$390,000

S has to receive a down payment of at least $390,000 to be able to apply the accrual method of accounting.

---

36   EITF Issue No. 87-9
37   FAS 66, paragraph 53
38   Based on minimum percentages in paragraph 54 of FASB Statement No. 66
39   Sales value ($2,000,000) less 115% of permanent loan commitment ($1,610,000): $390,000

EXAMPLE—INITIAL INVESTMENT[40]

Ace LLC (A) has a 75% interest in a real estate property; Bloom Co. (B) holds the other 25% interest. A sells its interest to B and receives a 10% cash down payment and a note for the balance of the sales price. For this type of sales transaction, paragraph 54 of Statement 66 requires a 15% minimum initial investment. B pledges its 100% interest in the property as security for the note to A. No debt is outstanding on the property.

Is the down payment sufficient to enable A to recognize profit on the sale under the accrual method of accounting?

No. Under paragraph 9 of Statement 66, only the 10% cash down payment qualifies as initial investment. The purchased property pledged as security for the note is not included as part of the buyer's initial investment. Since B makes a 10% down payment for a sale transaction that requires a 15% down payment in order for the accrual method of accounting to be appropriate, the initial investment is not sufficient to allow for the use of the accrual method of accounting.

SIZE OF CONTINUING INVESTMENT

Both the initial and the continuing investment criteria must be met for the seller to be able to recognize profit under the accrual method of accounting. After the seller has made the determination that the initial investment meets or exceeds the amounts required by Statement 66, the buyer needs to determine whether—until all amounts due to the seller are received from the buyer[41]—the buyer meets the continuing investment criterion. For purposes of determining the adequacy of the buyer's initial and continuing investments, the down payment (that is, the initial investment) and any subsequent payments (that is, the continuing investment) made by the buyer are evaluated on a combined basis. If the initial investment exceeds the minimum prescribed, the excess is applied toward the required annual increases in the buyer's investment.[42] The initial and continuing investment requirements are met if, at all times throughout the term of the buyer's note, the cumulative amounts of the down payment and the contractually required payments exceed the minimum amounts calculated in accordance with Statement 66. These minimum amounts are based on the *total indebtedness* of the buyer on the property, which includes not only the amounts owed to the seller, but also all other debt the buyer incurs for the purchase of the property. That is, when evaluating whether the criteria of initial and continuing investments are met, payments made by the buyer, rather than amounts received by the seller are determinative.

---

40   Adapted from EITF Issue No. 88-12

41   If the seller has unconditionally received all amounts it is entitled to receive from the sale and is not at risk related to the financing, a buyer's initial and continuing investments below the thresholds established by FASB Statement No. 66 will not preclude the use of the accrual method of profit recognition. See Section 3.7.4 of this chapter for further discussion.

42   FAS 66, paragraph 16

Statement 66 has put certain limits in place with respect to the time period over which a buyer's note has to be amortized for purposes of calculating the sufficiency of the buyer's investments to ensure that the continuing investment requirements remain at a level that would be expected under normal financing arrangements: Paragraph 12 of Statement 66 provides that a buyer's continuing investment in a real estate transaction does not qualify for the accrual method of accounting

> unless the buyer is contractually required to pay each year on its total debt for the purchase price of the property an amount at least equal to the level annual payment that would be needed to pay that debt and interest on the unpaid balance over no more than (a) 20 years for debt for land and (b) the customary amortization term of a first mortgage loan by an independent established lending institution for other real estate.

RELEASE PROVISIONS

When a sale occurs and the seller finances part of the purchase price, it is generally presumed that in the event of default by the buyer, the seller can recover the property and be in no worse position with respect to the property than before the sale. This is not the case if an agreement to sell property provides that part or all of the property is released from liens securing related debt by payment of a release price, or that payments by the buyer are assigned first to released property. Such release provisions are common in the sale of land to homebuilders. A homebuilder typically pledges lots to obtain home construction loans, and the construction lenders require a first lien on the land. If a sales contract includes release provisions, a buyer's initial investment needs to be sufficient to pay the release price on property released at the date of sale and to constitute an adequate initial investment on property not released in order to meet the criterion of adequate initial investment for the property as a whole.[43]

Additionally, the buyer's continuing investment needs to be sufficient, after the released property is paid for, to constitute an adequate continuing investment on property not released in order to satisfy the criterion of adequate continuing investment for the property as a whole.[44] If the amounts applied to unreleased portions do not meet the initial and continuing investment criteria with respect to the property not released, the released portions are treated as separate transactions, and profit is recognized on each released portion once the criteria for profit recognition are met.[45]

---

43   FAS 66, paragraph 13
44   FAS 66, paragraph 14
45   FAS 66, paragraph 15

EXAMPLE—RELEASE PROVISIONS

LakelandCo., a developer, sells 50 parcels of land for a total sales price (and sales value) of $5,000,000. The minimum down payment requirement for profit recognition under the accrual method is 20%. The buyer makes a down payment of $1 million (20%) at closing and signs a note to the seller for the remainder. The sales price of 10 of the lots is $120,000 each, and the remaining lots have sales prices of $95,000 each. According to the terms of the sales contract, the seller is required to release at closing five lots with sales prices of $120,000 each.

Is the buyer's initial investment sufficient to recognize gain on the sale of the 50 parcels under the accrual method of accounting?

No, the buyer's initial investment is not sufficient, as demonstrated by the following calculation:

Aggregate sales value of the lots	$5,000,000
Less: Sales value of lots released at closing	$ 600,000
Sales value of lots not released	$4,400,000

Required down payment for the accrual method on lots not released (20%): $880,000

Buyer's initial investment	$1,000,000
Applied to lots released at closing	$ 600,000
Buyer's initial investment, applied to lots not released	$ 400,000

The down payment has to be applied to the released lots first. The released lots have been paid in full; profit recognition under the accrual method is appropriate for the released lots. The remaining down payment of $400,000 is less than the required down payment for the remaining lots ($880,000); therefore, the application of the accrual method is not appropriate for the lots not released.

3.4.2.2 Seller's Receivable Not Subject to Future Subordination   When a seller finances part of the purchase price, it is generally assumed that—in the case of buyer default—the seller will be able to recover the property sold and be in at least as good a position with respect to the property as before the sale. If the seller's receivable is subordinated to other loans, however, the seller may not be able to recover the property sold. For example, the buyer may have financed part of the purchase price with a mortgage from a lending institution; if the seller's receivable were subordinated to that mortgage, the lending institution, rather than the seller, would recover (foreclose on) the property. Recognizing the detrimental

impact of an existing *or future* subordination of the seller's receivable on the position of the seller with respect to the property sold, Statement 66 requires for the use of the accrual method of accounting that the seller's receivable not be subject to future subordination, with the following two exceptions:[46]

1. A receivable is subordinate to a first mortgage on the property *existing* at the time of sale. However, for liens on loan amounts that have not been funded (drawn), this exception does not apply, because the unfunded portions are in essence new, rather than existing loans.

2. A future loan is provided for by the terms of the sale and the proceeds of the loan are applied first to the payment of the seller's receivable.

3.4.2.3 Absence of Continuing Involvement   Additionally, the accrual method of accounting requires that there be no continuing involvement by the seller with a property after it is sold in any way that results in retention of *substantial* risks or rewards of ownership, except a participation in profits without further risk of loss.[47] If this is not the case, the absence-of-continuing-involvement criterion has not been met, and profit recognition under the accrual method of accounting is generally not appropriate. There are many different ways a seller may be involved with the property after its sale that result in the retention of substantial risks or rewards of ownership, as outlined later in this chapter.

3.5 FAILURE TO MEET CRITERIA FOR THE APPLICATION OF THE ACCRUAL METHOD

If a real estate sale transaction does not satisfy the criteria for recognition of profit by the accrual method, Statement 66 prescribes different profit recognition methods to be used (see Exhibit 3.3), depending on the reason for failing the criteria for the application of the accrual method. In situations, in which more than one factor preclude the use of the accrual method of accounting, the seller would consider all such factors when determining the accounting method to be used (see matrix in Section 3.6).

3.5.1 INADEQUATE INITIAL INVESTMENT   If the buyer's initial investment does not meet the criteria for recognition of profit by the accrual method, the profit recognition method to be used depends on whether the recovery of the cost of the property is reasonably assured if the buyer defaults:[48]

- If recovery of the cost of the property is reasonably assured if the buyer defaults, the installment or cost recovery methods are appropriate to recognize profit.

---

46   FAS 66, paragraph 17
47   FAS 66, paragraph 43
48   FAS 66, paragraph 22; this assumes that all other criteria for the use of the accrual method have been met

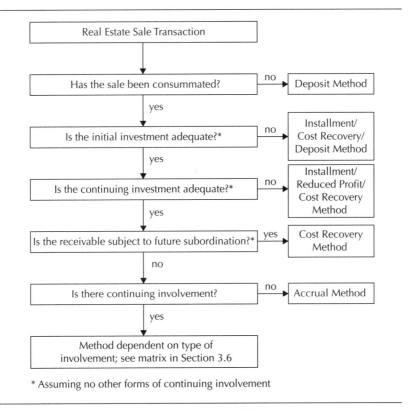

EXHIBIT 3.3   FLOWCHART—METHODS OF PROFIT RECOGNITION

- If recovery of the cost of the property is not reasonably assured if the buyer defaults, or if cost has already been recovered and the collection of additional amounts is uncertain, the cost recovery or deposit method should be used.

3.5.2 INADEQUATE CONTINUING INVESTMENT   In a situation in which the initial, but not the continuing, investment meets the criteria specified by Statement 66 (and all other criteria for the use of the accrual method have been met), profit is recognized by the reduced profit method at the time of sale, if payments by the buyer each year will at least cover both of the following:[49]

- Interest and principal amortization on the maximum first mortgage loan that could be obtained on the property
- Interest, at an appropriate rate,[50] on the excess of the aggregate actual debt on the property over such maximum first mortgage loan

---

49   FAS 66, paragraph 23
50   Paragraphs 13 and 14 of APB Opinion No. 21, *Interest on Receivables and Payables*, provide criteria for selecting an appropriate interest rate for present value calculations.

If these criteria for the use of the reduced profit method are not met, profit on the sale is recognized by the installment or the cost recovery method.

3.5.3 RECEIVABLE SUBJECT TO FUTURE SUBORDINATION   If the seller's receivable is subject to future subordination, profit is generally recognized by the cost recovery method.[51] As outlined in Section 3.4.2.2, a receivable subject to future subordination would not preclude the use of the accrual method of accounting if (1) that receivable is subordinate to a first mortgage on the property existing at the time of sale or (2) the terms of the sale provide for a loan, the proceeds of which are applied first to the payment of the seller's receivable.

3.5.4 CONTINUING INVOLVEMENT   If the seller has some continuing involvement with the property and does not transfer substantially all of the risks and rewards of ownership, recognition of all of the profit is generally not appropriate. Whether or not a sale may be recorded and—if the recording of a sale is appropriate—the amount of profit to be recognized is determined by the nature and extent of the seller's continuing involvement.[52] If the amount of the seller's loss of profit because of continued involvement with the property is limited by the terms of the sales contract, it is generally appropriate to recognize profit; however, the profit calculated in accordance with Statement 66 is reduced by the *maximum exposure* to loss.[53] Applying the FASB Statement No. 5 concept of a *probable loss* is not appropriate in this circumstance.

Statement 66 describes certain types of continuing involvement commonly encountered in real estate transactions and sets forth the accounting methods to be applied. If some other form of continuing involvement exists, the sale is accounted for based on the nature of the continuing involvement.[54] In certain sales transactions, several forms of continuing involvement may be present, for which Statement 66 may prescribe different accounting methods. In that situation, the selection of the appropriate method is subject to significant judgment.

When structuring a transaction that exposes the seller to loss contingencies, the seller should consider including a provision in the sales contract that limits the amount of the seller's responsibility in order for the seller to be able to recognize profit on the sale.

---

51   FAS 66, paragraph 24; this assumes that all other criteria for the use of the accrual method have been met
52   Additionally, the seller has to consider whether this continuing involvement constitutes a variable interest in a variable interest entity governed by FIN 46(R), *Consolidation of Variable Interest Entities*. FIN 46(R)-considerations are not further discussed in this chapter.
53   FAS 66, paragraph 25
54   FAS 66, paragraph 25

EXAMPLE—MAXIMUM EXPOSURE TO LOSS

SuperSale Inc. (S) has entered into a purchase and sale agreement to sell six parcels of developed property for $30 million to a third-party buyer (B), who pays the sales price in cash at the date of closing. Two of the parcels are sites of former gas stations. Investigation reveals high levels of residual contamination on the sites. S has agreed to retain responsibility for the remediation of these two parcels for a period of ten years, based on present and future environmental laws, and to pay for the remediation up to an amount of $5 million. S estimates that the cost of the environmental remediation will amount to $2 million. The gain on sale, before taking into consideration S's responsibilities for environmental remediation, amounts to $20 million; all other criteria for the accrual method are met.

How much profit should S recognize at the time of sale?

S should recognize $15 million profit at the time of sale. Based on the provisions of the sales contract, S is responsible for environmental remediation for up to $5 million. In accordance with paragraph 25 of FASB Statement No. 66, the profit to be recognized needs to be reduced by the maximum exposure to loss ($5 million), rather than S's cost estimate ($2 million). Without a contractual provision limiting S's exposure to $5 million, S would not have been able to recognize any profit at the time of sale.

3.5.4.1 Obligation or Option to Repurchase Property   A seller that has an obligation or an option to repurchase real estate property sold or that can be required to repurchase the property sold cannot recognize a sale. Paragraph 26 of Statement 66 provides:

> The seller has an obligation to repurchase the property, or the terms of the transaction allow the buyer to compel the seller or give an option[*] to the seller to repurchase the property. The transaction shall be accounted for as a financing, leasing, or profit-sharing arrangement rather than as a sale.
>
> [*]A right of first refusal based on a bona fide offer by a third party ordinarily is not an obligation or an option to repurchase.

Statement 66 does not distinguish between contingent and noncontingent options, nor does it provide for an evaluation of the probability of exercise. Thus, an option that is contingent on a future event—whether or not within the control of the seller—generally precludes the recording of a sale.[55]

When determining whether to use the financing, leasing, or profit sharing method for obligations or options to repurchase, the seller has to evaluate the relationship of the parties to the transaction, the substance of the transaction, and

---

55   FAS 66, paragraph 26; a narrow exception is provided in EITF Issue No. 86-6, as discussed later in this section

the terms of the option or obligation to repurchase. The following general rules have evolved in practice and may serve as guidelines on how to account for repurchase obligations.

- Obligations to repurchase real estate property sold at a fixed price that exceeds the sales value are generally accounted for under the financing method by recognizing interest expense (using the effective interest method) for the difference between the sales value and the repurchase price, so that at the expected date of repurchase the financing obligation equals the repurchase price.
- Obligations to repurchase the property sold at fair value (or another amount indeterminate at the time of sale) are generally also accounted for under the financing method. If the repurchase obligation is at fair value, the financing obligation should be trued up to fair value at the end of each reporting period. That adjustment amount, similar to a debt discount, is amortized into income prospectively until the expected date of repurchase. This is consistent with the accounting by a participating mortgage loan borrower, as provided for in SOP 97-1, *Accounting by Participating Mortgage Loan Borrowers.*
- For obligations to repurchase real estate at a fixed price that is lower than the sales value, the transaction may in substance be a lease, and the leasing method may be the appropriate method to use.

When (1) the buyer has an option to put the property back to the seller, or (2) the seller has an option to repurchase the property sold and the exercise of the option is likely, that option is accounted for like an obligation to repurchase.

If the exercise of the option to repurchase is not considered likely at the time of sale, the seller has to evaluate whether the use of the profit-sharing method is more reflective of the substance of the transaction than the use of the financing method. If the use of the financing method is determined to be appropriate in a scenario, in which the exercise price is at fair value (or another amount indeterminate at the time of sale) and exercise of the option is not deemed likely at the time of sale, views differ as to whether the financing obligation should be trued up at the end of each reporting period. The following arguments are made: Since FASB Statement No. 66 does not differentiate based on whether or not an option is contingent or not, nor based on the likelihood of exercise, the likelihood of option exercise should not impact the application of the financing method. Others believe that in situations, in which exercise of the option is not likely, the financing obligation should not be trued up at the end of each reporting period, because doing so would distort interest expense. Practice is diverse with respect to the application of the financing method in scenarios such as the one described in this paragraph.

Ultimately, the accounting depends on the individual facts and circumstances of the transaction; as the authoritative literature does not provide any specific guidance, there may be more than one acceptable accounting alternative. This is particularly true in transactions in which multiple forms of continuing involvement are present.

ANTISPECULATION CLAUSE

The following is a narrow exception to the general rule that the mere existence of an option precludes the recording of a sale: Land sale agreements sometimes contain antispeculation clauses that require the buyer to develop the land in a specific manner or within a stated period of time. If the buyer *fails to comply* with the provisions of the sales contract, the seller has the right to reacquire the property. The Emerging Issues Task Force (EITF) dealt with this issue in EITF Issue No. 86-6, *Antispeculation Clauses in Real Estate Sales Contracts*, and reached a consensus that such arrangement does not preclude recognition of a sale if the probability of the buyer not complying with the provisions of the sales contract is *remote*. Factors the Task Force deemed relevant in that probability assessment were the economic loss to the buyer from repurchase and the buyer's perceived ability to comply with the provisions of the sales contract. However, a probability test is not appropriate if the seller's repurchase option is not contingent upon compliance by the buyer.

RIGHT OF FIRST REFUSAL

Statement 66 specifically provides that a right of first refusal based on a bona fide offer by a third party is ordinarily not an obligation or option to repurchase that in and of itself precludes the recording of a sale.[56] A right of first refusal gives the seller the right to purchase the property *under the same terms and conditions* that the buyer negotiates with a third party, if the buyer decides at some point in the future to sell the real estate property purchased. Thus, a right of first refusal based on a bona fide offer by a third party allows the seller to continue to exercise some control over the property without precluding sale recognition. If buyer and seller were to agree, however, that the seller could buy back the property at a price different from the price negotiated with the prospective purchaser, the agreement would *not* be considered a right of first refusal.

ECONOMIC COMPULSION TO REPURCHASE

Statement 66 precludes sale accounting not only when options or obligations to repurchase exist, but also in instances in which arrangements between buyer and seller could effectively compel the seller to repurchase the property sold. If such economic compulsion exists, sale accounting is precluded. The arrangements between seller and buyer have to be carefully evaluated as to their substance when determining whether the recording of a sale is appropriate.[57]

---

56   FAS 66, paragraph 26, footnote 7
57   See also Section 3.5.4.6 in this chapter

3.5.4.2 Seller is General Partner of Buyer and Holds Receivable   The sale of an interest in real property to a partnership by a general partner may not be recorded as a sale, if the general partner holds a receivable from the partnership for a significant portion of the sales price; the transaction is accounted for as a financing, leasing, or profit-sharing arrangement.[58] Additionally, since a general partner is liable for all of the partnership's liabilities, with the exception of liabilities that are explicitly nonrecourse to the partnership, the general partner would also be precluded from recognizing a sale if the partnership obtained a loan to finance the property with recourse to the partnership.

If sale recognition is not precluded, the general partner (seller of the property) needs to defer profit on the sale to the extent of its interest in the partnership, or, if the general partner controls the partnership, defer all of the profit until the profit is realized from transactions with third parties through sale or operations of the property.[59] Additionally, when determining the appropriate accounting for the sale, consideration should be given to any support obligations the general partner may have, either contractually or from being the general partner.[60]

3.5.4.3 Guarantee of Investment or on Investment[61]   A seller may guarantee the return *of* the buyer's investment or a return *on* that investment through guarantees of cash flows, subsidies, or tax benefits, for example. The accounting for such guarantees depends on the nature and the time period of the guarantee.[62]

GUARANTEES OF INVESTMENT OR GUARANTEES ON INVESTMENT COVERING AN EXTENDED PERIOD
If the seller's guarantee, whether a guarantee of investment or a guarantee on investment, covers an extended period (a guarantee period of at least five years),[63] the transaction is accounted for as a financing, leasing, or profit sharing arrangement. Sale recognition is not appropriate.

---

58   FAS 66, paragraph 27; a significant receivable is a receivable in excess of 15% of the maximum first-lien financing that could be obtained from an independent established lending institution for the property. Forms of financing could include:
1. A construction loan made or to be made by the seller to the extent that it exceeds the minimum funding commitment for permanent financing from a third party for which the seller will not be liable
2. An all-inclusive or wraparound receivable held by the seller to the extent that it exceeds prior-lien financing for which the seller has no personal liability
3. Other funds provided or to be provided directly or indirectly by the seller to the buyer
4. The present value of a land lease when the seller is the lessor. [FAS 66, footnote 8]

59   FAS 66, paragraph 34
60   Such support obligations are described in FASB Statement No. 66, paragraphs 28–33.
61   FAS 66, paragraph 28
62   Additionally, the seller needs to consider whether there are any recognition or disclosure requirements under FIN 45, *Guarantor's Accounting and Disclosure Requirements for Guarantees, Including Guarantees of Indebtedness of Others*.
63   The term "extended period" is not defined in FASB Statement No. 66. It has generally been interpreted to mean a guarantee period of at least five years by some or of more than five years by others.

EXAMPLE—GUARANTEE FOR EXTENDED PERIOD

Buggs (B) owns limited partnership interests in several partnerships that invest in low-income housing projects eligible for tax credits. B intends to sell these limited partnership interests with a guarantee that the investor in the limited partnership will receive a certain amount of tax credits over a seven-year period. The third party buyer pays the purchase price in cash.

How should B account for this transaction?

Limited partnership interests in a partnership that invests in low-income housing are in substance real estate; sale and profit recognition follow the provisions of Statement 66.[64] Because B, through its guarantee, provides a guaranteed return for an extended period, the real estate transaction may not be recognized as a sale. Instead, the transaction is accounted for according to its substance as either a financing, leasing, or profit-sharing arrangement.

GUARANTEES ON INVESTMENT COVERING A LIMITED PERIOD

Guarantees covering less than five years are considered guarantees for a limited period.[65] The deposit method is used until the operations of the real estate property cover all operating expenses, debt service, and contractual payments. At that time, profit is recognized on the basis of performance of the services required. Performance of those services is measured by the ratio of costs incurred to total costs incurred and expected to be incurred over the period during which the services are performed.[66]

3.5.4.4 Support of Operations   A seller may be required to initiate or support operations or continue to operate the property at its own risk, or may be presumed to have such a risk:

- For an extended period
- For a specified limited period
- Until a specified level of operations has been obtained; for example, until rentals of a property are sufficient to cover operating expenses and debt service[67]

When evaluating the seller's support obligations, the facts and circumstances surrounding the support arrangement have to be considered. Though not contractually required to provide support, a seller may provide such support for

---

64   EITF Issue No. 98-8

65   The term "limited period" is not defined in FASB Statement No. 66. It has generally been interpreted to mean a guarantee period of less than five years by some or of five years or less by others.

66   The performance-of-services method is described in paragraphs 84–88 of FASB Statement No. 66; an example is provided in Section 3.6.9 of this chapter.

67   FAS 66, paragraph 29

moral or economic reasons, to protect its reputation or the value of the project. Paragraph 29 of Statement 66[68] provides that support is "presumed to be required" in the following circumstances:

- A seller obtains an interest as a general partner in a limited partnership that acquires an interest in the property sold
- A seller retains an equity interest in the property, such as an undivided interest or an equity interest in a joint venture that holds an interest in the property[69]
- A seller holds a receivable from a buyer for a significant part of the sales price, and collection of the receivable depends on the operation of the property
- A seller agrees to manage the property for the buyer on terms not usual for the services to be rendered, and the agreement is not terminable by either the seller or the buyer

If support is required or presumed to be required for an *extended period of time*,[70] the transaction is accounted for as a financing, leasing, or profit-sharing arrangement. If support is required or presumed to be required for a *limited period of time*,[71] profit on the sale is recognized on the basis of performance of the services required. Performance of services is measured by the costs incurred and to be incurred over the period during which the services are performed.

Statement 66 provides specific guidance relating to profit recognition, tailored to income-producing property:[72] Profit recognition begins when there is reasonable assurance that future rent receipts will cover operating expenses and debt service, including payments due the seller under the terms of the transaction. Objective information regarding occupancy levels and rental rates in the immediate area are used to provide such reasonable assurance. Paragraph 29 of Statement 66 states with respect to the methodology that should be used in that evaluation: "In assessing whether rentals will be adequate to justify recognition of profit, total estimated future rent receipts of the property shall be reduced by one-third as a reasonable safety factor unless the amount so computed is less than the rents to be received from signed leases. In this event, the rents from signed leases shall be substituted for the computed amount." If the period during which the seller is obligated to

---

68   FAS 66, paragraph 29, footnote 10
69   Paragraph 33 of FASB Statement No. 66 provides specific guidance if a seller retains an equity interest in the property; that guidance should be followed absent any indication of support obligations.
70   The term "extended period" is not defined in FASB Statement No. 66. It has generally been interpreted to mean a guarantee period of at least five years by some or of more than five years by others.
71   The term "limited period" is not defined in FASB Statement No. 66. It has generally been interpreted to mean a guarantee period of less than five years by some or of five years or less by others.
72   FAS 66, paragraph 29

support the operations of the property is not stated in the sales contract, support is presumed for at least two years from the time of initial rental, unless actual rental operations cover operating expenses, debt service, and other contractual commitments before that time.[73]

If the sales contract requires the seller to provide management services relating to the property after the sale without compensation or at compensation less than prevailing rates for the service required, paragraph 31 of Statement 66 requires that compensation be imputed when the sale is recognized and that it be recognized in income as the services are performed over the term of the management contract.

However, one first has to determine whether that management contract meets the definition of a lease. If the management contract were to meet the definition of a lease, the accounting for the transaction would follow the guidance for sale-leaseback transactions,[74] and profit on the sale of the real estate would generally be amortized over the term of the management agreement. An example could be the sale of a hotel that continues to be managed by the seller.

3.5.4.5 Option to Purchase Property
SALE IS IN SUBSTANCE AN OPTION TO PURCHASE PROPERTY[75]
A sale transaction may in substance constitute an option for the purchase of real estate property. For example, undeveloped land may be "sold" under terms that call for a very small initial investment by the buyer and postponement of additional payments until the buyer obtains zoning changes or building permits, or until other contingencies specified in the sales agreement are satisfactorily resolved. Whenever the down payment is relatively small compared to the minimum initial investment percentages specified by Statement 66, and the buyer has little economic stake in the property (colloquially referred to as little "skin in the game"), the down payment may be more akin to an option premium than to a down payment on the property. For the purchase of land, down payments of less than five percent are generally treated as payments to obtain an option to purchase the property, if financing provided by the seller is nonrecourse to the buyer. Such small down payments are accounted for under the deposit method until the buyer makes additional payments that indicate the buyer's financial commitment.

OPTION TO PURCHASE PROPERTY
The seller may grant an option for the purchase of real property. The seller accounts for any option premiums received as deposits. Profit is not recognized until the option either expires or is exercised.[76]

---

73   FAS 66, paragraph 30
74   See Chapter 5
75   FAS 66, paragraph 32
76   FAS 66, paragraph 32

If an option to purchase real estate is sold by an option holder, and the buyer's initial and continuing investments are not adequate for profit recognition under the full accrual method, the seller of the option recognizes income using the cost recovery method to the extent that nonrefundable cash proceeds exceed the seller's cost of the option.[77] When determining the minimum initial and continuing investment requirements, the sales value includes the sales price of the option, as well as the price the option holder has to pay for the real estate upon acquisition.

EXAMPLE—SALE OF OPTION BY OPTION HOLDER[78]

OregonHousing Co. (OH) bought an option to purchase a parcel of land at a price of $500,000. OH's cost of the option is $60,000. Subsequently, OH sells the option to Benjamin (B) for $150,000 ($50,000 cash and a note receivable in the amount of $100,000). Development of the land is not planned within the next few years.

How should OH account for this transaction?

When an option to purchase real estate is sold by an option holder, the sales value includes the exercise price of the option and the sales price of the option.

Sales value:	
Sales price of the option	$150,000
Exercise price of the option	$500,000
Sales value	$650,000
Minimum initial investment (25%)[79]	$162,500

The cash payment made by B is measured against the sum of the exercise price of the option and the sales price of the option, not only against the sales price of the option. Since the cash received by OH at the time of the sale of the option is less than the minimum initial investment required for the accrual method of accounting, OH cannot use the accrual method of accounting. Until the payments received from B exceed OH's cost of the option ($60,000), OH would not recognize any income; any subsequent payments received from B would be recorded as income.

3.5.4.6 Partial Sale[80]   A partial sale is a form of continuing involvement commonly encountered in the real estate industry. A sale is a partial sale if the seller retains an equity interest in the property or has an equity interest in the buyer, such

---

77   FAS 66, paragraph 32

78   Adapted from FASB Statement No. 66, paragraph 32, footnote 11

79   FAS 66, paragraph 54: minimum initial investment percentage for land when development is expected not to commence within two years

80   FAS 66, paragraph 33

as an interest in a real estate venture.[81] A partial sale generally results in profit recognition to the extent the property is considered sold. No profit is recognized on the part of the property that is retained by the seller through equity interests in the property or in the buyer.

Profit on the part of the property sold to outside parties is recognized if all of the following conditions are met:[82]

- The buyer is independent of the seller.
- Collection of the sales price is reasonably assured.
- The seller is not required to support the operations of the property or its related obligations to an extent greater than its proportionate interest.

Paragraph 35 of Statement 66 provides that the cost recovery or installment method of recognizing profit are to be used if collection of the sales price is not reasonably assured in a partial sale. Additionally, if the seller controls the buyer, no profit on the sale is recognized until it is realized from transactions with outside parties through the sale or through operations of the property.[83] Similarly, if the seller and the buyer of a property are under common control, no profit on the sale is recognized.

Partners to a venture often have multiple contractual relationships that need to be considered when determining the appropriate accounting. A partner selling real estate to a venture may assume support obligations, either directly, or through granting its venture partner preferences as to profits, cash flows, or a specified return on investment. If the sale of a partial interest involves such support obligations, profit on the portion of the sale to the outside parties can only be recognized to the extent that proceeds from the sale exceed all of the seller's costs related to the entire property.[84]

Frequently, venture agreements include buy-sell clauses that allow either partner to request a buy-out of the other partner's interest. If a buy-sell clause is triggered, the offeree can either elect to sell its interest in the venture to the offeror or elect to buy the offeror's interest in the venture. When a partner sells real estate to the venture, it has to be evaluated whether such buy-sell clause is a form of continuing involvement that precludes sale accounting. In EITF Issue No. 07-6, *Accounting for the sale of Real Estate subject to the Requirements of FASB Statement No. 66 when the Agreement contains a Buy-Sell Clause*, the EITF has addressed the issue of buy-sell clauses and has reached a consensus that a buy-sell clause, in and of itself, does not constitute a prohibited form of

---

81   See also Chapter 6, which deals with transactions between a real estate venture and its partners.
82   FAS 66, paragraph 33
83   FAS 66, paragraph 34
84   FAS 66, paragraph 36

continuing involvement that would preclude the recording of a partial sale under Statement 66; however, all relevant facts and circumstances of the transaction must be considered when determining whether the seller has transferred the usual risks and rewards of ownership and does not have substantial continuing involvement.

3.5.4.7 Sale of Condominium Units During Construction   Because of the length of time required to construct condominium projects, profit from the sale of individual units is recognized under the percentage-of-completion method during the period of construction if all of the following requirements are met:[85]

- Construction is beyond the preliminary stage.[86]
- The buyer is not entitled to a refund of the amounts paid except for non-delivery of the unit or interest.[87]
- Sufficient units have already been sold to ensure that the entire property will not revert to rental property.[88]
- The sales price is collectible.
- Aggregate sales proceeds and costs can be reasonably estimated.[89]

Until all of the above criteria are met, all proceeds received from the buyer are accounted for as deposits; sale and profit recognition is not appropriate. When determining whether the buyer's investment is sufficient for the recognition of a sale, the seller has to apply the initial *and continuing* investment tests described in paragraphs 8 through 12 of Statement 66.[90] The continuing investment test is performed using a hypothetical loan from the seller to the buyer for the amount of the purchase price less the buyer's initial investment.

Condominium developers have to be cognizant of the limits on nonrefundable down payment percentages imposed by state laws; any amounts paid by a buyer that exceed these percentages would not be "nonrefundable" and thus would not be included in the initial and continuing investments.

---

85   FAS 66, paragraph 37
86   Construction is *not* considered beyond the preliminary stage if engineering and design work, execution of construction contracts, site clearance and preparation, excavation, and completion of the building foundation are incomplete. [FAS 66, paragraph 37, footnote 13]
87   A buyer may be entitled to a refund under state law or based on the terms of the contract. State law may provide a right to refund until a "Declaration of Condominium" is filed; until a minimum status of completion of the project has been reached; or until the condominium units have been registered. [FAS 66, paragraph 37, footnote 14]
88   In determining whether this condition has been met, the seller needs to consider the requirements of state laws; the condominium contracts, which might provide buyers with the right of rescission until a certain percentage of units is sold; and the terms of the financing agreements.
89   Paragraph 37(e) of FASB Statement No. 66 requires that when estimating sales proceeds and costs, consideration be given to sales volume, trends of unit prices, demand for the units including seasonal factors, developer's experience, geographical location, and environmental factors.
90   EITF Issue No. 06-8

EXAMPLE—APPLICATION OF THE CONTINUING INVESTMENT CRITERION
TO THE SALE OF CONDOMINIUMS

On January 1, 2008, Britney (B) buys a luxury condominium unit from SpearCo. (S). The sales price amounts to $2 million, and B makes a down payment of $200,000 at the time of purchase. The condominium building is expected to be ready for occupancy on December 31, 2009; at that point in time, all remaining consideration will be paid in cash.

How much additional payment must B be required to make on (or before) January 1, 2009 for S to be able to recognize profit under the percentage-of-completion method at the time of sale?

This example uses the following assumptions:

- The amount of minimum initial investment is $200,000.
- The customary amortization term of a first mortgage loan by an independent established lending institution is ten years.
- The appropriate interest rate is 10%.
- All other requirements for the percentage-of-completion method are met.
- The sale is expected to qualify for the accrual method at closing.

B would have to be required to make an additional payment of $ 292,942 on or before January 1, 2009 for S to be able to recognize profit under the percentage-of-completion method at the time of sale.[91] Alternatively, if B were to make a down payment of $500,000, for example, B's investment would also be sufficient to allow for the application of the percentage-of-completion method.

When applying the percentage-of-completion method, costs are largely incurred for the condominium project as a whole, rather than directly for an individual unit. When allocating costs to individual units, a developer generally uses the relative sales value of the units, rather than the ratio of the number of units sold to the total number of units in the project, so that any differences in

---

91   The continuing investment requirements are calculated on a hypothetical loan of $1.8 million. The level annual payment that would be needed to pay that debt and interest at 10% over 10 years amounts to $292,942, see amortization table below.

YEAR	HYPOTHETICAL LOAN	INTEREST	PRINCIPAL	PAYMENT, END OF YEAR
2008	1,800,000	180,000	112,942	292,942
2009	1,687,058	168,706	124,236	292,942
2010	1,562,823	156,282	136,660	292,942
2011	1,426,163	142,616	150,326	292,942
2012	1,275,838	127,584	165,358	292,942
2013	1,110,480	111,048	181,894	292,942
2014	928,586	92,859	200,083	292,942
2015	728,503	72,850	220,092	292,942
2016	508,411	50,841	242,101	292,942
2017	266,311	26,631	266,311	292,942

the value of the units are appropriately reflected in the cost of sales amount. An example for the application of the relative sales value method is provided in Chapter 7, Section 7.3.1.3.

3.5.4.8 Sale of Property Improvements with Lease of the Underlying Land [92]

Improvements may be sold separately from the land on which they are situated. The sale of property improvements without a sale or lease of the underlying land is not governed by the provisions of Statement 66.[93] However, even if a land lease has not been entered into, such land lease may be implicit in the terms of the sale transaction.[94] An example for the sale of improvements without a lease of the underlying land would be the sale of machines[95] used in the seller's factory that are removed by the buyer and reinstalled in the buyer's factory.

Statement 66 establishes special profit recognition rules if the seller sells property improvements and leases the underlying land to the buyer of the improvements, because the transactions are interdependent and the FASB deemed it impracticable to distinguish between profits on the sale of the improvements and profits under the related lease.[96]

ACCOUNTING TREATMENT AS LEASE

The transaction is accounted for as a lease of both the land and the improvements if the term of the land lease to the buyer from the seller of the improvements falls within either of the following two categories:

- The term does not cover substantially all of the economic life of the property improvements.
- The term is for a period of less than 20 years, which is not considered a substantial period of time.

ACCOUNTING TREATMENT AS SALE

If the land lease covers substantially all of the economic life of the improvements and extends for at least 20 years, the transaction is accounted for as a sale of the

---

92   FAS 66, paragraphs 38 and 39
93   The sale of property improvements or integral equipment subject to an existing lease of the underlying land are also subject to the provisions of Statement 66. [FIN 43, paragraph 3(a), footnote 1]
94   FIN 43, paragraph 3(a), footnote 1
95   This assumes that the machines meet the definition of integral equipment as established in EITF Issue No. 00-13.
96   FAS 66, paragraph 38

improvements and a lease of the underlying land. The sale and profit recognition criteria of Statement 66 apply to the sale of the improvements. The profit attributable to the land lease is deferred and recognized over the lease term.

That raises the question: What portion of the profit is attributable to the sale of the improvements? Paragraph 39 of Statement 66 provides the following formula:

FORMULA—CALCULATION OF PROFIT ON THE SALE OF PROPERTY IMPROVEMENTS

Present value of the rental payments over period specified in FASB Statement No. 66[97]
    (not in excess of the seller's cost of the land)
Plus: Sales value of the improvements
Less: Carrying value of the improvements and the land
Profit on the sale of the improvements

The rental payments included in the above calculation are limited to the rental payments over the term of the primary indebtedness on the improvements (or the customary amortization term of primary indebtedness on the type of improvements), which differs based on the type of improvements. Additionally, the rental payments are limited to the seller's cost of the land. Statement 66 also prescribes the interest rate to be used to determine the present value of the future rental payments: An interest rate appropriate for primary debt is used if the lease is not subordinated to loans with prior liens on the property; an interest rate appropriate for secondary debt is used if the lease is subordinated.[98] Profit on the buyer's rental payments on the land in excess of the seller's cost of the land and from rentals that are not included in the above calculation are recognized when the land is sold or the rentals in excess of the seller's cost of the land accrue under the lease.[99] The effect of applying the above formula to the determination of profit on the sale of the improvements is that any losses relating to the land lease are recognized currently,

---

97   "The present value of the specified rental payments is the present value of the lease payments specified in the lease over the term of the primary indebtedness, if any, on the improvements, or over the customary amortization term of primary debt instruments on the type of improvements involved. The present value is computed at an interest rate appropriate for (a) primary debt if the lease is not subordinated or (b) secondary debt if the lease is subordinated to loans with prior liens." [SFAS 66, paragraph 39, footnote 15]

98   FAS 66, paragraph 39, footnote 15; Paragraphs 77–83 of FASB Statement No. 66 illustrate in four different scenarios the accounting for the sale of improvements with a lease of the underlying land.

99   FAS 66, paragraph 39

EXAMPLE—SALE OF PROPERTY IMPROVEMENTS WITH LEASE OF UNDERLYING LAND[100]

BetterStore Co. (B) purchases a storage building and leases the land for a period of 99 years. The sales price of the storage building is $875,000. B makes a cash down payment of $125,000 and receives a $750,000 loan from an insurance company over a 28-year term, bearing 8.5% interest, payable in equal monthly installments of principal and interest. The loan is not subordinated and is secured by the property. The land lease payments are $1,583.33 per month. The carrying value of the improvements on the seller's books is $600,000. The seller's cost of the land amounts to $250,000. For the application of the accrual method of accounting, a 20% initial investment is required.

Is the down payment sufficient to apply the accrual method of accounting?

No. The down payment received ($125,000) is insufficient for the application of the accrual method.

Down payment	$ 125,000
Loan from insurance company	$ 750,000
Present value of land lease payments[101]	$ 204,000
Sales value	$1,079,000
Down payment required:	$ 215,800

If the buyer determines that the installment method of accounting is appropriate, how much profit can the buyer recognize at time of closing (before any payments under the lease have been made)?

Determination of profit from the sale of the improvements:

Sales value	$1,079,000
Less: Carrying amount of land and improvements	$ 850,000
Profit on the sale of the improvements	$ 229,000

Cash received and to be received by the seller, other than proceeds of the primary loan:

Down payment	$ 125,000
Present value of land lease payments	$ 204,000
	$ 329,000

Under the installment method, the profit to be recognized in the period of sale amounts to $87,006, calculated as:

$125,000/$329,000 × $229,000 = $87,006

---

100   Adapted from FASB Statement No. 66, paragraphs 80–83
101   Lease payments are limited to the term of the primary indebtedness (28 years). The present value of the monthly lease payments of $1,583.33 over 28 years (i.e., 336 months) discounted at 8.5% (interest rate from insurance company) amounts to $204,000. [Calculation in FASB Statement No. 66, paragraph 80: $1,583.33 + ($1,583.33 × 127.9071)]

whereas profits attributable to the land lease are deferred and recognized in future periods.

The initial and continuing investment requirements are determined based on the sales value of the improvements plus the discounted present value of the land lease payments over the actual or customary term of the primary indebtedness on the improvements.

Seller Sells Property Improvements Subject to Land Lease

A seller may not own the land; rather, the seller may lease the land under a land lease and sell the real estate improvements to the buyer subject to the existing land lease, as shown in Exhibit 3.4.

The accounting depends on the contractual arrangements between the land owner, the seller of improvements (lessee of land), and the buyer of improvements (sublessee of land).

Seller Relieved from All Obligations under the Land Lease

If the buyer assumes the seller's land lease and the seller is relieved from all further obligations under the land lease, the amount of profit to be attributed to the sale of the improvements is calculated as the difference between the sales value of the improvements and the seller's cost of the improvements.

Seller Not Relieved from All Obligations under the Land Lease

If seller and buyer of the improvements enter into a sublease and the seller of the improvements is not being relieved from its land lease obligations, any loss on the sublease (calculated as the excess of the present value of the lease payments to be made under the lease over the present value of the lease payments received) is recognized upon entering into the transaction. Any profit relating to the sublease would be recognized over the term of the sublease.

For purposes of determining the adequacy of the buyer's initial and continuing investments, the land lease obligation needs to be taken into consideration; that is, the down payment and continuing investment requirements must be applied against the sum of (1) the sales value of the improvements and (2) the discounted present value of the land lease obligation over the term of the primary

Exhibit 3.4   Seller of Improvements Leases Land under Land Lease

indebtedness of the property, if any, or over the customary amortization term of the primary indebtedness.

3.5.4.9 Development Activities by the Seller after the Sale[102]   Real estate properties are frequently sold before the seller has fulfilled its contractual obligations to construct amenities or complete improvements. If the cost to fulfill the seller's development and construction obligations can be reasonably estimated, profit is recognized under the percentage-of-completion method of accounting. If future costs cannot be reasonably estimated, no profit is recognized until either the seller has fulfilled its commitments or such future costs can be estimated. Under the percentage-of-completion method, a portion of the profit is recognized at the time of sale, and the remainder is deferred and recognized as the seller fulfills its contractual obligations for development and construction work. The profit to be recognized in any period is based on the ratio of costs incurred to total expected costs. The same rate of profit is attributed to each activity before and after the sale.[103] As long as the seller remains obligated under the contract, profit relating to the future obligations cannot be recognized, even if the seller "outsources" the development and construction work to a third-party contractor.

EXAMPLE—SALE OF LAND WITH REMAINING DEVELOPMENT ACTIVITIES

SaugaCo. (S) owns a parcel of land with a book value of $1 million and a fair value of $10 million. S sells the land to Tuck and agrees to build access roads and other improvements at an estimated cost of $1 million. S has determined that the application of the percentage-of-completion method is appropriate.

How much profit should S recognize in the period of sale?

S should recognize $4,000,000 profit in the period of sale.

Paragraph 42 of Statement 66 provides that the profit be allocated to the sale of the land and the later development work on the basis of the estimated costs of each activity.

Cost of the land:	$1,000,000
Cost of future improvements:	$1,000,000
Percentage of project completion:	50%
Total estimated profit from the sale of the land:	$8,000,000
Profit to be recognized in the current period:	$4,000,000

---

102   FAS 66, paragraph 41
103   FAS 66, paragraph 42

CALCULATION OF PROFIT UNDER THE PERCENTAGE-OF-COMPLETION METHOD[104]

$$\text{Profit in any period} = \frac{\text{Costs to date}}{\text{Total costs}} \times \text{Profit from sale} \quad \text{less} \quad \frac{\text{Profit recognized}}{\text{in prior periods}}$$

3.5.4.10 Profit Participation by the Seller Seller and buyer may agree that the seller has the right to participate in future profits from the resale of the property or its operations without risk of loss (such as a participation in operating profits). If the transaction otherwise qualifies for recognition of profit by the full accrual method, the transfer of risks and rewards of ownership and absence of continuing involvement criteria are considered met. Profit recognition is based on the sales value without giving consideration to any amounts that may be received in the future. Such contingent future profits are recognized when they are realized. The cost of the sale is recognized in full at the time of sale; no costs are deferred to periods in which contingent profits are expected to be recognized.[105]

EXAMPLE—FUTURE PROFIT PARTICIPATION BY THE SELLER

A developer sells land to a homebuilder. The sales contract states that the homebuilder will pay $20,000 per lot at the time of sale. Additionally, the homebuilder will pay $10,000 per lot at the issuance of a building permit for each home constructed. The seller's cost per lot amounts to $15,000.

How much profit should the developer recognize at the time of sale, assuming the criteria for profit recognition under the accrual method are met?

The seller should recognize $5,000 profit per lot at the time of sale. The additional payment of $10,000 at the time a building permit is issued is contingent upon the issuance of the building permit. Accordingly, any additional payments received from the homebuilder are treated as profit participation by the seller and recognized when they are realized, in accordance with paragraph 43 of Statement 66.

3.6 APPLICATION OF OTHER ACCOUNTING METHODS

The following matrix shows—in simplified form—the accounting methods applicable to real estate sales transactions.

3.6.1 DEPOSIT METHOD
The deposit method is appropriate when, in substance, no sale has occurred. For example, the seller's down payment is only nominal and

---

104 Under this calculation, a cumulative catch-up method is applied, as explained for construction contracts in paragraphs 82–84 of SOP 81-1, *Accounting for Performance of Construction-Type and Certain Production-Type Contracts.*

105 FAS 66, paragraph 43

	Accrual Method	Deposit Method	Installment Method	Cost Recovery Method	Reduced Profit Method	Percentage of Completion Method	Financing/Leasing Profit-Sharing Method	Performance-of-Services Method
Inadequate initial investment		x	x	x				
Inadequate continuing investment			x	x	x			
Receivable subject to future subordination				x				
Obligation/option to repurchase property							x	
Seller is general partner and holds receivable							x	
Guarantee of investment or on investment		x					x	x
Support of operations							x	x
Option to purchase property		x						
Partial sale[106]	x							
Sale of condominium units under development		x				x		
Sale of improvements with lease of land[107]	x	x	x	x	x	x	x	x
Development activities after sale						x		
Profit participation by seller	x							

Matrix-Accounting Methods for Real Estate Sales

---

106   Assuming no other forms of prohibited continuing involvement; profit recognition under the accrual method is proportionate to the interest in the property sold, if the seller does not control the buyer

107   As described in Section 3.5.4.8, the accounting treatment of a sale of improvements with a lease of the underlying land depends on the term of the lease. If the recording of a sale is appropriate, any of the profit recognition methods in this matrix may be applicable to the sale of the improvements.

the seller has "no skin in the game," or not all conditions precedent to closing have been performed, so the sale is not considered consummated.[108]

Under the deposit method, the seller does not recognize a sale. The seller continues to report the property and related existing debt in its financial statements—even if the debt has been assumed by the buyer—and discloses that the property and related debt are subject to a sales contract. Principal payments made by the buyer on any assumed debt are recorded as a reduction of debt and as additional deposits from the buyer.[109]

The seller continues to record revenues and expenses relating to the property sold, as well as depreciation expense, unless the property is a long-lived asset that has been classified as held for sale.[110] A long-lived asset that is classified as held for sale is not depreciated while it is classified as held for sale; however, interest and other expenses continue to accrue.[111]

ACCOUNTING FOR CASH REPRESENTING INTEREST

All cash received from the buyer, including the initial investment and subsequent collections of principal and interest, is reported as a deposit on the contract, with the following exception: Portions of cash received that are *not* subject to refund and that are designated by the contract as interest are recognized as income to the extent they offset carrying charges (property taxes and interest on existing debt) on the property.[112] All other interest payments received from the buyer before a sale is recorded are accounted for as part of the buyer's initial investment at the time the sale is recorded.[113] Such interest is also included as part of the sales value of the property.

Once the criteria for recording a sale are met, the transaction is recorded as a sale. At that time, all amounts recorded as deposits are included as part of the buyer's investment.[114] When changing from the deposit method to the accrual method of accounting, future continuing investment requirements are calculated from the date the transaction is first accounted for as a sale and not from the date at which the transaction was first accounted for on the deposit method.[115]

CANCELLATION OF SALES CONTRACT

If, in subsequent periods, the sales contract is canceled without a refund, deposits forfeited are recognized as income.[116]

108   FAS 66, paragraph 20
109   FAS 66, paragraph 67
110   FAS 66, paragraph 65
111   FAS 144, paragraph 34
112   This exception does not apply to retail land sales. [FAS 66, paragraph 65]
113   FAS 66, paragraph 65; SOP 78-4, Section titled "The Deposit Method"
114   FAS 66, paragraph 66
115   SOP 75-6, section titled "Cumulative Application of Tests When Recognition of Sale Is Delayed"
116   FAS 66, paragraph 66

EXAMPLE—APPLICATION OF THE DEPOSIT METHOD

BetterStore Co. (B) purchases a storage building from Sellco (S) for a sales price (sales value) of $1 million. S's carrying amount of the storage building is $600,000. B pays for the building as follows:

Cash down payment	$ 10,000
Note to seller	$ 490,000
Non-recourse mortgage assumed by buyer	$ 500,000
Sales price	$1,000,000

Subsequent to the sale, B makes principal payments of $25,000 on the first mortgage assumed by B, $35,000 on the note to S, and $10,000 interest payments ($6,000 on the first mortgage assumed and $4,000 on the note—both nonrefundable). At the time of sale, B's initial investment ($10,000) is minimal; therefore, the transaction is initially recorded under the deposit method of accounting, and the property remains on S's books. After B has made principal payments on the mortgage and the note, S continues to use the deposit method of accounting as a result of continuing involvement with the property sold.

How should S record the transaction in its books?

Journal entries:

AT THE TIME OF SALE

Cash	$10,000	
Deposit		$10,000

At the time of sale, the seller records cash payments received; the note received from the buyer is not reflected on the seller's books.

AT THE TIME PAYMENTS ARE MADE BY BUYER ON MORTGAGE ASSUMED

Mortgage loan	$25,000	
Interest expense	$ 6,000	
Deposit		$31,000

AT THE TIME PRINCIPAL AND INTEREST PAYMENTS ARE RECEIVED ON THE NOTE

Cash	$39,000	
Deposit		$39,000 (*)

(*) The interest portion of $4,000 would be recognized as income to the extent of any carrying charges (property taxes, interest) on the property.

Additionally, the seller would continue to record depreciation expense on the storage building; the journal entries are not presented in the example.

IMPAIRMENT LOSS RECOGNITION[117]

A loss arising from the sale of real estate cannot be deferred. Although under the deposit method no sale is recorded, an impairment loss needs to be recognized if the terms of the transaction indicate that the property is impaired. Paragraph 21 of Statement 66 requires specifically that a loss be recognized to the extent the carrying amount of the real estate sold exceeds the sum of any deposits received, the fair value of the (unrecorded) note receivable, and the debt assumed by the buyer. Additionally, if a buyer defaults or if it is probable that a buyer will default, the seller needs to perform an impairment analysis to determine whether the fair value of the property is below its carrying amount and, should the property sold be impaired, recognize the impairment loss.[118]

PRESENTATION AND DISCLOSURE

Paragraph 67 of Statement 66 requires the following disclosures: Presentation of nonrecourse debt assumed by the buyer among the liabilities; the debt assumed is not offset against the related property. The seller reports the buyer's principal payments on mortgage debt assumed as additional deposits with corresponding reductions of the carrying amount of the mortgage debt.

3.6.2 INSTALLMENT METHOD   Under the installment method, the seller recognizes a sale. The real estate property sold and any debt assumed by the buyer are removed from the books. The use of the installment method is appropriate when the initial and/or continuing investment does not qualify for the use of the accrual method, and the carrying amount of the property has already been recovered or its recovery is reasonably assured if the buyer defaults.[119] If, in a later period, the transaction meets the requirements for the accrual method of recognizing profit, the seller *may* change to the full accrual method. The profit not yet recognized under the installment method is recognized in income at that time.[120]

The installment method results in deferring profits from a sale and recording these profits as cash payments are collected. Each cash receipt (and principal payment by the buyer on debt assumed) is apportioned between cost recovered and profit in the same ratio as total cost and total profit bear to sales value.[121]

Under the installment method of accounting, interest income is recognized when received, rather than accrued into income. If the seller finances the sale with a note that carries a below-market interest rate, the seller needs to determine whether financing provided at market rates would have resulted in a loss on the sale. Any such loss should be recognized at the time of sale. Paragraph 57 of Statement 66 provides

---

117   See also discussion in Section 3.5.1.
118   FAS 66, paragraph 21
119   FAS 66, paragraph 22; the use of the reduced profit method, rather than the installment method, is required in certain circumstances, as outlined in Section 3.6.4 of this chapter.
120   FAS 66, paragraph 61
121   FAS 66, paragraph 56

that for sales transactions that result in a profit, it is acceptable not to adjust the interest rate to reflect market rates. Since interest is recognized in full when received, whereas principal payments are allocated between cost and profit, a stated interest rate below market generally results in reduced profit recognition in earlier years.

A seller must ensure that a receivable from the sale of property less profits not recognized does not exceed what the carrying amount would have been had the property not been sold.[122] For a sale of property with little down payment, a

---

EXAMPLE—PROFIT RECOGNITION UNDER THE INSTALLMENT METHOD[123]

BetterStore Co. (B) purchases a storage building from Sellco (S) for a sales price of $1 million. S's carrying amount of the storage building is $600,000. B pays for the building as follows:

Cash down payment	$ 150,000
Note from buyer	$ 350,000
Mortgage assumed by buyer (full recourse to seller)	$ 500,000
Sales price	$1,000,000

Subsequent to the sale, B makes principal payments of $25,000 on the first mortgage assumed by the buyer, $35,000 on the note to the seller, and $10,000 interest payments ($6,000 on the first mortgage assumed, $4,000 on the note (both nonrefundable)). The minimum initial investment is assumed to be 20%; all other criteria for the application of the accrual method are met. S assesses that a recovery of the property is reasonably assured should the buyer default.

How should S account for the transaction?

At the time of sale, the initial investment ($150,000) is inadequate for the use of the accrual method. S assesses that a recovery of the cost of the property is reasonably assured should the buyer default, therefore, S determines that the use of the installment method of accounting is appropriate.

Under the installment method, S can recognize profit of $60,000 upon receipt of the down payment, representing 40% ($400,000/$1,000,000) of $150,000.

Upon receipt of the principal payments by B on the mortgage and the note, S can recognize profit of $24,000, representing 40% of $60,000 ($25,000 + $35,000).

Journal entries:

AT THE TIME OF SALE

Cash	$ 150,000	
Debt on property	$ 500,000	
Note from buyer	$ 350,000	
Storage building		$ 600,000
Deferred Profit		$ 400,000
Deferred profit	$ 60,000	
Profit recognized		$ 60,000

---

122   FAS 66, paragraph 58
123   Adapted from FASB Statement No. 66, Appendix C, paragraph 90

TO RECORD PRINCIPAL PAYMENTS ON THE NOTE/ON ASSUMED DEBT
Cash	$35,000	
Deferred profit	$24,000	
Note from buyer		$35,000
Profit recognized		$24,000

TO RECORD INTEREST PAYMENTS ON THE NOTE
Cash	$ 4,000	
Interest Income		$ 4,000

The interest payments on the debt assumed do not result in any journal entries on S's books.

seller needs to monitor the amount of the receivable from the buyer and compare it to the "hypothetical" depreciated book value of the property sold to determine whether this requirement is met in periods after the sale. This provision was included in Statement 66 to prevent a seller from avoiding loss recognition in circumstances where, as a result of small down payment received, risk of ownership might not have passed to the buyer.

PRESENTATION AND DISCLOSURE
Paragraph 59 of Statement 66 requires that the income statement or related notes present the sales value, the gross profit that has not yet been recognized, and the total cost of the sale. Revenue and cost of sales (or gross profit) are presented as separate items on the income statement or are disclosed in the notes to the financial statements when profit is recognized.

3.6.3 COST RECOVERY METHOD   Like the installment method, the cost recovery method provides for the recording of a sale. The principal difference between the cost recovery and the installment method is that the cost recovery method does not permit the recognition of profit on sale nor the recognition of interest income until interest and principal payments made by the buyer, including payments on assumed debt, equal the carrying amount of the property sold. All payments from the buyer to the seller are credited to balance sheet accounts (principal is credited to notes receivable and interest to deferred profit) until the carrying amount of the property is recovered. Once cost is recovered, the entire amount of any subsequent payments received is credited to income.

Any losses arising from the sale of real estate properties are recognized at the date of sale.

In certain situations, Statement 66 allows for the use of either the installment method or the cost recovery method. The decision whether to use the cost recovery method or the installment method is a matter of judgment: The seller has to determine whether the carrying amount of the property is recoverable in the event of buyer default. The cost recovery method is used if recovery of the cost

---

EXAMPLE—PROFIT RECOGNITION UNDER THE COST RECOVERY METHOD

BetterStore Co. (B) purchases a storage building from Sellco (S) for a sales price of $1 million. S's carrying amount of the storage building is $600,000. B pays for the building as follows:

Cash down payment	$ 150,000
Note from buyer	$ 350,000
Mortgage assumed by buyer (full recourse to seller)	$ 500,000
Sales price (equals sales value)	$1,000,000

Subsequent to the sale, the buyer makes principal payments of $25,000 on the first mortgage assumed by the buyer, $35,000 on the note to the seller, and interest payments ($6,000 on the mortgage assumed, $4,000 on the note). The minimum initial investment is assumed to be 20%. All other criteria for the accrual method are met. S assesses that a recovery of the property is not reasonably assured should the buyer default.

How should S account for the transaction?

At the time of sale, the initial investment ($150,000) is inadequate for profit recognition under the accrual method. As the recovery of cost is not reasonably assured, the seller applies the cost recovery method of accounting.

Under the cost recovery method, no profit is recognized, since the sum of the down payment ($150,000) and the subsequent payments by the buyer ($70,000) are less than the cost of the property ($600,000).

Journal entries:

AT THE TIME OF SALE

Cash	$150,000	
Debt on property	$500,000	
Note from buyer	$350,000	
Storage building		$600,000
Deferred profit		$400,000

UPON RECEIPT OF PRINCIPAL PAYMENTS ON THE NOTE/ON ASSUMED DEBT

Cash	$35,000	
Note from buyer		$35,000

UPON RECEIPT OF INTEREST PAYMENTS

Cash	$4,000	
Deferred profit		$4,000

The interest payments on debt assumed by the buyer do not result in any journal entries on the books of the seller. However, interest and principal payments on debt assumed by the buyer need to be monitored to determine when the cost of the property has been recovered.

of the property is not reasonably assured if the buyer defaults. This may occur in a transaction in which the seller does not have a lien on the property after the sale, or in which the seller has a receivable from the buyer that is subordinate to other liens on the property. Statement 66 also permits the use of the cost recovery method in lieu of the installment method.[124]

The cost recovery method contains the same limitation on the amount of the seller's receivable as the installment method: The note receivable from the buyer less any profits not recognized should not exceed what the depreciated property value would have been had the property not been sold.[125]

If the transaction meets the requirements for the accrual method in periods after the sale, the seller *may* change to the accrual method and recognize the remaining profit into income at that time.[126]

PRESENTATION AND DISCLOSURE
Paragraph 63 of Statement 66 requires a presentation of the sales value, the gross profit that has not yet been recognized, and the total cost of the sale. The amount of gross profit not yet recognized is offset against the related receivable on the balance sheet. Principal collections reduce the receivable, and interest collections on the receivable increase the unrecognized gross profit on the balance sheet. Gross profit is presented as a separate item of revenue on the income statement when recognized as earned.

3.6.4 REDUCED PROFIT METHOD   The reduced profit method is used in transactions in which the buyer's initial investment meets the criteria for the application of the accrual method of accounting, but the buyer's continuing investment, while exceeding certain requirements, fails to meet the criteria for the application of the accrual method. Specifically, for the reduced profit method to be appropriate, paragraph 23 of Statement 66 requires that the buyer's payment each year cover both [footnote omitted]:

a. The interest and principal amortization on the maximum first mortgage loan that could be obtained on the property

b. Interest, at an appropriate rate, on the excess of the aggregate actual debt on the property over such a maximum first mortgage loan

If these requirements are not met, the seller should use the installment or cost recovery method.[127] A "reduced profit" is calculated by substituting the receivable from the buyer with the present value of the lowest level of annual payments required by the sales contract over 20 years (for the sale of land) or the customary amortization term of a first mortgage loan by an independent established

---

124   FAS 66, paragraph 22
125   FAS 66, paragraph 62
126   FAS 66, paragraph 64
127   FAS 66, paragraph 23

lending institution (for all other real estate);[128] any scheduled lump sum payments are excluded from that calculation. The present value is calculated using an appropriate interest rate,[129] but not less than the rate stated in the sales contract. This method of profit recognition permits profit to be recognized from level payments on the buyer's debt over 20 years (for the sale of land) or the customary amortization term of a first mortgage loan by an independent established lending institution (for all other real estate) and postpones recognition of other profits until lump sum or other payments are made.[130]

The application of the reduced profit method is best explained in an example.

EXAMPLE—PROFIT RECOGNITION UNDER THE REDUCED PROFIT METHOD[131]

Summerland Inc. (S) sells land with a cost of $800,000 for $1,000,000 to a homebuilder. The homebuilder does not intend to commence development activities within the next two years. The transaction is financed as follows:

Buyer's initial investment	$ 250,000
First mortgage note payable to an independent lending institution (Terms—15% interest payable annually over 20 years: $79,881 per year including principal and interest)	$ 500,000
Second mortgage note payable to seller (Terms—12% interest payable annually over 25 years: $31,875 per year including principal and interest)	$ 250,000
Total selling price	$1,000,000

The market rate of interest on the second mortgage is 16%.

What amount of profit should S recognize upon sale of the land, assuming there are no other forms of prohibited continuing involvement?

For a sale of land that is not scheduled to be developed within two years after the sale, the minimum investment requirement for the application of the accrual method is 25% of the sales price.[132] This requirement is met. The amortization term of the second mortgage (25 years) exceeds the term permitted by paragraph 12 of Statement 66 (20 years for the sale of land). Therefore, the continuing investment requirements for the application of the accrual method are not met. S calculates the present value of the receivable on the second mortgage as $188,982[133] and calculates the reduced profit as follows:

---

128 FAS 66, paragraphs 12 and 68
129 Paragraphs 13 and 14 of APB Opinion No. 21 provide criteria for selecting an appropriate rate for present value calculations.
130 FAS 66, paragraph 68
131 Adapted from FASB Statement No. 66, paragraph 69
132 FAS 66, paragraph 54
133 The present value of $31,875 per year for 20 years at a market rate of 16% is $31,875 × 5.92884 = $188,982.

Homebuilder's initial investment	$ 250,000
First mortgage note payable to an independent lending institution (Terms—15% interest payable annually over 20 years: $79,881 per year including principal and interest)	$ 500,000
Present value of receivable on second mortgage note payable	$ 188,892
Less: S's cost	($800,000)
Reduced profit	$ 138,892

   Upon sale of the land, S should recognize profit of $138,892. The remaining profit will be recognized in the years 21 through 25, as payments on the second mortgage are received.

3.6.5 PERCENTAGE-OF-COMPLETION METHOD

Under the accrual, installment, cost recovery, and reduced profit methods, the entire sales price and related cost of goods sold are reflected in the income statement; depending on the profit recognition method, part or all of the profit may have to be deferred.

EXAMPLE—PROFIT RECOGNITION UNDER THE PERCENTAGE-OF-COMPLETION METHOD

BetterStore Co. (B), a construction company, purchases land and constructs a shopping center. B expects the total project costs to amount to $8,380,000. At the beginning of Period 1, B sells the shopping center at a sales price of $11,000,000. The sales price is paid in installments over the period of construction, based on the percentage of completion of the project.
The costs are incurred as follows:

Period 1:	$2,370,000
Period 2:	$6,010,000
Total Project Costs:	$8,380,000

   Accordingly, B expects to realize a profit from the sale of the shopping center of $2,620,000, or approximately 31.3% of project costs.
Profit to be recognized in Period 1:

$$\frac{\$2,370,000}{\$8,380,000} \times \$2,620,000 = \qquad \$ \ 740,979$$

Profit to be recognized in Period 2:

$$\frac{\$8,380,000}{\$8,380,000} \times \$2,620,000 \text{ less } \$740,979 = \qquad \$1,879,021$$

Under the percentage-of-completion method, the application of which requires that future costs of development be reasonably estimable, costs are reported in the period they are incurred, and gross profit is reported based on the ratio of costs incurred to date as compared to total expected project costs.[134] The revenue to be reported in any one period is calculated as the sum of the costs incurred in that period and the related gross profit. If it is expected that a contract results in a loss, the entire loss has to be recognized in full; Statement 66 does not provide for loss deferral.

In the example above, the costs are incurred as planned. In reality, project cost estimates may change during the construction phase. Statement 66 does not directly address what method to use for the "true-up" of expected amounts. The examples relating to the performance-of-services method,[135] as well as the accounting pre-scribed for the "true-up" of costs incurred related to time-share sales,[136] support a retrospective "true-up" via the cumulative catch-up method.[137] The cumulative catch-up method, outlined in paragraph 83 of SOP 81-1, *Accounting for Performance of Construction-Type and Certain Production-Type Contracts*, is also used to account for a change in estimate in construction-type contracts. Under the cumulative catch-up method, a change in estimate is accounted for in the period of change; the balance sheet at the end of the period of change and subsequent periods reflect the revised cost and revenue estimates as if they had been the original estimates.

3.6.6 FINANCING METHOD   The financing method is appropriate when, in substance, the transaction is not a sale, but akin to a financing arrangement, with the loan (the proceeds from the sale) secured by the property sold. The financing method is also the appropriate method for some forms of continuing involvement, such as a guarantee provided by a seller for an extended period of time.

Under the financing method, no sale is recorded. The property and any debt assumed by the buyer remain on the seller's books, and the seller continues to report the results of the operations of the property. If a sale transaction subsequently quali-fies for sale recognition, a sale is recorded. Any results of operations of the property (other than depreciation) that do not accrue to the seller should be offset by a corre-sponding increase or decrease in interest[138] expense, consistent with the accounting by a participating mortgage loan borrower. As a general rule, a real estate sale trans-action that does not initially qualify for sale recognition must not result in a "sched-uled loss" at the time the transaction is expected to qualify for sale recognition.[139]

---

134   This assumes that no facts and circumstances exist that would require the deferral of profit, such as inad-equate initial and continuing investments or forms of continuing involvement.
135   FAS 66, paragraphs 84–88
136   See Chapter 7, Section 7.3.1.3
137   For retail land sales, changes in cost and revenue estimates are accounted for prospectively. [FAS 66, para-graph 76]
138   SOP 97-1, paragraph 13
139   See also Section 5.2.1.2 in Chapter 5 for further discussion.

No specific guidance is provided in Statement 66 regarding the application of the financing method,[140] and frequently questions arise with respect to (1) the "gross" vs. "net" recording of the transaction, (2) the appropriate interest rate to use, and (3) the presentation in the income statement.

RECORDING OF THE TRANSACTION "GROSS" VS. "NET"

Views differ on whether a seller should record the transaction "gross" or "net," that is, whether the seller should record the cash received and a corresponding financing obligation ("net recording"), or whether—in addition to the cash received—the seller should also record a note received from the buyer as part of the consideration ("gross recording"). The following arguments are made: In a financing transaction, the property owner receives cash from a lender, which is collateralized by real estate. Accordingly, the property owner should record a loan in the amount of cash received; any note received from the buyer does not fit into the framework of a financing transaction and should therefore not be reflected on the seller's balance sheet. On the other hand, it can be argued that consideration received from the buyer includes not only the cash received, but also a note (or other assets received) from the buyer. A note from the buyer represents a legal obligation of the buyer that the seller may be able to monetize. Therefore, why would the note not be recognized as an asset? Additionally, if the financing method is used in scenarios in which no option or obligation to repurchase the property sold exists, the transactions may not necessarily be akin to a "loan" collateralized by real estate.

INTEREST RATE TO BE USED

A topic of discussion is also the interest rate to be used when applying the financing method. As outlined in Section 3.5.4.1 of this chapter, in the case of an obligation to repurchase the property sold at a price greater than the sales value,[141] the difference between the sales value and the repurchase price is deemed to be interest and is charged to income using the effective interest method. If continuing involvement other than an obligation or option to repurchase trigger the use of the financing method, it may be appropriate to apply the seller's incremental borrowing rate to the amount of the financing obligation, consistent with the rationale that in a financing transaction, the seller would have to borrow funds at its incremental borrowing rate. If the application of the seller's incremental borrowing rate leads to atypical results, however, such as a negative amortization of the financing obligation, the use of an interest rate different from the seller's incremental borrowing rate may be more appropriate.

---

140   Paragraphs 34 – 39 of FASB Statement No. 98 describe the application of the financing method as it relates to the sale-leaseback of real estate. In the examples provided in FASB Statement No. 98, the seller records cash received from the buyer and a corresponding financing obligation; a note from the buyer is not recorded.

141   The sales price may have to be adjusted to arrive at the sales value. For example, if the interest rate on the buyer's note is below market, the seller would adjust the sales price to reduce the receivable to its present value. [FAS 66, paragraph 7(b)]

INCOME STATEMENT PRESENTATION

Another frequently asked question relates to the income statement presentation when the financing method is applied. Under the financing method, the seller is deemed the accounting owner of the property: Should the seller continue to reflect rental revenue, depreciation, and operating expenses relating to the property, or should the seller reflect depreciation expense relating to the property sold, and present only the results of the operations of the property (net of depreciation) on the seller's income statement? Some believe that the seller of the real estate property remains the accounting owner and therefore should record rental revenues, depreciation, and operating expenses like a property owner. This presentation is criticized by others, however, based on the indicators set forth in EITF Issue No. 99-19, *Reporting Revenue Gross as a Principal versus Net as an Agent,* which will frequently not support a gross presentation. The author believes that net presentation is in many cases the more appropriate presentation.

There is no one "right" answer to these questions: The application of the financing method to real estate sales transactions is dependent on facts and circumstances and is subject to significant judgment.[142] Additional complexities arise in situations in which multiple forms of continuing involvement are present.

EXAMPLE—FINANCING METHOD
At the beginning of Period 1, SandyCove (S) sells land for a cash sales price of $5 million. At the same time, S enters into an obligation to repurchase the land at the end of Period 1 for $5.5 million. The seller's incremental borrowing rate is 10%.
How should S account for the transaction?
In substance, the sale is a financing transaction; $500,000, the difference between the sales price and the repurchase price, represents interest, which has to be recorded as interest expense in Period 1, using the effective interest method.

3.6.7 LEASING METHOD   A real estate sale transaction may in substance be a lease. The leasing method is often appropriate when the seller has an obligation or option to repurchase the property at a price lower than the sales price paid by the buyer.

Under the leasing method, the seller leaves the property and any related debt on its books and continues to report the property's operating results. Any cash received from the buyer is recorded as a liability. Under the leasing method, the difference between the repurchase price and the sales price represents, in substance, prepaid rent, which is accrued into income using the straight-line method. The liability is reduced by the amount of "lease income" recognized, so that at the time of expected repurchase, the liability account is equal to the repurchase price of the property.

---

142   The application of the financing method in sale-leaseback transactions is discussed in Chapter 5, section 5.2.1.2.

> ### EXAMPLE—LEASING METHOD
>
> At the beginning of Period 1, SellCo (S) sells a warehouse to BetterStore Inc. (B) for $5 million, and enters into an obligation to repurchase the warehouse at the end of Period 5 for $3 million.
>
> How should S account for the transaction?
>
> In substance, the sale is a lease with $2 million prepaid rentals. The property and related debt remain on the books of S. The rental income received from B is straight-lined over the lease period. The seller records rental income of $400,000 in periods 1 through 5.

3.6.8 PROFIT-SHARING METHOD   Real estate sale transactions frequently involve venture arrangements in which two or more parties undertake a real estate project or in which one party sells land to the other party and participates in future profits. These venture arrangements may or may not, involve a separate legal entity. If these transactions don't qualify for sale accounting as a result of continuing involvement by the seller, the profit-sharing method may be the appropriate method to use.

Like the financing method, the profit-sharing method is not further explained in the authoritative literature. One way the profit-sharing method is applied in practice is as follows: The seller leaves the property and any debt assumed by the buyer on its books and records a "profit-sharing obligation" or "co-venture obligation" for any consideration received from the buyer/venture partner. The seller continues to record depreciation and the results of the property's operations on its books. The total of the income and expense amounts attributable to the buyer/venture partner is presented in the income statement caption "profit-sharing expense/income" or "co-venture expense" or "co-venture income."

The arrangements between buyer/venture partner and seller may provide for payments as consideration for management services, payments to support operations, or payments to share profits from the operations or upon the sale of the property. Because the operations of the property are reflected on the books of the seller, any arrangements between buyer and seller need to be evaluated as to their impact on the financial statements. For example, payments between the parties may result in additional expense or in a reduction of expense.

The way the profit-sharing method is implemented will depend on the individual facts and circumstances of the transaction; as the authoritative literature does not provide any specific guidance, there may be more than one acceptable alternative.

3.6.9 PERFORMANCE-OF-SERVICES METHOD   The performance-of-services method is appropriate in situations in which the seller agrees to guarantee a return to the seller or to support the operations of a property for a limited period of time,[143] when the operations of the property cover all operating expenses, debt

---

143   FAS 66, paragraphs 28–30: The term "limited period" is not defined in FASB Statement No. 66. It has generally been interpreted to mean a guarantee period of at least five years by some or of more than five years by others.

service, and contractual payments.[144] Under the performance-of-services method, a sale is recorded; profit deferred is based on the ratio of cost incurred to date in relation to cost expected to be incurred for the project until the end of the guarantee or support period, similar to the percentage-of-completion method.

If the revenues expected from the project cannot be estimated over the support period, because no objective information is available regarding occupancy levels and rental rates for similar properties, profit recognition is not appropriate, unless the amount of the maximum support obligation can be quantified.

When the seller of income-producing property guarantees a return on investment to the buyer for a limited period of time, Statement 66 requires that certain adjustments be made when estimating the property's rental revenues over the guarantee period to allow for unforeseen circumstances: Expected rental revenues from the property sold are to be reduced by a safety factor of one-third, but not below the amount expected to be received from signed leases.[145] Once signed leases have been obtained, it can be assumed that the level of occupancy from signed leases is sustainable over future periods, unless there is evidence to the contrary.[146] Actual amounts are substituted for estimated amounts once actual amounts are known, and any subsequent changes in estimates of revenues and costs are taken into consideration when determining the amount of profit to be recognized in future periods.[147]

EXAMPLE—PROFIT RECOGNITION UNDER THE PERFORMANCE-OF-SERVICES METHOD[148]

SellCo (S) has constructed a shopping center (project cost of $8,380,000) and, upon completion, sells the shopping center to BetterBuy Co. (B) at a sales price of $11,000,000. The sales price is paid in cash at closing. S will reimburse B for cash flow deficits for a period of three years. At the time of sale, S has signed leases in place for $600,000 per year. Based on S's experience with similar projects, S expects the following revenues and costs relating to the shopping center over the three-year guarantee period:

	Rental Revenue	Rental Expense and Debt Service
Year 1	$ 750,000	$1,300,000
Year 2	$1,500,000	$1,510,000
Year 3	$1,800,000	$1,510,000

For simplification purposes, it is assumed that the actual amounts of revenues and expenses equal the expected amounts.

---

144   The deposit method is used until the operations of the property cover all operating expenses, debt service, and contractual payments.

145   FAS 66, paragraph 86(b)(3); additionally, the expected revenues (before adjustment for the one-third safety factor), should not exceed rental revenues based on 95% of gross scheduled rents. [FAS 66, paragraph 85(g)]

146   FAS 66, paragraph 88, footnote to Schedule B

147   FAS 66, paragraph 86(b)(1)

148   Adapted from FASB Statement No. 66, paragraphs 84–87

How much profit should S recognize in years 1, 2, and 3 under the performance-of-services method?

Calculation of adjusted rental revenues:

	Rental Revenues	Safety Factor	Adjusted Revenues
Year 1	$ 750,000	$250,000	$ 600,000[149]
Year 2	$1,500,000	$500,000	$1,000,000
Year 3	$1,800,000	$600,000	$1,200,000
Total adjusted rental revenues			$2,800,000

Calculation of profit expected from the project:

Revenues

Sales Value	$11,000,000
Adjusted Rental Revenues	$ 2,800,000
Total Revenues	$13,800,000
Costs	
Project Costs	$ 8,380,000

Estimated rental expenses and debt services:

Year 1	$ 1,300,000
Year 2	$ 1,510,000
Year 3	$ 1,510,000
Total Costs	$12,700,000
Total Profit	$ 1,100,000

Profit to be recognized in Year 1: $838,425

Calculated as:

$$\frac{\$\ 9,680,000^{150}}{\$12,700,000} \times \$1.1 \text{ million} = \$838,425$$

Profit to be recognized in Year 2: $130,788

Calculated as:

$$\frac{\$11,190,000}{\$12,700,000} \times \$1.1 \text{ million} = \$969,213 \text{ less } \$838,425 \text{ recognized in Year 1} = \$130,788$$

Profit to be recognized in Year 3: $130,787

Calculated as:

$$\frac{\$12,700,000}{\$12,700,000} \times \$1.1 \text{ million} = \$1.1 \text{ million less } \$969,213 \text{ recognized in Years 1 and 2}$$

$$= \$130,787$$

Note: Actual cost may not equal expected costs over the term of a project. Actual amounts are substituted for estimated amounts as the actual amounts become known.

---

149   Revenues are not reduced below revenues expected to be received from signed leases.

150   Calculated as the sum of the project cost ($8,380,000) and expenses in Year 1 ($1,300,000).

3.7 SPECIAL ACCOUNTING ISSUES

3.7.1 IMPAIRMENT AND LOSS ON SALE   The accounting for impairment and loss recognition of real estate depends on the type of real estate property (e.g., property held for development or completed real estate project) and the intent of the owner with respect to its use, once a project is completed. Paragraph 24 of FASB Statement No. 67, *Accounting for Costs and Initial Rental Operations of Real Estate Projects*, provides, in part:

> The provisions in Statement 144 for long-lived assets to be disposed of by sale shall apply to a real estate project, or parts thereof, that is substantially completed and that is to be sold. The provisions in that Statement for long-lived assets to be held and used shall apply to real estate held for development, including property to be developed in the future as well as that currently under development, and to a real estate project, or parts thereof, that is substantially completed and that is to be held and used (for example, for rental).

3.7.1.1 Impairment of Real Estate Properties   Real estate properties are subject to the impairment provisions in FASB Statement No. 144, *Accounting for the Impairment or Disposal of Long-Lived Assets*. A long-lived asset is considered impaired when the carrying amount of the asset exceeds its fair value. For purposes of recognition and measurement of an impairment loss, a long-lived asset needs to be grouped with other assets and liabilities at the lowest level for which identifiable cash flows are largely independent of the cash flows of other assets and liabilities.[151] In the case of an office building that a company has acquired to hold for rental, for example, the asset group acquired may include intangible assets, such as in-place leases.[152] In the case of the company's headquarters facility, the asset group may include all assets and liabilities of the company, because a corporate headquarters building does not have identifiable cash flows that are largely independent of the cash flows of other assets and liabilities.[153]

The guidance for the recognition of impairment losses is fundamentally different for properties to be held and used than for properties to be disposed of by sale.[154]

IMPAIRMENT OF PROPERTIES TO BE HELD AND USED
Real estate properties to be held and used encompass all real estate properties of a company that are not to be disposed of by sale (held for sale). Properties to be held and used may include properties a company holds for rental, as well as properties a company uses in its own operations, such as a factory or its corporate headquarters facility. The provisions of FASB Statement No. 144 for long-lived assets to be held and used also apply to real estate under development and to real estate to be developed in the future.

---

151   FAS 144, paragraph 10
152   The acquisition of income-producing properties is discussed in Section 1.6 of Chapter 1.
153   FAS 144, paragraph 11
154   Section 3.8.2 in this chapter discusses the criteria for classification of properties as held for sale.

Two-Step Impairment Analysis under FASB Statement No. 144.   FASB Statement No. 144 prescribes the following two-step impairment test to evaluate for impairment property[155] to be held and used (Step 1) and to determine the amount of any impairment loss to be recognized (Step 2):

Step 1: Determine whether the carrying amount of the long-lived asset is recoverable through the sum of the undiscounted cash flows expected to result from the use and eventual disposition of the asset. These undiscounted cash flows exclude payments made by the owner for interest that is recognized as expense when incurred.[156] If the carrying amount of the property is recoverable through undiscounted cash flows, no impairment loss needs to be recognized, even if the carrying amount of the asset exceeds its fair value. If the carrying amount is not recoverable through undiscounted cash flows, an impairment loss needs to be recognized, the amount of which is determined as described in Step 2 of the analysis.

Step 2: Determine the amount of impairment loss to be recognized by comparing the carrying amount of the asset to its fair value. The excess of the carrying amount of an asset over its fair value is the amount of impairment loss to be recognized in the financial statements.[157]

Real estate properties that are "to be held and used" need to be evaluated for impairment whenever events or changes in circumstances indicate that their carrying amounts may not be recoverable. The following are examples of impairment indicators:[158]

- A significant decrease in the market price of real estate properties
- A significant adverse change in the extent or manner in which the real estate properties are being used or in their physical condition

---

155   In the remainder of this section, it is assumed that such property represents the lowest level for which identifiable cash flows are largely independent of the cash flows of other assets and liabilities.

156   Estimates of future cash flows relating to an asset that is under development are based on the expected service potential of the asset when development is substantially complete. Those estimates include cash outflows associated with all future expenditures necessary to develop the long-lived asset, including interest payments that will be capitalized as part of the cost of the asset. [FAS 144, paragraphs 20 and 21]

157   FAS 144, paragraph 7; if long-lived assets are grouped with other assets and liabilities at the lowest level for which identifiable cash flows are largely independent of the cash flows of other assets and liabilities, the impairment loss needs to be allocated to the assets and liabilities in the group. Paragraph 14 of FASB Statement No. 144 provides with respect to such allocation: "An impairment loss for an asset group shall reduce only the carrying amounts of a long-lived asset or assets of the group. The loss shall be allocated to the long-lived assets of the group on a pro rata basis using the relative carrying amounts of those assets, except that the loss allocated to an individual long-lived asset of the group shall not reduce the carrying amount of that asset below its fair value whenever that fair value is determinable without undue cost and effort . . ." If an asset group includes intangibles, as, for example, in an office building held for rental with in-place leases, the in-place leases would also be subject to the provisions in FASB Statement No. 144 as they relate to impairment. [FAS 142, paragraphs 15–17]

158   FAS 144, paragraph 8

- A significant adverse change in legal factors or in the business climate that could affect the value of the real estate properties
- An accumulation of costs significantly in excess of the amount originally expected for the acquisition or construction of the real estate properties
- A current-period operating or cash flow loss combined with a history of operating or cash flow losses or a projection or forecast that demonstrates continuing losses associated with the use of the real estate properties
- A current expectation that, more likely than not, real estate properties will be sold or otherwise disposed of significantly before the end of their previously estimated useful lives

Insufficient demand for a rental project currently under development may also indicate that the property is impaired.[159]

When an impairment loss is recognized, the adjusted carrying amount of the real estate property becomes its new basis; restoration of a previously recognized impairment loss is inappropriate.[160]

IMPAIRMENT OF PROPERTIES TO BE DISPOSED OF BY SALE

If a company decides to sell a real estate property, such as its corporate headquarters facility or a rental property, the property may meet the criteria for being classified as "to be disposed of by sale" (held for sale).[161] A property classified as held for sale is measured at the lower of its carrying amount or fair value less cost to sell.[162] While classified as held for sale, the property is not depreciated. The provisions in Statement 144 for long-lived assets to be disposed of by sale also apply to a real estate project that is substantially completed and that is to be sold.[163]

One-Step Impairment Analysis under FASB Statement No. 144.   FASB Statement No. 144 requires a comparison of the carrying amount of the property held for sale with its fair value less cost to sell.[164] If the carrying amount exceeds fair value less cost to sell, an impairment loss needs to be recognized. Any subsequent recoveries in fair value are recognized up to the amount of impairment losses (for a write-down to fair value less cost to sell) previously recognized.[165]

The reclassification of property to be held and used as property held for sale may result in the recognition of an impairment loss, as it is no longer

---

159   FAS 67, paragraph 25
160   FAS 144, paragraph 15
161   The criteria that a property must meet to qualify as property held for sale and the presentation and disclosure requirements for such property are discussed in Section 3.8.2 of this chapter.
162   FAS 144, paragraph 34
163   FAS 67, paragraph 24
164   FAS 144, paragraph 34
165   FAS 144, paragraph 37

appropriate to perform the two-step impairment analysis for properties held and used, described above.

3.7.1.2 Loss on Sale of Real Estate Properties
As a result of the requirement to recognize impairment losses for both (1) properties to be held and used and (2) properties to be disposed of by sale, loss recognition in the period in which the sale is recorded is expected to occur only in limited circumstances. In a situation in which, as a result of a decline in fair values, a company becomes aware during contract negotiations that the fair value of the property (less cost to sell) is less than its carrying amount, the company would generally recognize an impairment loss at that time rather than deferring the recognition of a loss on sale until the time of closing.

The impact of recording an impairment loss vs. a loss on the sale of real estate properties is especially significant for real estate companies, such as REITs, that use Funds from Operations (FFO) as a performance measure. When adjusting net income to arrive at FFO, impairment losses are not added back; however, losses on the sale of real estate are added back. Thus, a classification of "losses" as losses on sale rather than impairment losses leads to higher performance numbers.

3.7.2 EXTINGUISHMENT OF DEBT WITH THE SALE OF PROPERTY
Assume that a property owner has entered into a transaction to sell an income-producing property at a gain or loss. The property is financed with a mortgage that is required to be repaid at closing. The prepayment of the mortgage will trigger a prepayment penalty. Additionally, the seller has deferred loan costs on its books, which will have to be written off. The loss on the extinguishment of debt and any gain or loss on disposal of the property should be treated as separate transactions; they should not be combined for accounting purposes.[166]

If the real estate property sold represents a component of a company—that is, if it has operations and cash flows that can be clearly distinguished (operationally and for financial reporting purposes) from the rest of the company[167]—the reporting of discontinued operations may be required.[168] Under a discontinued operations presentation, any gain or loss on disposal, as well as any prepayment penalty and write-off of deferred loan costs, would all be part of discontinued operations. If prepayment penalties and debt issuance costs are related to the debt

---

166   By analogy to the requirement that an impairment loss for a long-lived asset that is subject to nonrecourse debt is measured as the amount by which the carrying amount of the asset exceeds its fair value. Paragraph B34 of FASB Statement No. 144 states, in part: "The recognition of an impairment loss and the recognition of a gain on the extinguishment of debt are separate events, and each event should be recognized in the period in which it occurs. The Board believes that the recognition of an impairment loss should be based on the measurement of the asset at its fair value and that the existence of nonrecourse debt should not influence that measurement."

167   FAS 144, paragraph 41

168   See Section 3.8.3 of this chapter.

that is required to be repaid in connection with the sale of the property, and cash flows relating to the property will be eliminated from the ongoing operations of the entity as a result of the disposal transaction, the write-off of debt issuance cost and prepayment penalties will be included in discontinued operations. This is consistent with the treatment of interest on debt that is required to be repaid as a result of an asset disposal transaction.[169]

3.7.3 WRAP-AROUND MORTGAGE   A seller may sell a real estate property and provide financing to the buyer for the difference between the sales price and the down payment, secured by a second lien note on the property; the note is "wrapped around" the existing mortgage.

Under a wrap-around mortgage, the seller remains the primary obligor under the existing mortgage. Accordingly, the seller does not remove the debt from its books and continues to record interest and principal payments on the debt. The note receivable, net of any interest discount, is reported as an asset on the seller's balance sheet.

However, if the buyer assumes responsibility for a mortgage and the lender accepts the buyer as the new primary obligor, the arrangement is not considered a wrap-around mortgage; the seller is allowed to remove the liability from its balance sheet. If the seller remains secondarily liable should the buyer default, the seller needs to evaluate any accounting and reporting requirements under FIN 45, *Guarantor's Accounting and Disclosure Requirements for Guarantees, Including Guarantees of Indebtedness of Others.*

3.7.4 EFFECT OF NONRECOURSE FINANCING ON PROFIT RECOGNITION
EITF Issue No. 88-24, *Effect of Various Forms of Financing under FASB Statement No. 66*, addresses the issue of sufficient initial and continuing investments. The Task Force reached a consensus that any amounts borrowed that are secured by the property purchased do not demonstrate commitment of the buyer and may not be included in the amounts of initial and continuing investments. However, if the seller has unconditionally received all amounts it is entitled to receive from the sale and is not at risk related to the financing, the size of the buyer's initial and continuing investment below the thresholds established by FASB Statement No. 66 does not preclude the use of the accrual method of profit recognition.

Additionally, the Task Force reached the following consensus: If the profit deferred as a result of insufficient initial and continuing investments exceeds the sum of the outstanding amount of seller financing and the outstanding amount of buyer's debt secured by the property for which the seller is contingently liable, the seller can recognize any excess in income.[170]

---

169   EITF Issue No. 87-24
170   That assumes that no other forms of continuing involvement are present that preclude profit recognition under the accrual method.

EXAMPLES—APPLICATION OF EITF ISSUE NO. 88-24

SellCo (S) sells a real estate property (cost $70 million) for sales price of $100 million. The initial investment requirement is 20%. All mortgage obligations meet the continuing investment requirements of Statement 66.

The following two examples illustrate how financing can impact profit recognition.

EXAMPLE 1[171]
The sales price is financed as follows:

Cash down payment	$10 million
Assumption of seller's recourse mortgage[172]	$80 million
Seller financing	$10 million

The initial investment requirement of $20 million is not met. Therefore, the use of the accrual method is not appropriate. The seller determines that the use of the installment or cost recovery method of accounting for this transaction is appropriate.

In this example, the seller remains contingently liable for the payment of the recourse mortgage. Thus, the assumption of the seller's recourse mortgage ($80 million) cannot be considered when calculating the profit to be recognized.

PROFIT UNDER THE INSTALLMENT METHOD
Under the installment method, the seller recognizes profit of $3 million, calculated as follows:

$$\frac{\text{Cash payment (\$10 million)}}{\text{Sales price (\$100 million)}} \times \text{profit on the sale (\$30 million)} = \$3 \text{ million}$$

PROFIT UNDER THE COST RECOVERY METHOD
Under the cost recovery method, the seller cannot recognize any profit, since the payment ($10 million) is less than the cost of the property ($70 million).

EXAMPLE 2[173]
The sales price is financed as follows:

Cash down payment	$10 million
Assumption of seller's nonrecourse mortgage	$80 million
Seller financing	$10 million

The difference between Example 2 and Example 1 is that this example assumes a *non*recourse mortgage, in which the seller is relieved from all obligations.

The seller would make the same profit calculation as presented in Example 1. However, following the consensus reached in EITF Issue No. 88-24, the profit that is to be deferred is limited to amounts due to the seller ($10 million). Therefore, under both the installment method and the cost recovery methods, the seller can recognize profit of $20 million.

---

171 Adapted from EITF Issue No. 88-24, example 18
172 Seller remains contingently liable.
173 Adapted from EITF Issue No. 88-24, example 17

3.8 FINANCIAL STATEMENT PRESENTATION AND DISCLOSURE

This section outlines financial statement presentation and disclosure requirements other than those relating to individual accounting methods, which are discussed in Section 3.6 of this chapter.

3.8.1 PRESENTATION OF GAIN ON SALE OF LAND OPTION   A real estate company may have acquired land options that it sells in subsequent periods. Any gains or losses realized from the sale of the land options that are reported in the balance sheet as other assets are presented as other gains/other income or other losses in the seller's income statement, rather than presented "gross" as revenues and cost of sales.

3.8.2 PRESENTATION OF PROPERTIES AS HELD FOR SALE   A real estate property to be disposed of other than by sale (for example, by abandonment, in an exchange not measured at fair value under the provisions of APB Opinion No. 29, *Accounting for Nonmonetary Transactions*, or distributed to owners in a spinoff) is considered held and used until the property is disposed of.[174] The depreciable life of the property that is to be disposed of other than by sale needs to be revised in accordance with paragraphs 19–22 of FASB Statement No. 154, *Accounting Changes and Error Corrections*, to reflect the use of the property over its shortened useful life.[175]

If a company has the intention to sell real estate properties, the real estate properties need to be classified as held for sale in the period in which all of the following criteria are met:[176]

- Management with the authority to approve the sale commits to a plan to sell the properties.
- The properties are available for immediate sale in their present condition.
- An active program to locate a buyer and other actions required to sell the properties have been initiated.
- The sale of the real estate properties is probable, and transfer of the properties is expected to qualify for sale recognition within one year. There is a narrow exception to this one-year rule, if certain specified events or circumstances beyond a company's control extend the period to complete the sale.[177]
- The properties are being actively marketed for sale at a price that is reasonable in relation to their current fair value.
- Actions required to complete the plan indicate that it is unlikely that significant changes to the plan will be made, or that the plan will be withdrawn.

---

174   FAS 144, paragraph 27
175   FAS 144, paragraph 28
176   FAS 144, paragraph 30
177   FAS 144, paragraph 31

If these criteria are met after the balance sheet date but before the issuance of the financial statements, the real estate to be sold will continue to be classified as held and used. However, footnote disclosures are required, as if the properties had met the criteria for held for sale properties before the balance sheet date.[178]

DISCLOSURE REQUIREMENTS

Paragraph 47 of FASB Statement No. 144 requires the following disclosures for periods in which real estate properties either have been sold or are classified as held for sale:

- A description of the facts and circumstances leading to the expected disposal, the expected manner and timing of that disposal, and, if not separately presented on the face of the statement, the carrying amount(s) of the major classes of assets and liabilities included as part of a disposal group
- Any losses that have been recognized for a write-down to fair value less cost to sell, and any gains that have been recognized for any subsequent increase in fair value less cost to sell, but not in excess of cumulative losses previously recognized, and if not separately presented on the face of the income statement, the caption in the income statement that includes that gain or loss
- If applicable, amounts of revenue and pretax profit or loss reported in discontinued operations
- If applicable, the segment in which the long-lived asset is reported under FASB Statement No. 131, *Disclosures about Segments of an Enterprise and Related Information*

Circumstances may arise that lead to a change in the company's plans to sell real estate property previously classified as held for sale. Once the criteria for "held for sale" are no longer met, the real estate property is reclassified from "held for sale" to "held and used" property.[179] The facts and circumstances leading to the decision to change the plan to sell the property and its effects on the results of operations for the current period and any prior periods presented need to be disclosed in the notes to the financial statements that include the period of that decision.[180]

3.8.3 DISCONTINUED OPERATIONS PRESENTATION   FASB Statement No. 144 retained the basic provisions of APB Opinion No. 30, *Reporting the Results of Operations—Reporting the Effects of Disposal of a Segment of a Business, and Extraordinary, Unusual, and Infrequently Occurring Events and Transactions*, for presentation of discontinued operations in the income statement, but it broadened

---

178   FAS 144, paragraph 33
179   FAS 144, paragraph 38; upon such reclassification, the reclassified asset is measured at the lower of its
       (1) carrying amount before the asset was classified as held for sale, adjusted for any depreciation/amortization expense that would have been recognized had the asset been continuously classified as held and used, or (2) fair value at the date of the decision not to sell.
180   FAS 144, paragraph 48

that presentation to include a component of an entity rather than a segment of a business. As such, Statement 144 may require the reporting of discontinued operations if a real estate property represents a component of an entity, that is, if it comprises operations and cash flows that can be clearly distinguished from the rest of the entity and that component either has been disposed of or is classified as held for sale. This generally would be the case in the sale of an income-producing real estate property.

The discontinued operations presentation requirements of Statement 144 also apply to properties that have been developed to be sold if they are being leased up before their sale, such as apartment or office buildings.

The results of operations of a component that either has been disposed of or is classified as held for sale need to be reported as discontinued operations, if the following two conditions are met:

- The operations and cash flows have been (or will be) eliminated from the ongoing operations as a result of the disposal transaction.
- The entity will not have any significant continuing involvement in the operations of the component after the disposal transaction.

The reporting of discontinued operations is required even for the sale of individual real estate properties, if the above criteria are met. The questions "When are operations and cash flows eliminated from operations?" and "What is significant continuing involvement?" have been clarified by EITF Issue No. 03-13, *Applying the Conditions in Paragraph 42 of FASB Statement No. 144 in Determining Whether to Report Discontinued Operations.*

In 2006, the FASB received an agenda request from the National Association of Real Estate Investment Trusts (NAREIT) for a reconsideration of the criteria in Statement 144 as they relate to the presentation of discontinued operations. In January 2007, the FASB and the IASB discussed that the disposition of operating segments as defined in FASB Statement No. 131, *Disclosures about Segments of an Enterprise and Related Information*, rather than components, should trigger the reporting requirements for discontinued operations. The FASB has not added a separate project to its technical agenda to reconsider the criteria for reporting discontinued operations; rather, the FASB staff will work with the IASB to converge the definition of discontinued operations in the financial statement presentation project. Any modification to the current discontinued operations definition is not expected to be effective before the year 2009.

Statement 144[181] includes certain presentation and disclosure requirements in the period (for current and prior periods) in which a component of an entity either has been disposed of or is classified as held for sale:

- Presentation of the results of operations of the component, including any impairment losses and subsequent recoveries in fair value in discontinued

---

181   FAS 144, paragraph 43

operations; the results of operations of a component classified as held for sale are reported in discontinued operations in the period(s) in which they occur

- Reporting of the results of discontinued operations, less applicable income taxes (benefits), as a separate component of income before extraordinary items and the cumulative effect of accounting changes
- Disclosure of gain or loss recognized on disposal either on the face of the income statement or in the notes to the financial statements

Statement 144 provides an example for the presentation of discontinued operations in a company's income statement:

REPORTING OF DISCONTINUED OPERATIONS IN THE INCOME STATEMENT[182]		
Income from continuing operations before income taxes	$XXX	
Income taxes	XXX	
Income from continuing operations		$XXX
Discontinued operations		
Gain/loss from operations of discontinued component (including loss on disposal of $XXX)		XXX
Income taxes (benefit)		XXX
Gain/loss on discontinued operations		XXX
Net income/loss		$XXX

PRESENTATION OF DISCONTINUED OPERATIONS IN THE STATEMENT OF CASH FLOWS
FASB Statement No. 95 permits, but does not require, a separate disclosure of cash flows relating to discontinued operations:[183]

Separate disclosure of cash flows pertaining to extraordinary items or discontinued operations . . . is not required. An enterprise that nevertheless chooses to report separately operating cash flows of discontinued operations shall do so consistently for all periods affected, which may include periods long after sale of the operation.

As Statement 95 requires that *all* cash flows be reported as operating, investing, or financing activities, the cash flows relating to discontinued operations have to be segregated into operating, investing, or financing activities, if disclosed separately; a "lump-sum" disclosure of cash flows from discontinued operations in one of the three categories, irrespective of their nature, would not meet the requirements in Statement 95.

---

182   Adapted from FASB Statement No. 144, paragraph 43
183   FAS 95, paragraph 26, footnote 10

3.8.4 DISCLOSURES UPON RECOGNITION OF IMPAIRMENT LOSS Paragraph 26 of FASB Statement No. 144 requires the disclosure of the following information if an impairment loss has been recognized:

- A description of the impaired asset and the facts and circumstances leading to the impairment
- If not presented separately in the income statement, the amount of the impairment loss and the caption in the income statement that includes that loss
- The methods used for determining fair value, that is, the valuation techniques used
- The segment in which the impaired asset is reported under FASB Statement No. 131

3.9 INTERNATIONAL FINANCIAL REPORTING STANDARDS

At present, the International Financial Reporting Standards do not have a separate standard that deals with revenue and profit recognition of real estate sales; rather IAS 18, *Revenue*, applies to revenue recognition of real estate sales transactions. However, in July 2007, the International Financial Reporting Interpretations Committee (IFRIC) issued for comment IFRIC Draft Interpretation D21, *Real Estate Sales*, to provide guidance on when a company should recognize revenue from the sale of real estate:

- It clarifies whether sale agreements entered into before construction is complete should be considered construction contracts within the scope of IAS 11, *Construction Contracts*, or agreements for the sale of goods within the scope of IAS 18.
- It revises guidance on the application of IAS 18 to real estate sales in general.

Until D21 is issued and becomes effective, the provisions of IAS 11, *Construction Contracts*, and IAS 18, *Revenue*, apply. Under IAS 18, revenue from the sale of goods is recognized when all of the following conditions have been satisfied:[184]

- The entity has transferred to the buyer the significant risks and rewards of ownership of the goods
- The entity retains neither continuing managerial involvement to the degree usually associated with ownership nor effective control over the goods sold
- The amount of revenue can be measured reliably
- It is probable that the economic benefits associated with the transaction will flow to the entity
- The costs incurred or to be incurred in respect of the transaction can be measured reliably

---

184   IAS 18, paragraph 14

Paragraph 9 of Appendix A to IAS 18 provides some general guidelines relating to specific circumstances encountered in real estate transactions. Paragraph 9 explicitly states that if the seller is obliged to perform any significant acts after the transfer of the equitable and/or legal title, revenue is recognized as the acts are performed. Other forms of continuing involvement and a buyer's financial commitment necessary to record a sale are being raised as issues, but no specific accounting guidance is provided.

Unlike FASB Statement No. 66,[185] IAS 18 does not provide for the percentage-of-completion method when recognizing revenue from the sale of real estate properties with a long construction period, such as office buildings, apartments, condominiums, and shopping centers. Rather, under IAS, the percentage-of-completion method is permissible only for construction contracts, when the outcome of that construction contract can be estimated reliably.[186] A construction contract is defined as "a contract specifically negotiated for the construction of an asset or a combination of assets that are closely interrelated or interdependent in terms of their design, technology and function or their ultimate purpose or use."[187]

DISCLOSURES
Under IAS 18, the seller of real estate property has to disclose the following:[188]

- The accounting policies adopted for the recognition of revenue, including the methods adopted to determine the stage of completion of transactions involving the rendering of services.
- The amount of each significant category of revenue recognized during the period, including revenue arising from:
  - The sale of goods
  - The rendering of services
  - Interest
  - Royalties
  - Dividends
  - Exchanges of goods or services included in each significant category of revenue

Paragraphs 39–45 of IAS 11 set forth disclosure requirements for contracts that are construction contracts.

3.10 SYNOPSIS OF AUTHORITATIVE LITERATURE

FASB STATEMENT NO. 66, ACCOUNTING FOR SALES OF REAL ESTATE
FASB Statement No. 66 provides sale and profit recognition guidance for all real estate sales transactions without regard to the nature of the seller's business.

185   FAS 66, paragraph 20
186   IAS 11, paragraph 22
187   IAS 11, paragraph 3
188   IAS 18, paragraph 35

Sales of real estate are classified as *other than retail land sales* or *retail land sales*. FASB Statement No. 66 establishes detailed rules and bright lines that need to be considered when determining whether a sale can be recorded and what profit recognition method to use. In October 1982, the FASB extracted the specialized sale and profit recognition principles and practices from the AICPA Industry Accounting Guides, *Accounting for Profit Recognition on Sales of Real Estate* and *Accounting for Retail Land Sales*, and the AICPA Statements of Position No. 75-6, *Questions Concerning Profit Recognition on Sales of Real Estate*, and No. 78-4, *Application of the Deposit, Installment, and Cost Recovery Methods in Accounting for Sales of Real Estate*, and issued them as FASB Statement No. 66.

FASB Statement No. 144, Accounting for the Impairment or Disposal of Long-Lived Assets

FASB Statement No. 144 provides accounting and reporting guidance relating to the impairment or disposal of long-lived assets.

FASB Interpretation No. 43, Real Estate Sales, an Interpretation of FASB Statement No. 66

In FIN 43, FASB clarifies that FASB Statement No. 66 applies to all sales of real estate, including sales of real estate with property improvements or integral equipment. The terms *property improvements* and *integral equipment* refer to any physical structure or equipment attached to real estate that cannot be removed and used separately without incurring significant costs.

Proposed FASB Staff Position (FSP) FAS 144-c, Classifying and Accounting for a Depreciable Asset as Held-for-Sale When an Equity Method Investment Is Obtained[189]

The FASB staff has received inquiries on classifying and accounting for a depreciable long-lived asset when it is expected that once the asset is sold, the entity will account for its interest in the entity that holds the long-lived asset as an equity method investment.

Proposed FASB Staff Position. An entity shall classify the entire long-lived asset as held-for-sale and cease depreciating the long-lived asset once the long-lived asset meets the held-for-sale criteria, even if the entity plans to account for its direct or indirect interest in the long-lived asset under the equity method of accounting subsequent to its sale.

EITF Issue No. 84-17, Profit Recognition on Sales of Real Estate with Graduated Payment Mortgages or Insured Mortgages

Issue. For sales of real estate financed by graduated payment mortgages that involve initial negative amortization of principal or that are financed by mortgages

---

189   The FASB decided not to finalize the proposed FSP.

that are partially or fully insured, how should the profit recognition criteria in FASB Statement No. 66 be applied?

Consensus/Status. A sale involving a graduated payment mortgage that does not meet the continuing investment test in FASB Statement No. 66 should not result in full immediate profit recognition.

EITF ISSUE NO. 86-6, ANTISPECULATION CLAUSES IN REAL ESTATE SALES CONTRACTS

Issue. Land sale agreements may contain antispeculation clauses that require the buyer to develop the land in a specific manner or within a stated period of time or prohibit certain uses of the property. If the buyer fails to comply with the provisions of the sales contract, the seller may have the right to reacquire the property. The issue is whether FASB Statement No. 66 precludes the seller from accounting for the transaction as a sale when an antispeculation clause exists.

Consensus/Status. The Task Force reached a consensus that the contingent option to repurchase the real estate does not preclude sale recognition if the probability of the buyer not complying is remote.

EITF ISSUE NO. 86-7, RECOGNITION BY HOMEBUILDERS OF PROFIT FROM SALES OF LAND AND RELATED CONSTRUCTION CONTRACTS

Issue. A homebuilder enters into a contract for the construction of a single-family home on the homebuilder's lot. The homebuilder does not relinquish title to the lot until closing. How should the homebuilder recognize earnings from the contract related to the lot sale and the construction of the house?

Consensus/Status. The Task Force reached a consensus that profit recognition is not appropriate until the conditions in paragraph 5 of FASB Statement No. 66 are met: consummation of a sale; adequate initial and continuing investments; seller's receivable not subject to future subordination; and transfer of usual risks and rewards of ownership. Until these conditions are met, the deposit method of accounting should be used for both the construction activity and the land.

EITF ISSUE NO. 87-9, PROFIT RECOGNITION ON SALES OF REAL ESTATE WITH INSURED MORTGAGES OR SURETY BONDS

Issues. The issues are:

1. Should a financial instrument, such as a surety bond, be considered the equivalent of an irrevocable letter of credit in determining whether it is appropriate to recognize profit under the accrual method of accounting?
2. Should government or private mortgage insurance covering a part of the mortgage balance be considered equivalent to an irrevocable letter of credit and included as part of the buyer's initial and continuing investment in

determining whether it is appropriate to recognize profit under the accrual method?

3. Should the minimum down payment percentages set forth in FASB Statement No. 66 apply, or may the loan limits in the government programs be used if a buyer of single-family residential property qualifies for a Federal Housing Administration (FHA) or Veterans Administration (VA) loan that requires little (less than 5%) or no down payment and the principal amount of the mortgage is insured or guaranteed either in full or in part by the FHA or VA?

Consensuses/Status.   The Task Force reached the following consensuses:

1. An irrevocable financial instrument, such as a surety bond from an established independent insuring institution, which provides for the same rights and obligations as an irrevocable letter of credit, may be considered equivalent to an irrevocable letter of credit.
2. Mortgage insurance should not be considered the equivalent of an irrevocable letter of credit in determining whether the seller can recognize profit on the sale by the accrual method, because the purchase of mortgage insurance is not deemed to demonstrate a commitment by the buyer to honor its obligation to pay for the property.
3. A seller of owner-occupied single-family residential homes that finances a sale under a VA or FHA government-insured program may use the normal down payment requirements or loan limits established by those programs instead of the down payment criteria set forth in paragraphs 53 and 54 of FASB Statement No. 66. The seller may record profit under the accrual method provided that the mortgage receivable is insured from loss under the VA or FHA program.

EITF ISSUE 87-24, ALLOCATION OF INTEREST TO DISCONTINUED OPERATIONS

Issues.   An enterprise sells a component of an enterprise and reports the sale separately as a discontinued operation. The enterprise has debt on its balance sheet.
   The issues are:

1. May interest expense be allocated to discontinued operations based on the principal amount of debt that will be or could be paid with the proceeds from the sale of such operations? If so, what method of allocation should be used?
2. May general corporate overhead expenses be allocated to discontinued operations?

Consensuses/Status.   The Task Force reached the following consensuses:

1. Interest on debt that is to be assumed by the buyer and interest on debt that is required to be repaid as a result of the disposal transaction should

be allocated to discontinued operations. The allocation to discontinued operations of other consolidated interest that is not directly attributable to or related to other operations of the enterprise is permitted but not required. EITF Issue No. 87-24 outlines a methodology for the allocation of interest to continuing and discontinued operations.

The SEC staff expects that registrants that allocate interest in accordance with the consensus clearly disclose the accounting policy and the amount allocated to and included in discontinued operations for all periods presented.

2. General corporate overhead may not be allocated to discontinued operations.

EITF ISSUE NO. 88-12, *TRANSFER OF OWNERSHIP INTEREST AS PART OF DOWN PAYMENT UNDER FASB STATEMENT NO. 66*
Issues.   The issues are:

1. Should the buyer's ownership interest in a purchased property that is pledged as security for a note be included as part of the buyer's initial investment in determining whether profit may be recognized under the accrual method?
2. Should assets other than the purchased property that collateralize the buyer's note be included as part of the buyer's initial investment in determining whether profit may be recognized under the accrual method?

Consensuses/Status.   The Task Force reached a consensus that FASB Statement No. 66 precludes profit recognition under the accrual method in the scenarios addressed in Issues 1 and 2, because purchased property or other assets pledged as security for a note should not be included as part of the buyer's initial investment.

EITF ISSUE NO. 88-24, *EFFECT OF VARIOUS FORMS OF FINANCING UNDER FASB STATEMENT NO. 66, ACCOUNTING FOR SALES OF REAL ESTATE*
Issue.   How should profit be recognized under FASB Statement No. 66 when a real estate sale transaction involves various forms of financing?

Consensus/Status.   If the profit that is deferred as a result of inadequate buyer investment exceeds the sum of the outstanding amount of seller financing and the outstanding amount of buyer's debt secured by the property for which the seller is contingently liable, the seller must recognize such excess in income. When the seller has unconditionally received all amounts it is entitled to from the sale and is not at risk related to the financing, the buyer's commitment to pay for the property is not a factor in the seller's profit recognition. The requirements for the consummation of a real estate sale transaction and the appropriate accounting for forms of continuing involvement are not affected by the consensus reached in the EITF.

EITF Issue No. 98-8, *Accounting for Transfers of Investments That Are in Substance Real Estate*

Issue. Should the sale or transfer of an investment in the form of a financial asset that is in substance real estate be accounted for in accordance with FASB Statements No. 66 or No. 140?

Consensus/Status. The Task Force reached a consensus that the sale or transfer of an investment in the form of a financial asset that is in substance real estate should be accounted for in accordance with FASB Statement No. 66. Acquisition, development, and construction loans that are in substance real estate investments are subject to this consensus. However, a marketable investment in a REIT that is accounted for in accordance with FASB Statement No. 115 is not considered an investment that is in substance real estate; a sale of that investment should be accounted for in accordance with FASB Statement No. 140.

EITF Issue No. 00-13, *Determining Whether Equipment Is "Integral Equipment" Subject to FASB Statements No. 66 and No. 98*

Issue. Sales of integral equipment are within the scope of FASB Statement No. 66. FIN 43 defines integral equipment as any physical structure or equipment attached to real estate that cannot be removed and used separately without incurring significant cost. How should one determine whether equipment is integral equipment?

Consensus/Status. When the combined total of both the cost to remove the equipment plus the decrease in its value exceeds 10% of the fair value of the equipment, the equipment is integral equipment. At a minimum, the decrease in value of the equipment as a result of its removal is the estimated cost to ship and reinstall the equipment at a new site.

EITF Issue No. 03-13, *Applying the Conditions in Paragraph 42 of FASB Statement No. 144 in Determining Whether to Report Discontinued Operations*

Issues. Paragraph 42 of FASB Statement No. 144 provides that the results of operations of a component of an entity that either has been disposed of or is classified as held for sale have to be reported in discontinued operations if (1) the operations and cash flows of the component have been (or will be) eliminated from the ongoing operations of the entity as a result of the disposal transaction, and (2) the entity will not have any significant continuing involvement in the operations of the component after the disposal transaction.

The issues are:

1. How should an ongoing entity evaluate whether the operations and cash flows of a disposed component have been or will be eliminated from the ongoing operations of the entity?

2. What types of continuing involvement constitute significant continuing involvement in the operations of the disposed component?

Consensuses/Status.   The following consensuses were reached:

1. Operations and cash flows should be considered eliminated from the ongoing operations if no direct cash flows are expected to be generated. The determination of whether any continuing cash flows are direct or indirect is made based on their nature and significance. EITF Issue No. 03-13 provides guidance for the evaluation of whether continuing cash flows are to be considered direct cash flows.
2. Continuing involvement in the operations of the disposed component provides the ongoing entity with the ability to influence the operating and/or financial policies of the disposed component. An interest in the disposed component and contractual arrangements needs to be evaluated to determine whether the ongoing entity has continuing involvement with the disposed component. EITF Issue No. 03-13 provides factors to be considered in evaluating whether continuing involvement constitutes significant continuing involvement.

EITF Issue No. 06-8, *Applicability of the Assessment of a Buyer's Continuing Investment under FASB Statement No. 66 for Sales of Condominiums*
Issues.   The issues are:

1. Does an entity need to evaluate the adequacy of the buyer's continuing investment pursuant to paragraph 12 of FASB Statement No. 66 to recognize profit under the percentage-of-completion method?
2. Should an entity that is reassessing the criteria in paragraph 37 of FASB Statement No. 66 apply the initial and continuing investment tests on a cumulative basis from the contract date or prospectively from the reassessment date (that is, the date on which an entity not previously eligible to recognize profit under the percentage-of-completion method reassesses whether it is now eligible to recognize profit under the percentage-of-completion method by meeting the criteria in paragraph 37 of FASB Statement No. 66)?

Consensuses/Status

1. The Task Force reached a consensus that in assessing the collectibility of the sales price, an entity should evaluate the adequacy of the buyer's initial and continuing investment to conclude that the sales price is collectible.
2. The Task Force reached a consensus that on a reassessment date, an entity should reassess all of the criteria in paragraph 37 of FASB Statement No. 66 to determine whether profit should be recognized under the percentage-of-completion method; in reassessing the collectibility of the sales price,

the initial and continuing investment tests should be applied prospectively from the reassessment date (as if the deposit was received on the reassessment date).

EITF Issue No. 07-6, *Accounting for the Sale of Real Estate Subject to the Requirements of FASB Statement No. 66 When the Agreement Includes a Buy-Sell Clause*

Issue.   When investors enter into an arrangement to create a jointly owned entity and one investor sells real estate to that entity, a buy-sell clause may be included in the agreement between the investors. Is a buy-sell clause a prohibited form of continuing involvement that precludes partial sales treatment under FASB Statement No. 66?

Consensus/Status.   A buy-sell clause, in and of itself, does not constitute a prohibited form of continuing involvement that precludes partial sales treatment. However, all the relevant facts and circumstances need to be considered to determine whether the buy-sell clause gives the buyer an in-substance option to put its interest in the jointly owned entity back to the seller or gives the seller an in-substance option to acquire the buyer's interest in the jointly owned entity thereby reacquiring the real estate sold.

International Accounting Standard 11, *Construction Contracts*

IAS 11 provides accounting guidance relating to construction contracts. A construction contract is a contract specifically negotiated for the construction of an asset or assets. When the outcome of a construction contract can be reliably estimated, revenue and related expenses are recognized based on the stage of completion of the contract activity. When the outcome of a construction contract cannot be reliably estimated, revenue is recognized to the extent of the contract costs incurred that are probable of being recovered, and contract costs are recognized as an expense in the period in which they are incurred.

International Accounting Standard 18, *Revenue*

Revenue is recognized when it is probable that future economic benefits will flow to the entity and these benefits can be measured reliably. IAS 18 identifies the circumstances when the criteria for revenue recognition are met. That Standard also provides guidance on the application of these criteria.

Draft IFRIC Interpretation D21, *Real Estate Sales*

D21 provides guidance on when an entity selling real estate should recognize revenue from the sale of real estate. It clarifies whether sale agreements entered into before construction is complete should be within the scope of IAS 11 or IAS 18, and it revises guidance on how to apply IAS 18 to real estate sales in general.

CHAPTER 4

REAL ESTATE LEASES

4.1 OVERVIEW

What agreements are considered leases? Financial Accounting Standards Board (FASB) Statement No. 13, *Accounting for Leases*, defines a lease as an agreement conveying the right to use property, plant, or equipment (land or depreciable assets or both) usually for a stated period of time.[1]

Agreements that transfer the right to use property, plant, or equipment meet the definition of a lease even though substantial services by the lessor may be called for in connection with the operation or maintenance of the asset under lease. The evaluation of whether an arrangement contains a lease within the scope of Statement 13 is based on the substance of the transaction,

---

1   FAS 13, paragraph 1

rather than its legal form. An agreement may not be designated as "lease," but nevertheless meet the definition of a lease, such as a heat supply contract for nuclear fuel.[2] Similarly, certain agreements designated as "leases" may not meet the definition of a lease. The accounting guidance for leases does not apply to lease agreements relating to the rights to explore for or to exploit natural resources, such as oil, gas, minerals, or timber; nor to licensing agreements for items such as motion picture films, plays, manuscripts, patents, and copyrights.[3]

Statement 13 provides the basic framework for determining whether a contract is within its scope. Before the issuance of Emerging Issues Task Force (EITF) Issue No. 01-8, *Determining Whether an Arrangement Contains a Lease*, that determination was largely judgmental. EITF Issue No. 01-8 provides specific guidance to be considered when making that determination. Besides the typical lease arrangement, in which a piece of equipment or real property is leased for a certain period of time, a lease also encompasses other contractual arrangements that historically, before the issuance of EITF Issue No. 01-8, may not have been considered "leases." A few examples of contractual arrangements that may meet the definition of a lease are:

- Power supply agreements
- Take-or-pay contracts
- Throughput arrangements
- Hotel management agreements
- Other service arrangements involving the use of specified property

While the guidance in EITF Issue No. 01-8 does not need to be applied to an arrangement entered into before May 29, 2003, a change in the contractual terms of that arrangement generally requires a reassessment based on the guidance provided in EITF Issue No. 01-8.[4]

The accounting for leases reflects the view that a lease that transfers substantially all of the benefits and risks of ownership should be accounted for as the acquisition of an asset and the incurrence of an obligation by the lessee (capital lease) and as a sale or financing by the lessor (sales-type, direct financing, or leveraged lease). Other leases should be accounted for as operating leases, that is, the rental of property.[5] The existing lease model is applied to both lessee and lessor, and often leads to symmetrical lease classification.

The accounting literature for leases is very fragmented. Several FASB Statements (FASs), Technical Bulletins (TBs), EITF Issues and FASB Staff

2   FAS 13, paragraph 1, footnote 1
3   FAS 13, paragraph 1
4   EITF Issue No. 01-8, paragraphs 13 and 16
5   FAS 13, paragraph 60

	Lease Classification Lessee	Lease Classification Lessor
Substantially All of the Risks and Rewards of Ownership Transferred to Lessee	Capital Lease	Sales-Type Lease Direct Financing Lease Synthetic Lease
Not Substantially All of the Risks and Rewards of Ownership Transferred to Lessee	Operating Lease	Operating Lease

Positions (FSPs) provide rule-driven, bright-line guidance on how to account for leasing transactions. In spite of the existing guidance, accounting for leases (mainly the accounting for lease incentives and rent holidays) resulted in hundreds of restatements on the books of retailers and restaurants in early 2005.

Additionally, since the issuance of FASB Interpretation (FIN) No. 46(R), *Consolidation of Variable Interest Entities*, companies have to evaluate their leasing arrangements to determine whether they are variable interests in a variable interest entity. Particularly in situations in which single-purpose entities are used in structuring leases, the provisions of FIN 46(R) may have a significant impact on the accounting and financial statement disclosures.

ON THE HORIZON—NEW LEASE ACCOUNTING

The FASB and the International Accounting Standards Board (IASB) have recognized the need for revised accounting guidance relating to leases, and "Leases" was added to the agendas of both the FASB and the IASB in July 2006. This joint project of the FASB and the IASB sets out to reconsider all aspects of lease accounting. The project is expected to fundamentally revise the way lease contracts are accounted for in the financial statements of both lessees and lessors. In December 2006, an international working group was established to assist the FASB and the IASB in reconsidering the accounting for leases. The first due process discussion paper that expresses the boards' preliminary views is expected to be published in 2008; a final standard is not expected to be issued before the year 2009.

4.2 DEFINITION OF A LEASE

A lease[6] is an agreement that conveys

- The right to use
- Property, plant, or equipment (land and/or depreciable assets)
- Usually for a stated period of time

When specific property is explicitly identified and the benefits of that property are conveyed based on time, the contract likely contains a lease. The difficulty in

---

6   FAS 13, paragraph 1

determining whether an arrangement contains a lease arises when the right to use property is conveyed in some other manner, such as granting the right to the output of the property.

Before the issuance of EITF Issue No. 01-8, the determination of whether or not a contract is (or contains) a lease was a matter of judgment and the evaluation of how to account for a lease arrangement generally started with the determination of lease classification. After the issuance of EITF Issue No. 01-8, the first step in lease accounting will often be the determination of whether or not a contract is within the scope of FASB Statement No. 13. The three components that must be considered when making that determination are discussed in this section.

4.2.1 RIGHT TO USE   EITF Issue No. 01-8 provides three conditions that need to be evaluated when determining whether a right to use has been conveyed. If *any* of these conditions is met, a right to use has been conveyed. Paragraph 12 of EITF Issue No. 01-8, the concept of which is depicted in Exhibit 4.1, states:

> An arrangement conveys the *right to use* property, plant, or equipment if the arrangement conveys to the purchaser (lessee) the right to control the use of the underlying property, plant, or equipment. The right to control the use of the underlying property, plant, or equipment is conveyed if any one of the following conditions is met:
>
> a. The purchaser has the ability or right to operate the property, plant, or equipment or direct others to operate the property, plant, or equipment in a manner it determines while obtaining or controlling more than a minor amount of the output or other utility of the property, plant, or equipment,
> b. The purchaser has the ability or right to control physical access to the underlying property, plant, or equipment while obtaining or controlling more than a minor amount of the output or other utility of the property, plant, or equipment, or

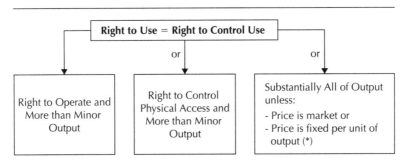

(*) The term "fixed per unit of output" has been interpreted very narrowly and does not allow for adjustment based on volume.

EXHIBIT 4.1   RIGHT TO USE

c. Facts and circumstances indicate that it is remote that one or more parties other than the purchaser will take more than a minor amount of the output or other utility that will be produced or generated by the property, plant, or equipment during the term of the arrangement, and the price that the purchaser (lessee) will pay for the output is neither contractually fixed per unit of output nor equal to the current market price per unit of output as of the time of the delivery of the output.

In many contracts for the purchase of products or services, an evaluation has to be made as to whether the payments are made for products or services purchased, or whether in essence they are made for the time that property, plant, or equipment is made available to produce the products or services.

Take-or-pay arrangements, for example, may commit the purchaser to pay the supplier irrespective of whether the purchaser actually uses a plant, or whether the purchaser obtains the output from a plant. In these circumstances, the purchaser may in essence be paying for the right to use the plant, rather than for the output from the plant.[7] Depending on the terms of the contractual arrangement, the contract may be within the scope of FASB Statement No. 13.[8]

EXAMPLE—RIGHT TO USE[9]

PurePower Inc. (P), a producer of silicon wafers, enters into an arrangement with a third party to supply a specific part for a specified period of time. The supplier designs and constructs a plant adjacent to P's manufacturing facility to produce the part, and the contract specifies that the part is to be produced in that facility. The designed capacity of the plant exceeds P's current needs, and the supplier maintains ownership and control over all significant aspects of operating the plant. P does not have the ability or right to control physical access to the facility. The contract specifies that the supplier must stand ready to deliver a minimum quantity of the part. If P purchases less than that stated minimum quantity.

Will only have to pay a fixed price per unit for the actual quantity taken. The supplier has the right to sell any parts not purchased by P to other customers, and it is expected that parties other than P will take more than a minor amount of the parts produced at that facility.

Does the arrangement convey to P the right to use the facility?

No. P has not obtained the right to use the facility because:

1. P does not have the ability or right to operate the facility, or to direct others to operate the facility.
2. P does not have the ability or right to control physical access to the facility.
3. The likelihood that parties other than the purchaser will take more than a minor amount of the component parts produced at the plant is more than remote.

---

7   EITF Issue No. 01-8, paragraph B15
8   Whether a take-or-pay contract is subject to FASB Statement No. 13, to FASB Statement No. 133, or to neither of these depends on its terms. FASB Statement No. 13 should be applied first, as leases within the scope of FASB Statement No. 13 are not derivative instruments subject to FASB Statement No. 133. However, a derivative embedded in a lease would be subject to FASB Statement No. 133. [EITF Issue No. 01-8, paragraphs B18–B20]
9   Adapted from EITF Issue No. 01-8, Exhibit 01-8A, Example 2

4.2.2 SPECIFIED PROPERTY, PLANT, OR EQUIPMENT   FASB Statement No. 13 applies to contracts that convey the use of *specified* property, plant, or equipment. Paragraph 9 of EITF Issue No. 01-8 explains:

> Property, plant, or equipment, as used in Statement 13, includes only land and/or depreciable assets. Therefore, inventory (including equipment parts inventory) and minerals, precious metals, or other natural resources cannot be the subject of a lease for accounting purposes because those assets are not depreciable. Additionally, intangibles (for example, motion picture film licensing rights or workforce) and rights to explore for minerals, precious metals, or other natural resources are not depreciable assets (they are amortized or depleted) so they may not be the subject of a lease.

A contract that conveys the right to use property, plant, or equipment is not necessarily a lease, if the lessor has the choice of which property, plant, or equipment to use to fulfill its contractual obligations. The determination of whether *specified* property, plant, or equipment has to be used to fulfill the contractual obligations is not an issue in a typical lease arrangement, such as the lease of a building. However, in arrangements that provide for the delivery of products, such as take-or-pay contracts, that determination often requires an in-depth analysis. The identification of the property in the arrangement need not be explicit; it may be implicit. The following example is provided in EITF Issue No. 01-8:[10]

> . . . in the case of a power purchase contract, if the seller of the power is an SPE that owns a single power plant, that power plant is implicitly specified in the contract because it is unlikely that the SPE could obtain replacement power to fulfill its obligations under the contract because an SPE generally has limited capital resources. Similarly, in the case of a throughput contract, the seller may have only a single pipeline and the prospect of obtaining access to a second pipeline may not be economically feasible. In that case, the seller's pipeline is implicitly specified in the contract.

> EXAMPLE—SPECIFIED PROPERTY, PLANT, OR EQUIPMENT[11]
>
> PurePower Inc. (P), a producer of silicon wafers, enters into an arrangement with a third party to supply a minimum quantity of specialty gas needed in its production process for a specified period of time. The supplier designs and constructs a facility adjacent to P's plant to produce the needed gas.
>
> Although the facility is explicitly identified in the arrangement, the supplier has the contractual right to supply gas from other sources. However, supplying gas from other sources is not economically feasible or practicable.
>
> Does the facility constitute specified property, plant, or equipment?
>
> Yes. Property, plant, or equipment (the facility) is explicitly identified in the arrangement, and fulfillment of the arrangement is dependent on the facility. While the supplier has the right to supply gas from other sources, its ability to do so is nonsubstantive.

---

10   EITF Issue No. 01-8, paragraph B9
11   Adapted from EITF Issue No. 01-8, Exhibit 01-8A, Example 1

4.2.3 STATED PERIOD OF TIME   Rights to use specified property are leases if they convey the right to use the property, plant, or equipment for a stated period of time. A contract that conveys the right to use property, plant, or equipment is within the scope of FASB Statement No.13, even if no period of time is explicitly stated in the contract if the terms of the contract specify another measure of use, such as number of units produced.[12]

However, if a contract conveys the right to use property for an indefinite period, such as an easement, the arrangement is not within the scope of Statement 13.

4.2.4 REASSESSMENT OF THE ARRANGEMENT   The determination of whether an arrangement conveys the right to use specified property, plant, or equipment (that is, whether it is within the scope of FASB Statement No. 13) is made at the inception of the arrangement. A reassessment has to be made (and can only be made) in the following four circumstances:[13]

- Change in contractual terms[14]
- Exercise of a renewal option, or extension of the term of the arrangement
- Change in the determination as to whether or not fulfillment is dependent on specified property, plant, or equipment
- Substantial physical change to the specified property, plant, or equipment

That reassessment is made (and would impact the accounting) on a prospective basis.

Example—Reassessment of Arrangement

PurePower Inc. (P) enters into a power purchase arrangement for a period of 10 years, with an option to renew the power purchase arrangement for an additional term of 10 years. Based on the guidance in EITF Issue No. 01-8, it is determined that the arrangement conveys the right to use specified property, plant, and equipment; that is, the arrangement meets the definition of a lease. The terms of the lease provide for a significant penalty if P does not renew the lease after the 10-year base term, such that it is deemed reasonably assured at the inception of the lease that the renewal option will be exercised. Accordingly, the lease term is determined to be 20 years.
 	
    Would the exercise of the renewal option trigger a reassessment of whether or not the arrangement contains a lease?
 	
    No. The lease term (as determined at the inception of the lease) includes the term under the renewal option; the exercise of that renewal option does not trigger a reassessment.

---

12   EITF Issue No. 01-8, paragraph B10
13   EITF Issue No. 01-8, paragraph 13
14   Other than extensions and renewals [EITF Issue No. 01-8, paragraph 13(a)]

EXERCISE OF A RENEWAL OPTION OR EXTENSION OF THE TERM OF THE ARRANGEMENT[15]
A renewal or extension of the term of the arrangement that does not include a modification of other terms of the arrangement triggers a reassessment of the arrangement, with the following exception: The exercise of a renewal option that was included in the lease term at the inception of the arrangement is not considered a renewal for the purpose of reassessing the arrangement.

A reassessment may impact the accounting for the renewal or extension period; the accounting for the remaining period of the original arrangement is not impacted.

CHANGE IN THE DETERMINATION AS TO WHETHER FULFILLMENT IS DEPENDENT ON SPECIFIED PROPERTY, PLANT, OR EQUIPMENT
EITF Issue No. 01-8 provides the following example for a change in the determination as to whether fulfillment is dependent on specified property, plant, or equipment:[16]

> . . . if an arrangement was initially determined to include a lease because . . . fulfillment of the arrangement was initially dependent upon specific property, plant, or equipment and an event or events occurred subsequent to the inception of the arrangement such that fulfillment was no longer dependent upon the specific property, plant, or equipment (for example, an active market for the product develops subsequent to inception of the arrangement), the arrangement would be reassessed to determine if the arrangement contains a lease as of the date that the arrangement is no longer dependent upon specific property, plant, or equipment.

Another example would be a supplier that has one facility and decides to build a second facility to increase its production capacity; in that situation, the

---

EXAMPLE—SUBSTANTIAL PHYSICAL CHANGE TO SPECIFIED PROPERTY, PLANT, OR EQUIPMENT[17]

PurePower Inc. enters into a contract for the purchase of power from a specified power plant, PowerMine. The owner of PowerMine intends to increase power production by 100% and considers the two alternatives: (1) increase the capacity of PowerMine, or (2) build a second plant on adjacent land.

Would (1) the increase in the capacity of PowerMine or (2) the construction of a second plant constitute a substantial physical change to specified property, plant, or equipment?

The contractual arrangements specify that the power has to be delivered from PowerMine, that is, PowerMine constitutes specified property, plant, or equipment. An increase in the capacity of PowerMine is a substantial change to the specified property, plant, or equipment. Constructing a second plant on adjacent land would not constitute a change to that specified property, plant, or equipment.

---

15   EITF Issue No. 01-8, paragraph 13(b)
16   EITF Issue No. 01-8, paragraph 13(c)
17   Adapted from EITF Issue No. 01-8, paragraph 13(d)

fulfillment of the supplier's obligations to provide certain products may no longer be dependent on the first facility.

SUBSTANTIAL PHYSICAL CHANGE TO THE SPECIFIED PROPERTY, PLANT, OR EQUIPMENT
A substantial physical change to the specified property, plant, or equipment may also lead to a reassessment event as to whether the contract contains a lease, depending on the facts and circumstances.

4.3   LEASE CLASSIFICATION—GENERAL

The classification of leases involving real estate builds upon the general lease classification criteria established by Statement 13 for all leases.

The lease classification criteria are generally applied on an asset-by-asset basis, with functionally interdependent equipment (such as computer desktop, monitor, and keyboard) being considered one asset. Statement 13 does not provide for the application of the lease classification criteria to groups of assets.

The classification of a lease is determined at lease inception (which is the date of the lease agreement or commitment, if earlier)[18] and not at the beginning of the lease term. For accounting purposes, the beginning of the lease term is the date the lessee takes physical possession of the leased asset, which does not necessarily coincide with the beginning of the lease term stated in the lease agreement (see Exhibit 4.2).

4.3.1   LEASE CLASSIFICATION—LESSEE   From the perspective of the lessee, a lease is classified as either:

- Capital lease
- Operating lease

A lease that transfers substantially all of the benefits and risks of ownership is accounted for as the acquisition of an asset and the incurrence of an obligation by the lessee (capital lease). All other leases are accounted for as operating leases,

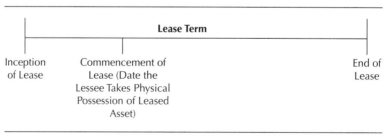

EXHIBIT 4.2   LEASE TERM

---

18   The term "inception of the lease" is defined as the date of the lease agreement or commitment, if earlier. That commitment must be in writing, signed by the parties in interest to the transaction, and must be specific as to the principal provisions of the transaction. If any of the principal provisions are yet to be negotiated, such a preliminary agreement or commitment does not qualify for purposes of this definition. [FAS 13, paragraph 5(b)]

that is, the rental of property. FASB Statement No. 13 contains certain bright lines that establish when a lease is deemed to have transferred substantially all of the benefits and risks of ownership. If a particular lease meets any one of the following criteria,[19] it is classified as a capital lease:

OVERVIEW—LEASE CLASSIFICATION CRITERIA (LESSEE)
1. The lease *transfers ownership* of the property to the lessee by the end of the lease term.
2. The lease contains a *bargain purchase option* for the purchase of the leased property.
3. The *lease term* is equal to or greater than 75% of the estimated economic life of the leased property ("75% of economic life test"). However, if the beginning of the lease term falls within the last 25% of the total estimated economic life of the leased property, this criterion is not used for purposes of lease classification.
4. The *present value of the minimum lease payments* equals or exceeds 90% of the fair value of the leased property[20] ("90% of fair value test"). However, if the beginning of the lease term falls within the last 25% of the total estimated economic life of the leased property, this criterion does not apply.

Minimum lease payments are the payments that the lessee is obligated to make or can be required to make in connection with the leased property.[21] For purposes of computing the present value of rental and other minimum lease payments, a lessee should use its incremental borrowing rate,[22] unless the following two conditions apply:

- It is practicable for the lessee to learn the implicit rate computed by the lessor.
- The implicit rate computed by the lessor is *lower* than the lessee's incremental borrowing rate.[23]

If the lessee has knowledge about the implicit rate computed by the lessor, and the lessor's rate is lower than the lessee's incremental borrowing rate, the lessor's implicit borrowing rate is used. Using the lower implicit rate of the lessor rather than the lessee's incremental borrowing rate results in a higher amount of present value of minimum lease payments; it increases the likelihood that the 90% of fair value test leads to capital lease classification.

---

19   FAS 13, paragraph 7

20   If investment tax credits are retained by the lessor: The threshold for meeting this criterion is 90% of the fair value of the leased property less any investment tax credits expected to be realized by the lessor. [FAS 13, paragraph 7(d)]

21   FAS 13, paragraph 5(j)

22   Incremental borrowing rate is the rate that the lessee would have incurred to borrow over a similar term the funds necessary to purchase the leased asset. A lessee is not proscribed from using its secured borrowing rate as its incremental rate if that rate is determinable, reasonable, and consistent with the financing that would have been used in the particular circumstance. [FAS 13, paragraph 5(l); FTB 79-12]

23   FAS 13, paragraph 7(d)

If none of the four criteria listed in the overview is met, the lease is classi-fied as an operating lease by the lessee. Often, lease agreements are purposefully structured around these thresholds established by paragraph 7 of Statement 13 to achieve a certain lease classification—generally, operating lease classification—and corresponding accounting treatment.

4.3.2 LEASE CLASSIFICATION—LESSOR   From the lessor's perspective, a lease is classified as one of the following:

- Sales-type lease
- Direct financing lease
- Leveraged lease
- Operating lease

Leases that transfer substantially all of the benefits and risks of ownership are classified as sales-type leases if the lease gives rise to a manufacturer's or deal-er's profit, or as direct financing or leveraged lease if the lease does not give rise to a manufacturer's or dealer's profit. Other leases are accounted for as operating leases, that is, the rental of property. A lessor does not have to be a dealer to real-ize a "dealer's" profit (or loss) on a transaction. For example, if a lessor leases an asset that at the inception of the lease has a fair value that is greater or less than its carrying amount, such transaction may be a sales-type lease, assuming the other criteria for a sales-type lease are met.[24]

Leases are classified as sales-type, direct financing, or leveraged leases if they meet one or more of the criteria for capital leases for lessees (Lease Classification Criteria (Lessee) 1. through 4.) and *both* of the following criteria:[25]

Overview—Additional Lease Classification Criteria (Lessor)
- Collectibility of the minimum lease payments is reasonably predictable. - There are no important uncertainties relating to the amount of unreimbursable costs yet to be incurred by the lessor under the lease.

For purposes of computing the present value of rental and other minimum lease payments, a lessor should use the interest rate implicit in the lease.[26]

---

24   FAS 13, paragraph 6; special rules apply for extensions and renewals, see section 4.6.1.2
25   FAS 13, paragraph 8
26   FAS 13, paragraph 7(d): The interest rate implicit in the lease is defined as follows: The discount rate that, when applied to (i) the minimum lease payments (as defined in paragraph 5(j)), excluding that portion of the payments representing executory costs to be paid by the lessor, together with any profit thereon, and (ii) the unguaranteed residual value (as defined in paragraph 5(i)) accruing to the benefit of the lessor [footnote omitted], causes the aggregate present value at the beginning of the lease term to be equal to the fair value of the leased property (as defined in paragraph 5(c)) to the lessor at the inception of the lease, minus any investment tax credit retained by the lessor and expected to be realized by him. [FAS 13, paragraph 5(k)]

A *leveraged lease* is a direct financing lease that additionally has all of the following characteristics:[27]

- It involves at least three parties: a lessee, a long-term creditor, and a lessor.
- The financing provided by the long-term creditor is substantial to the transaction and is nonrecourse to the lessor.
- The lessor's net investment[28] declines during the early years and increases during the later years of the lease term.

Appendix E of FASB Statement No. 13 includes illustrations of accounting for leveraged leases.

4.3.3 LEASE CLASSIFICATION CRITERIA   As discussed in Section 4.3.1, the classification of leases is based on the following four criteria:[29]

1. Transfer of ownership
2. Bargain purchase option
3. 75% of economic life test
4. 90% of fair value test

If any one of these criteria is met, a lease meets the definition of a capital lease and is capitalized by the lessee. The period over which the leased asset is amortized depends on the lease classification criterion that resulted in the classification as capital lease. If the lease is classified as capital lease, because of transfer of ownership or bargain purchase option, the leased asset is amortized over the estimated useful life of the leased asset.[30] If the lease qualifies as a capital lease because it meets either the 75% of economic life test or the 90% of fair value test (or both of these criteria) at the inception of the lease, the asset is amortized over the lease term.[31]

4.3.3.1 Transfer of Ownership   FASB Statement No. 13 provides that a lease that transfers ownership of the property at the end of the lease is classified as a capital lease by the lessee. The "transfer of ownership" criterion is also met in situations in which the lease agreement provides for the transfer of title at or shortly after the end of the lease term in exchange for the payment of a nominal fee, such as the minimum fee required by statutory regulation to transfer ownership.[32]

However, if the terms of the lease specify that ownership of the leased asset is *not* transferred if the lessee *elects not to* pay a specified fee, the criterion of transfer of ownership would not be considered met.[33]

---

27   FAS 13, paragraph 42
28   Paragraph 43 of FASB Statement No. 13 defines the term "net investment" for purposes of leveraged lease classification.
29   Additionally, lessors need to consider whether collectibility of the minimum lease payments is reasonably predictable and whether there are uncertainties regarding the amount of unreimbursable costs that will be incurred by the lessor under the lease. [FAS 13, paragraph 8(a) and (b)]
30   FAS 13, paragraph 11(a)
31   FAS 13, paragraph 11(b)
32   FAS 13, paragraph 7(a)
33   EITF Issue No. 00-11, paragraph 5

4.3.3.2 Bargain Purchase Option   When is an option a bargain purchase option?

Paragraph 5(d) defines a bargain purchase option as a "provision allowing the lessee, at his option, to purchase the leased property for a price which is sufficiently lower than the expected fair value of the property at the date the option becomes exercisable that exercise of the option appears, at the inception of the lease, reasonably assured." The estimated fair value of the leased property at the date the bargain purchase option becomes exercisable is based on price levels and market conditions at the inception of the lease and does not include the impact of inflation. When determining whether or not the exercise of a purchase option is reasonably assured, one would consider, for example:

- *Time from lease inception to the date the option becomes exercisable.* The longer the time period, the more difficult it generally is to conclude that the exercise of the option is reasonably assured.
- *Type of asset.* The fair value of leased personal property, such as vehicles or computer equipment, is generally expected to decline more than the fair value of real estate.
- *Existence of any penalty provisions in the lease* that are triggered if the purchase option is not exercised.

Purchase options that are reasonably assured of exercise for factors *other than price* (or penalty provisions in the lease agreement) are also considered bargain purchase options; in certain situations, a lessee may incur costs or economic penalties[34] in such amount that the exercise of the purchase option appears reasonably assured at the inception of the lease. That is, an economic disincentive may create a bargain purchase option.

The following are illustrative factors to be considered in the evaluation whether a bargain purchase option exists:

- Costs to relocate to another location when a company leases its headquarters or manufacturing facilities
- Location of the property and availability of replacement property
- Value of leasehold improvements at the time the option becomes exercisable
- Exercise price of option if at other than fair value

---

34   The term "penalty" has been defined rather broadly in FASB Statement No. 13 as: Any requirement that is imposed or can be imposed on the lessee by the lease agreement or by factors outside the lease agreement to disburse cash, incur or assume a liability, perform services, surrender or transfer an asset or rights to an asset or otherwise forego an economic benefit, or suffer an economic detriment. Factors to consider when determining if an economic detriment may be incurred include, but are not limited to, the uniqueness of purpose or location of the property, the availability of a comparable replacement property, the relative importance or significance of the property to the continuation of the lessee's line of business or service to its customers, the existence of leasehold improvements or other assets whose value would be impaired by the lessee vacating or discontinuing use of the leased property, adverse tax consequences, and the ability or willingness of the lessee to bear the cost associated with relocation or replacement of the leased property at market rental rates or to tolerate other parties using the property. [FAS 13, paragraph 5(o)]

Statement 13 does not provide any specific criteria to be considered in making the evaluation whether economic penalties are present that make the exercise of a purchase option reasonably assured; that evaluation depends on the facts and circumstances and is subject to significant judgment.

4.3.3.3 Lease Term   Determining the appropriate "lease term" is critical for arriving at the appropriate lease classification, since the lease term impacts the assessment under the 75% of economic life test (paragraph 7(c) of Statement 13), as well as the 90% of fair value test (paragraph 7(d) of Statement 13).

The lease term is comprised of the following:[35]

- Fixed noncancelable term of the lease. A lease that is cancelable only upon the occurrence of some remote contingency, only with the permission of the lessor, only if the lessee enters into a new lease with the same lessor, or only if the lessee incurs a penalty in such amount that continuation of the lease appears reasonably assured is considered noncancelable.[36] If a fiscal funding clause is present in a lease with a governmental unit, and the likelihood of exercise of that clause is not assessed as being remote, the lease is considered cancelable. A fiscal funding clause generally provides that the lease is cancelable if the funding authority does not appropriate the funds necessary for the governmental unit to fulfill its obligations under the lease agreement.[37]
- All periods covered by bargain renewal options. A bargain renewal option is a provision allowing the lessee to renew the lease for rentals sufficiently lower than the fair rental of the property at the date the option becomes exercisable so that exercise of the option appears to be reasonably assured at lease inception.[38] That evaluation is, like the evaluation of a bargain purchase option discussed in Section 4.3.3.2, dependent on the facts and circumstances of the arrangement, and requires significant judgment.
- All periods for which failure to renew imposes a penalty on the lessee in such amount that a renewal appears reasonably assured at the inception of the lease. The term "penalty" is defined very broadly and encompasses not only any payments due to the lessor or third parties, but any economic detriment suffered by the lessee if a lease renewal option is not exercised. A penalty includes:[39]
  - Any requirement that is imposed or can be imposed on the lessee by the lease agreement to:
    - ◊ Disburse cash
    - ◊ Incur or assume a liability

---

35   FAS 13, paragraph 5(f)
36   FAS 13, paragraph 5(f)
37   FTB 79-10
38   FAS 13, paragraph 5(e)
39   FAS 13, paragraph 5(o)

◇ Perform services
◇ Surrender or transfer an asset or rights to an asset
◇ Otherwise forgo an economic benefit
◇ Suffer an economic detriment

- Factors to consider when determining whether an economic detriment may be incurred include, but are not limited to:
  ◇ The uniqueness of purpose or location of the property
  ◇ The availability of a comparable replacement property
  ◇ The relative importance or significance of the property to the continuation of the lessee's line of business or service to its customers
  ◇ The existence of leasehold improvements or other assets whose value would be impaired by the lessee vacating or discontinuing use of the leased property
  ◇ Adverse tax consequences
  ◇ The ability or willingness of the lessee to bear the cost associated with relocation or replacement of the leased property at market rental rates or to tolerate other parties using the leased property

- All periods covered by ordinary renewal options during which a guarantee by the lessee of the lessor's debt directly or indirectly related to the leased property is expected to be in effect
- All periods during which a loan from the lessee to the lessor directly or indirectly related to the leased property is expected to be outstanding
- All periods covered by ordinary renewal options preceding the date as of which a bargain purchase option is exercisable
- All periods representing renewals or extensions of the lease at the lessor's option

Notwithstanding the above, the lease term would never extend beyond the date a bargain purchase option becomes exercisable.

4.3.3.4 Minimum Lease Payments   The components of the minimum lease payments differ depending on whether they are being evaluated from the lessor's or the lessee's perspective.

MINIMUM LEASE PAYMENTS: LESSEE'S PERSPECTIVE
Minimum lease payments are payments the lessee is obligated to make or can be required to make in connection with the leased property (see Exhibit 4.3).[40] They include the minimum rental payments, any guarantee of residual value by the lessee, and any payments the lessee can be required to make upon failure to

---

COMPONENTS OF MINIMUM LEASE PAYMENTS: LESSEE'S PERSPECTIVE

Minimum rental payments
Plus: Residual value guarantee
Plus: Penalties for failure to renew the lease
Plus: Payment for exercise of bargain purchase option
Plus: Other payments the lessee can be required to make[1]
Minimum Lease Payments

---

[1]Other than executory costs and profit thereon

renew or extend the lease term. If the lease includes a bargain purchase option, the amount required to be paid under the bargain purchase option is also included in the minimum lease payments. Minimum lease payments exclude any unguaranteed residual value; the portion of the lease payments representing executory costs such as insurance, maintenance, and taxes to be paid by the lessor; and any profit thereon. If the portion of the minimum lease payments representing executory costs, including profit thereon, is not determinable from the provisions of the lease, the amount is estimated.

MINIMUM LEASE PAYMENTS: LESSOR'S PERSPECTIVE

When evaluated from the lessor's perspective, minimum lease payments include, aside from the components described from the lessee's perspective, any guarantee of the residual value or of rental payments beyond the lease term by a party that is unrelated to either lessee or lessor, if that third party is deemed financially capable of performing under that guarantee.[41]

DISCOUNT RATE TO BE USED

FASB Statement No. 13 prescribes the following discount rates to be used when computing the present value of the minimum lease payments:[42]

- A lessee should use its incremental borrowing rate, unless it is practicable for the lessee to learn the implicit rate computed by the lessor and the implicit rate computed by the lessor is lower than the lessee's incremental borrowing rate.
- A lessor should use the interest rate implicit in the lease, which is the discount rate that causes the present value of the lessor's minimum lease payments to equal the fair value of the leased property at the inception of the lease.[43]

The following two examples depict some common provisions in leases and their impact on the calculation of minimum lease payments.

---

41   FAS 13, paragraph 5(j)(ii)
42   FAS 13, paragraph 7(d)
43   The interest rate implicit in the lease is defined in FASB Statement No. 13, paragraph 5(k).

EXAMPLE—PENALTY FOR FAILURE NOT TO RENEW

I-Rentco (R) leases a facility for a period of 20 years. The lease imposes a penalty of $1 million if, at the termination of the original lease term, the lease is not renewed for a period of 10 years.

As a result of the penalty, R considers the renewal of the lease reasonably assured.

Questions
1. What is the lease term?
2. Is the penalty payment of $1 million included in minimum lease payments?

Answers
1. The lease term is 30 years, as the renewal of the lease is reasonably assured.
2. No. As the renewal of the lease is reasonably assured, rentals over the 30-year lease term are included in, and the penalty is excluded from, minimum lease payments.[44]

[Note: If the renewal of the lease were not reasonably assured, the lease term would be 20 years, and the amount of the penalty payment of $1 million would be included when calculating minimum lease payments.]

EXAMPLE—DEFAULT PROVISION WITH PENALTY[45]

A lease agreement between Lazy-Pay and a lessor contains a default provision that imposes a penalty on Lazy-Pay, if Lazy-Pay fails to meet certain financial ratios. Based on Lazy-Pay's financial condition at the inception of the lease, it is not reasonable to assume that the event of default will not occur.

Does the penalty have to be included in the amount of minimum lease payments for purposes of lease classification?[46]

Yes, the maximum amount that Lazy-Pay could be required to pay under the default covenant needs to be included in minimum lease payments for purposes of lease classification.

4.4 LEASE CLASSIFICATION—LEASES INVOLVING REAL ESTATE

Leases involving real estate are categorized based on the general lease classification criteria for leases as:

- Operating lease or capital lease by the lessee
- Operating lease, sales-type lease, direct financing lease, or leveraged lease by the lessor

For a lease involving real estate with a fair value different from its carrying amount, the lease is classified as a sales-type lease only if the lease transfers ownership of the property to the lessee by the end of the lease term. Otherwise, such lease is classified as operating lease.

---

44   FAS 13, paragraph 5(j)(i)(c)
45   See EITF Issue No. 97-1, Question 2
46   Note that although the amount of potential penalty is considered a minimum lease payment for purposes of lease classification, it would not be accrued over the term of the lease.

Leases involving real estate can be divided into four categories:[47]

- Leases involving land only
- Leases involving land and building
- Leases involving equipment as well as real estate
- Leases involving only part of a building

Additionally, special accounting rules apply to leases involving facilities owned by governmental units.[48]

4.4.1 LEASES INVOLVING LAND ONLY

4.4.1.1 Leases Involving Land Only: Lease Classification—Lessee
If land is the sole item of property leased, and either of the following criteria are met:

- Transfer of title (criterion 1.)
- Bargain purchase option (criterion 2.)

the lessee accounts for the lease as a capital lease, otherwise as an operating lease. Criteria 3. (75% of economic life test) and 4. (90% of fair value test) are not applicable to land leases.

4.4.1.2 Leases Involving Land Only: Lease Classification—Lessor
TRANSFER OF TITLE[49]
If land is the sole item of property leased and the criterion of transfer of title is met, the lessor classifies the lease as a *sales-type lease* for property whose fair value at the inception of the lease is greater or less than its carrying amount.

If the criterion of transfer of title is met for property whose fair value at the inception of the lease is equal to its carrying amount, the lessor accounts for the lease either as a *direct financing lease* or as a *leveraged lease*, if both of the following criteria are met:

- Collectibility of the minimum lease payments is reasonably predictable.
- No important uncertainties surround the amount of unreimbursable costs yet to be incurred by the lessor under the lease.

If the lease does not meet both of these criteria, the lessor accounts for the lease as an operating lease.

BARGAIN PURCHASE OPTION
Land for which the fair value does not equal its carrying amount is always classified as an operating lease by the lessor, unless the lease provides for a transfer of title.

---

47   FAS 13, paragraph 24
48   FAS 13, paragraph 28; see Section 4.4.4.1 for further discussion
49   FAS 13, paragraph 25

Land with fair value equal to its carrying amount, for which the lease agreement contains a bargain purchase option, is classified as a *direct financing lease* or as a *leveraged lease*, if both of the following criteria are met:

- Collectibility of the minimum lease payments is reasonably predictable.
- No important uncertainties surround the amount of unreimbursable costs to be incurred by the lessor under the lease.

If the lease does not meet these two criteria, the lessor accounts for the lease as an operating lease.[50]

CRITERIA 3. AND 4.
Criteria 3. and 4. (75% of economic life test; 90% of fair value test) are not applicable to land leases.[51]

4.4.2 LEASES INVOLVING LAND AND BUILDING
4.4.2.1 Leases Involving Land and Building: Lease Classification—Lessee
TRANSFER OF TITLE OR BARGAIN PURCHASE OPTION
If a lease involves land and building, and either of the following criteria are met:

- Transfer of title (criterion 1.)
- Bargain purchase option (criterion 2.)

the lessee accounts for the lease as a capital lease.

If the lease is classified as a capital lease, land and building are capitalized separately by the lessee. The present value of the minimum lease payments (after deducting executory costs and any profit thereon) is allocated between land and building in proportion to their fair values at the inception of the lease.[52] The building is amortized consistent with the lessee's normal depreciation policy for owned assets.[53]

75% OF ECONOMIC LIFE TEST AND 90% OF FAIR VALUE TEST
If the lease does not transfer title to the real property and does not contain a bargain purchase option, the lessee has to determine the fair value of the land as compared to the fair value of the real estate property leased. If the fair value of the land is less than 25% of the fair value of the leased property, land and building are considered a single unit for purposes of applying criteria 3. and 4. (75% of economic life test; 90% of fair value test).

---

50   FAS 13, paragraph 25
51   FAS 13, paragraph 25
52   If the lease agreement or commitment, if earlier, includes a provision to escalate minimum lease payments for increases in construction or acquisition cost of the leased property or for increases in some other measure of cost or value, such as general price levels, during the construction or preacquisition period, the effect of any increases that have occurred is taken into consideration when determining the "fair value of the leased property at the inception of the lease." [FAS 13, paragraph 26(a)(i), footnote 22a]
53   Land capitalized under a lease that transfers title or contains a bargain purchase option is generally not amortized. [FAS 13, paragraph 26(a)(i)]

FAIR VALUE OF LAND IS LESS THAN 25% OF THE FAIR VALUE OF LEASED PROPERTY
For a lease of land and building that does not transfer title and does not contain a
bargain purchase option, with the fair value of the land being less than 25% of the
total fair value of the leased property at the inception of the lease, the following
rules apply:

If either criterion 3. (75% of economic life test) or 4. (90% of fair value test)
is met, the lessee capitalizes land and building as a single unit and amortizes that
unit consistently with the lessee's normal depreciation policy for buildings, except
that the period of amortization is the lease term. The leased asset is amortized to
its expected value to the lessee at the end of the lease term. For example, if the
lessee guarantees a residual value at the end of the lease term and has no interest
in any excess that may be realized, the expected value of the leased property to
the lessee is the amount that can be realized by the lessee from the leased property
at the end of the lease term, up to the amount of the residual value guarantee.[54]

If the lease meets neither the 75% of useful life test nor the 90% of fair
value test, land and building are accounted for as a single operating lease.[55]

FAIR VALUE OF LAND EQUALS OR EXCEEDS 25% OF THE FAIR VALUE OF LEASED PROPERTY[56]
For a lease of land and building that does not transfer title and does not contain a
bargain purchase option, land and building are considered separately for purposes
of applying the 75% of economic life test and the 90% of fair value test, if the
fair value of the land equals or exceeds 25% of the total fair value of the leased
property at the inception of the lease. The minimum lease payments (after deducting executory costs including any profit thereon) applicable to the land and the
building are separated by determining the fair value of the land and applying
the lessee's incremental borrowing rate to it to determine the annual minimum
lease payments applicable to the land element. The remaining minimum lease
payments are attributed to the building element.

If the building element of the lease meets the 75% of economic life test or
the 90% of fair value test, the building element is accounted for as a capital lease
and amortized consistently with the lessee's normal depreciation policy, except
that the period of amortization is the lease term rather than the useful life of the
building. The building is amortized to its expected value to the lessee at the end
of the lease term, up to the amount of a residual value guarantee.

The land element of the lease is accounted for separately as an operating
lease.

If the building element of the lease meets neither the 75% of economic life
test nor the 90% of fair value test, both the building element and the land element
are accounted for as a single operating lease.

---

54   FAS 13, paragraph 11(b)
55   FAS 13, paragraph 26(b)(i)(a)
56   FAS 13, paragraph 26(b)(ii)(a)

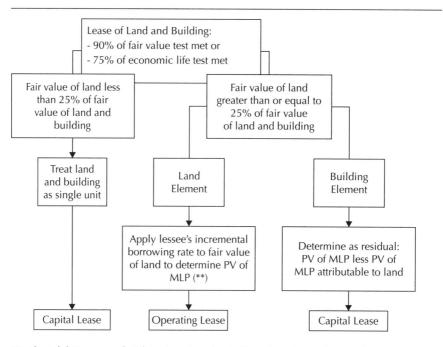

(*)   The Exhibit assumes that there is no transfer of title or bargain purchase option.
(**) MLP = Minimum lease payments.

Exhibit 4.3   Leases Involving Land and Building: Lease Classification—Lessee (*)

Exhibit 4.3 illustrates the lease classification for leases involving land and building from the perspective of the lessee.

4.4.2.2 Leases Involving Land and Building: Lease Classification—Lessor
Transfer of Title[57]

If a lease that involves land and building transfers title at the end of the lease, and the fair value of the leased property at the inception of the lease is greater or less than its carrying amount, the lessor classifies the lease as a sales-type lease. The lessor accounts for the lease like an owner of land and buildings that sells real estate.

If the fair value of the leased property at the inception of the lease equals its carrying amount, the lessor classifies the lease as a direct financing lease or a leveraged lease, if both of the following two criteria are met:

- Collectibility of the minimum lease payments is reasonably predictable.
- No important uncertainties surround the amount of unreimbursable costs yet to be incurred by the lessor under the lease.

If the lease does not meet both of these criteria, the lessor accounts for the lease as an operating lease.

---

57   FAS 13, paragraph 26(a)(ii)

BARGAIN PURCHASE OPTION[58]

If a lease that involves land and building contains a bargain purchase option and the fair value of the leased property at the inception of the lease is greater or less than its carrying amount, the lessor classifies the lease as an operating lease. If the fair value of the leased property at the inception of the lease equals its carrying amount, the lessor classifies the lease as a direct financing lease or a leveraged lease[59] if both of the following two criteria are met:

- Collectibility of the minimum lease payments is reasonably predictable.
- No important uncertainties surround the amount of unreimbursable costs yet to be incurred by the lessor under the lease.

Otherwise, the lessor accounts for the lease as an operating lease.

75% OF ECONOMIC LIFE TEST AND 90% OF FAIR VALUE TEST

If the lease does not transfer title and does not contain a bargain purchase option, the accounting depends on the proportion of the fair value of the land as compared to the total value of the leased property.

FAIR VALUE OF LAND IS LESS THAN 25% OF THE FAIR VALUE OF LEASED PROPERTY[60]

If the fair value of the land is less than 25% of the total fair value of the leased property at the inception of the lease, and the lease neither transfers title nor contains a bargain purchase option, the lessor considers land and building as a single unit for purposes of applying criteria 3. and 4. (75% of economic life test and 90% of fair value test). For purposes of the 75% of economic life test, the estimated economic life of the building is considered to be the estimated economic life of the unit.

If the fair value of the leased property equals its cost or carrying amount,[61] and either criterion 3. or 4. *and* both of the following criteria are met:

- Collectibility of the minimum lease payments is reasonably predictable
- No important uncertainties surround the amount of unreimbursable costs yet to be incurred by the lessor under the lease

the lessor accounts for the lease as a single unit as a direct financing lease or a leveraged lease. Otherwise, the lease is accounted for as an operating lease.[62]

FAIR VALUE OF LAND EQUALS OR EXCEEDS 25% OF THE FAIR VALUE OF LEASED PROPERTY[63]

The lessor should consider land and building separately for purposes of applying the 75% of economic life test and the 90% of fair value test[64] if the fair value of

---

58   FAS 13, paragraph 26(a)(iii)
59   If fair value does not equal the carrying amount, the lease would be classified as operating lease.
60   FAS 13, paragraph 26(b)(i)
61   If fair value does not equal the carrying amount, the lease would be classified as operating lease.
62   FAS 13, paragraph 26(b)(i)(b)
63   FAS 13, paragraph 26(b)(ii)
64   The allocation of the minimum lease payments is based on the methodology outlined in section 4.4.2.1; the minimum lease payments (after deducting executory costs including any profits thereon) applicable to the land and building are separated by determining the fair value of the land and applying the lessee's

the land equals or exceeds 25% of the total fair value of the leased property at the inception of the lease and the lease does not either transfer title or contain a bargain purchase option.

The following rules apply for lease classification: If the building element of the lease with a fair value equal to its cost or carrying amount[65] meets either the 90% of fair value test or the 75% of economic life test *and* both of the following criteria:

- Collectibility of the minimum lease payments is reasonably predictable
- No important uncertainties surround the amount of unreimbursable costs yet to be incurred by the lessor under the lease

the building element is accounted for as a direct financing lease or a leveraged lease.[66]

The land element of the lease is accounted for separately as an operating lease.

Otherwise, both the building element and the land element are accounted for as a single operating lease.[67]

4.4.3 LEASES INVOLVING EQUIPMENT AS WELL AS REAL ESTATE   This Section refers to leases that involve equipment other than integral equipment. Integral equipment subject to a lease is considered real estate. In EITF Issue No. 00-13, *Determining Whether Equipment is "Integral Equipment" Subject to FASB Statements No. 66 and No. 98*, the Task Force addressed the issue of when equipment constitutes integral equipment. The Task Force reached a consensus that if the cost to remove the equipment plus the decrease in value[68] is in excess of 10% of the equipment's fair value, the equipment is considered "integral equipment." Section 5.2 of Chapter 5 includes an example relating to integral equipment.

If a lease involving real estate includes equipment that does not meet the criteria of integral equipment, the equipment lease is considered a lease separate from the lease of the land and building. Accordingly, the portion of the minimum lease payments applicable to the equipment element of the lease needs to be estimated. FASB Statement No. 13 does not specify any particular methodology to be used for that allocation.[69]

4.4.4 LEASES INVOLVING PART OF A BUILDING   When the leased property is part of a larger whole, the carrying amount of the leased portion or its fair value may not be objectively determinable, as for example, when an office or floor of a building is leased. The accounting for leases involving only part of a building

---

incremental borrowing rate to it to determine the annual minimum lease payments applicable to the land element. The remaining minimum lease payments are attributed to the building element.

65   If fair value does not equal the carrying amount, the lease would be classified as an operating lease.
66   FAS 13, paragraph 26(b)(ii)(b)
67   FAS 13, paragraph 26(b)(ii)(b)
68   At a minimum, the decease in the value of the equipment as a result of its removal is the estimated cost to ship and reinstall the equipment at a new site. [EITF Issue No. 00-13, paragraph 4]
69   FAS 13, paragraph 27

depends on whether the carrying amount and fair value of the leased property are objectively determinable.[70]

4.4.4.1 Leases Involving Part of a Building: Lease Classification—Lessee

FAIR VALUE OBJECTIVELY DETERMINABLE[71]

If the fair value of the leased property is objectively determinable, the lessee classifies and accounts for the lease according to the provisions for leases involving land and building.

FAIR VALUE NOT OBJECTIVELY DETERMINABLE[72]

If the fair value of the leased property is not objectively determinable, the lessee accounts for the lease as an operating lease, unless the 75% of economic life test is met, using the estimated economic life of the building in which the leased premises are located. If the 75% of economic life test is met, the leased property is capitalized as a single unit and amortized in a manner consistent with the lessee's normal depreciation policy, except that the period of amortization is the lease term. The asset is amortized to its expected value to the lessee at the end of the lease term.[73]

Leased Property Owned by Governmental Unit   Because of special provisions normally present in leases involving *terminal space* and other *airport facilities* owned by a governmental unit or authority,[74] the economic life of such facilities for purposes of classifying the lease is essentially indeterminate. Similarly, the concept of fair value is not applicable to leases of terminal space and other airport facilities. Since such leases do not provide for a transfer of ownership or a bargain purchase option, they are classified as operating leases. Paragraph 8 of FIN 23 provides that this "automatic" classification as an operating lease applies only if all of the following conditions are met:

- The leased property is owned by a governmental unit or authority.
- The leased property is part of a larger facility, such as an airport, operated by or on behalf of the lessor.
- The leased property is a permanent structure or a part of a permanent structure, such as a building, that normally could not be moved to a new location.
- The lessor, or in some cases a higher governmental authority, has the explicit right under the lease agreement or existing statutes or regulations applicable to the leased property to terminate the lease at any time during the lease term, such as by closing the facility containing the leased property or by taking possession of the facility.

---

70   FAS 13, paragraph 28
71   FAS 13, paragraph 28(a)
72   FAS 13, paragraph 28(a)(ii)
73   FAS 13, paragraph 11(b)
74   By virtue of its power to abandon a facility during the term of the lease, the governmental body can effectively control the lessee's continued use of the property for its intended purpose, thus making its economic life indeterminate. [FAS 13, paragraph 106]

- The lease neither transfers ownership of the leased property to the lessee nor allows the lessee to purchase or otherwise acquire ownership of the leased property.
- The leased property or equivalent property in the same service area cannot be purchased, nor can such property be leased from a nongovernmental unit or authority.

Leases of terminal space or other airport facilities that do not meet all of these criteria are classified in accordance with the real estate lease classification criteria in Statement 13.[75]

Leases of other facilities owned by a governmental unit or authority that grant essentially the same rights to the parties as in the lease of airport facilities are also classified as operating leases. Facilities at ports and bus terminals are examples of such leases.[76]

4.4.4.2 Leases Involving Part of a Building: Lease Classification—Lessor

CARRYING AMOUNT AND FAIR VALUE DETERMINABLE[77]

If the carrying amount and fair value of the leased property are objectively determinable, the lessor classifies and accounts for the lease according to the provisions of leases involving land and building.

CARRYING AMOUNT OR FAIR VALUE NOT OBJECTIVELY DETERMINABLE[78]

If either the carrying amount or the fair value of the leased property is not objectively determinable, the lessor accounts for the lease as an operating lease.

4.5 ACCOUNTING FOR LEASES

4.5.1 ACCOUNTING FOR LEASES—LESSEE   As outlined above, from the perspective of the lessee, a lease is classified as either of the following:

- Operating lease
- Capital lease

The accounting for operating leases and capital leases is as follows:

4.5.1.1 Operating Lease   Statement 13 provides that "rentals" under an operating lease are charged to expense on a straight-line basis over the lease term, unless another systematic and rational basis is more representative of the time pattern the leased property is physically employed.[79]

Section 4.6.5 discusses accounting considerations to be made when leases provide for scheduled rent increases or rent holidays.

---

75   FIN 23, paragraph 9
76   FAS 13, paragraph 28
77   FAS 13, paragraph 28
78   FAS 13, paragraph 28(b)
79   FAS 13, paragraph 15; FTB 85-3

4.5.1.2 Capital Lease   The lessee records a capital lease as an asset and a related lease obligation at an amount equal to (1) the present value of minimum lease payments over the lease term or (2) the fair value of the assets, if the fair value of the leased asset is lower than the present value of minimum lease payments.[80] Each minimum lease payment is allocated between a reduction of the lease obligation and interest expense in a manner that results in a constant periodic rate of interest on the remaining balance of the obligation.[81]

RESIDUAL VALUE GUARANTEES
Some lease agreements include residual value guarantees, that is, the lessee guarantees a certain value of the leased asset to the lessor at the end of the lease. The minimum lease payments are allocated between a reduction of the obligation and interest expense so that the balance of the lease obligation at the end of the lease term equals the amount of the residual value guarantee.[82] If the fair value of the asset at the end of the lease term is greater than or equal to the guaranteed residual amount, the lessee incurs no additional obligation. However, if the fair value of the leased asset is less than the guaranteed residual value, the lessee must make up the difference. The guaranteed residual value is often used as a tool to reduce the periodic payments by substituting periodic lease payments with a lump-sum residual value amount.

A residual value guarantee has to be taken into consideration when computing amortization to avoid a gain or loss at the end of the lease term: The leased asset is amortized to the lesser of its guaranteed residual value or expected residual value, unless the lessee benefits, if the fair value of the leased asset at the end of the lease term is greater than the guaranteed residual amount.[83] This results in a rational and systematic allocation of amortization expense over the lease term.

4.5.2 ACCOUNTING FOR LEASES—LESSOR   From the lessor's point of view, a lease can be classified as one of the following:

- Operating Lease
- Sales-Type Lease
- Direct Financing Lease
- Leveraged Lease.

The lessor accounts for these leases as follows:

4.5.2.1 Operating Lease   The property under lease remains on the lessor's books and is depreciated following the lessor's depreciation policy for that type of property.

---

80   FAS 13, paragraph 10
81   FAS 13, paragraph 12
82   FAS 13, paragraph 12
83   FAS 13, paragraph 11(b)

Rental payments received are recorded as rental revenues by the lessor on a straight-line basis over the lease term, unless another basis of systematic allocation is more representative of the time pattern over which the lessee has possession of or controls the physical use of the property.[84] Lessors are prohibited from taking into consideration factors such as the time value of money, anticipated inflation, or expected future revenues.[85] If any scheduled increase is due to additional property leased, the escalated rents should be considered rental expense or rental revenue attributable to the leased property and recognized in proportion to the additional leased property during the periods that the lessee has control over the use of the additional leased property.[86] The amount of rental expense or rental revenue attributed to the additional leased property should be proportionate to the relative fair value of the additional property as determined at the inception of the lease, in the applicable time periods during which the lessee controls its use.

Any initial direct costs incurred by the lessor in negotiating and consummating leasing transactions, such as commissions and legal fees, are amortized over the lease term; alternatively, these costs may be charged to expense as they are incurred if the effect is not materially different.[87]

A lease agreement may include incentives for the lessee to sign the lease, such as cash payments made to or on behalf of the lessee. Such incentives are considered reductions of rental revenue by the lessor, and recognized straight-line over the term of the lease.[88]

4.5.2.2 Sales-Type Leases

A sales-type lease generates two types of revenue for the lessor:

- Profit on the sale
- Interest earned on the lease receivable

At the beginning of a sales-type lease, the lessor generally records the following items on its books:[89]

1. *Gross investment in the lease (lease receivable).* The gross investment in the lease is computed as the minimum lease payments plus the unguaranteed residual value accruing to the benefit of the lessor.[90]

   The estimated residual value at the end of the lease has to be evaluated for impairment at least annually.[91]

---

84   FAS 13, paragraph 19(b)
85   FTB 85-3
86   FTB 88-1, Question 1
87   FAS 13, paragraph 19(c)
88   FTB 88-1, Question 2; see section 4.6.7 for further discussion of lease incentives in operating leases.
89   FAS 13, paragraph 17
90   The minimum lease payments include guaranteed residual value.
91   FAS 13, paragraph 17(d)

2. *Unearned income.* The difference between the gross investment in the lease and the present value of the gross investment in the lease (referred to as "net investment in the lease") is recorded as unearned income. The discount rate used to determine the net investment in the lease is the interest rate implicit in the lease. The unearned income is amortized to income over the lease term using the effective interest method. However, FASB Statement No. 13[92] allows for the use of other methods of income recognition if the results are not materially different.

3. *Sales price.* The present value of the minimum lease payments computed at the interest rate implicit in the lease represents the sales price.[93]

4. *Cost relating to sale.* The carrying amount of the leased property, plus any initial direct cost, less the present value of any unguaranteed residual value, computed at the interest rate implicit in the lease, is charged against income in the period the sale is recorded. For sales-type leases of real estate, sale and profit recognition is determined in accordance with the sale and profit recognition guidance for real estate. This leads to a deferral of profit until the criteria for the accrual method of accounting specified in FASB Statement No. 66 have been met. Particularly the provisions relating to adequate initial and continuing investments often preclude full profit recognition in the period of sale.

Exhibit 4.4 illustrates the elements of a sales-type lease.

Gross Investment	Minimum lease payments plus unguaranteed residual value
Net Investment	Present value of minimum lease payments plus present value of unguaranteed residual value
Unearned Income	Gross investment less net investment
Sales Price	Present value of minimum lease payments
Cost Relating to Sale	Cost or carrying amount of the leased asset plus initial direct cost less present value of unguaranteed residual value

EXHIBIT 4.4 ELEMENTS OF A SALES-TYPE LEASE[94]

4.5.2.3 Direct Financing Lease
The accounting for a direct financing lease is similar to the accounting for a sales-type lease. The primary difference is that under a direct financing lease, the lessor only records interest income; no profit is recognized from the sale of the asset.

At the beginning of the lease, the lessor records the following items on its books:

1. *Gross investment in the lease (lease receivable).* This is determined the same way as for a sales-type lease.

---

92   FAS 13, paragraph 17(b)
93   This assumes that the leased asset is inventory on the lessor's balance sheet. If the leased asset were classified as fixed asset, the lessor would record gain on sale, rather than sales and cost of goods sold.
94   FAS 13, paragraph 17

2. *Unearned income.* This is determined as the difference between the gross investment in the lease and the cost or carrying amount of the leased asset.

3. *Initial direct costs.* Initial direct costs are deferred and amortized over the lease term based on the effective interest method.[95]

Exhibit 4.5 illustrates the elements of a direct financing lease.

Gross Investment	Minimum lease payments plus unguaranteed residual value
Unearned Income	Gross investment less cost or carrying amount
Net Investment	Gross investment plus initial direct costs less unearned income

EXHIBIT 4.5   ELEMENTS OF A DIRECT FINANCING LEASE[96]

4.6 SPECIAL ACCOUNTING ISSUES

4.6.1 EXTENSIONS AND RENEWALS OF A LEASE   Generally, the extension of a lease beyond the expiration of its existing lease term (e.g., through the exercise of a lease renewal option) creates a new agreement, which is classified according to the lease classification criteria outlined in Sections 4.3 and 4.4 and accounted for accordingly.[97] The accounting rules established in FASB Statement No. 13 relating to extensions and renewals of leases are very specific; the accounting depends on a number of factors, including the type of lease and the existence of residual value guarantees. Therefore, when dealing with extensions or renewals, it is advisable to carefully consider the guidance provided by Statement 13. The following sections provide an overview over the rules, without attempting to cover all scenarios.

4.6.1.1 Accounting for Extensions and Renewals of a Lease—Lessee
EXISTING LEASE: OPERATING LEASE; NEW LEASE: CAPITAL LEASE
If the original lease is classified as operating lease and the new lease is classified as capital lease, the lessee should record an asset and lease obligation at the present value of the remaining minimum lease payments or the fair value of the leased asset, if lower, pursuant to paragraph 10 of Statement 13, which provides, in part:

> The lessee shall record a capital lease as an asset and an obligation at an amount equal to the present value at the beginning of the lease term of minimum lease payments during the lease term, . . . However, if the amount so determined exceeds the fair value of the leased property at the inception of the lease, the amount recorded as the asset and obligation shall be the fair value.

The change in lease classification is reflected on the books of the lessee at the time of lease extension or renewal. The term of the new lease includes the remaining term of the original lease plus the extension/renewal.

---

95   In a sales-type lease, initial direct costs are included in the cost relating to the sale. [See discussion in section 4.5.2.2.]
96   FAS 13, paragraph 18
97   FAS 13, paragraph 9

EXISTING LEASE: CAPITAL LEASE; NEW LEASE: OPERATING LEASE[98]

If the original lease is classified as an capital lease and the new lease is classified as operating lease, the existing lease continues to be accounted for as a capital lease until the end of its original term, and the renewal or extension is accounted for as an operating lease.[99]

EXISTING LEASE: CAPITAL LEASE; NEW LEASE: CAPITAL LEASE[100]

If both the original lease and the new lease meet the lease classification criteria for capital leases, the balance of the leased asset and lease obligation is adjusted by an amount equal to the difference between the present value of the future minimum lease payments under the new agreement and the present balance of the obligation, with no gain or loss being recognized. In computing the present value of the future minimum lease payments under the modified agreement, the rate of interest should be the same rate that was used initially to record the lease obligation.[101]

EXISTING LEASE: OPERATING LEASE; NEW LEASE: OPERATING LEASE

If the original lease is classified as an operating lease and the new lease is also classified as an operating lease, the remaining lease payments under the original operating lease and the lease payments over the extension or renewal period are straight-lined over the new lease term. Similarly, deferred rent credits on the lessee's balance sheet should also be recognized over the new lease term.

CAPITAL LEASE WITH RESIDUAL VALUE GUARANTEE OR PENALTY FOR FAILURE TO RENEW THE LEASE

In leases containing a residual value guarantee by the lessee or a penalty for failure to renew the lease at the end of the lease term, the balance of the obligation at the end of the lease term equals the amount of the guarantee or penalty at that date. In the event that a renewal of the lease, an extension of the lease term, or a new lease under which the lessee continues to lease the same property renders the guarantee or penalty inoperative, the asset and the obligation under the lease are adjusted by an amount equal to the difference between the present value of the future minimum lease payments under the revised agreement and the present balance of the obligation. The present value of the future minimum lease payments under the revised agreement is computed using the rate of interest used to record the lease initially.[102]

---

98   Special rules apply to capital leases with residual value guarantees or penalties for failure to renew the lease, as outlined later in this section.

99   FAS 13, paragraph 14(b)

100 Special rules apply to capital leases with residual value guarantees or penalties for failure to renew the lease, as outlined later in this section.

101 FAS 13, paragraph 14(a) and (b)

102 FAS 13, paragraph 12

4.6.1.2 Accounting for Extensions and Renewals of a Lease—Lessor

EXISTING LEASE: OPERATING LEASE; NEW LEASE: SALES-TYPE LEASE OR DIRECT
FINANCING LEASE

If, in a lease involving real estate, the original lease is classified as an operating lease and the new lease is classified as a sales-type lease,[103] the lessor has to consider the provisions in FASB Statement No. 66, *Accounting for Sales of Real Estate*,[104] in determining whether it is appropriate to remove the property from the books and recognize profit on the transaction. As the carrying amount of the leased asset at the time of extension or renewal of an operating lease generally does not equal its fair value, a change from operating lease classification to direct finance lease classification rarely ever occurs.[105]

EXISTING LEASE: SALES-TYPE OR DIRECT FINANCING LEASE; NEW LEASE:
OPERATING LEASE[106]

If the original lease is classified as sales-type lease or a direct financing lease, and the new lease is classified as an operating lease, the existing lease continues to be accounted for as a sales-type lease or direct financing lease under the existing agreement until the end of its original term, and the renewal or extension is accounted for as an operating lease.[107]

EXISTING LEASE: SALES-TYPE OR DIRECT FINANCING LEASE; NEW LEASE: SALES-TYPE LEASE

If a renewal or extension of an original sales-type or direct financing lease that occurs at or near the end[108] of the lease term of the existing lease meets the criteria for a sales-type lease, the renewal or extension is accounted for as a sales-type lease;[109] a renewal or extension of a sales-type lease or a direct financing lease that does not occur at or near the end of the existing lease term, but would ordinarily meet the criteria of a sales-type lease, is accounted for as a direct financing lease. Paragraph 6(b)(i) of Statement 13 provides with respect to the classification of sales-type leases: "A renewal or an extension of an existing sales-type or direct financing lease that otherwise qualifies as a sales-type lease shall be classified as a direct financing lease unless the renewal or extension occurs at or near the end of the original term specified in the existing lease, in which case it shall be classified as a sales-type lease."

---

103   For leases involving real estate, sales-type lease classification is appropriate only if title to the leased asset is transferred.

104   FAS 13, paragraph 17(a)

105   See FTB 88-1 for further discussion

106   Special rules apply to leases with residual value guarantees or penalties for failure to renew the lease.

107   FAS 13, paragraphs 17(f)(ii)(b) and 18(c)

108   A renewal or extension that occurs in the last few months of an existing lease is considered to have occurred at or near the end of the existing lease term. [FAS 13, paragraph 6(b)(i) footnote 9a]

109   FAS 13, paragraph 17(f)(ii)(c); paragraph 18(c)

EXISTING LEASE: SALES-TYPE OR DIRECT FINANCING LEASE; NEW LEASE:
DIRECT FINANCING LEASE

If the original lease is classified as a sales-type lease or direct financing lease, and the new lease is classified as a direct financing lease,[110] the balance of the minimum lease payments receivable and the estimated residual value are adjusted based on the provisions of the new lease, and the net adjustment is charged or credited to unearned income,[111] subject to the following restrictions:

- FASB Statement No. 13 prohibits an upward adjustment of residual value.[112]
- A decline in residual value that results from an other-than-temporary decline in value of the leased asset is recorded as a loss in the period, rather than deferred over the term of the lease.[113] Deferring a reduction in the estimated residual value of the leased asset is only appropriate in situations where such change is directly related to the changed provisions of the lease, such as a change due to normal wear and tear over the new lease term, or a change in residual value sharing provisions.

EXISTING LEASE: OPERATING LEASE; NEW LEASE: OPERATING LEASE

If the original lease is classified as an operating lease and the new lease is also classified as an operating lease, the remaining lease payments under the original operating lease and the lease payments over the extension or renewal period are straight-lined over the revised lease period.

SALES-TYPE LEASES AND DIRECT FINANCING LEASES WITH RESIDUAL VALUE GUARANTEE OR PENALTY FOR FAILURE TO RENEW THE LEASE

In leases containing a residual guarantee by the lessee or a penalty for failure to renew the lease at the end of the lease term, the balance of the obligation at the end of the lease term equals the amount of the guarantee or penalty at that date. In the event that a renewal of the lease, an extension of the lease term, or a new lease under which the lessee continues to lease the same property renders the guarantee or penalty inoperative, the asset and the obligation under the lease are adjusted for the changes resulting from the revised agreement,[114] and the net adjustment is charged or credited to unearned income.[115]

---

110   In direct financing leases, the carrying amount and fair value of the leased property are the same at the inception of the lease. An exception arises when an existing sales-type or direct financing lease is renewed or extended during the term of the existing lease. In such cases, the fact that the carrying amount of the property at the end of the original lease term is different from its fair value at that date does not preclude the classification of the renewal or extension as a direct financing lease. [FAS 13, paragraph 6(b)(ii)]

111   FAS 13, paragraph 17(f)(ii)(a); FAS 13, paragraph 17(f)(i); FAS 13, paragraph 18(c)

112   FAS 13, paragraph 17(f)(i); FAS 13, paragraph 17(d)

113   FAS 13, paragraph 17(d)

114   Except that no upward adjustment of the estimated residual value is permitted. [FAS 13, paragraph 17(d) and 17(e)]

115   FAS 13, paragraph 17(e); FAS 13, paragraph 18(c)

4.6.2 MODIFICATIONS TO THE PROVISIONS OF A LEASE   A change in the provisions of the lease, other than the renewal or extension of an existing lease, may or may not be considered a new agreement. Such modifications may result from adjusting contingent rentals, shortening the lease term, or adjusting minimum lease payments, for example. Generally, if modifications to the provisions of a lease are made in connection with the extension of the lease term, the rules for extensions and renewals are applicable.[116]

To evaluate whether a modification to the provisions of a lease, other than a lease extension or renewal is considered a new agreement, a determination needs to be made whether the provisions of the *revised_*lease would have resulted in a different lease classification had these terms been in effect at the inception of the lease.[117] If the provisions of the revised lease would *not* have resulted in a different lease classification had these terms been in effect at the inception of the lease, *no new lease agreement* has been created, and any adjustments to the existing lease agreement are accounted for prospectively. However, if the provisions of the revised lease would have resulted in a different lease classification had the changed terms been in effect at the inception of the lease, the lease classification and corresponding accounting is determined using current assumptions as of the date of modification, for example with respect to the fair value of the leased asset, the residual value, and the implicit and incremental borrowing rates.

4.6.2.1 Accounting for Lease Modifications—Lessee
CAPITAL LEASE REMAINS CAPITAL LEASE
If the original lease is a capital lease and the modification of the lease terms either:

- Does not result in a new agreement[118]
- Results in a new agreement that is also classified as a capital lease

then the balances of the asset and the lease obligation are adjusted by an amount equal to the difference between the present value of the future minimum lease payments under the modified agreement and the current balance of the lease obligation, with no resulting gain or loss being recognized. The present value of the future minimum lease payments under the modified agreement is computed using the same rate of interest as the rate that was used initially to record the lease obligation.[119]

EXISTING LEASE: CAPITAL LEASE; NEW LEASE: OPERATING LEASE
If the existing lease is a capital lease and the new agreement is classified as an operating lease, the transaction is accounted for as a sale-leaseback transaction and

---

116   FAS 13, paragraph 9
117   For example, if lease rentals are modified, the lease rentals used for calculating minimum lease payments at the inception of the lease should be those specified in the original lease up to the date of modification, and the modified rentals thereafter.
118   The provisions of the revised lease would not have resulted in a different lease classification of the lease had the changed terms been in effect at the inception of the lease.
119   FAS 13, paragraph 14(a)

is accounted for in accordance with the provisions of FASB Statements No. 13 and No. 98.[120]

EXISTING LEASE: OPERATING LEASE; NEW LEASE: CAPITAL LEASE
If the existing lease is an operating lease and the new agreement is classified as a capital lease, the asset and lease obligation are recorded—at the date of lease modification—at the present value of the remaining minimum lease payments or the fair value of the leased asset, if lower.[121]

OPERATING LEASE REMAINS OPERATING LEASE
Changes in lease provisions of an operating lease that do not result in a different lease classification are rent adjustments that are accounted for prospectively.[122]

4.6.2.2 Accounting for Lease Modifications—Lessor
SALES-TYPE OR DIRECT FINANCING LEASE REMAINS SALES-TYPE OR DIRECT FINANCING LEASE
If an existing lease is classified as a sales-type or direct financing lease, and the lease under the revised terms also results in the classification of a sales-type or direct financing lease, the lessor accounts for the change in the provisions of the lease as follows: The balances of the minimum lease payments receivable and the estimated residual value are adjusted, and the net adjustment is charged or credited to unearned income[123] subject to the following restrictions:

- The estimated residual value is not adjusted upward as a result of a change in lease terms.[124]
- A decline in residual value that results from an other-than-temporary decline in the value of the leased asset is recorded as a loss in the period, rather than deferred over the term of the lease.[125] Deferring a reduction in the estimated residual value of the leased asset is only appropriate in situations where such change is directly related to the changed provisions of the lease, such as a change due to normal wear and tear over the new lease term or a change in residual value sharing provisions.

EXISTING LEASE: SALES-TYPE OR DIRECT FINANCING LEASE; NEW LEASE: OPERATING LEASE
If the existing lease is a sales-type lease or direct financing lease and the new lease is classified as operating lease, the remaining net investment is removed from the lessor's books. The leased asset is recorded at the lower of its original cost, fair value, or carrying amount; the net adjustment is charged to income of the period.[126]

---

120   FAS 13, paragraph 14(a)
121   FAS 13, paragraphs 9 and 10
122   Section 4.6.3.3 of this chapter discusses considerations to be made when determining whether lease modifications should be considered lease terminations.
123   FAS 13, paragraph 17(f)(i)
124   FAS 13, paragraph 17(f)(i)
125   FAS 13, paragraphs 17(f)(i) and 17(d)
126   FAS 13, paragraph 17(f)(i)

EXISTING LEASE: OPERATING LEASE; NEW LEASE: SALES-TYPE OR DIRECT FINANCING LEASE
If the existing lease is classified as an operating lease at the inception of the lease, and the revised lease is classified as a sales-type lease,[127] the revised lease is reflected on the books of the lessor at the date of the lease modification as a sales-type lease following the accounting described in Section 4.5.2. As the carrying amount of the leased asset at the time of modification of an operating lease generally does not equal its fair value, a change from operating lease classification to direct finance lease classification rarely ever occurs.[128]

4.6.3 LEASE TERMINATION

4.6.3.1 Lease Termination—Capital Lease At the termination of a capital lease, the asset and related obligation are removed from the books and a gain or loss is recognized for any difference.[129]

4.6.3.2 Lease Termination—Sales-Type Lease and Direct Financing Lease A termination of a sales-type lease or direct financing lease is accounted for by removing the net investment from the lessor's books, recording the asset at the lower of its original cost, fair value, or present carrying amount, and charging the net adjustment to income of the period.[130]

4.6.3.3 Determining whether a Lease Modification is a Lease Termination A modification of a lease may, in substance, be a lease termination. In some circumstances, a change in terms may be a combination of a lease termination and a lease modification, such as a lessee vacating part of the office space leased and modifying the terms of the remaining space rented.

The EITF[131] addressed the following issue: An entity leases an asset under an operating lease for use in its operations. Prior to the expiration of the original lease term, lessee and lessor agree to modify the lease by shortening the lease term and increasing the lease payments over the shortened lease period. The modifications do not change the lease classification, and no other changes are made to the lease. The Task Force concluded that the appropriate accounting treatment of the increase in the lease payments over the shortened lease period depends on the relevant facts and circumstances and is a matter of judgment. If the increase is, in substance, only a modification of future lease payments, the increase is accounted for prospectively over the term of the modified lease. If the increase is, in substance, a termination penalty, it is charged to income in the period of the lease modification.

---

127 For leases involving real estate, sales-type lease classification is appropriate only if title to the leased asset is transferred.
128 See FTB 88-1 for further discussion
129 FAS 13, paragraph 14(c)
130 FAS 13, paragraph 17(f)(iii); FAS 13, paragraph 18(c)
131 EITF Issue No. 95-17

4.6.3.4 Treatment of Costs Incurred when Terminating an Operating Lease

FASB Statement No. 146, *Accounting for Costs Associated with Exit or Disposal Activities*, provides guidance for the treatment of costs associated with exit or disposal activities, which includes costs to terminate an operating lease.[132]

Costs to terminate an operating lease or other contract include both

- Costs to terminate the contract before the end of its term
- Costs that will continue to be incurred under the contract for its remaining term without economic benefit to the entity

COSTS TO TERMINATE THE CONTRACT BEFORE THE END OF ITS TERM

A liability for costs to terminate an operating lease contract before the end of its term is recognized and measured at its fair value in the period in which the liability is incurred, assuming its fair value can be reasonably estimated.[133] Statement 146 clarifies that only present obligations to others are considered "liabilities" for this purpose;[134] an obligation to others may be created, for example, when a lessee gives written notice of the termination of a lease to the lessor. If the fair value cannot be reasonably estimated in the period in which the liability is incurred, the liability is recognized in the period in which fair value can reasonably be estimated.[135]

Any subsequent change in the amount of the liability arising from a revision in the amount or the timing of estimated cash flows is recognized as an adjustment to the liability in the period of change. The fair value of such change is measured using the interest rate initially used to measure the liability. Changes due to the passage of time are recognized as an increase in the carrying amount of the liability and as (accretion) expense.[136] Accretion expense is not considered interest cost for purposes of applying FASB Statement No. 34, *Capitalization of Interest Cost*, or for purposes of income statement classification.[137]

COSTS INCURRED OVER THE REMAINING LEASE TERM

A liability for costs that continue to be incurred under a lease contract for its remaining term without economic benefit to the entity is recognized and measured at its fair value when the entity ceases using the leased property (referred to as "cease-use" date).

For an operating lease contract, the fair value of the liability at the cease-use date is determined based on the remaining lease rentals, reduced by estimated

---

132 Costs to terminate capital leases are not within the scope of FASB Statement No. 146. They are addressed in paragraph 14(c) of FASB Statement No. 13. [FAS 146, paragraph 2(b)]
133 FAS 146, paragraph 3
134 FAS 146, paragraph 4
135 FAS 146, paragraph 3
136 FAS 146, paragraph 6; the expense is not considered interest cost for purposes of income statement classification.
137 FAS 146, paragraph 6, footnote 6

sublease rentals that could be reasonably obtained for the property, even if the entity does not intend to enter into a sublease. Remaining lease rentals are not reduced to an amount less than zero.[138]

Any subsequent changes in the amount of the liability arising from the revision of the amount or the timing of estimated cash flows are recognized as an adjustment to the liability in the period of change. The fair value of such changes

---

EXAMPLE—COSTS TO TERMINATE AN OPERATING LEASE[139]

Laguna Inc. (L) leases a facility under an operating lease that requires L to pay rentals of $100,000 per year for 10 years. After using the facility for 6 years, L ceases to use the facility. At that point in time, the remaining rentals amount to $400,000 ($100,000 per year for the remaining term of 4 years).

Based on market rentals for similar leased property, L determines that it could sublease the facility and receive sublease rentals of $300,000 ($75,000 per year for the remaining lease term of 4 years). However, for competitive reasons, L decides not to sublease the facility at the cease-use date. The fair value of the liability at the cease-use date is $89,427, determined using a credit-adjusted risk-free interest rate of 8%.[140]

How should L account for the termination of the operating lease?

L should recognize a liability and expense of $89,427 at the cease-use date. L will incur rental expense over the remaining lease term. At the cease-use date, L should measure the fair value of the remaining lease rentals, reduced by estimated sublease rentals that could reasonably be obtained for the facility.

Accretion expense is recognized after the cease-use date to reflect the passage of time. The impact of not subleasing the property over the remaining lease period is recognized over the period the facility is not subleased; in Years 7 through 10, L would recognize an expense of $75,000 for sublease rentals it could have obtained, but, for competitive reasons, decided to forego.

CHANGE IN CIRCUMSTANCES

At the end of Year 7, the competitive factors referred to above are no longer present. L decides to sublease the facility and enters into a sublease. L enters into an agreement to sublease the facility for rentals of $250,000 ($83,333 per year for the remaining lease term of 3 years), which are based on market rentals for similar leased property at the sublease date.

How should L account for this change in circumstances?

L should adjust the carrying amount of the liability at the sublease date to $46,388 to reflect the revised expected net cash flows of $50,000 ($16,667 per year[141] for the remaining lease term of 3 years), which are discounted at a rate of 8%, the rate that was used to measure the liability initially. L should continue to record accretion expense to reflect the passage of time.

---

138   FAS 146, paragraph 16
139   Adapted from FASB Statement No. 146, paragraph A11, Example 4
140   The expected net cash flows of $100,000 ($25,000 per year for the remaining lease term of 4 years) are discounted using a credit-adjusted risk free rate of 8%.
141   Calculated as: $100,000 rental expense less $83,333 rentals from sublease.

is measured using the interest rate that was used to measure the liability initially. Changes due to the passage of time are recognized as an increase in the carrying amount of the liability and as an (accretion) expense.[142] Accretion expense is not considered interest cost for purposes of applying Statement 34 or for purposes of income statement classification.[143]

4.6.4 PURCHASE AND SALE OF LEASED ASSET BEFORE THE END OF THE LEASE TERM

4.6.4.1 Purchase of Leased Asset

ASSET LEASED UNDER CAPITAL LEASE

The termination of a capital lease[144] that results from the purchase of a leased asset by the lessee is not the type of transaction contemplated by the provisions relating to lease termination, but rather should be considered an integral part of the purchase of the leased asset. Paragraph 5 of FIN 26, *Accounting for Purchase of a Leased Asset by the Lessee during the Term of the Lease*, states, in part [footnote omitted]:

> The purchase by the lessee of property under a capital lease shall be accounted for like a renewal or extension of a capital lease that, in turn, is classified as a capital lease, that is, any difference between the purchase price and the carrying amount of the lease obligation shall be recorded as an adjustment of the carrying amount of the asset.

The purchased asset under lease needs to be evaluated for impairment following the provisions in FASB Statement No. 144, *Accounting for the Impairment or Disposal of Long-Lived Assets*. If the carrying amount of the asset is less than the undiscounted cash flows, but exceeds the purchased asset's fair value, loss recognition, while not required by FASB Statement No. 13 or FIN 26, is not precluded.[145]

ASSET LEASED UNDER OPERATING LEASE

The accounting for a purchase of an asset leased under an operating lease is not addressed in the authoritative guidance; rather, the accounting for the purchase of an asset leased under capital lease is generally applied by analogy. If a leased asset classified as operating lease is purchased before the end of the lease term, any deferred credits resulting from straight-line recognition of rentals should be recorded as an adjustment to the cost of the purchased asset rather than recognized as income at the time of purchase.

---

142 FAS 146, paragraphs 6 and 16
143 FAS 146, paragraph 6, footnote 6
144 FAS 13, paragraph 14(c)
145 FIN 26, paragraph 4

4.6.4.2 Sale of Leased Asset

ASSET LEASED UNDER OPERATING LEASE

The lessor accounts for the sale of an asset leased under an operating lease as a sale and recognizes profit. If the asset under lease is a real estate asset, the seller has to take into consideration the provisions of FASB Statement No. 66, *Accounting for Sales of Real Estate*, which may preclude sale or profit recognition of the transaction at the time of the transaction.[146] Any deferred costs or deferred rent resulting from straight-line recognition of rentals are included in the determination of profit on the sale.

ASSET LEASED UNDER SALES-TYPE OR DIRECT FINANCING LEASE

If a lessor sells a leased asset accounted for as a sales-type or direct financing lease, the assets and liabilities on the books of the lessor that relate to the leased asset are removed from the books and charged or credited to income.

4.6.5 RENT HOLIDAY AND SCHEDULED RENT INCREASES/DECREASES Lease agreements may specify scheduled rent increases/decreases, or they may include a payment schedule specifying the timing of rental payments over the lease term. Such agreements may have been designed to reflect the anticipated effects of inflation and time value of money; to take into consideration any specific cash flow situation of the lessee; or to provide an inducement or "rent holiday" to the lessee.

OPERATING LEASES

Rental payments are recognized on a straight-line basis over the lease term unless another systematic and rational basis is a better representation of the time pattern in which the leased property is physically employed.[147] The determination of what constitutes the "leased asset" is critical in determining the lease commencement date, which marks the beginning of the lease term. Take a lessee that leases retail space in a shopping mall, for example. If the lessee leases an "empty shell," which it intends to build out and use as retail space, that lease would commence at the date the lessee takes possession and obtains control over the leased space, regardless of whether the lease agreement allows for a rent-free period at the beginning of the lease. If the lessee were to lease the space *built-out to its specifications*, on the other hand (i.e., the lessor is responsible for building out the space), the lease would commence at the time the build-out is complete.

In the example above, if the lessee leases an "empty shell," recognition of rental expense or rental revenue should commence at the date the lessee takes possession of or controls the physical use of the leased space, even if the lessee

---

146   FASB Statement No. 66 does not permit the deferral of a loss on sale.
147   FTB 85-3; FTB 88-1

does not have to make any lease payments until store-opening. Since rentals under an operating lease are recognized straight-line over the term of the lease, the lessee would record rental expense and a corresponding liability, and the lessor would record a receivable and corresponding rental revenue over this rent-free time period.

EXAMPLE—RENT HOLIDAY

Rowing Gear Retailers, Inc. (R), leases rental space under an operating lease over a lease term of 10 years. The lease agreement provides that the lease term commences on January 1, 2001, which coincides with the date of the retailer's store opening. The parties agree that R gets free access to the rental space 90 days before the beginning of the lease term so it can build out the space to its specifications. The property under lease is the empty shell, rather than the built-out space.

How should this free access period of 90 days be considered on R's books?

For purposes of determining the lease term under FASB Statement No. 13, gaining access to and control over the property marks the beginning the lease term. Therefore, the lease payments under the 10-year lease have to be recognized over the lease term, which encompasses a period of 10 years and 90 days. The 90-day period over which the lessee has control over the property is part of the lease term.

LEASES OTHER THAN OPERATING LEASES

In leases accounted for as capital leases (lessee) or sales-type/direct financing leases (lessor), interest expense/revenue is recorded using the effective interest method over the lease term. The considerations discussed above under operating leases relating to the questions "What is the property under lease?" and: "When does the lease term commence?" apply equally to leases that are not operating leases.

TIME PATTERN OF THE PHYSICAL USE OF THE PROPERTY

FASB considers the right to control the physical use of the leased property the equivalent to physical use.[148] When the lessee controls the use of the leased property, recognition of rental expense or rental revenue should not be affected by the extent to which the lessee contemplates utilizing that property; for operating leases, the rental payments are recognized as rental expense or rental revenue on a straight-line basis.[149] However, if scheduled rent increases are due to the lessee gaining access to and control over *additional* leased property over the lease term, such increases in rentals attributable to additional leased property are recognized

---

148   FTB 88-1, paragraph 2(b)
149   FAS 13, paragraph 15; FTB 85-3

straight-line over the portion of the lease term in which the lessee has control over the use of the additional leased property. The amount of rental expense or rental revenue attributed to the additional leased property is based on the relative fair value of the additional property leased and the period during which the lessee has the right to control the use of the additional property.[150]

4.6.6 CONTINGENT RENTALS   Lease agreements may include a base rental and a contingent rental amount. Contingent rentals are rental amounts that depend on factors occurring subsequent to the inception of the lease, except for increases of minimum lease payments relating to increases in the cost of leased property or similar fact patterns.[151]

For example, rent for retail space often consists of two parts: a fixed or base amount per square foot, and additional rent if certain targets are met. Such targets may be linked to the lessee achieving a certain level of operating income, revenue, or another measure agreed upon between lessor and lessee. Similarly, lease payments that depend on a factor directly related to the future use of the leased property, such as machine hours of use or sales volume during the lease term, are contingent rentals and, accordingly, are excluded from minimum lease payments in their entirety.

A probability-based approach to determine whether rentals should be considered minimum lease payments or contingent rentals was rejected by the FASB because of the subjectivity involved in that approach.[152] Nevertheless, the substance of the transaction should be considered when determining whether "contingent" rental payments are in substance disguised minimum lease payments. Some lease agreements may provide for rentals that are seemingly contingent, although in reality they are virtually assured. For example, the lease may provide for an increase in lease payments based on the lesser of 3% or 5 times the change in CPI. The Securities and Exchange Commission (SEC) staff has taken the view that if such rent increase is virtually certain (3% in the example), that contingent rent should be included in minimum lease payments, rather than treated as contingent rentals.

If a leverage factor is used, such as rentals that increase by two times the change in the CPI, the lease agreement may contain an embedded derivative that must be bifurcated pursuant to the provisions of FASB Statement No. 133, *Accounting for Derivative Instruments and Hedging Activities*.

CONTINGENT RENT BASED ON INDEX
Lease payments that are related to an existing index or rate, such as the consumer price index or the prime interest rate, are included in minimum lease payments

---

150   FTB 88-1, paragraph 2(b)
151   FAS 13, paragraph 5(n)
152   FAS 29, paragraph 7

based on the index or rate existing at the inception of the lease; any increases or decreases in lease payments that result from subsequent changes in the index or rate are contingent rentals. If the increase or decrease in lease payments is based on a *change* in the index or rate, however, rather than the index or rate itself, such increase or decrease would be considered contingent rent.[153]

EXAMPLE—CONTINGENT RENTALS VS. MINIMUM LEASE PAYMENTS

RENTALS BASED ON PRIME RATE

RetailCo leases space in a shopping mall for a period of two years. The lease agreement provides for annual lease payments of $100,000 multiplied by the sum of 1 plus the lesser of 5% or the prime rate in effect at the beginning of each year. The prime rate at the inception of the lease is 4%. At the beginning of Year 2, the prime rate is 3%.

What is the amount of contingent rentals?

The amount of contingent rentals is minus $1,000. The minimum lease payments are $208,000 ($104,000 for two years). The difference between the actual amounts paid by R ($104,000 for Year 1 and $103,000 for Year 2) and the minimum lease payments is the amount of contingent rentals.

RENTALS BASED ON CONSUMER PRICE INDEX (CPI)

Like RetailCo, OrangeRep leases space in a shopping mall for a period of two years. The lease agreement provides for annual lease payments of $100,000 adjusted for changes in the Consumer Price Index (CPI). The lease agreement provides for lease payments of $100,000 for Year 1. For Year 2, the rentals are adjusted by the same percentage as the change in the CPI in Year 1. The CPI as of the beginning of Year 2 is 415, the CPI as of the beginning of Year 1 (lease inception) is 400, the CPI one year prior to lease inception was 390.

What is the amount of contingent rentals?

The amount of contingent rentals is $3,750 (calculated as: (415—400)/400 multiplied by $100,000).

[Note: While some may argue that the CPI is an index existing at lease inception (expressed as the change in the CPI from the previous year) and therefore should be included in minimum lease payments,[154] others point to the explicit language in paragraph 5(n) of FASB Statement No. 13, which provides that increases or decreases in rentals based on the change of an index should be considered contingent rentals. In practice, rentals based on a change in CPI are treated as contingent rentals.]

ACCOUNTING BY THE LESSEE

A lessee should recognize contingent rental expense in accordance with the criteria for recognizing a liability:[155] A liability is recorded prior to the achievement of the

---

153 FAS 13, paragraph 5(n); FAS 29, Appendix A
154 Paragraph 5(n) of FASB Statement No. 13 provides, in part: " . . . lease payments that depend on an existing index or rate, such as the consumer price index or the prime interest rate, shall be included in minimum lease payments based on the index or rate existing at the inception of the lease; any increases or decreases in lease payments that result from subsequent changes in the index or rate are contingent rentals and thus affect the determination of income as accruable."
155 FAS 5, paragraph 8

specified target that triggers the contingent rental expense, if the achievement of that target is considered probable and if the amount can be reasonably estimated.

Contingent rental expense recorded in prior periods is reversed into income at the time it becomes probable that the specified target will not be met.[156]

ACCOUNTING BY THE LESSOR

A lessor should defer the recognition of contingent rental income until the specified target that triggers the contingent rental income is achieved. Prior to the lessee's achievement of the target on which contingent rentals are based, the lessor has no legal claims on the contingent amounts. Consequently, it is inappropriate to recognize rental income prior to that time.[157]

EXAMPLE—CONTINGENT RENTALS[158]
Shop-REIT (lessor) renews a lease with Bargain-4-U Inc. (B), a retailer, that is classified as operating lease. The lease term is one year, and lease payments are $1.2 million, payable in monthly installments, plus 1% of B's net sales in excess of $25 million (contingent rentals). The lessee has historically experienced annual net sales in excess of $25 million in the space being leased, and it is probable that the lessee will generate in excess of $25 million net sales during the term of the lease.
Should Shop-REIT recognize income from contingent rentals before the lessee actually achieves the $25 million net sales threshold?
No. Shop-REIT's contingent rental income is contingent upon B achieving net sales of $25 million. The contingent rentals should not be recognized until B's net sales actually exceed $25 million. Once the $25 million threshold is met, Shop-REIT should recognize the contingent rental income as it becomes accruable.

4.6.7 LEASE INCENTIVES IN OPERATING LEASES[159] An operating lease agreement may include incentives for the lessee to sign the lease, such as an up-front cash payment to the lessee; payment of costs on behalf of the lessee, such as moving expenses; or the assumption by the lessor of the lessee's pre-existing lease with a third party. Payments made to or on behalf of the lessee represent lease incentives that should be considered reductions of rental expense by the lessee and reductions of rental revenue by the lessor over the term of the new lease. Similarly, losses incurred by the lessor as a result of assuming a lessee's pre-existing lease with a third party should be considered an incentive by both the lessor and the lessee. Incentives are recognized on a straight-line basis over the term of the new lease.[160]

---

156   EITF Issue No. 98-9
157   SAB Topic 13.A.4.c. (SAB 101); EITF Issue No. 98-9
158   Adapted from SAB Topic 13.A.4.c. (SAB 101)
159   FTB 88-1, Question 2
160   FAS 13, paragraph 15; FTB 85-3; FTB 88-1

EXAMPLE—LEASE INCENTIVE IN AN OPERATING LEASE[161]

Lessor LeaseMax (L) enters into an eight-year operating lease for one of its properties at annual rentals of $1.2 million. As an incentive for the lessee to enter into the lease, L assumes the lessee's pre-existing lease with a third party that has four years remaining. The lease payment under the lessee's previous lease is $800,000 per year. L estimates it will incur a loss of $1 million on the assumed lease over its remaining term, based on the ability to sublease the property for $550,000 per year.[162] The lessee estimates that the incentive amounts to $960,000 based on a comparison of the pre-existing lease rate to current rates for similar property. The accounting for that incentive is as follows:

JOURNAL ENTRIES

LESSOR ACCOUNTING

AT INCEPTION

Incentive to lessee	$1,000,000	
Liability on sublease assumed		$1,000,000

To record deferred cost and liability related to loss on assumption of remaining lease

RECURRING JOURNAL ENTRIES IN YEARS 1–4

Liability on sublease assumed ($1 million/4 years)	$ 250,000	
Sublease expense	$ 550,000	
Cash		$ 800,000

To record cash payment on sublease assumed and amortization of the liability on the sublease assumed

Cash	$ 550,000	
Sublease revenue		$ 550,000

To record cash received from sublease of the property

RECURRING JOURNAL ENTRIES IN YEARS 1–8

Cash	$1,200,000	
Rental revenue		$1,075,000
Incentive to lessee ($1 million 8 years)		$ 125,000

To record cash received on new lease and amortization of incentive over new lease term

LESSEE ACCOUNTING AT

INCEPTION

Loss on sublease assumed by lessor	$ 960,000	
Incentive from lessor		$ 960,000

To record loss on sublease assumed in conjunction with new lease agreement

RECURRING JOURNAL ENTRIES IN YEARS 1–8

Lease expense	$1,080,000	
Incentive from lessor ($960,000/8 years)	$ 120,000	
Cash		$1,200,000

To record cash payment on new lease and amortization of incentive over the new lease term

---

161   Adapted from FTB 88-1

162   $800,000 (annual payment on assumed lease) less $550,000 (sublease income) = $250,000/year over four years

Lease Incentives vs. Leasehold Improvements.   A lessor may provide the tenant with leasehold improvements (tenant improvements), such as fixtures or new carpets in the leased space. The lessor may install such leasehold improvements for the tenant, or provide the tenant with an allowance to build out the leased space. Lessor funding of leasehold improvements may be direct or indirect—cash paid directly to the lessee, or cash paid to third parties on behalf of the lessee.

LEASEHOLD IMPROVEMENTS—ACCOUNTING BY THE LESSEE

The accounting for lease incentives led to numerous restatements on the books of lessees in early 2005, triggered—in part—by a letter from Donald T. Nicolaisen, then Chief Accountant of the SEC, in which he clarified his views regarding the accounting for lease incentives from the perspective of the lessee:[163]

- Leasehold improvements made by a lessee that are funded by landlord incentives or allowances under an operating lease should be recorded by the lessee as leasehold improvement assets and amortized over the shorter of their economic lives or the lease term.
- The incentives should be recorded as deferred rent and amortized as reductions to lease expense over the lease term in accordance with paragraph 15 of FASB Statement No. 13 and the response to Question 2 of FTB 88-1; it is inappropriate to net the deferred rent against the leasehold improvements.
- The statement of cash flows should reflect cash received from the lessor that is accounted for as a lease incentive within operating activities and the acquisition of leasehold improvements for cash within investing activities.

LEASEHOLD IMPROVEMENTS—ACCOUNTING BY THE LESSOR

Lessors also face the question as to how to account for leasehold improvements: Should funds provided to a tenant that are intended for the construction of lease-hold improvements be recorded as leasehold improvements (i.e., property, plant, and equipment) or lease incentives? The determination of whether amounts pay-able under the lease are lease incentives or leasehold improvements depends on the property under lease (for example, empty shell versus built-out space) and the contractual rights of lessee and lessor.

An agreement may specify that the allowance is intended to be used by the tenant to fund leasehold improvements, but if it does not require that the tenant provide the landlord with proof of spending for tenant improvements or other-wise provide for a mechanism under which the landlord can monitor the usage of the tenant allowance, the payment to the tenant may be more akin to a lease incentive than the acquisition of property, plant, and equipment. Similarly, an agreement that

---

163   Letter dated February 7, 2005, addressed to the Center for Public Audit Firms

allows the tenant to retain any funds not used to construct leasehold improvements indicates that the payment by the lessor is in substance a lease incentive.

The classification of such lessor funding of leasehold improvements as incentives vs. property, plant and equipment has a major impact on lessors of real estate, such as Real Estate Investment Trusts (REITs), that use Funds from Operations (FFO) as a performance measure: Real estate-related depreciation is added back to net income to arrive at FFO, whereas the amortization of incentives provided to tenants are not added back. Therefore, a lessor's classification of payments as leasehold improvements rather than lease incentives results in higher FFO and may lead to a perception of higher performance by investors.

4.6.8 SUBLEASES AND LEASE SUBSTITUTIONS   Subleases and lease substitutions include the following three types of arrangements:[164]

1. *Sublease.* The leased property is re-leased by the original lessee to a third party; the lease agreement between the lessor and the original lessee remains in effect.
2. *Substitution of lessee under original lease agreement, no cancellation of original lease agreement.* The new lessee becomes the primary obligor under the agreement; the original lessee may or may not be secondarily liable.
3. *Substitution of lessee through new agreement, and cancellation of original lease agreement.*

4.6.8.1 Accounting by the Original Lessor   If the original lessee enters into a sublease (Arrangement Type 1) or if the original lease agreement is transferred by the original lessee to a third party (Arrangement Type 2), the original lessor continues to account for the lease as before.[165]

If the original lease agreement is replaced by a new agreement with a new lessee (Arrangement Type 3), the lessor accounts for the replacement of the lease as a termination of the original lease. The new lease is classified and accounted for as a separate transaction.[166]

4.6.8.2 Accounting by the Original Lessee   The original lessee's accounting for the sublease or lease substitution depends on the obligations retained by the lessee:

- The lessee may be relieved of its primary obligation.
- The lessee may not be relieved of its primary obligation.

ORIGINAL LESSEE RELIEVED OF PRIMARY OBLIGATION
The original lessee is relieved of the primary obligation under the original lease if a new lessee is substituted under the original lease agreement and the new lessee

---

164   FAS 13, paragraph 35
165   FAS 13, paragraph 36
166   FAS 13, paragraph 37

becomes the primary obligor (the original lessee may remain secondarily liable) (Arrangement Type 2) or if a new lease agreement is substituted for the original agreement and the original lease is cancelled (Arrangement Type 3). The lessee accounts for such "termination" of the original lease agreement as follows:

Original Lease is Capital Lease.[167]   The lessee removes the asset and related lease obligation from its books and recognizes a gain or loss for the difference. Any consideration paid or received by the lessee is included in the determination of gain or loss on the substitution or cancellation. For a real estate lease, the provisions of FASB Statement No. 66 relating to sale and profit recognition must be followed when determining whether the real estate asset and related lease obligation should be removed from the lessee's books and what profit recognition method should be used. Any loss arising from the transaction would be recognized immediately.

If the asset and related lease obligation are removed from the lessee's books, but the lessee remains secondarily liable, the lessee would record a guarantee obligation in accordance with paragraph 114 of FASB Statement No. 140, *Accounting for Transfers and Servicing of Financial Assets and Extinguishments of Liabilities.* That guarantee obligation is initially measured at fair value and reduces the gain or increases the loss on the transaction.

Original Lease is Operating Lease.[168]   The lessee removes any deferred amounts (e.g., lease incentives, amounts relating to the straight-lining of rent) from its books and recognizes a gain or loss.

A guarantee obligation is recognized by the original lessee in accordance with paragraph 114 of Statement 140 if the lessee remains secondarily liable. That guarantee obligation reduces the gain or increases the loss on the transaction.

ORIGINAL LESSEE NOT RELIEVED OF PRIMARY OBLIGATION
The original lessee is not relieved of its primary obligation if the lessee enters into a sublease (Arrangement Type 1). In that case, the accounting for the original lease contract by the original lessee does not change as a result of the lessee entering into the sublease.

The following describes the accounting consequences for the original lessee in its role as sublessor:

Original Lease is Capital Lease.   If the original lease contains a bargain purchase option or transfers ownership by the end of the lease term, the original lessee (as sublessor) classifies the new lease with the sublessee based on the lease classification criteria of Statement 13 for lessors.[169]

---

167   FAS 13, paragraphs 38(a) and (b)
168   FAS 13, paragraph 38(c)
169   FAS 13, paragraphs 7 and 8

If the original lease agreement does not transfer ownership and does not contain a bargain purchase option, the new lease (sublease) is classified as an operating lease except in the following two situations:[170]

1. The new lease (sublease) meets the 75% of economic life test and additionally both of the following lease classification criteria for lessors are met:
    a. Collectibility of the minimum lease payments is reasonably predictable.
    b. There are no important uncertainties relating to the amount of unreimbursable costs yet to be incurred by the lessee under the lease.

If these criteria are met, the lease is classified as a direct financing lease, with the unamortized balance of the asset under the original lease treated as cost of the leased property.

2. The new lease (sublease) was intended as an integral part of the overall transaction in which the original lessee serves only as an intermediary. In that case, the new lease (sublease) is classified based on the 75% of economic life test, the 90% of fair value test, and both of the following lease classification criteria for lessors:
    a. Collectibility of the minimum lease payments is reasonably predictable.
    b. There are no important uncertainties relating to the amount of unreimbursable costs yet to be incurred by the lessee under the lease.

When applying the 90% of fair value test, the fair value of the leased property is the fair value to the original lessor at the inception of the original lease.

Original Lease is Operating Lease. If the original lease meets the criteria of an operating lease, the original lessee accounts for both the original lease and the new lease as operating leases.[171]

4.6.8.3 Accounting by the New Lessee A new lessee under a sublease or similar transaction classifies and accounts for the lease as an operating or capital lease in accordance with the lease classification criteria in Statement 13.[172]

4.6.9 LEASES AND LEASEHOLD IMPROVEMENTS ACQUIRED IN A BUSINESS COMBINATION

ACQUISITION OF LEASES

In a business combination, the purchase price is assigned to the assets acquired and liabilities assumed based on their fair values. Accordingly, lease agreements need to be evaluated as to whether they represent assets or liabilities. Leases may represent assets to the acquirer even if lease terms are at-market, because the acquirer does not have to incur the time and expense involved in securing a lease.

---

170   FAS 13, paragraph 39(b)
171   FAS 13, paragraph 39(c)
172   FAS 13, paragraph 40

This can have a significant impact, such as in the acquisition of rental properties, as outlined in Section 1.6.3 of Chapter 1.

Statement 13[173] requires that the classification of a lease be determined at the inception of the lease. Once that determination has been made, the classification of the lease is not re-examined unless one of the following two conditions is present:

- Both parties to the lease agree to a revision that would have resulted in a different lease classification had the changed terms been in effect at the inception of the lease.
- The lease is extended or renewed beyond the existing lease term.

In a business combination, the acquiring company retains the classification of the leases it acquires, unless the provisions of the leases are modified in a way that results in the revised agreements being considered *new agreements* under paragraph 9 of Statement 13. Such "new agreements" would be classified according to the lease classification criteria outlined above, based on the conditions as of the date of the modification of the leases.[174]

Deferred assets or liabilities on the books of the seller arising from the straight-lining of rent or the amortization of initial direct costs are not carried over to the acquirer, since they do not represent assets or liabilities. Deferred revenues of an acquired entity are recognized only in certain instances, such as in the acquisition of a building with in-place leases that were prepaid. The acquirer would recognize the fair value of its obligation to lease space to the tenant that prepaid the rent, and, at the same time recognize an intangible asset relating to the lease.[175]

ACQUISITION OF LEVERAGED LEASES

The acquisition of leveraged leases requires special accounting considerations due to the unique accounting, reporting, and disclosure requirements for leveraged leases. Appendix A of FIN 21 illustrates the accounting for a leveraged lease in a business combination.

ACQUISITION OF LEASEHOLD IMPROVEMENTS

In EITF Issue No. 05-6, *Determining the Amortization Period for Leasehold Improvements Purchased after Lease Inception or Acquired in a Business Combination*, the Task Force addressed the issue of how to determine the amortization period for leasehold improvements acquired in a business combination. The Task Force reached a consensus that any leasehold improvements acquired in

---

173   FAS 13, paragraph 7
174   FIN 21, paragraph 13; additionally, arrangements entered into prior to the effective date of EITF Issue No. 01-8 lose their grandfathering upon any substantive modification after the effective date of the consensus in EITF Issue No. 01-8.
175   EITF Issue No. 01-3, FAS 142, paragraph 8

a business combination should be amortized over the shorter of their useful lives or a term that includes required lease periods and renewals that are deemed to be reasonably assured *at the date of acquisition.*

4.6.10 IMPAIRMENT OF ASSETS UNDER LEASE AND LOSSES ON LEASING ACTIVITIES

4.6.10.1 Impairment of Assets under Lease   The impairment of long-lived assets accounted for as capital leases (by lessees) or operating leases (by lessors) is within the scope of FASB Statement No. 144, *Accounting for the Impairment or Disposal of Long-Lived Assets.*[176]

For purposes of recognition and measurement of an impairment loss, a long-lived asset first needs to be grouped with other assets and liabilities at the lowest level for which identifiable cash flows are largely independent of the cash flows of other assets and liabilities.[177] A long-lived asset (asset group) to be held and used, such as real estate property under lease, is considered impaired when the carrying amount of the long-lived asset (asset group) exceeds its fair value; FASB Statement No. 144 prescribes a two-step impairment test.[178] Step 1 is performed to evaluate whether the carrying amount of a long-lived asset (asset group) to be held and used is recoverable. If Step 1 is not met, Step 2 is performed to determine the amount of any impairment loss that needs to be recognized.

Step 1: Determine whether the carrying amount of the long-lived asset (asset group) is recoverable through the sum of the *undiscounted cash flows* expected to result from the use and eventual disposition of the asset (asset group).[179]

If the carrying amount is recoverable, no impairment loss needs to be recognized, even if the carrying amount of the asset (asset group) exceeds the asset's (asset group's) fair value. If the carrying amount is not recoverable, an impairment loss needs to be recognized, the amount of which is determined in Step 2 of the analysis.

Step 2: Determine the amount of the impairment loss to be recognized by comparing the carrying amount of the asset (asset group) to its fair value. The excess of the carrying amount over the fair value of the asset (asset group) is the amount of impairment loss to be recognized in the financial statements.

Statement 144 provides examples of events and changes in circumstances that require a recoverability test, which are outlined in Section 3.7.1.1 of Chapter 3.

4.6.10.2 Losses Incurred by Lessee Arising from Operating Leases   Lessees leasing assets under operating leases may incur losses under a lease contract if they discontinue the use of the leased asset and terminate the lease contract. FASB

---

176   FAS 144, paragraph 3
177   FAS 144, paragraph 10
178   Impairment considerations for long-lived assets to be disposed of are not addressed in this section.
179   FAS 144, paragraph 7

Statement No. 146 provides guidance with respect to costs associated with such exit or disposal activity.[180] Costs to terminate a lease contract may either be costs to terminate the contract before the end of its term or costs that will continue to be incurred under the contract for its remaining term.[181] The accounting treatment of such costs is discussed in Section 4.6.3.4 of this Chapter.

4.6.10.3 Losses on Subleasing Activities[182]

Losses resulting from subleasing property may arise in situations in which a lessee subleases leased property for amounts that are less than the rental payments the lessee is required to make under the lease. If costs expected to be incurred under an operating sublease exceed anticipated revenue from the operating sublease, the lessee needs to record a loss for the excess; such loss should not be deferred and amortized over the lease term. Similarly, if the sublease qualifies as a direct financing lease, the lessee would record as loss the excess of the carrying amount of the investment in the sublease over the total of rentals, estimated residual value, and tax benefits from the sublease transaction.[183]

A lessor may "absorb" losses incurred by a lessee in a sublease to induce the lessee to enter into a new lease with the lessor. This assumption of the lessee's losses under the sublease by the lessor is considered a lease incentive: The lessee would record a loss on the sublease and recognize the incentive as reduction of rent expense over the term of the lease.[184] Similarly, the lessor would record a lease incentive, which is recognized over the term of the lease as a reduction of rental revenue.

4.6.11 BUILD-TO-SUIT LEASES

In a build-to-suit lease, a lessee is involved in constructing the asset it will lease, once constructed. Build-to-suit leases are commonly encountered in the lease of new headquarter buildings, distribution facilities, data centers, and retail locations. Build-to-suit lease transactions are often structured as synthetic leases. A synthetic lease is a hybrid financing arrangement: For financial reporting purposes, the lessee accounts for a synthetic lease as an operating lease, whereas for income tax purposes, the lessee is deemed the owner of the leased property.

LESSEE INVOLVEMENT IN A BUILD-TO-SUIT LEASE TRANSACTION
In some build-to-suit transactions, a lessee's involvement in the construction of the asset is minimal; for example, the lessee's involvement may be limited to approving engineering drawings for the construction project. In other cases, the lessee may serve as construction agent, general contractor, or developer of the project.

---

180   Costs to terminate a contract that is a capital lease are not within the scope of FASB Statement No. 146. [FAS 146, paragraph 2]
181   FAS 146, paragraph 14
182   FTB 79-15
183   FTB 79-15
184   See section 4.6.7 for further discussion.

Depending on the lessee's involvement during the asset's construction, the lessee may be deemed the owner of the property during the construction period. If that is the case, the lessee has to record the property on its books during the construction phase (e.g., construction in progress). After the construction of the property is complete, it has to be determined whether the lessee can derecognize the property following sale-leaseback guidance. In a sale-leaseback transaction involving real estate, any continuing involvement by the seller-lessee with the leased property—other than a "normal leaseback"—that results in the seller-lessee not transferring the risks or rewards of ownership precludes the derecognition of the real estate property.[185] Since in real estate build-to-suit transactions, such prohibited continuing involvement is often present in the form of purchase options, financing provided to the owner-lessor, and guarantees and indemnities, the asset under lease often remains on the books of the lessee subsequent to construction completion.

Several EITF Issues deal with the circumstances that would lead a lessee in a build-to-suit lease to be considered the owner of the asset during the construction phase.[186] The primary guidance is provided by EITF Issue No. 97-10, *The Effect of Lessee Involvement in Asset Construction*. The guidance in EITF Issue No. 97-10 is rule-driven and has been interpreted very strictly. This Section intends to provide a brief overview of the major concepts of that EITF Issue, rather than a complete listing of the specific provisions.

As a general rule, the lessee is considered the owner of the asset, if the lessee bears substantially all of the construction period risks. EITF Issue No. 97-10 establishes the following maximum guarantee test: A lessee is considered to have substantially all of the construction period risks if the lessee could be required, *under any circumstance*, to pay 90% or more of the project costs, excluding land acquisition costs, as of any time during the construction period. EITF Issue No. 97-10 provides: ". . . that assessment should test whether, at each point during the construction period, the sum of (1) the accreted value of any payments previously made by the lessee and (2) the present value of the maximum amount the lessee can be required to pay as of that point in time (whether or not construction is completed) is less than 90 percent of the total project costs incurred to date (excluding land acquisition costs, if any). If that test is not met, the lessee will be considered the owner of the real estate project during construction."

For purpose of making this assessment, amounts the lessee can be required to pay include not only payments for construction costs incurred, but all payments that the lessee is obligated to make or can be required to make in connection with the construction project, including, for example, obligations that could arise

---

185   See section 5.2.2.1 in chapter 5 for further discussion

186   EITF Issue No. 96-21, *Implementation Issues in Accounting for Leasing Transactions involving Special-Purpose Entities*; EITF Issue No. 97-1, *Implementation Issues in Accounting for Lease Transactions, including Those involving Special-Purpose Entities*; EITF Issue No. 97-10, *The Effect of Lessee Involvement in Asset Construction*.

from being the developer or general contractor, lease payments that must be made regardless of whether the project is complete, payments for indemnities or guarantees, and an obligation to fund construction cost overruns. The likelihood of the lessee actually having to make these payments is not considered when performing that assessment.

In addition to the maximum guarantee test, a number of other factors have to be considered when determining whether the lessee is deemed the owner during the construction period. These factors can be categorized as follows:

1. Costs incurred prior to lease inception
2. Activities during the construction period
3. Indemnification provisions

Costs Incurred Prior to Lease Inception

EITF Issue No. 96-21 discusses the nature of costs that may be incurred by a lessee prior to lease inception. To maintain off-balance sheet treatment for a build-to-suit lease, a lessee may not commence construction activities. Construction activities have commenced if the lessee has broken ground, if the lessee has incurred any "hard costs," such as site preparation and construction costs, or if it has incurred "soft costs," such as architectural fees, survey costs and zoning fees, of more than 10% of the expected fair value of the leased property.

Activities during the Construction Period

In EITF Issue No. 97-10, the Task Force concluded that a lessee should capitalize the leased asset under construction if, in connection with the project:

- The lessee or any party related to the lessee that is involved with construction on behalf of the owner-lessor makes or is required to make an equity investment in the owner-lessor that is considered in substance an investment in real estate.
- The lessee is responsible for paying directly (in contrast to paying those costs through rent payments under a lease) any cost of the project other than (1) pursuant to a contractual arrangement that includes a right of reimbursement, (2) payment of certain environmental remediation costs, or (3) "normal tenant improvements." In that context, "normal tenant improvements" exclude not only structural elements of the project, but also any amounts for tenant improvements included in the original project budget that the owner-lessor agrees to pay regardless of the nature of the costs. A requirement that the lessee pay more of the cost of tenant improvements than originally budgeted for if construction overruns occur could, in effect, obligate the lessee to pay for 90 percent or more of the total project costs, which would violate the maximum guarantee test.
- The lessee takes title to the real estate at any time during the construction period or provides supplies or other components used in constructing the

project other than materials purchased subsequent to the inception of the lease (or the date of the applicable construction agreement, if earlier), for which the lessee is entitled to reimbursement.

- The lessee either owns the land and does not lease it to the owner-lessor or leases the land and does not sublease it (or provide an equivalent interest in the land; for example, a long-term easement) to the owner-lessor before construction commences.

EXAMPLE—TENANT IMPROVEMENTS

Tootsyco. (T) has entered into a build-to-suit lease transaction for its new office building. Per the contractual arrangements, T is required to make lease payments over the term of the lease. Additionally, T will pay for the costs of the Heat, Ventilation, and Air-Conditioning (HVAC) system and the elevators.

Will the fact that T pays for the elevators and the HVAC system cause T to be the owner of the building?

Yes. HVAC systems and elevators are not considered normal tenant improvements. Pursuant to the consensus reached by the Task Force, the lessee should be considered the owner of the office building, if it pays for tenant improvements other than normal tenant improvements.

INDEMNIFICATION PROVISIONS
EITF Issue No. 97-10 limits the nature of indemnities related to construction completion that a lessee can provide. Except for indemnities relating to pre-existing environmental risks for which the risk of loss is remote, the lessee is not permitted to provide indemnities or guarantees to any party other than the owner-lessor. Additionally the indemnifications or guarantees provided to the owner-lessor must be limited to damage claims caused by or resulting from the lessee's own actions or failures to act while in possession or control of the construction project.[187]

EITF Issue No. 97-10 provides an analysis of indemnification/guarantee provisions, which is reproduced in Exhibit 4.6.

4.6.12 LEASES BETWEEN RELATED PARTIES   The classification and accounting of leases between related parties is the same as for leases between unrelated parties, except in cases in which it is clear that the terms of the transaction have been significantly affected by the fact that lessee and lessor are related. In such cases, classification and/or accounting are modified to recognize the economic substance of the lease transaction rather than its legal form. FASB Statement No. 13 requires disclosures relating to the nature and extent of leasing transactions with related parties.[188]

---

187   If the lessee is acting in the capacity of a general contractor, the lessee's own actions or failures to act include the actions or failures to act of its subcontractors.
188   FAS 13, paragraph 29

	INCLUDE IN MAXIMUM GUARANTEE TEST	AUTOMATIC INDICATION OF SUBSTANTIVE OWNERSHIP	NO IMPACT ON THE FINANCIAL REPORTING
Indemnities/Guarantees to owner-lessor			
1. Pre-existing environmental risk			
a. When risk of loss is remote			X
b. When risk of loss is more than remote		X	
2. Damage claims caused by or resulting from lessee's own actions or failures to act (including third-party claims caused by or resulting from the lessee's own actions or failure to act)			
a. Related to construction completion	X		
b. Not related to construction completion—for example, "slip and fall" claims that occur on the construction site			X
3. Damage claims unrelated to lessee's own actions or failures to act (including third-party claims unrelated to the lessee's own actions or failure to act)		X	
Indemnities/Guarantees to anyone other than owner-lessor			
1. Pre-existing environmental risk			
a. When risk of loss is remote			X
b. When risk of loss is more than remote		X	
2. Any risk other than pre-existing environmental risk		X	

EXHIBIT 4.6   ANALYSIS OF INDEMNIFICATION/GUARANTEE PROVISIONS

In consolidated financial statements or in financial statements for which an interest in an investee is accounted for under the equity method of accounting, any profit or loss on a leasing transaction with the related party is accounted for in accordance with the principles for consolidation or equity method of accounting.[189]

CAPITAL LEASES BETWEEN PARTIES UNDER COMMON CONTROL
Capital lease transactions between entities under common control are accounted for analogous to transfers of assets between companies under common control, as

189   FAS 13, paragraph 30

described in paragraph D12 of FASB Statement No. 141, *Business Combinations*, which states:

> When accounting for a transfer of assets or exchange of shares between entities under common control, the entity that receives the net assets or the equity interests shall initially recognize the assets and liabilities transferred at their carrying amounts in the accounts of the transferring entity at the date of transfer.

For an asset transferred that is accounted for as an asset under capital lease, the lessee should record the asset based on the lessor's carrying amount. A capital lease obligation is recorded in the amount of the present value of minimum lease payments. Any difference between the carrying amount of the asset and the present value of minimum lease payments is treated as a contribution or distribution of capital.

4.7 FINANCIAL STATEMENT PRESENTATION AND DISCLOSURE

4.7.1 Presentation and Disclosure—Lessee   Paragraph 16(d) of FASB Statement No. 13 requires a general description of a lessee's leasing arrangements, including:

- The basis on which contingent rental payments are determined
- The existence and terms of renewal or purchase options and escalation clauses
- Restrictions imposed by lease agreements, such as those concerning dividends, additional debt, and further leasing

Disclosures Required for Capital Leases   For assets recorded under capital leases, the accumulated amortization and any related lease obligations need to be separately identified in the lessee's balance sheet or in the footnotes. Also, separate presentation or disclosure of amortization expense relating to assets under capital leases is required, unless the amortization of leased assets is included in depreciation expense of the lessee's fixed assets and that fact is disclosed.[190]

Additionally, paragraph 16(a) of Statement 13 requires that the following be disclosed:

a. The gross amount of assets recorded under capital leases as of the date of each balance sheet, presented by major classes (this information may be combined with the comparable information for owned assets)
b. Future minimum lease payments as of the date of the latest balance sheet presented, in the aggregate and for each of the five succeeding fiscal years (amounts representing executory costs, including profit thereon, and imputed interest to reduce minimum lease payments to present value need to be deducted from the amount of future minimum lease payments and presented separately)

---

190   FAS 13, paragraph 13

c. The total of minimum sublease rentals to be received in the future under non-cancelable subleases as of the date of the latest balance sheet presented

d. Total contingent rentals actually incurred for each period for which an income statement is presented

Disclosures Required for Operating Leases[191]   For all operating leases, lessees need to disclose rental expense for each period for which an income statement is presented, with separate amounts for minimum rentals, contingent rentals, and sublease rentals. Rental payments under leases with terms of a month or less that were not renewed need not be included.

For operating leases that have initial or remaining noncancelable lease terms in excess of one year, the following additional disclosures are required:[192]

a. Future minimum rental payments required as of the date of the latest balance sheet presented, in the aggregate and for each of the five succeeding fiscal years

b. The total of minimum rentals to be received in the future under noncancelable subleases as of the date of the latest balance sheet presented

4.7.2 PRESENTATION AND DISCLOSURE—LESSOR   When leasing[193] is a significant part of the lessor's business activities in terms of revenue, net income, or assets, paragraph 23 of FASB Statement No. 13[194] requires that the financial statements include a general description of the leasing arrangement. Additionally, a disclosure of the following information is required:

1. For sales-type and direct financing leases:[195]
    a. The components of the net investment in sales-type and direct financing leases as of the date of each balance sheet presented:
        i. Future minimum lease payments to be received, with separate deductions for amounts representing executory costs, including any profit thereon, included in the minimum lease payments and the accumulated allowance for uncollectible minimum lease payments receivable
        ii. The unguaranteed residual values accruing to the benefit of the lessor
        iii. Unearned income
        iv. Initial direct costs for financing leases

191   FAS 13, paragraph 16(c)
192   FAS 13, paragraph 16(b)
193   other than leveraged leasing
194   FAS 13, paragraph 23
195   FAS 13, paragraph 23

    b. Future minimum lease payments to be received for each of the five succeeding fiscal years as of the date of the latest balance sheet presented

    c. Total contingent rentals included in income for each period for which an income statement is presented

2. For operating leases:[196]

    a. The cost and carrying amount of property on lease or held for leasing by major classes of property and the amount of accumulated depreciation in total as of the date of the latest balance sheet presented

    b. Minimum future rentals on noncancelable leases as of the date of the latest balance sheet presented, in the aggregate and for each of the five succeeding fiscal years

    c. Total contingent rentals included in income for each period for which an income statement is presented

4.8 INTERNATIONAL FINANCIAL REPORTING STANDARDS

International Accounting Standard (IAS) 17, *Leases*, and several Interpretations establish guidance on how to account for leases. The scope of IAS 17 is broader than the scope of FASB Statement No. 13. IAS 17 applies to all leases other than (1) leases to explore for or use minerals, oil, natural gas and similar non-regenerative resources and (2) licensing arrangements for such items as motion picture films, video recordings, plays, manuscripts, patents and copyrights. The general principles for the recording of leases are very similar to U.S. Generally Accepted Accounting Principles (U.S. GAAP): For example, IAS 17 distinguishes between operating leases and capital leases (called finance leases under IFRS); it sets standards for lease classification that are similar to the criteria in FASB Statement No. 13; it provides for cost deferral of initial direct costs. However, the Standard contains no bright lines, such as a 75% of economic life test or a 90% of fair value test. Rather than bright lines, IAS 17 includes indicators that serve as guidelines for the classification of leases. Additionally, special rules apply for real estate leases of income-producing properties that are accounted for at fair value.

    Presently, the agendas of both the IASB and the FASB include a project on leases in which the fundamental approach to the accounting for leases will be reconsidered.

4.8.1 LEASE CLASSIFICATION   The classification of leases is based on the extent to which risks and rewards of ownership of a leased asset lie with the lessor or the lessee.[197]

---

196   FAS 13, paragraph 23(b)
197   IAS 17, paragraph 7

IAS 17 establishes the following classifications for leases for both lessee and lessor:[198]

- Finance lease if substantially all the risks and rewards incident to ownership are transferred to the lessee
- Operating lease if not substantially all the risks and rewards incident to ownership are transferred to the lessee

Whether a lease is a finance lease or an operating lease depends on the substance of the transaction, rather than the form of the contract. IAS 17 provides the following examples of situations that would normally lead to a lease being classified as a finance lease:[199]

1. The lease transfers ownership of the asset to the lessee by the end of the lease term.
2. The lessee has the option to purchase the asset at a price that is expected to be sufficiently lower than the fair value at the date the option becomes exercisable such that, at the inception of the lease, it is reasonably certain that the option will be exercised.
3. The lease term is for the major part of the economic life of the asset.
4. At the inception of the lease, the present value of the minimum lease payments amounts to at least substantially all of the fair value of the leased asset.
5. The leased assets are of a specialized nature such that only the lessee can use them without major modifications.

Additionally, certain other indicators could also lead to a lease being classified as a finance lease:[200]

1. Upon a lessee's cancellation of the lease, the lessee is required to bear the lessor's losses associated with the cancellation.
2. Gains or losses from the fluctuation in the fair value of the residual accrue to the lessee (e.g., in the form of a rent rebate equaling most of the sales proceeds at the end of the lease).
3. The lessee has the ability to extend the lease at a rent that is substantially lower than market rent.

LEASE OF REAL ESTATE PROPERTY
When classifying a lease of real estate property, the land and building elements of the lease are considered separately, unless the amount of the land element is immaterial.[201] The minimum lease payments are allocated between land and buildings

---

198   IAS 17, paragraph 9
199   IAS 17, paragraph 10
200   IAS 17, paragraph 11
201   For a lease of land and buildings in which the amount that would initially be recognized for the land element is immaterial, the land and buildings may be treated as a single unit for the purpose of lease

based on the *relative fair values* of the leasehold interests in the land and building elements of the lease. The land element is classified as an operating lease, unless title passes to the lessee at the end of the lease term. The building element of the lease is classified as an operating or finance lease based on the lease classification criteria in IAS 17.[202] If the lease payments cannot be allocated reliably between these two elements, the entire lease is classified as a finance lease, unless it is clear that both elements are operating leases, in which case the entire lease is classified as an operating lease.[203]

INVESTMENT PROPERTY

Investment property is real estate held by the owner or by a lessee under a finance lease to earn rentals or for capital appreciation or both.[204] Special rules have been developed for investment property held under leases:

- Separate measurement of the land and building element is not required when the lessee's interest in both land and buildings is classified as investment property in accordance with IAS 40, *Investment Property*, and the fair value model is adopted.[205]
- In accordance with IAS 40, a property interest held by a lessee under an operating lease may be classified as investment property if the following criteria are met:
  - The definition of investment property is otherwise met.
  - The operating lease is accounted for as if it were a finance lease in accordance with IAS 17.
  - The lessee uses the fair value model set out in IAS 40 for the asset recognized.[206]

The lessee is required to continue to account for the lease as a finance lease, even if a subsequent event changes the nature of the lessee's interest so that it is no longer classified as investment property.

4.8.2 ACCOUNTING AND DISCLOSURES—LESSEE

4.8.2.1 Finance Leases   Lessees recognize finance leases as assets and liabilities in their balance sheets at the lower of the fair value of the leased property or the present value of the minimum lease payments. Initial direct costs may be

---

classification and classified as a finance or operating lease in accordance with paragraphs 7–13. In such a case, the economic life of the building element is regarded as the economic life of the entire leased asset. [IAS 17, paragraph 17]

202   IAS 17, paragraphs 15 and 16
203   IAS 17, paragraph 16
204   IAS 40, paragraph 5
205   IAS 17, paragraph 18
206   IAS 17, paragraph 19; IAS 40, paragraph IN5

incurred in connection with specific leasing activities, such as costs incurred in negotiating and securing leasing arrangements. The costs identified as directly attributable to activities performed by a lessee for a finance lease are included as part of the amount recognized as leased asset.[207] In calculating the present value of the minimum lease payments, the discount factor is the interest rate implicit in the lease,[208] if it is practicable to determine; otherwise, the lessee's incremental borrowing rate should be used.

A finance lease results in a depreciation expense for depreciable assets, as well as a finance expense, for each accounting period. The depreciation policy for depreciable leased assets should be consistent with that for depreciable assets that are owned, and the depreciation recognized should be calculated according to IAS 16, *Property, Plant and Equipment*, and IAS 38, *Intangible Assets*. If there is no reasonable certainty that the lessee will obtain ownership by the end of the lease term, the asset should be fully depreciated over the shorter of the lease term or its useful life.[209]

DISCLOSURES
For finance leases, lessees should disclose the following:[210]

- For each class of asset, the net carrying amount at the balance sheet date
- Reconciliation between the total of minimum future lease payments at the balance sheet date, and their present value. In addition, a company should disclose the total of minimum lease payments at the balance sheet date, and their present value, for each of the following periods:
  - (i)   Not later than one year
  - (ii) Later than one year and not later than five years
  - (iii) Later than five years
- Contingent rents recognized in income for the period
- The total of future minimum sublease payments expected to be received under noncancelable subleases at the balance sheet date
- A general description of the lessee's material leasing arrangements, including:
  - (i)   The basis on which contingent rent payments are determined
  - (ii) The existence and terms of renewal or purchase options and escalation clauses
  - (iii) Restrictions imposed by lease arrangements, such as those concerning dividends, additional debt, and further leasing

---

207   IAS 17, paragraphs 20 and 24
208   The interest rate implicit in the lease is defined as the discount rate that, at the inception of the lease, causes the aggregate present value of (a) the minimum lease payments and (b) the unguaranteed residual value to be equal to the sum of (i) the fair value of the leased asset and (ii) any initial direct costs of the lessor. [IAS 17, paragraph 4]
209   IAS 17, paragraph 27
210   IAS 17, paragraph 31; These disclosures are in addition to the disclosure requirements under IFRS 7.

4.8.2.2 Operating Leases   Lease payments under an operating lease should be recognized as an expense in the income statement on a straight-line basis over the lease term unless another systematic basis is more representative of the time pattern of the user's benefit.[211]

For operating leases, lease payments (excluding costs for services such as insurance and maintenance) are recognized as an expense in the income statement on a straight-line basis unless another systematic basis is more representative of the time pattern of the user's benefit.[212]

Disclosures

Lessees should, in addition to the disclosures required by International Financial Reporting Standards (IFRS) 7, *Financial Instruments: Disclosures* make the following disclosures for operating leases:[213]

- The total of future minimum lease payments under noncancelable operating leases for each of the following periods:
    - **(i)**   Not later than one year
    - **(ii)**   Later than one year and not later than five years
    - **(iii)**   Later than five years
- The total of future minimum sublease payments expected to be received under noncancelable subleases at the balance sheet date
- Lease and sublease payments recognized into income for the period, disclosing separately amounts for minimum lease payments, contingent rents, and sublease payments
- A general description of the lessee's significant leasing arrangements, including:
    - **(i)**   The basis on which contingent rent payments are determined
    - **(ii)**   The existence and terms of renewal or purchase options and escalation clauses
    - **(iii)**   Restrictions imposed by lease arrangements, such as those concerning dividends, additional debt, and further leasing

4.8.3 ACCOUNTING AND DISCLOSURES—LESSOR

4.8.3.1 Finance Leases   Under a finance lease, substantially all the risks and rewards of ownership are transferred by the lessor. Lessors should recognize a receivable at an amount equal to the net investment in the lease.[214] Lease payments are treated by the lessor as repayment of principal and finance income.[215]

---

211   IAS 17, paragraph 33
212   IAS 17, paragraph 34
213   IAS 17, paragraph 35
214   IAS 17, paragraph 36
215   IAS 17, paragraph 37

Finance income is recognized to reflect a constant periodic rate of return on the lessor's net investment in the finance lease.[216]

A finance lease of an asset by a manufacturer or dealer lessor gives rise to two types of income:[217]

1. Profit or loss equivalent to the profit or loss resulting from an outright sale of the asset being leased, at normal selling prices
2. Finance income over the lease term

The sales revenue recognized at the commencement of a finance lease term by a manufacturer or dealer lessor is the lower of the fair value of the asset or the present value of the minimum lease payments accruing to the lessor, computed at a market rate of interest. The cost of sale recognized at the commencement of the lease term is the cost, or carrying amount if different, of the leased property less the present value of the unguaranteed residual value. The difference between the sales revenue and the cost of sale is the selling profit, which is recognized in accordance with the policy followed by the company for sales.[218]

Initial direct costs incurred by a manufacturer or dealer in connection with negotiating and arranging a financing lease are recognized as an expense at the commencement of the lease term, because they are mainly related to earning the manufacturer's or dealer's selling profit.[219] For finance leases other than leases involving manufacturer or dealer lessors, the initial direct costs are included in the finance lease receivable; they reduce the amount of income recognized over the lease term.[220]

DISCLOSURES

In addition to the disclosures required by in IFRS 7, lessors need to disclose the following:[221]

- Reconciliation between the gross investment in the lease at the balance sheet date and the present value of minimum lease payments receivable at the balance sheet date. In addition, a company should disclose the gross investment in the lease and the present value of minimum lease payments receivable at the balance sheet date, for each of the following periods:
  - (i)   Not later than one year
  - (ii) Later than one year and not later than five years
  - (iii) Later than five years
- Unearned finance income
- The unguaranteed residual values accruing to the benefit of the lessor

---

216   IAS 17, paragraph 39
217   IAS 17, paragraph 43
218   IAS 17, paragraph 44
219   IAS 17, paragraph 46
220   IAS 17, paragraph 38
221   IAS 17, paragraph 47

- The accumulated allowance for uncollectible minimum lease payments receivable
- Contingent rents recognized in income
- A general description of the lessor's material leasing arrangements

4.8.3.2 Operating Leases
Lessors present assets subject to operating leases in their balance sheets according to the nature of the asset.[222]

Lease income from operating leases is recognized in income on a straight-line basis over the lease term, unless another systematic basis is more representative of the time pattern in which use benefit derived from the leased asset isdiminished.[223]

Costs, including depreciation, incurred in earning the lease income are recognized as an expense. Lease income (excluding receipts for services provided, such as insurance and maintenance) is recognized in income on a straight-line basis over the lease term, unless another systematic basis is more representative of the time pattern in which use benefit derived from the leased asset is diminished.[224]

Initial direct costs incurred in negotiating and arranging an operating lease are added to the carrying amount of the leased asset and recognized as expense over the lease term on the same basis as lease income.[225]

The leased assets should be depreciated consistent with the lessor's normal depreciation policy for similar assets, with the depreciation charge being calculated as set forth in IAS 16, *Property, Plant and Equipment*, and IAS 38, *Intangible Assets*.[226]

DISCLOSURES

For operating leases, lessors should disclose the following in addition to the disclosures required by IFRS 7:

- The future minimum lease payments under noncancelable operating leases in the aggregate and for each of the following periods:
  - **(i)** Not later than one year
  - **(ii)** Later than one year and not later than five years
  - **(iii)** Later than five years
- Total contingent rents recognized in income
- A general description of the lessor's leasing arrangements

4.9 SYNOPSIS OF AUTHORITATIVE LITERATURE

FASB STATEMENT NO. 13, *ACCOUNTING FOR LEASES*

FASB Statement No. 13 establishes lease classification, accounting, and reporting standards for both lessee and lessor. Additionally, FASB Statement No. 13

---

222   IAS 17, paragraph 49
223   IAS 17, paragraph 50
224   IAS 17, paragraph 51
225   IAS 17, paragraph 52
226   IAS 17, paragraph 53

provides accounting guidance for sale-leaseback transactions involving personal property. Since its issuance in November 1976, FASB Statement No. 13 has been amended by several FASB Statements and clarified by FASB Interpretations.

FASB STATEMENT NO. 23, *INCEPTION OF THE LEASE*, AN AMENDMENT OF FASB STATEMENT NO. 13

In FASB Statement No. 23, FASB reconsidered the application of FASB Statement No. 13 to leasing transactions in which lessor and lessee agree on lease terms prior to the construction or acquisition of the asset to be leased. The amendments to FASB Statement No. 13 include a redefinition of the term *inception of the lease* to make it the date of the lease agreement or any earlier commitment.

FASB STATEMENT NO. 29, *DETERMINING CONTINGENT RENTALS*, AN AMENDMENT OF FASB STATEMENT NO. 13

FASB Statement No. 29 defines contingent rentals as the increases or decreases in lease payments that result from changes occurring subsequent to the inception of the lease in the factors on which lease payments are based, with the exception of increases of minimum lease payments relating to increases in the cost of the leased property. Lease payments that depend on a factor that exists and is measurable at the inception of the lease, such as the prime interest rate, would be included in minimum lease payments based on that factor at the inception of the lease. Lease payments that depend on a factor that does not exist or is not measurable at the inception of the lease, such as future sales volume, are considered contingent rentals in their entirety, and are excluded from minimum lease payments. Contingent rentals are included in income as they accrue.

FASB STATEMENT NO. 91, *ACCOUNTING FOR NONREFUNDABLE FEES AND COSTS ASSOCIATED WITH ORIGINATING OR ACQUIRING LOANS AND INITIAL DIRECT COSTS OF LEASES*, AN AMENDMENT OF FASB STATEMENTS NO. 13, 60, AND 65 AND A RESCISSION OF FASB STATEMENT NO. 17

FASB Statement No. 91 establishes accounting and reporting standards for nonrefundable fees and costs associated with lending activities. Loan origination fees and direct costs are deferred and recognized over the life of the loan as an adjustment of yield. The provisions of FASB Statement No. 91 also apply to the accounting for fees and initial direct costs associated with leasing.

FASB INTERPRETATION NO. 19, *LESSEE GUARANTEE OF THE RESIDUAL VALUE OF LEASED PROPERTY*, AN INTERPRETATION OF FASB STATEMENT NO. 13

FASB Interpretation No. 19 clarifies certain provisions in FASB Statement No. 13 relating to a lessee's residual value guarantees:

- A lease provision requiring the lessee to make up a residual value deficiency that is attributable to damage, extraordinary wear and tear, or excessive usage does not constitute a lessee guarantee of residual value.

- If a lease limits the amount of the lessee's obligation to make up a residual value deficiency to an amount less than the stipulated residual value of the leased property at the end of the lease term, the amount of the lessee's guarantee to be included in minimum lease payments is limited to the specified maximum deficiency the lessee can be required to make up.
- A guarantee of the residual value obtained by the lessee from an unrelated third party for the benefit of the lessor cannot be used to reduce the amount of the lessee's minimum lease payments, unless the lessor releases the lessee from the obligation. Amounts paid in consideration for a guarantee by an unrelated third party are executory costs, which are not included in minimum lease payments.

FASB INTERPRETATION NO. 21, *ACCOUNTING FOR LEASES IN A BUSINESS COMBINATION*, AN INTERPRETATION OF FASB STATEMENT NO. 13
FASB Interpretation No. 21 provides that the classification of a lease is not changed as a result of a business combination unless the provisions of the lease are modified. If in connection with a business combination, the provisions of a lease are modified in a way that requires the revised agreement to be considered a new agreement following the provisions of FASB Statement No. 13, this "new" lease is classified according to the lease classification criteria in FASB Statement No. 13.

FASB INTERPRETATION NO. 23, *LEASES OF CERTAIN PROPERTY OWNED BY A GOVERNMENTAL UNIT OR AUTHORITY*, AN INTERPRETATION OF FASB STATEMENT NO. 13
FASB Interpretation No. 23 provides clarification regarding the requirement in paragraph 28 of FASB Statement No. 13 to classify certain leases of property owned by a governmental unit as operating leases.

FASB INTERPRETATION NO. 24, *LEASES INVOLVING ONLY PART OF A BUILDING*, AN INTERPRETATION OF FASB STATEMENT NO. 13
In FASB Interpretation No. 24, FASB clarifies that the fair value of the leased property involving only part of a building may be objectively determinable, even if there are no sales of property similar to the leased property; evidence, such as an independent appraisal of the leased property or estimated replacement cost information, may provide a basis for an objective determination of fair value.

FASB INTERPRETATION NO. 26, *ACCOUNTING FOR PURCHASE OF A LEASED ASSET BY THE LESSEE DURING THE TERM OF THE LEASE*, AN INTERPRETATION OF FASB STATEMENT NO. 13
FASB Interpretation No. 26 clarifies that the termination of a capital lease that results from the purchase of a leased asset by the lessee is an integral part of the purchase of the leased asset; any difference between the purchase price and the carrying amount of the lease obligation is recorded as an adjustment of the carrying amount of the asset.

FASB Interpretation No. 27, *Accounting for a Loss on a Sublease*, an interpretation of FASB Statement No. 13 and APB Opinion No. 30
This interpretation clarifies that FASB Statement No. 13 does not prohibit the recognition of a loss by a lessee that disposes of leased property or mitigates the cost of an existing lease commitment by subleasing the property.

FASB Staff Position FAS13-1, *Accounting for Rental Costs Incurred during a Construction Period*
A lessee may take possession of leased property prior to the lessee commencing operations. During this period, the lessee has the right to use the leased property and does so for the purpose of constructing leasehold improvements. Rental costs relating to the period in which leasehold improvements are constructed should be recognized as rental expense, rather than capitalized.

FASB Staff Position FAS13-2, *Accounting for a Change or Projected Change in the Timing of Cash Flows Relating to Income Taxes Generated by a Leveraged Lease Transaction*
In leveraged lease transactions, the lessor is the owner of the assets for income tax purposes, depreciates the assets, and receives accelerated tax depreciation deductions. FSP FAS13-2 addresses how a change or projected change in the timing of cash flows relating to income taxes generated by leveraged lease transactions affects the lessor's accounting.

FASB Technical Bulletin No. 79-10, *Fiscal Funding Clauses in Lease Agreements*
A fiscal funding clause is commonly found in a lease agreement in which the lessee is a governmental unit. A fiscal funding clause generally provides that the lease is cancelable if the legislature or other funding authority does not appropriate the funds necessary for the governmental unit to fulfill its obligations under the lease agreement. The existence of a fiscal funding clause in a lease agreement necessitates an assessment of the likelihood of lease cancellation through exercise of the fiscal funding clause. If the likelihood of exercise of the fiscal funding clause is assessed as being remote, a lease agreement containing such a clause is considered a noncancelable lease; otherwise, the lease is considered cancelable.

FASB Technical Bulletin No. 79-11, *Effect of a Penalty on the Term of a Lease*
Superseded by FASB Statement No. 98

FASB Technical Bulletin No. 79-12, *Interest Rate Used in Calculating the Present Value of Minimum Lease Payments*
Paragraph 7(d) of FASB Statement No. 13 generally requires that the lessee use its incremental borrowing rate to calculate the present value of minimum lease payments. FTB 79-12 provides that the lessee's use of a secured borrowing rate is not proscribed by paragraph 5(l) of FASB Statement No. 13, if that rate is determinable,

reasonable, and consistent with the financing that would have been used in the particular circumstances.

FASB TECHNICAL BULLETIN NO. 79-13, *APPLICABILITY OF FASB STATEMENT NO. 13 TO CURRENT VALUE FINANCIAL STATEMENTS*
FTB 79-13 states that FASB Statement No. 13 is applicable to financial statements prepared on a current value basis.

FASB TECHNICAL BULLETIN NO. 79-14, *UPWARD ADJUSTMENT OF GUARANTEED RESIDUAL VALUES*
FASB Statement No. 13 prohibits the upward adjustment of the estimated residual value of sales-type leases, direct financing leases, and leveraged leases. FTB 79-14 provides that this prohibition is also applicable to upward adjustments that result from renegotiations of the guaranteed portions of residual values.

FASB TECHNICAL BULLETIN NO. 79-15, *ACCOUNTING FOR LOSS ON A SUBLEASE NOT INVOLVING THE DISPOSAL OF A SEGMENT*
If costs expected to be incurred under an operating sublease exceed anticipated revenue on the operating sublease, a loss should be recognized by the sublessor. Similarly, a loss should be recognized on a direct financing sublease if necessitated by the terms of the transaction.

FASB TECHNICAL BULLETIN NO. 85-3, *ACCOUNTING FOR OPERATING LEASES WITH SCHEDULED RENT INCREASES*
FTB 85-3 provides that scheduled rent increases included in minimum lease payments under FASB Statement No. 13 should be recognized by lessors and lessees on a straight-line basis over the lease term unless another systematic and rational allocation basis is more representative of the time pattern in which the leased property is physically employed.

FASB TECHNICAL BULLETIN NO. 86-2, *ACCOUNTING FOR AN INTEREST IN THE RESIDUAL VALUE OF A LEASED ASSET: ACQUIRED BY A THIRD PARTY OR RETAINED BY A LESSOR THAT SELLS THE RELATED MINIMUM RENTAL PAYMENTS*
The FASB staff has responded to inquiries received as follows:

Accounting for a Residual Value Interest Acquired by a Third Party.   The acquisition of an interest in the residual value of a leased asset should be accounted for as the acquisition of an asset, generally at the amount of cash disbursed, the fair value of other consideration given, and the present value of liabilities assumed at the date the right is acquired. Subsequent to initial recognition, any subsequent increase in the fair value of the residual interest would not be recognized; an other-than-temporary decline in value would require a write-down.

Accounting for a Residual Value Interest Retained by a Lessor That Sells the Related Minimum Rental Payments.   A lessor retaining an interest in the residual value of the leased asset should not recognize increases in the value of the lease residual over the remaining lease term. Any other-than-temporary declines in value require a write-down to fair value.

FASB TECHNICAL BULLETIN NO. 88-1, ISSUES RELATING TO ACCOUNTING FOR LEASES: TIME PATTERN OF THE PHYSICAL USE OF THE PROPERTY IN AN OPERATING LEASE, LEASE INCENTIVES IN AN OPERATING LEASE, APPLICABILITY OF LEVERAGED LEASE ACCOUNTING TO EXISTING ASSETS OF THE LESSOR, MONEY-OVER-MONEY LEASE TRANSACTIONS, WRAP LEASE TRANSACTIONS

The FASB staff responded to inquiries received as follows:

Time Pattern of the Physical Use of the Property in an Operating Lease.   If rents escalate in contemplation of the lessee's physical use of the leased property, but the lessee takes possession of or controls the physical use of the property at the beginning of the lease term, all rental payments should be recognized on a straight-line basis. If rents escalate because a lessee gains access to and control over additional leased property, rental expense or rental revenue should be attributed to the additional leased property proportionate to the relative fair value of the additional leased property.

Lease Incentives in an Operating Lease.   Incentives in an operating lease should be recognized on a straight-line basis by both the lessee and the lessor.

Applicability of Leveraged Lease Accounting to Existing Assets of the Lessor.   The requirement that the carrying amount of a leased asset must equal its fair value at the inception of the lease to qualify as a leveraged lease applies literally to a lease of a lessor's existing assets. The carrying amount of an asset previously placed in service is likely not the same as its fair value; therefore, leveraged lease accounting is generally not appropriate in such circumstance.

Money-Over-Money Lease Transactions.   In a money-over-money lease transaction, an enterprise manufactures or purchases an asset, leases the asset to a lessee, and obtains nonrecourse financing in excess of the asset's cost using the leased asset and the future lease rentals as collateral. Other than the recognition of manufacturer's or dealer's profit in a sales-type lease, an enterprise should not recognize as income any proceeds from the borrowing in a money-over-money lease transaction at the beginning of the lease term.

Wrap Lease Transactions.   A wrap lease transaction is a transaction in which an enterprise purchases an asset, leases the asset to a lessee, obtains nonrecourse financing using the lease rentals or the lease rentals and the asset as collateral, sells the asset subject to the lease and the nonrecourse debt to a third-party investor, and leases the asset back while remaining the substantive principal lessor under the original lease. Wrap lease transactions are accounted for as sale-leaseback transactions. Wrap lease transactions of real estate should be accounted for following the sale-leaseback provisions of FASB Statement No. 98.

EITF Issue No. 85-27, Recognition of Receipts from Made-Up Rental Shortfalls
Outline provided in Chapter 1.

EITF Issue No. 87-7, Sale of an Asset Subject to a Lease and Nonrecourse Financing: "Wrap Lease Transactions"
Issues.   A lessor may lease an asset to a lessee and obtain nonrecourse financing using the lease receivable and the asset as collateral. The lessor may then sell the asset subject to the lease and the nonrecourse financing to a third party and lease the asset back. The lessor remains the principal lessor with the user of the asset. In exchange for the asset, the lessor receives cash and a note receivable and may also retain an interest in the residual value of the leased asset and remarketing rights.
The issues are:

- How should the cash proceeds be accounted for?
- Should an interest retained in the residual value of the leased asset be recorded as an asset and recognized as income in the period of the transaction?
- How should the fees for the remarketing of the asset at the end of the lease term be accounted for?

Consensuses/Status.   The Task Force reached a consensus that any revenue associated with future remarketing rights should be separated from other proceeds received in the transaction, deferred, and recognized in income by the original lessor at the time the remarketing services are performed.
Subsequent to the issuance of EITF Issue No. 87-7, FTB 88-1 was issued, which provides accounting guidance for wrap-lease transactions. Wrap-leases are accounted for following the guidance for sale-leaseback transactions.

EITF Issue No. 88-3, Rental Concessions Provided by Landlord
Resolved by FTB 88-1 and EITF Issues No. 88-10 and 94-3.

EITF Issue No. 88-10, Costs Associated with Lease Modification or Termination
Issues resolved or nullified by FASB Statement No. 146.

EITF Issue No. 90-15, Impact of Nonsubstantive Lessors, Residual Value Guarantees, and Other Provisions in Leasing Transactions
Nullified for entities within the scope of FIN 46(R).

EITF Issue No. 92-1, Allocation of Residual Value or First-Loss Guarantee to Minimum Lease Payments in Leases Involving Land and Building(s)
Issue.   A lease may include a residual value or first-loss guarantee by the lessee. What should the accounting treatment of the guarantee be for purposes of performing the 90% of fair value test?

Consensus/Status. The Task Force reached a consensus that pursuant to paragraph 26(b)(ii) of FASB Statement No. 13, the annual minimum lease payments applicable to the land are determined for both the lessee and the lessor by multiplying the fair value of the land by the lessee's incremental borrowing rate. The remaining minimum lease payments, including the full amount of the guarantee, are attributed to the building.

If the lease is classified as operating lease, the lessee may have to recognize a liability and provide certain disclosures pursuant to the provisions of FIN 45.

EITF ISSUE NO. 95-17, *ACCOUNTING FOR MODIFICATIONS OF AN OPERATING LEASE THAT DO NOT CHANGE THE LEASE CLASSIFICATION*

Issue.   Lessor and lessee may modify an operating lease by shortening the lease term and increasing the lease payments over the shortened lease period; the modifications do not change the lease classification. How should the adjustment to the lease term and the increase in the lease payments over the shortened lease period be accounted for?

Consensus/Status.   The treatment of the increase in the lease payments over the shortened lease period is a matter of judgment that depends on the facts and circumstances: If the increase is in substance a modification of future lease payments, the increase should be accounted for prospectively over the term of the modified lease. If the increase is in substance a termination penalty, it should be charged to income in the period of the modification.

The Task Force established the following factors to consider when making that determination:

- The term of the modified lease as compared with the remaining term of the original lease
- The relationship of the modified lease payments to comparable market rents

If the increase in lease payments represents a termination penalty, the amount of the charge may be calculated based on either undiscounted or discounted amounts.

EITF ISSUE NO. 96-21, *IMPLEMENTATION ISSUES IN ACCOUNTING FOR LEASING TRANSACTIONS INVOLVING SPECIAL-PURPOSE ENTITIES*
Partially nullified for entities within the scope of FIN 46(R).

Issues Not Nullified

1. In some build-to-suit lease transactions, the lessee may be obligated to make payments to the lessor prior to the completion of construction of the asset and the beginning of the lease term (sometimes referred to as "construction period lease payments"). How should construction period lease payments be considered in applying the 90% of fair value test of

paragraph 7(d) of FASB Statement No. 13? If the lease is an operating lease, how should the lessee account for those payments?[227]

2. The terms of some lease agreements require that the lessee pay fees for structuring the lease transaction (administrative fees). What is the accounting effect from both the lessee's perspective and the SPE's perspective when such fees are paid by the lessee to the owners of record of the SPE?[228]

3. In some build-to-suit lease transactions, the lessee may incur certain development costs prior to entering into a lease agreement with the developer-lessor. Those costs may include both "soft costs" and "hard costs." What are the nature and amount of such costs that the future lessee may incur prior to entering into the lease agreement before the lessee would be considered the owner of the construction in-progress and subject to a sale-leaseback transaction?[229]

4. If a lessee commences construction activities prior to the involvement of an SPE, and the subsequent transfer to the SPE is deemed to be within the scope of FASB Statement No. 98, how should the lessee apply the provisions of FASB Statement No. 98 to the transaction?[230]

5. A lease of real estate with an SPE may require rental payments equal to the sum of the interest on the SPE's debt plus a return on the SPE's equity, without providing for any amortization of principal over the lease term. The lessee provides the SPE-lessor with a residual value guarantee; the maximum deficiency that the lessee is required to pay would be limited such that the lease would be classified as an operating lease. Assuming the lease otherwise qualifies as an operating lease, what is the lessee's accounting for this "interest-only" lease?[231]

Consensuses/Status

1. Payments made prior to the beginning of the lease term are considered part of the minimum lease payments and included in the 90% of fair value test at their future value at the beginning of the lease term. If the lease is classified as an operating lease, such payments represent prepaid rent.

2. Fees that are paid by the lessee to the owners of the SPE for structuring the lease transaction are included as part of minimum lease payments for purposes of applying the 90% of fair value test.

3. A lessee who commences construction activities has to recognize the asset (construction in-progress) on its balance sheet. Construction activities have commenced if the lessee has (1) begun construction (broken ground),

---

227   EITF Issue No. 96-21, Question No. 4
228   EITF Issue No. 96-21, Question No. 6
229   EITF Issue No. 96-21, Question No. 10
230   EITF Issue No. 96-21, Question No. 11
231   EITF Issue No. 96-21, Question No. 12

(2) incurred hard costs, even if insignificant, or (3) incurred soft costs that represent more than 10% of the expected fair value of the leased property. If a lessee transfers an option to acquire real property that it owns to an SPE, the fair value of the option is included in incurred soft costs.

4. Because the lessee is considered the owner of the project, the transaction is evaluated as a sale-leaseback under FASB Statement No. 98.

5. The lessee would recognize rent expense over the lease term, generally on a straight-line basis. Although the maximum deficiency under the residual value guarantee is included in minimum lease payments for purposes of lease classification, those payments would not be considered in the amount to be straight-lined under paragraph 15 of FASB Statement No. 13 until it becomes probable that the value of the property at the end of the lease term will be less than the residual value guaranteed by the lessee. Beginning on the date the deficiency becomes probable, the expected deficiency up to the maximum for which the lessee is responsible) is accrued by the lessee. Additionally, FIN 45 requires the guarantor-lessee to recognize the fair value of the residual value guarantee at the inception of the lease, even though no deficiency is probable.

EITF Issue No. 97-1, *Implementation Issues in Accounting for Lease Transactions, Including Those Involving Special-Purpose Entities*

Issues

1. Some lease agreements include provisions that require that lessees provide indemnification against loss or damage arising from environmental contamination caused by the lessee during the term of the lease or from pre-existing environmental contamination. How do lessee environmental indemnification provisions affect the lessee's classification of the lease?

2. Some lease agreements contain default provisions that are unrelated to the lessee's use of the property, such as financial covenants. How do such nonperformance-related default covenants affect lease classification?

Consensuses/Status

1. A provision that requires lessee indemnifications for environmental contamination caused by the lessee during its use of the property over the term of the lease does not affect the lessee's classification of the lease. However, if the lessee is required to provide indemnification for pre-existing environmental contamination, then the lessee needs to assess the likelihood of loss before consideration of any recoveries from third parties. If the likelihood of loss is remote, the indemnity would not affect the lessee's classification of the lease. However, if the likelihood of loss is at

least reasonably possible, then the lessee is considered to have purchased, sold, and leased back the property; the transaction is subject to the sale-leaseback provisions of FASB Statement No. 98.

2. Non-performance-related default provisions do not affect lease classification when all of the following conditions exist: (1) the default covenant provision is customary in financing arrangements; (2) the occurrence of the event of default is objectively determinable; (3) predefined criteria, related solely to the lessee and its operations, have been established for the determination of the event of default; and (4) it is reasonable to assume that the event of default will not occur.

Regardless of whether the above conditions exist, if the lease is part of a sale-leaseback transaction subject to the provisions of FASB Statement No. 98, a default remedy that allows the buyer-lessor to put the leased property to the seller-lessee would violate the continuing involvement criteria in FASB Statement No. 98, and therefore the transaction is accounted for by the deposit method or as a financing, whichever is appropriate under FASB Statement No. 66.

EITF ISSUE NO. 97-10, *THE EFFECT OF LESSEE INVOLVEMENT IN ASSET CONSTRUCTION*
Issue.   A lessee may be involved on behalf of an owner-lessor with the construction of an asset that will be leased to the lessee when construction of the asset is completed. How should a lessee that is involved with the construction of an asset that it will lease when construction is completed determine whether it should be considered the owner of that asset during the construction period?

Consensus/Status.   The Task Force reached a consensus that a lessee should be considered the owner of a real estate project during the construction period if the lessee has substantially all of the construction period risks. An evaluation of whether the lessee has substantially all of the construction period risks should be based on a test that is similar to the 90% of fair value test described in paragraph 7(d) of FASB Statement No. 13.

If the documents governing the construction project could require, *under any circumstance*, that the lessee pay 90% or more of the total project costs (excluding land acquisition costs) as of any point in time during the construction period, the lessee should be deemed to have substantially all of the construction period risks and should be considered to be the owner of the real estate project during the construction period.

Additionally, a lessee should be considered the owner of a real estate project during construction, even if the 90% test described above is not violated, if certain other conditions outlined in that EITF Issue and EITF Issues No. 96-21 and 97-1 are met.

EITF Issue No. 98-9, Accounting for Contingent Rent

Issues.   Some rental agreements provide for minimum rental payments plus contingent rents based on the lessee's operations, such as a future specified sales target. The issues are:

1. How should a lessor account for contingent rental income that is based on future specified targets?
2. How should a lessee account for contingent rental expense that is based on future specified targets?

Consensuses/Status

1. EITF Issue No. 98-9 refers to guidance provided in SAB 101.[232] SAB 101 provides: Lessors should defer recognition of contingent rental income until the changes in the factors on which the contingent lease payments are based actually occur, that is until specified targets are met.
2. The Task Force reached a consensus that a lessee should recognize contingent rental expense prior to the achievement of the specified target that triggers the contingent rental expense, provided that achievement of that target is considered probable. Previously recorded rental expense should be reversed into income at such time that it is probable that the specified target will not be met.

EITF Issue No. 99-13, Application of EITF Issue No. 97-10 and FASB Interpretation No. 23 to Entities That Enter into Leases with Governmental Entities

Issue.   Should projects for the construction of government-owned properties involving a lease of the completed improvements that would be classified as an operating lease under FIN 23 be excluded from the scope of EITF Issue No. 97-10?

Consensus/Status.   The Task Force reached a consensus that the construction of government-owned properties subject to a future lease of the completed improvements should be included in the scope of EITF Issue No. 97-10.

EITF Issue No. 99-14, Recognition by a Purchaser of Losses on Firmly Committed Executory Contracts

Issue.   When should a purchaser under a firmly committed executory contract recognize an impairment of its remaining contractual right asset under the contract, and how should that impairment loss be measured if the purchaser will continue to use the asset or service to be received under the contract?

---

232   SAB Topic 13.A.4.c.

Consensus/Status. The Task Force discontinued discussions of this Issue. No consensus was reached.

EITF Issue No. 00-11, *Lessors' Evaluation of Whether Leases of Certain Integral Equipment Meet the Ownership Transfer Requirements of FASB Statement No. 13*

Issues

1. Should integral equipment subject to a lease be evaluated as real estate under FASB Statement No. 13?
2. If integral equipment subject to a lease is evaluated as real estate under FASB Statement No. 13, how should the requirement that the lease transfers ownership of the property to the lessee by the end of the lease term be evaluated, when no statutory title registration system exists for the leased assets?

Consensuses/Status

1. The Task Force reached a consensus that integral equipment subject to a lease should be evaluated as real estate under FASB Statement No. 13.
2. The Task Force reached a consensus that for integral equipment or property improvements for which no statutory title registration system exists, the criterion of transfer of ownership is met in lease agreements that provide that upon the lessee's performance in accordance with the terms of the lease, the lessor will execute and deliver to the lessee such documents as may be required to release the equipment from the lease and to transfer ownership to the lessee.

EITF Issue No. 00-26, *Recognition by a Seller of Losses on Firmly Committed Executory Contracts*

Issues. The issues are:

1. When should a seller or service provider under a firmly committed executory contract that requires the seller to deliver goods or services to the counterparty in the future for specified consideration recognize a loss under the contract?
2. If a loss should be recorded, how should the loss be measured?

Consensuses/Status. The Task Force discontinued discussions of this Issue. Consensuses were not reached.

EITF Issue No. 01-8, *Determining Whether an Arrangement Contains a Lease*

Issue. Paragraph 1 of FASB Statement No. 13 defines a lease as ". . . an agreement conveying the right to use property, plant, or equipment (land and/or depreciable assts) usually for a stated period of time."

How should one determine whether an arrangement contains a lease that is within the scope of FASB Statement No. 13?

Consensus/Status.   The evaluation of whether an arrangement contains a lcasc within the scope of FASB Statement No. 13 is based on the substance of the arrangement using the following guidance:

- Property, plant, or equipment includes only land and/or depreciable assets. Inventory minerals, precious metals, or other natural resources cannot be the subject of a lease for accounting purposes, because those assets are not depreciable. Intangibles and rights to explore minerals, precious metals, or other natural resources are not depreciable assets (they are amortized or depleted); therefore they may not be the subject of a lease.
- Property, plant, or equipment is not the subject of a lease if fulfillment of the arrangement is not dependent on the use of the specified property, plant, or equipment.
- An arrangement conveys the right to use property, plant, or equipment if the arrangement conveys to the purchaser (lessee) the right to control the use of the underlying property, plant, or equipment.

If an arrangement contains a lease and nonlease elements, the classification, recognition, measurement, and disclosure requirements of FASB Statement No. 13 are applied to the lease element of the arrangement. Payments and other considerations are separated into those for the lease and those for other services on a relative fair value basis consistent with the guidance in paragraph 4(a) of EITF Issue No. 00-21.

EITF Issue No. 01-12, *The Impact of the Requirements of FASB Statement No. 133 on Residual Value Guarantees in Connection with a Lease*
Issues.   There is a scope overlap between FASB Statement No. 13 and FASB Statement No. 133, for certain residual value guarantees.
The issues are:

1. How should the scope overlap between FASB Statement No. 13 and FASB Statement No. 133 with respect to such residual value guarantees be resolved?
2. Should a third-party residual value guarantor account for a residual value guarantee under the requirements of FASB Statement No. 133?

Consensuses/Status

1. Residual value guarantees that are subject to the requirements of the lease accounting literature are not subject to the requirements of FASB Statement No. 133.

2. A third-party residual value guarantor should consider the guidance in FASB Statement No. 133 to determine whether residual value guarantees provided by that guarantor are derivatives and whether they qualify for any of the scope exceptions in that Statement.

EITF ISSUE NO. 05-6, *DETERMINING THE AMORTIZATION PERIOD FOR LEASEHOLD IMPROVEMENTS PURCHASED AFTER LEASE INCEPTION OR ACQUIRED IN A BUSINESS COMBINATION*

Issues.   The issues are:

1. How should the amortization period for leasehold improvements acquired in a business combination be determined?

2. How should the amortization period of leasehold improvements that are placed in service significantly after and not contemplated at the beginning of the lease term be determined?

Consensuses/Status

1. Leasehold improvements acquired in a business combination should be amortized over the shorter of the useful life of the assets or a term that includes required lease periods and renewals that are deemed to be reasonably assured at the date of acquisition.

2. Leasehold improvements that are placed in service significantly after and not contemplated at or near the beginning of the lease term should be amortized over the shorter of the useful life of the assets or a term that includes required lease periods and renewals that are deemed to be reasonably assured at the date the leasehold improvements are purchased.

EITF TOPIC NO. D-8, *ACCRUING BAD-DEBT EXPENSE AT INCEPTION OF A LEASE*

Recognition of bad debts should be based on the guidance provided in FASB Statement No. 5.

EITF TOPIC NO. D-107, *LESSOR CONSIDERATION OF THIRD-PARTY RESIDUAL VALUE GUARANTEES*

The SEC staff has taken the position that when determining lease classification, lessors should not include residual value guarantees for a portfolio of leased assets in the amount of minimum lease payments, because residual value guarantees of a portfolio of leased assets preclude the lessor from determining the amount of the guaranteed residual value of any individual leased asset within the portfolio at lease inception.

INTERNATIONAL ACCOUNTING STANDARD 17, *LEASES*

IAS 17 establishes lease classification, accounting, and reporting standards for lessors and lessees; the general principles underlying the accounting and reporting for leases are similar to the provisions in FASB Statement No. 13.

IFRIC INTERPRETATION 4, *DETERMINING WHETHER AN ARRANGEMENT CONTAINS A LEASE*
Issues.   The issues are:

1. How does one determine whether an arrangement is, or contains, a lease as defined in IAS 17?
2. When should the assessment or a reassessment of whether an arrangement is, or contains, a lease be made?
3. If an arrangement is, or contains, a lease, how should the payments for the lease be separated from payments for any other elements in the arrangement?

Consensuses

1. The determination shall be based on the substance of the arrangement. That requires an assessment of whether the following two criteria are met:
   a. Fulfillment of the arrangement is dependent on the use of specific assets.
   b. The arrangement conveys a right to use the asset.
2. The assessment of whether an arrangement contains a lease shall be made at the inception of the arrangement. A reassessment of whether the arrangement contains a lease after the inception of the arrangement shall be made only if certain conditions are met.
3. Payments and other consideration required by the arrangement shall be separated at the inception of the arrangement or upon a reassessment of the arrangement into those for the lease and those for other elements on the basis of their relative fair values. IFRIC 4 includes special provision if it is impracticable to separate the payments reliably.

SIC INTERPRETATION 15, *OPERATING LEASES—INCENTIVES*
Issue.   In negotiating an operating lease, the lessor may provide incentives for the lessee to enter into the agreement. How should incentives in an operating lease be recognized in the financial statements of both the lessee and the lessor?

Consensus.   All such incentives should be recognized as an integral part of the net consideration agreed for the use of the leased asset, irrespective of the incentive's nature or form or the timing of payments. The benefit (lessee) or cost (lessor) of the incentive is recognized as a reduction of rental expense (lessee) or income (lessor) on a straight-line basis over the lease term, unless another systematic basis is more representative of the time pattern over which the use is derived (lessee) or the benefit of the leased asset is diminished (lessor).

SIC INTERPRETATION 27, *EVALUATING THE SUBSTANCE OF TRANSACTIONS INVOLVING THE LEGAL FORM OF A LEASE*
Issues.   When an arrangement between unrelated parties is made in the legal form of a lease, the issues are:

1. How should one determine whether a series of transactions is linked and should be accounted for as one transaction?

2. Does the arrangement meet the definition of a lease under IAS 17? And If not,

   a. Should a separate investment account and lease obligations that might exist be considered assets and liabilities of the entity?

   b. How should the entity account for other obligations resulting from the arrangement?

   c. How should the entity account for a fee received from an investor?

Consensuses. 1.   A series of transactions that involve the legal form of a lease shall be accounted for as one transaction when the overall economic effect cannot be understood without reference to the series of transactions as a whole. The accounting shall reflect the substance of the arrangement. IAS 17 applies when the substance of an arrangement includes the conveyance of the right to use an asset for an agreed-upon period of time.

2.a. Paragraphs 49–64 of the Framework provide guidance for the determination whether a separate investment account and lease payment obligations should be considered assets and liabilities of the entity.

2.b. Other obligations should be accounted for based on the guidance provided in IAS 37, IAS 39, or IFRS 4, depending on the terms.

2.c. The criteria in paragraph 20 of IAS 18 should be applied to the facts and circumstances of each arrangement in determining when a fee should be recognized as income.

SALE-LEASEBACK OF REAL ESTATE

5.1 OVERVIEW

Sale-leaseback transactions involve the sale of property by the owner and a lease of any or all of the property back to the seller, allowing the seller to retain the use of the property after ownership is transferred. The sale-and-leaseback of real estate, frequently used for the financing of warehouses, distribution centers, office buildings, hotels, research and development facilities, and many other types of real estate properties, is a form of asset-based financing. In a typical sale-leaseback transaction, the seller-lessee gives up the residual value of the property, which can be substantial for real estate assets. As a result, the periodic payments under the lease may be lower than interest payments on other forms of financing. Another reason for entering into sale-leaseback transactions may be the desire to move the property and related debt off a company's balance sheet, thereby improving a company's debt-to-equity ratio. Loan agreements or indentures with restrictive debt covenants may place a limit on the amount of debt a company may have outstanding. Through sale-leaseback transactions that allow for a derecognition of the asset and related debt, companies owning real estate may be able to enter into new borrowing arrangements that would otherwise not be available.

When entering into sale-leaseback transactions, seller-lessees need to consider the tax consequences: A tenant of the property is entitled to deduct rental payments on the property from its income, whereas an owner of the property deducts the interest portion of the debt service in addition to the depreciation on building and property improvements. The tax effects of a sale-leaseback transaction are complex and depend on the facts and circumstances of the individual transaction, such as the tax bracket of the tax payer, depreciation recapture, and taxable gain to the seller.

What are some of the advantages for a buyer-lessor? A buyer-lessor acquires real estate property together with a steady income stream over the term of the lease, which provides the buyer-lessor with a return that—absent a seller-lessee's default—is guaranteed. The acquisition of real property under a sale-leaseback agreement can be a good investment, especially when considering that the buyer benefits from any future appreciation of the real property. Ownership also provides for a stronger legal position than the position of a mortgage holder, if the lessee defaults on its lease payments. These advantages have to be weighed against the costs involved in structuring a sale-leaseback transaction, which needs to be tailored to the specific situation of the seller-lessee. Like the seller-lessee, the buyer-lessor must carefully evaluate the tax consequences before entering into a sale-leaseback transaction.

5.2 ACCOUNTING FOR SALE-LEASEBACK TRANSACTIONS INVOLVING REAL ESTATE

The two major building blocks for the accounting rules relating to real estate sale-leaseback transactions are Financial Accounting Standards Board (FASB) Statement No. 66, *Accounting for Sales of Real Estate,* and FASB Statement No. 13, *Accounting for Leases.* Real estate sale-leaseback transactions were originally addressed in Statement 13. The provisions of Statement 13 were interpreted rather liberally by the constituents: The principal perceived abuse was an interpretation that allowed a seller-lessee to achieve off-balance sheet accounting treatment for a sale-leaseback transaction of real estate that included a repurchase option. A seller that sold a real estate property, leased it back, and retained a fixed-price option to repurchase the property was not precluded from recording a sale for the property sold subject to the leaseback,[1] while a seller that sold real estate with a fixed-price

---

1   Assuming all other criteria for the recording of a sale were met.

repurchase option without a leaseback *was* precluded from recording a sale.[2] In May 1998, the FASB issued FASB Statement No. 98, *Accounting for Leases: Sale-Leaseback Transactions Involving Real Estate, Sales-Type Leases of Real Estate, Definition of the Lease Term, Initial Direct Costs of Direct Financing*, which replaced the provisions of Statement 13 with respect to sale-leaseback transactions involving real estate and limited the conditions under which accounting for the sale-leaseback of real estate as a sale and leaseback would be appropriate. The provisions of Statement 98 relating to sale-leaseback transactions involving real estate apply equally to sale-leaseback transactions involving real estate with equipment and equipment integral to real estate.[3]

Integral equipment is defined in FASB Interpretation (FIN) No. 43 as "any physical structure or equipment attached to the real estate that cannot be removed and used separately without incurring significant cost."[4] The Emerging Issues Task Force (EITF) dealt with the issue of determining whether equipment is integral equipment in EITF Issue No. 00-13, *Determining Whether Equipment Is "Integral Equipment" Subject to FASB Statements No. 66 and No. 98*, and concluded: When

---

EXAMPLE—INTEGRAL EQUIPMENT[5]

MFG-Company sells and leases back equipment it will continue to use in its manufacturing operations. The fair value of the production equipment (installed) at lease inception is $1,075,000. The estimated cost to remove the equipment after installation is $50,000. Additionally, it is expected that it will cost $30,000 to repair damage to the existing location as a result of the removal. The estimated cost to ship and reinstall the equipment at a new site is $85,000. This example assumes that there is no diminution in the fair value of the equipment as a result of the removal.

Does the equipment constitute "integral equipment"?

In accordance with the consensus in EITF Issue No. 00-13, MFG performs the following calculation:

	US-$
Equipment removal:	50,000
Damage repair:	30,000
Shipping and reinstallation:	85,000
Total:	165,000

$165,000/$1,075,000 = 15.3%

Because the cost of removal combined with the diminution in value exceeds 10% of the fair value (installed) of the production equipment, the cost to remove the equipment and use it separately is deemed to be significant. Therefore, the production equipment is integral equipment.

---

2   As discussed in Section 3.5.4.1 of Chapter 3, the mere existence of a repurchase option precludes sale accounting in real estate sale transactions under FASB Statement No. 66.

3   FAS 98, paragraph 43

4   FIN 43, paragraph 2

5   EITF Issue No. 00-13, Exhibit 00-13A

the combined total of both the cost to remove the equipment plus its decrease in value is in excess of 10% of the fair value of the equipment, including installation cost, the equipment should be considered integral equipment.

A sale-leaseback transaction involving real estate with equipment includes any sale-leaseback transaction in which the equipment and the real estate are sold and leased back as a package, irrespective of the relative value of the equipment and the real estate. Thus, sale-leaseback transactions of manufacturing facilities, power plants, and office buildings with furniture and fixtures are governed by the guidance for sale-leaseback transactions involving real estate.[6] Similarly, the sale of a power plant coupled with an electricity supply contract between the seller and the buyer of the plant is also subject to the real estate sale-leaseback provisions, if the electricity supply contract meets the definition of a lease. As discussed above, a sale-leaseback transaction involving equipment (whether integral or not) should not be separated into two separate transactions for accounting purposes (a sale-leaseback of equipment and a sale-leaseback of real estate), even if the real estate portion of the transaction is *de minimis*. This is important to realize, since the sale-leaseback provisions relating to equipment[7] are less restrictive than the provisions relating to the sale-leaseback of real estate.

Statement 98 also addresses sale-leaseback transactions in which the seller-lessee sells property improvements or integral equipment to a buyer-lessor and leases them back while retaining the underlying land.[8]

5.2.1 ACCOUNTING BY THE SELLER-LESSEE   Certain arrangements may inadvertently trigger the accounting consequences of a sale-leaseback transaction. For example, in build-to-suit leases with lessee involvement,[9] the lessee may be deemed the owner of the asset during the period of construction. After the construction of the asset is complete and the asset is leased to the lessee, the accounting for the transaction follows sale-leaseback rules. Similarly, a modification of a capital lease that results in operating lease classification is accounted for following the guidance for sale-leaseback transactions.

A sale-leaseback transaction of real estate is accounted for following one of three methods: Recognizing a sale of real estate and recording a leasing transaction (referred to as "sale-leaseback accounting") is appropriate only if certain criteria are met. A transaction that does not qualify for sale-leaseback accounting is accounted for under the deposit or financing method.

5.2.1.1 Sale-Leaseback Accounting   Sale-leaseback accounting is a method of accounting for a sale-leaseback transaction in which the seller-lessee records the

---

6   EITF Issue No. 01-8 provides guidance for determining whether an arrangement contains a lease.
7   See FASB Statement No. 13, paragraphs 32–34
8   FAS 98, paragraph 6
9   Section 4.6.11 of Chapter 4 discusses build-to-suit leases.

sale, removes all property and related extinguished liabilities from its balance sheet, recognizes gain or loss from the sale (in the current and future periods as provided for by paragraph 33 of FASB Statement No. 13),[10] and classifies the leaseback as an operating lease or a capital lease, depending on the terms of the lease.[11]

A common misconception is that under sale-leaseback accounting rules, the property is automatically removed from the books of the seller. While it is true that the recording of a sale triggers the removal of the asset from the seller's books, the leased-back property will be reflected on the seller-lessee's balance sheet as an asset if the lease is considered a capital lease. If the seller-lessee desires off-balance sheet treatment—for example, to improve its balance sheet ratios or to meet its debt covenants—the terms of the transaction have to be structured so that the lease does not meet the capital lease classification criteria.

The following three steps need to be performed to evaluate the appropriateness of sale-leaseback accounting and the amount of profit to be recognized at the time of sale:

Step One: Determine that sale recognition is appropriate following the guidance in FASB Statement No. 66.[12]

Step Two: If sale recognition is appropriate: Determine whether the criteria for sale-leaseback accounting in FASB Statement No. 98 are met.[13]

Step Three: If criteria for sale-leaseback accounting are met: Determine:

    a. Proper lease classification (capital vs. operating lease)

    b. Profit or loss on the sale, calculated in accordance with FASB Statement No. 66

    c. Portion of profit to be recognized at the time of sale, as provided for in FASB Statement No. 13

The criteria that must be met for a transaction to be accounted for as a sale of real estate (Step One) are explained in Chapter 3. The determination of whether the criteria for sale-leaseback accounting are met and the calculation of the portion of the profit to be recognized at the time of sale (Steps Two and Three) are outlined below.

---

10   In a sale-leaseback transaction of real estate, the amount of profit on the sale is determined in accordance with the provisions of FASB Statement No. 66. Profit or loss on the sale is recognized in accordance with paragraph 33 of FASB Statement No. 13.

11   FAS 98, paragraph 70

12   If sale recognition is not permitted, the transaction is accounted for under the deposit or financing method.

13   If the criteria for sale-leaseback accounting are not met, the transaction is accounted for under the deposit or financing method. Note that the criteria for sale-leaseback accounting (Step Two) subsume some of the criteria under Step One.

5.2.1.1.1 SALE-LEASEBACK ACCOUNTING—CRITERIA

Sale-leaseback accounting is only appropriate if a sale-leaseback transaction involving real estate satisfies all of the following three criteria:[14]

1. Normal leaseback
2. Adequate initial and continuing investment
3. Absence of continuing involvement

Normal Leaseback.   A normal leaseback is a lessee-lessor relationship that involves the active use of the leased back property by the seller-lessee in consideration for payment of rent. *Active use* of the property by the seller-lessee refers to the use of the property during the lease term in the seller-lessee's trade or business. Except for a minor sublease, the lessee is prohibited from subleasing the property leased back. A sublease is considered minor if the present value of a reasonable amount of rentals for the subleased portion represents 10% or less of the fair value of the asset sold.[15] *Active use* of the property may involve the providing of services where the occupancy of the property is generally transient or short-term and is integral to the ancillary services being provided. Those ancillary services include, but are not limited to, housekeeping, inventory control, entertainment, bookkeeping, and food services. Thus, the use of property by a seller-lessee engaged in the hotel or bonded warehouse business, or the operation of a golf course or a parking lot is considered active use.[16]

Adequate Initial and Continuing Investment.   The second criterion that must be met is sufficient initial and continuing investment by the buyer-lessor: Payment terms and provisions must adequately demonstrate the buyer-lessor's initial and continuing investment in the property. Whether a buyer-lessor's initial and continuing investment in the property is adequate is determined in accordance with the guidance provided in Statement 66; if the buyer's investment is considered inadequate, sale recognition is precluded. The requirement of "initial and continuing investment" referred to in paragraph 7(b) of Statement 98 can easily be misunderstood. It does not mean that the buyer-lessor must have made an investment adequate to qualify for the accrual method of accounting under Statement 66.[17] Rather, the investment made by the buyer has to be adequate to allow for sale accounting under Statement 66.[18]

Absence of Continuing Involvement.   Any form of continuing involvement by the seller-lessee with the leased property—other than a normal leaseback—that results in the seller-lessee not transferring the risks or rewards of ownership to the buyer-lessor precludes sale-leaseback accounting. The continuing involvement provisions

---

14   FAS 98, paragraph 7
15   FAS 98, paragraph 8
16   FAS 98, paragraph 8
17   Example 1 in Appendix A of FASB Statement No. 98 outlines a fact pattern in which a seller-lessee uses sale-leaseback accounting, with gain on the sale being recognized under the installment method of accounting.
18   FAS 98, paragraph 7(b)

for sale-leaseback accounting are more stringent that the continuing involvement provisions relating to the sale of real estate, established in Statement 66.[19]

The following are examples of continuing involvement that preclude sale-leaseback accounting:[20]

1. The seller-lessee has an obligation or an option[21] to repurchase the property, or the buyer-lessor can compel the seller-lessee to repurchase the property.

2. The seller-lessee guarantees the buyer-lessor's investment or a return on that investment for a limited or extended period of time.

3. The seller-lessee is required to pay the buyer-lessor at the end of the lease term for a decline in the fair value of the property below the estimated residual value on some basis other than excess wear and tear of the property.

4. The seller-lessee provides nonrecourse financing to the buyer-lessor for any portion of the sales proceeds, or provides recourse financing in which the only recourse is to the leased asset.[22]

5. The seller-lessee is not relieved of the obligation under any existing debt related to the property.

6. The seller-lessee provides collateral on behalf of the buyer-lessor other than the property directly involved in the sale-leaseback transaction; the seller-lessee or a related party to the seller-lessee guarantees the buyer-lessor's debt; or a related party to the seller-lessee guarantees a return of or a return on the buyer-lessor's investment.

7. The seller-lessee's rental payments are contingent on some predetermined or determinable level of future operations of the buyer-lessor.

8. The seller-lessee enters into a sale-leaseback transaction involving property improvements or integral equipment without leasing the underlying land to the buyer-lessor.[23]

---

19   *Substantial* continuing involvement with the property precludes profit recognition under the full accrual method in real estate sales transactions, whereas *any* continuing involvement other than a normal leaseback precludes sale-leaseback accounting. [FAS 66, paragraph 5(d); FAS 98, paragraph 10] Similarly, profit on real estate sales transactions can be recognized by the accrual method once the seller has transferred to the buyer *the usual* risks and rewards of ownership, whereas sale-leaseback accounting is appropriate only if *all* of the other risks and rewards of ownership have been transferred. [FAS 66, paragraph 5(d); FAS 98, paragraph 7(c)]

20   FAS 98, paragraphs 11-13; Examples 4, 5, and 9 in this list would not preclude profit recognition under FASB Statement No. 66.

21   A right of first refusal based on a bona fide offer by a third party ordinarily is not an obligation or an option to repurchase; however, an unusually long time granted to the seller-lessee to exercise the right of first refusal may indicate continuing involvement, as it could effectively constrain a buyer-lessor that attempts to sell the property. An agreement that allows the seller-lessee to repurchase the asset in the event no third-party offer is made is in substance an option to repurchase.

22   Sale-leaseback accounting is not precluded if a seller-lessee provides *recourse* financing to a substantive buyer-lessor, that is, a buyer-lessor with substantial net assets/operations other than the property sold and leased back.

23   Paragraph 38 of FASB Statement No. 66 precludes sale recognition for property improvements if the term of the land lease (1) does not cover substantially all of the economic life of the property improvements or (2) is not for a substantial period, for example, 20 years. If it is determined that a sale cannot be recognized for the improvements, sale-leaseback accounting is inappropriate.

9. The buyer-lessor is obligated to share with the seller-lessee any portion of the appreciation of the property.

10. Any other provision or circumstance that allows the seller-lessee to participate in any future profits of the buyer-lessor or the appreciation of the leased property—for example, a situation in which the seller-lessee owns or has an option to acquire any interest in the buyer-lessor.

The illustrative list of examples provided above is not all-inclusive. *Any* continuing involvement besides a normal leaseback that indicates that not all of the risks and rewards of ownership have been transferred needs to be avoided to meet the criteria for sale-leaseback accounting.[24] The terms of the sale-leaseback transaction have to be carefully evaluated to determine whether a form of such continuing involvement exists. For example, below-market rentals generally preclude sale-leaseback accounting, because lower rentals are presumed to have been negotiated in exchange for a below-market price for the asset sold. Through below-market rentals, the seller-lessee is considered to have provided financing to the buyer-lessor. Unless that financing is recourse to the buyer, or unless the seller has recourse to assets other than the asset subject to the sale-leaseback, a form of prohibited continuing involvement exists.[25] Similarly, rentals that are declining over the term of the lease may be an indication that the seller-lessee is in essence providing financing to the buyer-lessor, if the declining rentals are above-market at the beginning of the lease term and below-market during later periods.

However, if a form of continuing involvement does not impact the transfer of risks and rewards, it would not necessarily constitute prohibited continuing involvement, that is, it would not necessarily preclude sale-leaseback accounting under Statement 98.

EXAMPLE—RESTRICTIONS ON USE

Sale-Crop, Inc. (S) sells a parcel of land to a buyer, which intends to build a veterinary clinic on the land. S has been using the land for purposes of growing crops. S leases the land back for a period of one year to be able to harvest the crops already planted. S and the purchaser have agreed that the land should be used to build and operate a veterinary clinic, that is, the sale agreement contains a restriction on how the land can be used.

Does the restriction on how to use the land constitute a form of continuing involvement within the meaning of FASB Statement No. 98?

No. Restrictions on the use of real estate ordinarily do not constitute a form of continuing involvement, as the seller has transferred the risks and rewards of ownership.

---

24   FAS 98, paragraph 7(c)

25   Sale-leaseback accounting is not precluded if a seller-lessee provides *recourse* financing to a substantive buyer-lessor. Additionally, if a seller-lessee provides nonrecourse financing to a buyer-lessor and obtains a third-party guarantee or letter of credit from a substantive, credit-worthy party, sale-leaseback accounting is not precluded.

5.2.1.1.2 Recognition of Profit or Loss

In a sale-leaseback transaction, the provisions of the sale and the lease are intertwined and may not accurately reflect the fair value of the individual sale and lease transaction; that is, the stated sales price may be higher or lower than the fair value of the property, with a corresponding adjustment made to the lease payments. Because of this interdependence of the terms of the lease and the terms of the sale, profit is generally recognized over the term of the lease.

Nevertheless if the fair value of the property at the time of the sale-leaseback transaction is less than its carrying amount, a loss should be recognized immediately up to the amount of the difference between the carrying amount and fair value.[26]

General Rule for Profit Recognition.   Profit on the sale[27] is generally deferred and amortized as follows:

- In proportion to the amortization of the leased asset if the lease is classified as a capital lease
- In proportion to the related gross rentals charged to expense over the lease term if the lease is classified as an operating lease[28]

There are two exceptions to this general rule that the profit on the sale must be deferred and amortized over the lease term.

Exceptions

Seller Retains only Minor Portion of Use.   In a sale-leaseback transaction in which a seller retains only a minor portion of the use of the property sold, no portion of the profit[29] on the sale transaction is deferred. A leaseback is considered "minor" if the present value of a *reasonable amount* of leaseback rentals represents 10% or less of the fair value of the asset sold. In such a minor leaseback, the seller-lessee is presumed to have transferred to the purchaser-lessor the right to substantially all of the remaining use of the property sold, and the seller-lessee is presumed to have retained only a minor portion of its use.[30] Thus, a minor leaseback can result from the use of substantially all of the property sold for a relatively short period of time or from the use of a small portion of the property sold over a longer lease period.

---

26   FAS 13, paragraph 33(c)
27   Profit on the sale refers to the profit that would be recognized on the sale if there were no leaseback.
28   The lease term excludes any renewal options other than bargain renewal options. Upon exercise of a renewal option before the end of the lease term, any unamortized profit on the sale is amortized prospectively over the remaining lease term including the renewal period.
29   The profit to be recognized is determined in accordance with the provisions of FASB Statement No. 66.
30   FAS 13, paragraph 33(a)

EXAMPLE—MINOR LEASEBACK[31]

Mall-Builder Inc. (MB) constructs a shopping center (cost: $10 million) and sells it to a third-party buyer at a cash sales price of $11.2 million, which reflects its fair value. The sale meets the criteria for the accrual method of accounting pursuant to the provisions in FASB Statement No. 66. At the same time, MB leases back a portion of the shopping center for a period of 40 years. The present value of the rentals for the leased back portion amounts to approximately 8% of the fair value of the shopping center. The rentals are reflective of fair value.

MB determines that the transaction meets the criteria for sale-leaseback accounting:

- A normal leaseback
- Payment terms and provisions that adequately demonstrate the buyer-lessor's initial and continuing investments in the property
- Payment terms and provisions that transfer all of the other risks and rewards of ownership

How much profit should MB recognize at the time of sale?

MB should recognize $1.2 million profit at the time of sale. The leaseback is minor, as the present value of the rentals does not exceed 10% of the fair value of the asset sold.

The continuing involvement provisions of Statement 98 apply, even if the leaseback is "minor." That is, if a prohibited form of continuing involvement with the property exists for a sale-leaseback transaction with minor leaseback, the seller-lessee has to account for the transaction under the deposit or financing method. Below-market rentals in minor leasebacks are further discussed in Section 5.3.1 in this Chapter.

Seller Retains More than Minor Part, but Less than Substantially All of the Use.   If the seller-lessee retains more than a minor part but less than substantially all of the use of the property through the leaseback, special profit recognition rules apply. A seller-lessee is deemed to have retained more than a minor but less than substantially all of the use of the property through the leaseback if the present value of the lease payments exceeds 10%, but is less than 90% of the fair value of the asset sold.[32]

---

31   Adapted from FASB Statement No. 28, paragraph 23

32   " 'Substantially all' and 'minor' are used here in the context of the concepts underlying the lease classification criteria of FASB Statement No. 13. In that context, a test based on the 90% recovery criterion of FASB Statement No. 13 could be used as a guideline; that is, if the present value of a reasonable amount of rental for the leaseback represents 10% or less of the fair value of the asset sold, the seller-lessee could be presumed to have transferred to the purchaser-lessor the right to substantially all of the remaining use of the property sold, and the seller-lessee could be presumed to have retained only a minor portion of such use." [FAS 13, paragraph 33(b), footnote 23a]

At the time of sale, the seller should recognize a profit on the sale[33] in excess of:

1. The present value of the minimum lease payments over the lease term if the leaseback is classified as an operating lease
2. The recorded amount of the leased asset if the leaseback is classified as a capital lease

The remaining profit is deferred and amortized over the lease term.

For purposes of applying this provision, the present value of the minimum lease payments for an operating lease is computed using the interest rate that is used to apply the 90% of fair value test for lease classification purposes:[34] The seller-lessee's incremental borrowing rate is the appropriate interest rate to use,[35] unless the lessor's implicit rate is known and lower than the lessee's incremental borrowing rate.

EXAMPLE—LEASEBACKS THAT ARE NOT MINOR BUT DO NOT COVER SUBSTANTIALLY ALL OF THE USE OF THE PROPERTY SOLD[36]

Sandy Malls, Inc. (SM) sells an existing shopping center (carrying value: $1 million) to a third-party buyer (sales price: $3.5 million). At the same time, SM leases back part of the shopping center for its remaining economic life. The fair value of the land is less than 25% of the total fair value of the leased property at the inception of the lease.[37] The present value of the minimum lease payments amounts to $1.3 million, which equals the fair value of the leased space. The sale meets the criteria for full and immediate profit recognition,[38] as well as the criteria for sale-leaseback accounting.

How much profit should SM recognize at the time of sale?

SM should recognize $1.2 million profit at the time of sale, calculated as follows:

Sales Price:	$3,500,000
Carrying Value:	$1,000,000
Profit on the Sale	$2,500,000
Recorded amount of leased asset (capital lease)[39]	$1,300,000
Profit to be recognized at the time of sale	$1,200,000

---

33   Profit or loss on the sale refers to the profit or loss that would be recognized on the sale of real estate without a leaseback provision.

34   FAS 13, paragraph 7(d)

35   The lessee's incremental borrowing rate is the rate that, at the inception of the lease, the lessee would have incurred to borrow over a similar term the funds necessary to purchase the leased asset.

36   Adapted from FASB Statement No. 28, Appendix B, paragraph 25

37   If the fair value of the land were to exceed 25% of the total fair value of the leased property at the inception of the lease, land and building would have to be evaluated separately for purposes of determining the lease classification. This scenario is discussed in FASB Statement No. 28, Appendix B, paragraph 25.

38   Criteria to be met for the accrual method of accounting are outlined in paragraph 5 of FASB Statement No. 66.

39   SM leases a portion of the shopping center for its remaining economic life, which leads to capital lease classification pursuant to paragraph 7(c) of FASB Statement No. 13.

EXAMPLES—PROFIT RECOGNITION

Store-Long, Inc. (SL) sells its new warehouse and the underlying land for $18 million (carrying amount of property: $8 million), which equals the fair value of the property. The fair value of the land is less than 25% of the fair value of the property.[40] At the same time, SL enters into a leaseback transaction for the warehouse. SL evaluates the sale-leaseback transaction and determines that the criteria for sale-leaseback accounting are met.

Scenario 1: SL leases back the warehouse for all of its remaining useful life.

Scenario 2: SL leases back part of the building for its remaining useful life. The present value of the rentals for the leaseback represents 50% of the fair value of the asset sold. The lease meets the criteria for a capital lease; the leased asset is recorded at $9 million.

Scenario 3: SL leases back part of the building for its remaining useful life. The present value of a reasonable amount of rentals for the leaseback represents 5% of the fair value of the asset sold.

How should SL recognize the profit on the sale?

SL evaluates Scenarios 1 through 3 as follows:

SCENARIO 1

SL retains substantially all of the use of the property sold. The sale is classified as a capital lease, since SL retains substantially all of the use of the building. The profit on the sale is deferred and amortized over the lease term in proportion to the amortization of the leased asset, as the leased asset meets the criteria for a capital lease.

SCENARIO 2

Since SL leases back part of the building and has determined that the present value of the rentals for the leaseback represents 50% of the fair value of the asset sold, SL has retained more than a minor part, but less than substantially all of the use of the property. Special profit recognition criteria apply based on the amount of profit compared to the recorded amount of the leased asset. To the extent the profit on the sale ($10 million) exceeds the recorded amount of the leased asset ($9 million), it can be recognized at the time of sale—in this Scenario, $1 million. The remaining profit ($9 million) is deferred and amortized over the lease term in proportion to the amortization of the leased asset.

SCENARIO 3

SL has entered into a minor leaseback, since the present value of a reasonable amount of rentals for the leaseback represents 5% of the fair value of the asset sold. Under a minor leaseback, no profit deferral is necessary. SL can recognize the profit ($10 million) in full at the time of sale.

---

40   If the fair value of the land were to exceed 25% of the total fair value of the leased property, the leaseback of the land would have to be accounted for as a separate operating lease, in accordance with paragraph 26(b)(ii)(a) of FASB Statement No. 13. Since there is no transfer of title, the lease of the land would be classified as operating lease. Paragraph 25 of FASB Statement No. 28 provides an example for that fact pattern.

5.2.1.2 Deposit or Financing Method If sale-leaseback accounting is not appropriate for a sale-leaseback transaction, the seller-lessee uses the deposit or financing method, whichever is appropriate under FASB Statement No. 66.[41]

The *deposit method* is generally appropriate in the following circumstances:

- A sale has not been consummated.[42]
- Collection on the buyer-lessor's note is uncertain.
- The form of continuing involvement is a guarantee of a return on the buyer-lessor's investment for a *limited* time.[43]
- The buyer's initial investment is small compared to the sales value of the property.[44]

The *financing method* is generally used in the following situations:

- The seller-lessee guarantees a return *on* the buyer-lessor's investment for an *extended* period of time.
- The seller-lessee guarantees a return *of* the buyer-lessor's investment.
- Other forms of continuing involvement, such as the obligation or option to repurchase the property.[45]

If more than one form of prohibited continuing involvement is present, judgment must be exercised to determine whether the use of the deposit method or the use of the financing method is more reflective of the substance of the transaction.

Under the deposit method, the property and any related debt remain on the seller-lessee's balance sheet, and the seller-lessee continues to depreciate the property. Lease payments decrease (and, if the seller-lessee is providing financing, any collections on the buyer-lessor's note increase) the seller-lessee's deposit account. Under the deposit method, a loss is recognized if at any time the net carrying amount of the property exceeds the sum of the balance in the deposit account, the fair value of the unrecorded note receivable, and any debt assumed by the buyer;[46] a loss that would have to be recognized upon recognition of a sale cannot be deferred simply because the criteria for the recording of a sale have not been met.[47]

Similarly, under the financing method, the property and any related debt remain on the seller-lessee's balance sheet, and the seller-lessee continues to depreciate the property.

However, lease payments from the seller-lessee to the buyer-lessor (as well as collections on the buyer-lessor's note, if the seller-lessee provides financing) contain an interest portion. Lease payments and any collections on the buyer-lessor's

---

41 FAS 98, paragraphs 10, 30, and 34
42 FAS 66, paragraphs 6 and 20
43 FAS 66, paragraph 28
44 FAS 66, paragraph 22
45 FAS 66, paragraph 26
46 FAS 98, paragraph 30
47 See Section 5.3.2 in this Chapter for further discussion regarding impairment.

note, exclusive of the interest portion, are reflected as adjustments to the financing obligation. FASB Statement No. 98 does not specify the interest rate to be used when dividing lease payments into interest and principal. The specific facts and circumstances of each particular transaction need to be considered. In many cases, the seller's incremental borrowing rate will be the appropriate interest rate to use; however, in situations in which the incremental borrowing rate leads to atypical results, such as a negatively amortizing financing obligation, the use of the interest rate implicit in the lease or inherent in the expected cash flows from the sale-leaseback transaction may be more appropriate.[48] When determining whether and in which manner to amortize the financing obligation, care needs to be taken so as to avoid a "built-in" or "scheduled" loss. For example, if the financing method is being applied as a result of the seller-lessee guaranteeing a return of the buyer-lessor's investment for a period of one year, the sale-leaseback transaction would be expected to qualify for sale-leaseback accounting at the end of the guarantee period. The carrying amount of the leased-back real estate property at the end of the guarantee period should not exceed the financing obligation at that point in time.[49]

EXAMPLE—USE OF DEPOSIT AND FINANCING METHOD[50]

On January 1, year 1, Sun Lounge, Inc. (SL) sells a building to a buyer-lessor for $950,000 (which is equal to its fair value) and enters into an agreement to lease back the building for a period of 10 years at $150,000 per year. The property has a historical cost of $1.3 million, and accumulated depreciation at the date of the transaction is $400,000. Depreciation expense is $80,000 per year. At closing, SL receives a cash payment of $50,000 and a 10-year $900,000 recourse note with a 10% annual interest rate (SL's incremental borrowing rate) and annual payments of $146,471. SL determines that due to continuing involvement resulting from a guarantee provided by SL, the criteria for sale-leaseback accounting are not met.

> *Scenario 1*: SL provides a guarantee on the buyer-lessor's investment for a limited period of time.
> *Scenario 2*: SL provides a guarantee on the buyer-lessor's investment for an extended period of time.
>
> What journal entries would SL record in Year 1?

SCENARIO 1

The use of the deposit method is appropriate, and SL would record the following journal entries in Year 1:

Cash	$50,000	
Deposit		$50,000

To record the receipt of the cash at closing

---

48   FAS 98, Appendix A, example 3
49   See Section 3.6.6, which discusses the application of the financing method in a real estate sale.
50   Example adapted from FASB Statement No. 98, Appendix A, paragraphs 30–37

Cash	$146,471	
Deposit		$146,471

To record the receipt of principal and interest payments for the note

Deposit	$150,000	
Cash		$150,000

To record lease payments from SL to the buyer-lessor

Depreciation Expense	$80,000	
Accumulated Depreciation		$80,000

To record depreciation

SCENARIO 2

The use of the financing method is appropriate due to the guarantee provided for an extended period of time.

Cash	$50,000	
Financing Obligation		$50,000

To record the receipt of the initial down payment

Cash	$146,471	
Financing Obligation		$146,471[51]

To record the receipt of principal and interest payments for the note

Financing Obligation	$145,000	
Interest Expense	$ 5,000	
Cash		$150,000

To record lease payments from SL to buyer-lessor on down payment of $50,000 received at closing

Depreciation Expense	$80,000	
Accumulated Depreciation		$80,000

To record depreciation

5.2.1.3 Subsequent Change in Circumstances   When a sale-leaseback transaction, originally accounted for under the deposit or financing method, subsequently meets the criteria for sale-leaseback accounting, sale-leaseback accounting is applied. The leaseback is classified and accounted for in accordance with FASB Statement No. 13 as capital or operating lease, as if the sale had been recognized at the inception of the lease. Gain or loss on the sale transaction is recognized in accordance with the gain recognition criteria applicable to sale-leaseback transactions, as outlined above.[52] If the leaseback meets one of the criteria for classification as a capital lease, the asset and liability accounts relating to the leaseback are recorded to reflect accumulated

---

51   An acceptable accounting alternative may be the recording of the buyer-lessor's note in addition to the cash received from the buyer-lessor, rather than recording only the cash payments received. See Section 3.6.6 in Chapter 3 for further discussion.

52   FAS 98, Appendix A, paragraph 27; recognition of profit or loss is discussed in Section 5.2.1.1 in this Chapter.

amortization that would have been charged to expense had the lease been recorded as a capital lease at its inception. The change in the related lease accounts from the inception of the lease to the time of sale recognition is included in the computation of the gain or loss on sale.[53]

EXAMPLE—CHANGE FROM DEPOSIT METHOD TO SALE-LEASEBACK ACCOUNTING[54]

Store Long Inc. (SL) sells its warehouse to a buyer-lessor for $950,000 (fair value). The payment terms are as follows: $50,000 cash and a 10-year $900,000 recourse note with a 10% annual interest rate and annual payments of $146,471. SL enters into a lease agreement for 10 years at $150,000 per year. At the time of the transaction, the property has a historical cost of $1.3 million and accumulated depreciation of $400,000. Depreciation expense is $80,000 per year.

SL determines that deposit accounting is the appropriate method for recording the transaction. At the end of year 3, income recognition under the full accrual method becomes appropriate. SL determines that sale-leaseback accounting should be applied to the transaction and that the leaseback meets the criteria for a capital lease.

How should SL account for the transaction in years 1 through 3?

ACCOUNTING IN YEARS 1–3

Under the deposit method, SL continues to record depreciation on the real estate sold. Principal and interest received from the buyer are recorded as deposits, and lease payments made are deducted from the deposit recorded on the seller's books.

CHANGE TO SALE-LEASEBACK ACCOUNTING AT THE END OF YEAR 3

At the end of year 3, income recognition under the full accrual method is appropriate. SL determines that the lease met the criteria for a capital lease at the inception of the lease. Had the lease been recorded as capital lease at the beginning of year 1 (the beginning of the lease term), the balance sheet accounts at the end of year 3 would be as follows:

Asset under Capital Lease:	$950,000
Accumulated Amortization:	($285,000)[55]
Capital Lease Obligation:	($747,363)[56]
Note Receivable:	$713,082[57]

---

53   An example is provided in FASB Statement No. 98, Appendix A, paragraphs 30–33.

54   Adapted from FASB Statement No. 98, Appendix A, example 2; paragraphs 35–39 of FASB Statement No. 98 provide examples of sale-leaseback transactions accounted for as financing with subsequent sale recognition.

55   The asset under capital lease ($950,000) is amortized over the lease term (10 years). Amortization expense per year amounts to $95,000. Accumulated amortization at the end of year 3 amounts to $285,000.

56   The gross lease obligation of $1.5 million ($150,000 for 10 years) is amortized over 10 years, using a constant interest rate (9.301595%), which is assumed to be the buyer-lessor's incremental borrowing rate.

57   Present value of the remaining note payments at the end of year 3, discounted at 10%.

These amounts are compared to the amounts that the seller-lessee actually had recorded on its books at the end of year 3:

Fixed Assets:	$ 1,300,000
Accumulated Depreciation:	($ 640,000)[58]
Deposits:	($ 39,413)[59]

The seller-lessee records the following adjusting journal entry at the end of year 3:

Asset under Capital Lease	$ 950,000	
Note Receivable	$ 713,082	
Accumulated Depreciation	$ 640,000	
Deposits	$ 39,413	
Accumulated Amortization		$ 285,000
Capital Lease Obligation		$ 747,363
Fixed Assets		$1,300,000
Deferred Gain		$ 10,132

The deferred gain of $10,132 is amortized over the remaining term of the lease in proportion to the amortization of the leased asset.

When a sale-leaseback transaction, originally accounted for using sale-leaseback accounting, subsequently ceases to qualify for sale-leaseback accounting, a determination must be made whether sale-leaseback accounting continues to be appropriate. There is a presumption that the seller-lessee's subsequent change in involvement with the property was contemplated at the date the sale-leaseback transaction was executed, and any changes in the nature of the seller-lessee involvement with the real estate previously sold should be evaluated when determining whether that presumption can be overcome.

For example, if a seller-lessee—subsequent to entering into the sale-leaseback arrangement—decides to sublease the sold and leased back property, it is presumed that the sublease was contemplated at the time the transaction was entered into. If this presumption cannot be overcome with substantive, pervasive evidence, the seller-lessee needs to reverse its accounting for the sale. However, there are situations, in which sale-leaseback accounting remains appropriate. For example, there could be a scenario in which the economic situation of the seller-lessee deteriorates significantly in years subsequent to entering into the sale-leaseback transaction. As a result of that deterioration, executive management of the seller-lessee may decide to downsize operations and sublease more than a minor part of the property. If the seller-lessee can establish that the downsizing was not contemplated at the time the sale-leaseback transaction was executed, sale-leaseback accounting

---

58   Calculated as: $400,000 (accumulated depreciation at the beginning of Period 1) plus depreciation expense ($80,000) for 3 years.

59   Calculated as: $50,000 cash down payment plus 3 annual principal and interest payments of $146,471, less lease payments of $150,000 for 3 years.

would remain appropriate. The shorter the time period between the sale-leaseback transaction and the subsequent change in facts that lead to prohibited continuing involvement, the more difficult it will be for a seller-lessee to overcome that presumption.

5.2.2 ACCOUNTING BY THE BUYER-LESSOR   FASB Statement No. 98 provides guidance for the accounting of a seller-lessee only. No special provisions are included that relate to the buyer-lessor. The buyer-lessor records the purchase of the real estate assets at cost, allocating the purchase price to land and buildings (and any intangibles, such as lease contracts and tenant relationships,[60] if applicable). The sale-leaseback is recorded as a purchase and a direct financing lease if it meets the lease classification criteria in paragraphs 7 and 8 of FASB Statement No. 13; otherwise, the lessor records the transaction as a purchase and an operating lease.[61]

The accounting by the seller-lessee and the accounting by the buyer-lessor do not necessarily mirror each other, as FASB Statements No. 66 and No. 98 are not built on the concept of symmetry. For example, in a scenario in which the seller-lessee has to apply the deposit or financing method as a result of continuing involvement with the property, both the seller-lessee and the buyer-lessor would record the real estate property on their books.

The seller-lessee may enter into a master leaseback arrangement with the buyer-lessor. Master-leaseback arrangements are prevalent in situations in which a builder completes a project, sells it to a purchaser, and leases up the building for the purchaser. How should the buyer-lessor account for any rental proceeds—or payments for rental shortfalls—received from the seller-lessee under such agreements: Adjust the basis of the property or recognize rental revenues? The Emerging Issues Task Force addressed this question in EITF Issue No. 84-37, *Sale-Leaseback Transaction with Repurchase Option*,[62] That EITF Issue provides a list of factors that, while not necessarily conclusive, are helpful in identifying rental shortfall agreements "that warrant accounting as an adjustment of the purchase price by the buyer-lessor rather than as a sale-leaseback transaction:"[63]

- The seller receives a fee for entering into the lease agreement.
- The seller's lease commitment is for a short term, and the seller does not have any renewal options.

---

60   FAS 142, paragraph 9; Section 1.6 of Chapter 1 discusses purchase price allocation in purchases of income-producing properties.

61   FAS 13, paragraph 34

62   FASB Statement No. 133 applies if the agreement is not scoped out of that Statement and the terms of the agreement meet the definition of a derivative. Typically, an agreement like the one described above meets the scope exception in paragraph 10(e)(3) of FASB Statement No. 133. [EITF Issue No. 85-27; Status-Section]; see also EITF Issue No. 85-27 for further guidance

63   EITF Issue No. 84-37, Issue 4

- The seller is relieved of its lease obligations as it obtains tenants.
- The "subleases" extend beyond the "leaseback" period.
- When a building is currently leased up, the seller's lease commitment merely represents the difference between existing lease rentals and market rents over some period.

5.3 SPECIFIC ACCOUNTING ISSUES

5.3.1 UNUSUAL TERMS OF SALE-LEASEBACK TRANSACTIONS
Terms of a sale-leaseback transaction that are substantially different from terms that an independent third-party lessor or lessee would accept indicate an exchange of some stated or unstated rights or privileges. Any unusual terms must be carefully considered when evaluating whether there is (prohibited) continuing involvement by the seller-lessee. For example, a sales price substantially below the appraised fair value of the property is an indication that the seller-lessee is providing nonrecourse financing to the buyer-lessor to be repaid through below-market rental rates. Similarly, a requirement to prepay rent and the existence of below-market rentals indicate that the seller-lessee is providing nonrecourse financing to the buyer-lessor.[64] If the provisions in the terms of the arrangement lead to the conclusion that the seller has provided nonrecourse financing to the buyer-lessor, sale-leaseback accounting is precluded.[65]

For minor leasebacks, paragraph 33(a) of FASB Statement No. 13 provides, in part: "[I]f the amount of rentals called for by the lease is unreasonable under market conditions at the inception of the lease, an appropriate amount shall be deferred or accrued, by adjusting the profit or loss on the sale, and amortized as specified in the introduction of this paragraph to adjust those rentals to a reasonable amount."

One may question whether that provision in paragraph 33(a) of Statement 13 is applicable to sale-leaseback transactions involving real estate. While some point to an example in Appendix A of FASB Statement No. 28, *Accounting for Sales with Leasebacks*, which seems to allow for the use of sale-leaseback accounting in a real estate sale-leaseback transaction, in which the seller-lessee enters into a minor leaseback and the rentals are below market,[66] others argue that Statement 28 only deals with the *manner* in which profit in a sale-leaseback transaction is being recognized in the seller-lessee's financial statements *after* it has been determined that sale-leaseback accounting is appropriate. In a real estate sale-leaseback with below-market rentals, the seller is deemed to provide nonrecourse financing to the buyer-lessor, and as a result sale-leaseback accounting

---

64   FAS 98, paragraph 9
65   FAS 98, paragraph 12(b)
66   FAS 28, paragraph 24

is precluded;[67] the guidance on the *timing* of profit recognition would not be relevant. In other words, the provisions in Statement 28 relating to the *manner* of profit recognition in a sale-leaseback transaction cannot be used to *achieve* sale-leaseback accounting.

The author believes that it is appropriate to follow the guidance in FASB Statement No. 98; that is, as far as the appropriateness of sale-leaseback accounting is concerned, not to treat minor leasebacks any different from leasebacks that are more than minor.

5.3.2 IMPAIRMENT OF PROPERTY   When entering a sale-leaseback transaction, the seller has to evaluate whether the property is impaired and determine the proper accounting for any impairment loss. The calculation of the amount of impairment loss to be recognized and the presentation of the property in the seller-lessee's financial statements depends on the accounting method used.

5.3.2.1 Use of Sale-Leaseback Accounting   If the transaction qualifies for sale-leaseback accounting, the impairment loss is recognized in accordance with the provisions in Statement 13. Paragraph 33(c) of Statement 13 requires that a loss be recognized immediately up to the amount of the difference between carrying amount and fair value, if the fair value of the property at the time of the transaction is less than its carrying amount.

Property Classified as Held and Used.[68]   If a company commits to a plan to sell and lease back a real estate property, the real estate property continues to be classified as held and used if the seller-lessee retains *more than a minor portion*[69] of the use of the property. That is the case even in a situation in which the transaction is expected to qualify for sale-leaseback accounting within one year.[70] Nevertheless, if at the date of the sale-leaseback, the fair value of the property is less than its carrying amount, a loss must be recognized immediately up to the amount of the difference between the property's carrying amount and fair value in accordance with paragraph 33(c) of Statement 13.[71] While one may argue that the impairment guidance is more stringent than for other long-lived assets classified as held and used, immediate loss recognition is consistent with the principle

---

67   FAS 98, paragraph 12(b)

68   For property classified as held and used, the provisions in FASB Statement No. 144 require that an impairment loss be recognized if the carrying amount of a long-lived asset is not recoverable and exceeds its fair value. The carrying amount of a long-lived asset is deemed not to be recoverable, if it exceeds the sum of the undiscounted cash flows expected to result from the use and eventual disposition of the asset. [FAS 144, paragraph 7]

69   As outlined in Section 5.2.1.1, a leaseback is considered "minor" if the present value of a reasonable amount of rentals for the leaseback represents 10% or less of the fair value of the asset sold. [FAS 13, paragraph 33(a)]

70   FAS 144, Appendix A, example 8

71   FAS 144, Appendix A, footnote 30

underlying FASB Statement No. 66 that losses on real estate sales transactions must not be deferred.

Property Classified as Held for Sale. If the seller-lessee will retain only a *minor* portion of the use of the property, and the transaction is expected to qualify for sale-leaseback accounting within one year,[72] the real estate is classified as held for sale and measured at the lower of its carrying amount or fair value less cost to sell. In accordance with FASB Statement No. 144, the real estate property is not depreciated while it is classified as held for sale.[73] Even when classified as held for sale, the seller-lessee will have to monitor the fair value of the real estate property to determine whether—subsequent to the recognition of any impairment loss at the time of the sale-leaseback transaction—there is a further decline or recovery in value. Such decline or recovery in value triggers the following accounting consequences:

- A loss is recognized for any initial or subsequent write-down to fair value less cost to sell.
- A gain is recognized for any subsequent increase in fair value less cost to sell, but not in excess of the cumulative loss previously recognized (for a write-down to fair value less cost to sell).[74]

5.3.2.2 Use of Deposit or Financing Method   If sale-leaseback accounting is not appropriate, the seller is deemed to be the accounting owner of the property and the property remains on the books of the seller-lessee. Paragraph 30 of Statement 98 provides that a "seller-lessee that is accounting for any transaction by the deposit method . . . shall recognize a loss if at any time the net carrying amount of the property exceeds the sum of the balance in the deposit account, the fair value of the unrecorded note receivable, and any debt assumed by the buyer." If the financing method is used, an impairment analysis would ordinarily be performed in accordance with the provisions of FASB Statement No. 144, *Accounting for the Impairment or Disposal of Long-Lived Assets.*[75]

5.3.3 MINOR SUBLEASES   FASB Statement No. 98 precludes sale-leaseback accounting if the lessee subleases part of the property sold and the sublease is more than minor. A sublease is considered more than minor if the present value of a reasonable amount of rentals for the sublease represents more than 10% of the fair value of the asset sold.[76]

---

72   This assumes that all the other criteria specified in paragraph 30 of FASB Statement No. 144 have been met.
73   FAS 144, paragraph 34
74   FAS 144, paragraph 37
75   Sections 3.6.1 and 3.6.6 in Chapter 3 discuss the application of the deposit method and financing method, respectively.
76   FAS 98, paragraph 8

EXAMPLE—MINOR SUBLEASE

Store Long, Inc. (SL) sells its warehouse for $1 million and leases back a portion of the warehouse. The present value of a reasonable amount of rentals for the space leased back amounts to $100,000. SL subleases the warehouse space to a third party. The present value of reasonable rentals for the space subleased ($100,000) amounts to 10% of the fair value of the asset sold ($1 million).

Is the sublease a "minor" sublease?

Yes, the sublease is minor, since the present value of the rentals does not exceed 10% of the fair value of the warehouse sold.

If a portion of the property is subleased at the transaction date, the sublease term to be taken into consideration for purposes of determining whether the sublease is "minor" should include the initial term of the sublease as well as any renewal options available to the sublessee, since the seller-lessee has no control over the sublessee's exercise of any renewal options.

5.3.4 SALE OF A PARTIAL INTEREST   Paragraph 13(b) of FASB Statement No. 98 provides the following example for prohibited continuing involvement: "The buyer-lessor is obligated to share with the seller-lessee any portion of the appreciation of the property." The retention of a partial interest in the real property by the seller-lessee allows for profit participation by the seller-lessee, which constitutes continuing involvement and precludes sale-leaseback accounting. For example, if a partner in a real estate venture sells real estate to the venture and leases the real property back from the venture, sale-leaseback accounting is precluded.[77]

The FASB staff responded to the following technical inquiry involving the partial sale of an interest in real estate:[78] A utility that owns a 30% undivided interest in an electric generating facility is considering the sale-leaseback of a 7% undivided interest, which would leave the utility a 23% ownership interest and a 7% leasehold interest. The issue is whether the retention of a partial interest of a property in a sale-leaseback transaction violates the continuing involvement conditions of Statement 98.

The FASB staff believes that partial sale transactions, such as in the fact pattern described above, preclude sale-leaseback accounting due to the continuing involvement of the seller-lessee.

Unless the real estate sold is legally separated, a sale-leaseback transaction cannot be bifurcated into two transactions, an outright sale for the portion not leased back, and a sale-leaseback transaction for the portion leased back.

---

77   Paragraph 101 of FASB Statement No. 66 provides that the sale of partnership interests should be considered a real estate transaction, if the sale is in substance a sale of real estate. In EITF Issue No. 98-8, the Task Force reached a consensus that the sale or transfer of an investment in the form of a financial asset that is in substance real estate should be accounted for in accordance with FASB Statement No. 66.

78   EITF Topic No. D-24

5.3.5 LEASEBACK OF A PORTION OF THE PROPERTY SOLD   The leaseback of a portion of the property sold needs to be distinguished from the sale of a partial interest. Sale-leaseback accounting is permitted for sale-leaseback transactions involving the leaseback of a portion of the property sold. Paragraph 32 of FASB Statement No. 13 provides:

> Sale-leaseback transactions involve the sale of property by the owner and a lease of the property back to the seller. A sale of property that is accompanied by a leaseback of all or any part of the property for all or part of its remaining economic life shall be accounted for by the seller-lessee in accordance with the provisions of paragraph 33 [of Statement 13] and shall be accounted for by the purchaser-lessor in accordance with the provisions of paragraph 34 [of Statement 13].

In a leaseback of a portion of the property, any gain or loss is recognized as provided for in paragraph 33 of FASB Statement No. 13.

EXAMPLE—LEASEBACK OF A PORTION OF THE PROPERTY SOLD

Sun Lounge, Inc. (SL) owns an office building. It sells the office building and leases back part of the space for its own use. The sale-leaseback of the office building is subject to the sale-leaseback rules for real estate. The floors of the office building are legally divided into separate ownership interests, and the space SL leases back represents a divided interest.

How should SL account for the sale-leaseback transaction?

Depending on the facts and circumstances of the transaction, SL may be able to bifurcate the transaction as follows:

- A sale-leaseback transaction for the space it leases back
- A sale transaction for the space not subject to leaseback

Assuming that bifurcation is appropriate, only the sale of the property that SL leases back is subject to the sale-leaseback rules with the stringent provisions relating to continuing involvement. The sale of the real property that is not leased back would be subject to the provisions of FASB Statement No. 66.

5.3.6 SALE-LEASEBACK OF MULTIPLE ASSETS   In sale-leaseback transactions involving multiple properties with the same counterparty, sales prices and leaseback terms for the individual properties subject to sale-leaseback are intertwined. If the stated sales prices and market rentals for each individual property approximate fair value and are not impacted by the sale-leaseback of the other properties, the determination of the gain and the appropriate accounting should be evaluated on a property-by-property basis. There may be instances, however, in which a price is quoted for the portfolio as a whole, rather than for each individual property, or situations in which the agreed-upon sales price and rentals for a portfolio of real estate assets are reflective of the fair value of and market rentals for the properties in the aggregate, whereas the stated sales price and lease rentals for any individual property may not be reflective of the fair value and market rentals for that property. In a situation like this, it is more appropriate to compute the gain on the real estate sale transaction on a portfolio basis, rather than on a property-by-property basis.

However, the fair value and carrying amount of each property sold should be evaluated to determine whether there is an impairment loss. If the carrying amount of any individual property at the time of the sale exceeds its fair value, an impairment loss should be recognized.[79] The loss should not be netted against the gain realized from the sale of the portfolio, which is generally deferred and amortized over the term of the lease.[80]

5.3.7 CONTRIBUTION-LEASEBACK TRANSACTIONS   Contribution-leaseback transactions are transactions in which the owner of real property contributes the property to another entity in exchange for equity interests and then leases back the property. Contribution-leasebacks are similar to sale-leaseback transactions, except that the seller-lessee receives an equity interest as consideration for the property contributed, rather than cash or a note, and the accounting for contribution-leaseback transactions follows the accounting rules applicable to sale-leaseback transactions.

Paragraph 13(c) of FASB Statement No. 98 provides that "[a]ny other provision or circumstance that allows the seller-lessee to participate in any future profits of the buyer-lessor or the appreciation of the leased property, for example, a situation in which the seller-lessee owns or has an option to acquire any interest in the buyer-lessor" constitutes continuing involvement that precludes sale-leaseback accounting. In a contribution-leaseback, the contributor-lessee retains an equity interest in the buyer-lessor, and sale-leaseback accounting is not appropriate.

5.3.8 WRAP LEASE TRANSACTIONS   FASB Technical Bulletin 88-1[81] describes a wrap lease transaction as follows:

> An enterprise purchases an asset, leases the asset to a lessee, obtains nonre-course financing using the lease rentals or the lease rentals and the asset as collateral, sells the asset subject to the lease and the nonrecourse debt to a third-party investor, and leases the asset back while remaining the substantive principal lessor under the original lease.

FASB held that the provisions of FASB Statement No. 98 apply to a wrap lease transaction involving real estate, property improvements, or integral equipment. Since, in a wrap lease transaction, the company that sells the property subleases the property rather than using it in its own operations, the lease is not considered a normal leaseback,[82] and sale-leaseback accounting is precluded.[83]

---

79   FAS 13, paragraph 33
80   FAS 13, paragraph 33
81   FTB 88-1, Question 5
82   FAS 98, paragraph 8
83   No similar restriction exists for transactions not involving real estate.

5.3.9 LEASEBACK WITH FIXED-PRICE RENEWAL OPTIONS FOR SUBSTANTIALLY ALL OF THE PROPERTY'S ECONOMIC LIFE

Just like leases, sale-leaseback agreements often grant the lessee options to extend the lease term. Based on the terms of the lease agreement and the facts and circumstances of the transaction, periods covered by renewal options may or may not be included in the lease term.

The following interpretation, albeit not directly derived from authoritative guidance, is commonly accepted and should be followed by financial statement preparers: The existence of fixed-price renewal options for substantially all of the property's remaining useful life precludes sale-leaseback accounting. That view is based on the rationale that fixed-price renewal options allow a seller-lessee to benefit from the appreciation of the property,[84] putting a seller-lessee in a position similar to the position of an owner. Sale-leaseback accounting should be

---

EXAMPLE—FIXED PRICE RENEWAL OPTIONS

Smart LLC (SL) intends to sells and lease back its newly constructed headquarters building with an estimated economic life of 40 years. SL evaluates the following two lease arrangements:

ARRANGEMENT 1

Lease with an original lease term of ten years and three ten-year renewal options. The agreed-upon rentals are as follows:

Base Lease Term (Years 1–10): $500,000 in Year 1. For each subsequent year, annual rental amounts are adjusted for any increase in CPI.

Renewals (Years 11–40): Annual rental payments are based on the rentals in the preceding year increased by the lesser of 3 percent or the change in CPI.

ARRANGEMENT 2

Lease with an original lease term of ten years and three ten-year renewal options. The agreed-upon rentals are as follows:

Base Lease Term (Years 1–10): $500,000 in Year 1. For each subsequent year, annual rental amounts are adjusted for any increase in CPI.

Renewals (Years 11–30): Annual rental payments are based on the rentals in the preceding year increased by the lesser of three percent or the change in CPI.

Renewals (Years 31–40): Rentals based on fair value at the time of renewal.

For both arrangements, SL has determined that the lease term is ten years.

Are the renewal options fixed price renewal options for substantially all of the property's economic life?

The renewal option in Arrangement 1 would be considered fixed for substantially all of the economic life of the leased asset and would preclude sale-leaseback accounting. The renewal options in Arrangement 2 are not fixed for substantially all of the property's economic life, as the renewal option for Years 31–40 is based on fair value at the time of renewal.

---

84   A provision that allows a seller-lessee to participate in the appreciation of the leased property precludes sale-leaseback accounting. [FAS 98, paragraph 13(c)]

precluded for the land and building component of the sale-leaseback transaction, irrespective of the relative value of the land (with an indefinite life) and the building component.

5.3.10 SALE-LEASEBACK TRANSACTIONS BY REGULATED ENTERPRISES   FASB Statement No. 98[85] is applicable to sale-leaseback transactions entered into by regulated enterprises. The provisions of FASB Statement No. 71, *Accounting for the Effects of Certain Types of Regulation*, may provide for a timing of income and expense recognition that is different from the income and expense recognition required by FASB Statement No. 98.

Difference in Timing Results from Phase-in Plan.   If the difference in the timing of income and expense recognition constitutes all or a part of a phase-in plan, as defined in FASB Statement No. 92, *Regulated Enterprises—Accounting for Phase-in Plans*,[86] it should be accounted for in accordance with FASB Statement No. 92.[87]

Difference in Timing Does Not Result from Phase-in Plan.   If the difference in the timing of income and expense recognition does not constitute all or a part of a phase-in plan, the timing of income and expense recognition required under FASB Statement No. 98 needs to be modified to conform to FASB Statement No. 71. The following accounting guidance is provided for a sale-leaseback transaction that is recognized as a sale for rate-making purposes, but accounted for under the deposit or financing method under U.S. Generally Accepted Accounting Principles (GAAP):[88]

1. *Use of the deposit method under Statement 98*: The amortization of the asset needs to be modified to equal the total of the rental expense and the gain or loss allowable for rate-making purposes.
2. *Use of the financing method under Statement 98*: The total of interest imputed under the interest method for the financing and the amortization of the asset needs to be modified to equal the total rental expense and the gain or loss allowable for rate-making purposes.

---

85   FAS 98, paragraphs 14–16
86   The term phase-in plan is used in FASB Statement No. 92 to refer to any method of recognition of allowable costs in rates that meets all of the following criteria:
   1. The method was adopted by the regulator in connection with a major, newly completed plant of the regulated enterprise, or of one of its suppliers, or a major plant scheduled for completion in the near future.
   2. The method defers the rates intended to recover allowable costs beyond the period in which those allowable costs would be charged to expense under generally accepted accounting principles applicable to enterprises in general.
   3. The method defers the rates intended to recover allowable costs beyond the period in which those rates would have been ordered under the rate-making methods routinely used prior to 1982 by that regulator for similar allowable costs of that regulated enterprise. [FAS 92, paragraph 3]
87   FAS 98, paragraph 14(a)
88   FAS 98, paragraph 15

The difference between the amount of income or expense recognized on a transaction accounted for by the deposit method or as a financing under FASB Statement No. 98 and the amount of income or expense included in allowable cost for rate-making purposes should be capitalized or accrued as a separate regulatory-created asset or liability, if the criteria of FASB Statement No. 71 are met.[89]

5.3.11 SALE-LEASEBACK INVOLVING RELATED PARTIES[90]   Separate sale and leaseback agreements with the same counterparty or its related parties that are consummated at or near the same time should generally be evaluated as one sale-leaseback transaction.[91] The accounting for sale-and-leaseback transactions depends on the facts and circumstances (such as the terms of the transaction and the relationship between seller-lessee and buyer-lesser) of the arrangement. The following are two examples of the impact of related party relationships in sale-leaseback transactions:

- If a seller-lessee holds an equity interest in the buyer-lessor, sale accounting is precluded, as the seller, through its equity interest in the buyer-lessor, continues to participate in the appreciation of the property.[92]
- If a parent company provides a rental guarantee to the buyer-lessor, the sale-leaseback arrangement may have to be accounted for differently in the stand-alone financial statements and the consolidated financial statements of seller-lessee.

Some of the special circumstances arising from related party relationships have been addressed in EITF Issues, as outlined below.

SALE OF PROPERTY SUBJECT TO INTERCOMPANY LEASE
An entity has an investment in a partnership that owns a real estate property. That entity leases the real estate property from the partnership under an operating lease. The partnership subsequently sells its ownership interest in the property to a third party, and the entity continues to lease the property under the pre-existing lease.

---

89   FAS 98, paragraph 16
90   Paragraph 5(a) of FASB Statement No. 13 defines the term "[r]elated parties in leasing transactions" as follows: A parent company and its subsidiaries, an owner company and its joint ventures (corporate or otherwise) and partnerships, and an investor (including a natural person) and its investees, provided that the parent company, owner company, or investor has the ability to exercise significant influence over operating and financial policies of the related party, as significant influence is defined in APB Opinion No. 18, paragraph 17. In addition to the examples of significant influence set forth in that paragraph, significant influence may be exercised through guarantees of indebtedness, extensions of credit, or through ownership of warrants, debt obligations, or other securities. If two or more entities are subject to the significant influence of a parent, owner company, investor (including a natural person), or common officers or directors, those entities shall be considered related parties with respect to each other.
91   FAS 98, paragraph 6
92   FAS 98, paragraph 13(c)

Issues addressed by EITF Issue No. 88-21, *Accounting for the Sale of Property Subject to the Seller's Pre-existing Lease*, include the following:

Lease Agreement is Modified.   If the lease agreement is modified in connection with the sale, except for insignificant changes, the transaction should be considered a sale-leaseback transaction, subject to the provisions of FASB Statement No. 98. The exercise of a lease renewal option for a period that was not included in the original lease term is considered a new lease, and FASB Statement No. 98 should be applied.

Lease Agreement is Not Modified.   If the pre-existing lease is not modified in conjunction with the sale, except for insignificant changes, then the transaction is not subject to the provisions of FASB Statement No. 98, and the criteria for sale-leaseback accounting do not have to be met for purposes of determining whether a sale should be recognized. The profit on the sale-leaseback transaction should be deferred and recognized in accordance with FASB Statement No. 28.

SALE OF PROPERTY SUBJECT TO LEASE BETWEEN COMPANIES UNDER COMMON CONTROL[93]
In certain situations, the seller and the lessee may be under common control. For example, an entity may control the partnership that owns the property and a subsidiary of the entity may lease the property. The provisions of FASB Statement No. 98 should be applied to the sale of a real estate property, if the pre-existing lease is between parties under common control of the seller, rather than the seller itself. That is, the lease is not considered a pre-existing lease for purposes of that consensus. There is one exception to that rule: If one of the parties under common control is a regulated enterprise with a lease that has been approved by the appropriate regulatory agency, the lease should be considered a pre-existing lease. Unless that pre-existing lease is modified in connection with the sale, the transaction would not be within the scope of FASB Statement No. 98.

GUARANTEE OF LEASE PAYMENTS BY A MEMBER OF A CONSOLIDATED GROUP
EITF Issue No. 90-14, *Unsecured Guarantee by Parent of Subsidiary's Lease Payments in a Sale-Leaseback Transaction*, addresses the following fact pattern:

Subsidiary S (seller-lessee) enters into a sale-leaseback transaction for a building with a third-party buyer-lessor. The buyer-lessor requires the parent company of S to provide an unsecured guarantee of the lease payments. The transaction otherwise meets all of the provisions for sale-leaseback accounting under FASB Statement No. 98.

Should the parent company's unsecured guarantee of the subsidiary's lease payment be considered a form of continuing involvement that precludes the application of sale-leaseback accounting

---

93   EITF Issue No. 88-21, Issue 4

1. . . . in the parent company's consolidated financial statements?
2. . . . in S's separate financial statements?

The Task Force reached the following consensuses:

1. An unsecured guarantee of the lease payments of one member of a consolidated group by another member of the consolidated group is not a form of continuing involvement that precludes sale-leaseback accounting under FASB Statement No. 98 in the *consolidated* financial statements. From the perspective of the consolidated enterprise, it is an entity's unsecured guarantee of its own lease payments, which does not provide the buyer-lessor with additional collateral that reduces the buyer-lessor's risk of loss.
2. An unsecured guarantee of the lease payments of one member of a consolidated group by another member of the consolidated group is a form of continuing involvement that precludes sale-leaseback accounting under FASB Statement No. 98 in the *separate* financial statements of the seller-lessee, because such guarantee provides the buyer-lessor with additional collateral that reduces the buyer-lessor's risk of loss.

5.4 FINANCIAL STATEMENT PRESENTATION AND DISCLOSURE

In addition to the disclosure requirements of FASB Statements No. 13 and No. 66 and the related party disclosure requirements of FASB Statement No. 57, *Related Party Disclosures*,[94] the financial statements of a seller-lessee should include a description of the terms of the sale-leaseback transaction, including future commitments, obligations, provisions, and circumstances that require or result in the seller-lessee's continuing involvement.[95]

For a sale-leaseback transaction accounted for by the deposit or financing method, the following disclosures are required:[96]

- The obligation for future minimum lease payments as of the date of the latest balance sheet presented in the aggregate and for each of the five succeeding fiscal years
- The total of minimum sublease rentals to be received in the future under noncancelable subleases in the aggregate and for each of the five succeeding fiscal years

5.5 INTERNATIONAL FINANCIAL REPORTING STANDARDS

International Accounting Standard (IAS) 17 provides the primary accounting guidance for sale-leaseback transactions and for the way profits or losses resulting from sale-leaseback transactions are to be recognized; no distinction is made

---

94 FAS 57, paragraphs 2–4
95 FAS 98, paragraph 17
96 FAS 98, paragraph 18

between sale-leaseback transactions involving equipment and sale-leaseback transactions involving real estate.

The accounting treatment of sale-leaseback transactions differs depending on the classification of the lease as either a finance lease[97] or an operating lease, and the fair value of the asset as compared to the asset's carrying amount.

FINANCE LEASE

In a leaseback classified as a finance lease, the seller-lessee has not transferred substantially all of the risks and rewards of ownership of the asset to the lessor. The sale-leaseback transaction is considered a financing transaction with the buyer-lessor providing asset-backed financing to the lessee. The leased back property remains on the books of the seller-lessee. Any excess of the sales proceeds over the carrying amount is not recognized as income; rather, it is deferred and amortized over the lease term.[98]

For finance leases, it has to be assessed whether the sold and leased back asset is impaired.[99] If the asset is impaired, the carrying amount needs to be reduced to the recoverable amount in accordance with IAS 36, *Impairment of Assets,*[100] which involves a comparison of the carrying amount of the asset sold and leased back with the higher of that asset's fair value or its value in use.[101] A discounted cash flow approach is being used for determining the asset's value in use.[102]

OPERATING LEASE

In a sale-leaseback transaction classified as an operating lease, profit on the sale transaction is recognized at the time of sale if it can be established that both the lease payments and the sale price are at fair value and the fair value of the asset at the time of the sale-leaseback transaction equals or exceeds its carrying amount (see Exhibit 5.1).[103] If the fair value at the time of a sale-leaseback transaction is less than the carrying amount of the asset, a loss equal to the amount of the difference between the carrying amount and fair value must be recognized.[104]

---

97   A finance lease is a lease that transfers substantially all the risks and rewards incidental to ownership of an asset. [IAS 17, paragraph 4]
98   IAS 17, paragraph 60
99   IAS 17, paragraph 64
100 Paragraph 18 of IAS 36 defines recoverable amount as the higher of an asset's (or cash-generating unit's) fair value less costs to sell and its value in use. The calculation of an asset's value in use reflects the following elements: [IAS 36, paragraph 30]
   • An estimate of the future cash flows the entity expects to derive from the asset
   • Expectations about possible variations in the amount or timing of those future cash flows
   • The time value of money, represented by the current market risk-free rate of interest
   • The price for bearing the uncertainty inherent in the asset
   • Other factors, such as illiquidity, that market participants would reflect in pricing the future cash flows the entity expects to derive from the asset
101 IAS 36 does not apply to investment property that is measured at fair value. [IAS 36, paragraph 2(f)]
102 IAS 36, paragraphs 30–32
103 IAS 17, paragraph 62
104 IAS 17, paragraph 63

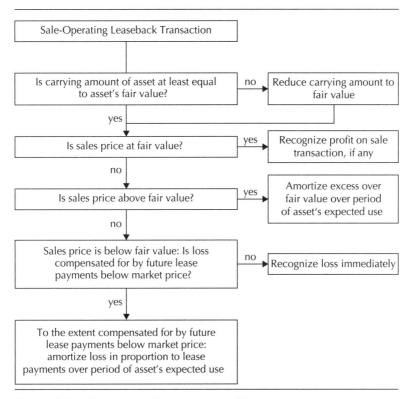

EXHIBIT 5.1   FLOWCHART—SALE-LEASEBACK TRANSACTION, LEASEBACK CLASSIFIED AS OPERATING LEASE

For a transaction in which the sale price is not reflective of fair value, the terms of the transaction need to be adjusted to reflect market terms. Paragraph 61 of IAS 17 provides:

> If the sale price is below fair value, any profit or loss shall be recognized immediately, except that, if the loss is compensated for by future lease payments at below market price, it shall be deferred and amortized in proportion to the lease payments over the period for which the asset is expected to be used. If the sale price is above fair vale, the excess over fair value shall be deferred and amortized over the period for which the asset is expected to be used.

DISCLOSURES

Both the seller-lessee and the buyer-lessor need to follow the disclosure requirements for leasing transactions. A description of material leasing arrangements and the disclosure of unique or unusual provisions of the agreement or terms of the sale-leaseback transaction are required.[105] Sale-leaseback transactions may also trigger the disclosure requirements in IAS 1, *Presentation of Financial Statements*.[106]

---

105   IAS 17, paragraph 65
106   IAS 17, paragraph 66

5.6 SYNOPSIS OF AUTHORITATIVE LITERATURE

FASB STATEMENT NO. 28, *ACCOUNTING FOR SALES WITH LEASEBACKS,* AN AMENDMENT OF FASB STATEMENT NO. 13

FASB Statement No. 28 establishes rules as to how a seller-lessee should recognize profit or loss in sale-leaseback transactions in the following two circumstances:

- The seller retains the use of only a minor part of the property or a minor part of its remaining useful life through the leaseback; the sale and the lease are accounted for based on their separate terms.
- The seller retains more than a minor part but less than substantially all of the use of the property; the profit exceeding the recorded amount of the leased asset (capital lease) or the present value of minimum lease payments (operating lease) is recognized as profit at the date of sale.

FASB STATEMENT NO. 98, *ACCOUNTING FOR LEASES: SALE-LEASEBACK TRANSACTIONS INVOLVING REAL ESTATE, SALES-TYPE LEASES OF REAL ESTATE, DEFINITION OF THE LEASE TERM, INITIAL DIRECT COSTS OF DIRECT FINANCING LEASES,* AN AMENDMENT OF FASB STATEMENTS NO. 13, 66, AND 91 AND A RESCISSION OF FASB STATEMENT NO. 26 AND TECHNICAL BULLETIN NO. 79-11

FASB Statement No. 98 specifies the accounting by a seller-lessee for a sale-leaseback transaction involving real estate, including real estate with equipment. In addition, FASB Statement No. 98 modifies the provisions of FASB Statement No. 13.

The provisions of FASB Statement No. 98 include:

- If a sale-leaseback transaction involving real estate, including real estate with equipment, does not qualify as a sale under FASB Statement No. 66, it should be accounted for by the deposit method or as a financing.
- A sale-leaseback transaction involving real estate, including real estate with equipment, that includes any continuing involvement other than a normal leaseback in which the seller-lessee intends to actively use the property during the lease should be accounted for by the deposit method or as a financing.
- A lease involving real estate may not be classified as a sales-type lease unless the lease agreement provides for the transfer of title to the lessee at or shortly after the end of the lease term. Sales-type leases involving real estate should be accounted for under the provisions of FASB Statement No. 66.

EITF ISSUE NO. 84-37, *SALE-LEASEBACK TRANSACTION WITH REPURCHASE OPTION*
Issues. EITF Issue No. 84-37 addresses the following issues:

1. What is the period of profit recognition in a sale-leaseback transaction with a short initial lease term and renewal options?

2. How should one account for a real estate sale-leaseback transaction with repurchase option or repurchase obligation?
3. In a real estate sale-leaseback transaction in which the seller finances the purchaser's acquisition, does the lease term include the renewal periods exercisable during the term of the loan?
4. How should rental shortfall agreements that would warrant accounting as an adjustment of the purchase price by the buyer-lessor be distinguished from a sale-leaseback transaction?

Consensuses/Status. Issues 1 through 3 have been affected by the issuance of FASB Statement No. 98.

1. FASB Statement No. 98 revised the definition of lease term. The period of profit recognition equals the lease term, as defined in FASB Statement No. 98.
2. FASB Statement No. 98 specifically precludes sale-leaseback accounting if the terms of the transaction include a repurchase option or obligation.
3. FASB Statement No. 98 revised the definition of lease term to include all periods during which a loan from the lessee to the lessor is expected to be outstanding.
4. The Task Force did not reach a consensus on this issue. However, the Task Force did provide the following criteria, which should be considered in identifying rental shortfall agreements that would warrant accounting as an adjustment of the purchase price by the buyer-lessor:

   a. The seller receives a fee as an inducement for entering into the lease agreement.
   b. The seller's lease commitment is for a short term, and the seller does not have any renewal options.
   c. The seller is relieved of its lease obligation as it obtains tenants for the building.
   d. The "subleases" extend beyond the leaseback period. The sublease may be in form a sublease from the seller-lessee over the remaining leaseback period and a separate lease from the buyer for an additional period.
   e. When a building is currently leased up, the seller's lease commitment merely represents the difference between existing lease rents and market rents.

   If the seller-lessee has a firm commitment, if it is not relieved of its primary obligation as the property is subleased, and if the agreement is for a longer term, the transaction resembles a typical sale-leaseback transaction.

EITF Issue No. 85-27, Recognition of Receipts from Made-Up
Rental Shortfalls

Issue.   A real estate developer sells an office building to a real estate syndication.
The syndication pays a fee to the seller for leasing back the office building under
a master leaseback agreement for a two-year period. The fee is held in escrow as
if it were a portion of the purchase price.

The seller subleases the rental space, and is then relieved from its future
lease payments for the space subleased. How should the syndication account for
the fee paid to the seller and the rent received from the seller?

Consensus/Status.   The Task Force reached a consensus that payments to and
receipts from the seller under this master-leaseback agreement should be treated
by the syndication as adjustments to the basis of the property, rather than as
current income and expense. The Securities and Exchange Commission (SEC)
Observer viewed the payment to the seller as an escrowed portion of the purchase
price contingent on the seller's ability to rent the space.

This consensus also applies if the property is fully rented at the time of
sale and the seller agrees to make up any decrease in rentals resulting from lease
terminations during a specified period after the sale.

EITF Issue No. 86-17, Deferred Profit on Sale-Leaseback Transaction with
Lessee Guarantee of Residual Value

Issue.   The Task Force discussed a sale-leaseback transaction in which the seller-
lessee retains more than a minor part but less than substantially all of the use of
the property through the leaseback, and the lease does not meet the criteria for
classification as a capital lease. How should the residual value guarantee affect
the determination of profit to be deferred on the sale in accordance with FASB
Statement No. 28?

Consensus/Status.   The Task Force reached a consensus that profit equal to the
present value of the periodic rents plus the gross amount of the guarantee should
be deferred at the date of sale. The FASB since issued FASB Statement No. 98,
which provides that sale-leaseback accounting cannot be used by a seller-lessee
for sale-leaseback transactions involving real estate if there is continuing involvement on the part of the seller. An example of continuing involvement specified in
FASB Statement No. 98 is the guarantee of the buyer-lessor's investment. FASB
Statement No. 98 precludes sale-leaseback accounting for transactions involving
real estate, if the lessee guarantees residual value.

EITF Issue No. 88-21, Accounting for the Sale of Property Subject to the
Seller's Preexisting Lease

Issues.   An entity owns an interest in property and is also a lessee under an operating lease for the property. Acquisition of an ownership interest in the property

and consummation of the lease occurred at or near the same time. This owner-lessee relationship can occur when the entity has an investment in a partnership that owns the leased property. The entity sells its interest in the partnership, or the partnership sells the property to an independent third party, and the entity continues to lease the property under the pre-existing operating lease.

The issues are:

1. Should the transaction be accounted for as a sale-leaseback transaction?
2. Should the amount of profit deferred, if any, be affected by the seller-lessee's prior ownership in the property?
3. Should FASB Statement No. 98 be applied to transactions if, pursuant to provisions in the pre-existing lease, the seller-lessee vacates and intends to sublease the property or exercises a renewal option?
4. Should FASB Statement No. 98 be applied to transactions if the pre-existing lease is between parties under common control of the seller?

Consensuses/Status

1. If the pre-existing lease is modified in connection with the sale, the transaction should be considered a sale-leaseback transaction. If the pre-existing lease is not modified in conjunction with the sale, profit should be deferred and recognized in accordance with FASB Statement No. 28.
2. Irrespective of lease modifications, the calculation of the amount of deferred profit should not be affected by the seller-lessee's prior ownership percentage in the property.
3. The exercise of a renewal option for a period that was included in the original minimum lease term or a sublease provision contained in the pre-existing lease does not affect the accounting for the transaction. However, the exercise of a renewal option for a period that was not included in the original lease term is considered a new lease, and FASB Statement No. 98 should be applied.
4. A lease between parties under common control should not be considered a pre-existing lease for purposes of this consensus, and FASB Statement No. 98 should be applied, with the following exception: If one of the parties under common control is a regulated enterprise with a lease that has been approved by the appropriate regulatory agency, that lease should be considered a pre-existing lease.

EITF Issue No. 89-16, *Consideration of Executory Costs in Sale-Leaseback Transactions*

Issue.   Executory costs of property leased in a sale-leaseback transaction may be paid by the buyer-lessor or by the seller-lessee. How should executory costs be considered in the calculation of profit to be deferred in a sale-leaseback transaction?

Consensus/Status.   The Task Force reached a consensus that executory costs of the leaseback should be excluded from the calculation of profit to be deferred on a sale-leaseback transaction, irrespective of who pays the executory costs or the classification of the leaseback.

EITF Issue No. 90-14, *Unsecured Guarantee by Parent of Subsidiary's Lease Payments in a Sale-Leaseback Transaction*

Issue.   Subsidiary S (seller-lessee), a subsidiary of Company A, enters into a sale-leaseback transaction for a building with Company B (buyer-lessor). B requires A to provide an unsecured guarantee of the lease payments.

Is A's unsecured guarantee of S's lease payments a form of continuing involvement that precludes the application of sale-leaseback accounting in S's separate financial statements and in the consolidated financial statements of A?

Consensus/Status.   The Task Force reached a consensus that the parent company guarantee does not result in a form of continuing involvement in the consolidated financial statements of A. However, the guarantee does preclude sale-leaseback accounting in the separate financial statements of S.

EITF Issue No. 90-20, *Impact of an Uncollateralized Irrevocable Letter of Credit on a Real Estate Sale-Leaseback Transaction*

Issue.   Company A (seller-lessee) enters into a real estate sale-leaseback transaction with unrelated Company B (buyer-lessor) and provides an irrevocable letter of credit securing the lease payments. The issuer of the letter of credit does not require Company A to pledge specific assets as collateral. Is Company A's uncollateralized, irrevocable letter of credit a form of continuing involvement that precludes sale-leaseback accounting under FASB Statement No. 98?

Consensus/Status.   The Task Force reached a consensus that an uncollateralized, irrevocable letter of credit is not a form of continuing involvement that precludes sale-leaseback accounting under FASB Statement No. 98. However, a financial institution's right of setoff of any amounts on deposit with that institution against any payments made under the letter of credit constitutes collateral and, therefore, is a form of continuing involvement that precludes sale-leaseback accounting under FASB Statement No. 98.

EITF Issue No. 97-1, *Implementation Issues in Accounting for Lease Transactions, including Those involving Special-Purpose Entities*
Outline provided in Chapter 4.

EITF Topic No. D-24, *Sale-Leaseback Transactions with Continuing Involvement*
FASB Statement No. 98 precludes the use of sale-leaseback accounting if the transaction includes any form of continuing involvement other than a normal leaseback.

The FASB staff received the following technical inquiries:

1. A utility that owns a 30% undivided interest in an electric generating facility is considering the sale-leaseback of a 7% undivided interest. Does the retention of a partial interest of a property in a sale-leaseback transaction violate the continuing involvement conditions of FASB Statement No. 98?

   FASB Staff Response: Partial sale transactions preclude the use of sale-leaseback accounting due to the continuing involvement of the seller-lessee.

2. A sale-leaseback agreement contains a provision that allows the seller-lessee to require the buyer-lessor to refinance debt related to the property and to pass through the interest savings to the seller-lessee. Would sale-leaseback accounting be precluded?

   FASB Staff Response: Such a provision would preclude sale-leaseback accounting for the transaction. However, changes in leaseback payments that are indexed to an interest rate would be considered contingent rental payments and would not preclude sale-leaseback accounting.

PART 2

ACCOUNTING FOR REAL ESTATE INDUSTRY-SPECIFIC TRANSACTIONS

CHAPTER 6

INTERESTS IN REAL ESTATE VENTURES

6.1 OVERVIEW

The ownership of real estate and the development of real estate projects often involve two or more parties. The cooperation between different parties may be limited to one real estate project; it may encompass several projects; or it may be of a continual nature, such as a venture that invests in office properties. One of the venturers may contribute land, another may contribute financial resources to develop the land, and a third may use its land development or home-building expertise. Particularly in large projects, the benefit of spreading risk among different investors is also a factor that is considered when entering into a venture.

Arrangements that involve a number of small investors who contribute capital, with one or more parties being responsible for the project development or project management, are referred to as syndications. Special accounting guidance has been developed for the syndicator's (sponsoring party's) accounting of income from syndication activities.[1]

Reflecting the different roles that venture partners assume to make a real estate venture successful, venture arrangements provide for different ways in which venturers participate in a venture's success. In one arrangement, a venturer may have an interest in the venture equity and share in the venture's future profits and losses; in another arrangement, the investor's interest may consist of sharing in future operating profits and losses and tax benefits; and in yet another arrangement, the venturer may receive a preferential return on its investment as return on capital the venturer has invested with the venture.

In 1978, the American Institute of Certified Public Accountants (AICPA) issued Statement of Position (SOP) No. 78-9, *Accounting for Investments in Real Estate Ventures*, to provide accounting guidance for investors in real estate ventures. As the application of the equity method of accounting proved to be challenging in venture arrangements with complex capital structures and/or income allocation provisions, the proposed SOP, *Accounting for Investors' Interests in Real Estate Ventures*, sought to replace the traditional method of income allocation provided for in Accounting Principles Board (APB) Opinion No. 18, *The Equity Method of Accounting for Investments in Common Stock*, with the hypothetical liquidation at book value method (HLBV method) to determine an investor's share in the income or losses of a real estate venture. The proposed SOP includes illustrations of the HLBV method that prove helpful in understanding on how to apply that method. Although that proposed SOP was never issued, the HLBV method is used in arrangements in which the traditional method of income allocation is not feasible or does not reflect the substance of the arrangements, and in determining the amount of equity method losses to be allocated to an investor.[2]

---

1   SOP 92-1, *Accounting for Real Estate Syndication Income*
2   EITF Issue No. 99-10

Phase 1 of the Financial Accounting Standards Board's (FASB's) Fair Value Option Project concluded with the issuance of FASB Statement No. 159, *The Fair Value Option for Financial Assets and Financial Liabilities,* in February 2007. That Standard affords investors in real estate ventures the option—generally on an instrument-by-instrument basis—to either continue to account for their nonconsolidated interests in ventures under the historical cost accounting model (using the cost or equity method of accounting, as appropriate), or to account for their interests in real estate ventures at fair value, assuming certain conditions are met.[3] As consolidated entities and wholly owned real estate assets are not accounted for at fair value, the financial community will be seeing a "mixed model" that allows for the use of fair value for nonconsolidated interests in ventures and requires the use of the historical cost model for real estate assets owned directly or through interests in consolidated entities. Providing companies with an instrument-by-instrument option to report financial assets and liabilities at fair value has been the subject of much controversy. One of the concerns is that the effect on earnings from using mixed measurement attributes may not be representative of the economics of the reporting company's activities.

This Chapter uses the terms "investor," venturer," and "venture partner" interchangeably; the use of one term vs. another is not intended to indicate any difference with respect to control or other features, and is not intended to denote any particular form of legal structure of the venture.

6.2 METHODS OF ACCOUNTING FOR INTERESTS IN REAL ESTATE VENTURES

When determining the appropriate method of accounting to be employed for interests in real estate ventures, a variety of factors need to be taken into consideration, such as ownership percentage and control exercised by the investor, and legal form of the venture.

Equity interests in real estate ventures are accounted for in one of four ways:[4]

1. Consolidation
2. Equity method of accounting
3. *Pro rata* consolidation
4. Cost method

6.2.1 CONSOLIDATION   Consolidated financial statements report the financial position and results of operations of the parent company and its subsidiaries as an economic entity; they "combine the assets, liabilities, revenues and expenses of subsidiaries with the corresponding items of the parent company. Intercompany

---

3   See Section 6.2.6 in this Chapter.

4   Additionally, FASB Statement No. 159 allows for the reporting of nonconsolidated equity interests in a venture at fair value; see Section 6.2.6 for further discussion.

items are eliminated to avoid double counting and prematurely recognizing income."[5]

Before the issuance of FASB Interpretation (FIN) No. 46 *Consolidation of Variable Interest Entities*, the determination of whether or not a real estate venture had to be consolidated was based on the concept of "control." Consolidated financial statements were considered necessary for a fair presentation when one of the venturers in a group directly or indirectly had a controlling financial interest in the real estate venture. Paragraph 3 of Accounting Research Bulletin (ARB) No. 51, *Consolidated Financial Statements*, states: "All majority-owned subsidiaries— all companies in which a parent has a controlling financial interest through direct or indirect ownership of a majority voting interest—shall be consolidated. . . ." ARB 51 provides for a very narrow exception to this rule:[6] "A majority-owned subsidiary shall not be consolidated if control does not rest with the majority owners (as, for instance, if the subsidiary is in legal reorganization or in bankruptcy or operates under foreign exchange restrictions, controls, or other governmentally imposed uncertainties so severe that they cast significant doubt on the parent's ability to control the subsidiary)."

The desire of many companies to keep assets and liabilities off–balance sheet has resulted in innovative financial concepts and complex legal structures. With the downfall of Enron in 2001, it became evident that "control," the traditional determinant for consolidation, was no longer a suitable means when determining whether certain entities should be consolidated. With FIN 46(R), the FASB introduced the concept of a variable interest entity (VIE). Benefits and risks, rather than control, are the determinants of consolidating an entity that meets the criteria of a VIE:[7]

As illustrated in the following, very simplified flowchart in Exhibit 6.1, FIN 46(R) has turned every analysis of whether an investor should consolidate an entity in which it holds an equity interest into a two-step process: After determining that no scope exception in FIN 46(R)[8] applies, an evaluation needs to be made whether (1) an entity (for example, a real estate venture) meets the criteria of a VIE[9] and should be consolidated based on risks and benefits, as measured by an entity's expected losses and expected residual returns, or (2) an entity is not a VIE, in which case the traditional "control-model"[10] applies.

That flow chart has been simplified to demonstrate the underlying concepts. FIN 46(R) analyses are often very complex and involve multiple steps. Following the provisions of FIN 46(R), holders of variable interests in the entity—other than equity holders—may absorb a majority of the VIE's expected losses or expected

---

5   APB 18, paragraph 4
6   ARB 51, paragraphs 2 and 3
7   FIN 46(R), paragraph E7
8   FIN 46(R), paragraph 4
9   Paragraph 5 of FIN 46(R) sets forth the criteria for a VIE.
10   ARB 51

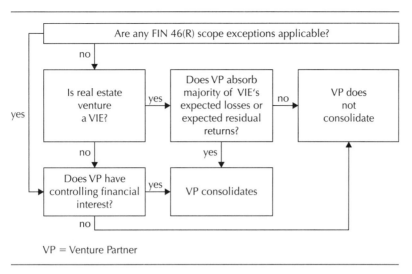

EXHIBIT 6.1 FLOWCHART—CONSOLIDATION

residual returns, and thus be required to consolidate. If the criteria for consolidation are not met, a VIE may not be consolidated by any of its variable interest holders.

6.2.1.1 Interests in Variable Interest Entities

FIN 46(R) sets forth two conditions that, if either one or both are present, trigger an entity's status as a VIE.[11] If (1) an entity has insufficient equity investment at risk, and/or (2) the holders of the equity investment at risk do not have the characteristics of typical "owners" of an entity, that is, the decision-making authority, the obligation to absorb the expected losses and the right to receive the expected residual returns of the entity, the entity is a VIE. Additionally, FIN 46(R) establishes that if the voting rights of some investors are not proportional to the risks and benefits they are entitled to receive, and substantially all of the entity's activities either involve or are conducted on behalf of an investor that has disproportionately few voting rights, the investors are deemed not to have the characteristics of typical owners, and therefore the entity is considered a VIE.[12]

The existence of multiple contractual relationships between a venture and its venture partners makes FIN 46(R)-analyses of interests in ventures particularly challenging. Variable interests are not only limited to equity interests in a venture, but may also be other arrangements, such as guarantees, options on land or other assets, supply arrangements, leases, management and service arrangements, and long-term fixed-price purchase contracts, to name a few. The identification of all of the variable interests in a venture is critical, because variable interests impact

---

11   FIN 46(R), paragraph 5
12   FIN 46(R), paragraph 5

(or may impact) whether or not a scope exception is applicable,[13] whether an entity is a variable interest entity, and whether a variable interest holder has to consolidate the entity.

6.2.1.2 Interests in Non-Variable Interest Entities

For an entity that is not a VIE, the determinant of consolidation is control. ARB 51 provides that consolidated financial statements are usually necessary for a fair presentation when one of the companies in the group directly or indirectly has a controlling financial interest in the other companies.[14] Paragraph 3 of ARB 51 creates a link between the ownership of a majority voting interest and control by establishing a general rule that entities in which a company has a controlling financial interest through majority ownership be consolidated.[15] In some entities, the powers of a shareholder with a majority voting interest may be restricted by approval or veto rights granted to the minority shareholders. The minority shareholders' rights may be so substantive as to overcome the presumption of control by the majority shareholder.[16]

The concept of control as the determinant for consolidation is not only applicable to entities in the legal form of a corporation, but also to partnerships, limited liability companies, and other legal structures.

When evaluating whether an investor has a controlling financial interest in an entity, consideration should be given to the legal form of the entity and the rights and obligations of the investors, as outlined below. Each venture arrangement and the facts and circumstances surrounding the investors' interests need to be analyzed before concluding whether consolidation is appropriate.

CORPORATE VENTURE[17]

In corporate venture arrangements, the powers of shareholders with majority voting interests may be restricted by approval or veto rights granted to the minority shareholders. If the minority shareholders have the ability to effectively participate in financial and operating decisions of the investee that are made in the ordinary course of business (referred to as substantive participating rights), the presumption of control by the majority shareholder is overcome. In EITF Issue No. 96-16, *Investor's Accounting for an Investee When the Investor Has a Majority of the Voting Interest but the Minority Shareholder or Shareholders Have Certain Approval or Veto*

---

13   For example, through a combination of variable interests, a variable interest holder may provide more than half of the total of the equity, subordinated debt, and other forms of subordinated financial support to the venture, and thus not be able to apply the business scope exception. [FIN 46(R), paragraph 4(h)(3)]

14   ARB 51, paragraph 1

15   Subject to the following exception: "A majority-owned subsidiary shall not be consolidated if control does not rest with the majority owners (as, for instance, if the subsidiary is in legal reorganization or in bankruptcy or operates under foreign exchange restrictions, controls, or other governmentally imposed uncertainties so severe that they cast significant doubt on the parent's ability to control the subsidiary)." [ARB 51, paragraph 2]

16   EITF Issue No. 96-16

17   This guidance also applies to limited liability companies with governing provisions that are the functional equivalent of corporations. [EITF Issue No. 96-16]

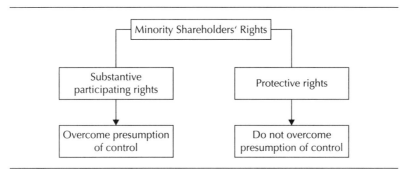

EXHIBIT 6.2   OVERVIEW—MINORITY SHAREHOLDERS' RIGHTS

Rights, the Task Force distinguishes between substantive participating rights, which overcome the presumption of control by the majority shareholder, and protective rights, which do not overcome such presumption. The assessment of whether or not the rights of minority shareholders overcome the presumption of control depends on the facts and circumstances and requires significant judgment (see Exhibit 6.2).

EITF Issue No. 96-16 explains:

> . . . the framework in which such facts and circumstances are judged should be based on whether the minority rights, individually or in the aggregate, provide for the minority shareholder to effectively participate in significant decisions that would be expected to be made in the "ordinary course of business." Effective participation means the ability to block significant decisions proposed by the investor who has a majority voting interest. That is, control does not rest with the majority owner because the investor with the majority voting interest cannot cause the investee to take an action that is significant in the ordinary course of business if it has been vetoed by the minority shareholder.

Rights of minority shareholders are considered *protective rights* that do not overcome the presumption of consolidation by the investor with a majority voting interest if they block corporate actions, such as the following:[18]

- Amendments to articles of incorporation of the investee
- Pricing on transactions between the owner of a majority voting interest and the investee and related self-dealing transactions
- Liquidation of the investee or a decision to cause the investee to enter bankruptcy or other receivership
- Acquisitions and dispositions of assets that are not expected to be undertaken in the ordinary course of business
- Issuance or repurchase of equity interests

---

18   EITF Issue No. 96-16

On the other hand, minority shareholders' *substantive participating rights* overcome the presumption of control by the majority investor. The following two rights are provided in EITF Issue No. 96-16 as examples of substantive participating rights:

1. Selecting, terminating, *and* setting the compensation of management responsible for implementing the investee's policies and procedures
2. Establishing operating *and* capital decisions of the investee, including budgets, in the ordinary course of business

Individual rights granted to minority shareholders, such as the right to veto the termination of management, should be assessed based on the facts and circumstances when determining whether they are substantive participating rights. Certain rights granted to minority shareholders may appear to be participating rights; however, the rights need to be *substantive* to overcome the presumption of consolidation by the investor with a majority voting interest. The Task Force identified the following six factors to be considered when determining whether minority rights that appear participating are *substantive* participating rights:[19]

1. Majority shareholder's percentage ownership interest in investee (as the disparity between the ownership interest of majority and minority shareholders increases, the rights of the minority shareholder are presumptively more likely to be protective rights)
2. Rights conveyed by the corporate governance arrangements
3. Related-party relationships between the majority and minority shareholders
4. Significance of rights to the ordinary course of business of the investee (minority rights that relate to decisions about the location of investee's headquarters, the name of investee, the selection of auditors, and the selection of accounting principles are provided as examples of rights the Task Force considered not to be significant rights)
5. Remote probability that an event or transaction that requires minority approval will occur
6. Existence of buy-out provision for fair value or less (if a contractual right to buy out the interest of the minority shareholder in the investee for fair value or less is prudent, feasible, and substantially within the control of the majority owner, the majority owner's contractual right to buy out the minority owner demonstrates that the participating right of the minority shareholder is not a substantive right)

GENERAL PARTNERSHIP

In a general partnership, the general partners assume joint and several liability. If one of the partners of the general partnership controls the general partnership, that

---

19   Exhibit 96-16A of EITF Issue No. 96-16 provides certain examples of how to assess individual minority rights under the consensus in EITF Issue No. 96-16.

controlling partner should consolidate the partnership. In partnerships in which voting interests are not clearly indicated, a condition that would usually indicate control is ownership of a majority (over 50%) of the financial interests in profits or losses.[20] However, the majority interest holder may not control the partnership if the other partners have substantive participating rights that permit them to effectively participate in significant decisions that are expected to be made in the ordinary course of the partnership's business. The determination of whether the rights of the other partners are substantive participating rights is based on the guidance provided in EITF Issue No. 04-5, *Determining Whether a General Partner, or the General Partners as a Group, Controls a Limited Partnership or Similar Entity When the Limited Partners Have Certain Rights,* discussed in Section 6.2.1.2 under "Limited Partnership."[21]

SOP 78-9, *Accounting for Investments in Real Estate Ventures,* acknowledges that the power to control may be conveyed by contract, lease, agreement with the other partners, or by court degree, and therefore, may exist even if a partner's ownership percentage is below 50%.[22]

If no general partner controls the partnership, the partners should account for their partnership interests under the equity method of accounting, regardless of the percentage of their partnership interests; accounting for general partnership interests under the cost method is not appropriate.[23]

LIMITED PARTNERSHIP[24]

General partners are presumed to control a limited partnership, regardless of the extent of the general partners' ownership interest in the limited partnership.[25] If there is more than one general partner, and one of them controls the partnership, that controlling general partner consolidates the partnership.[26] If there is only one general partner in the limited partnership, that partner is presumed to control the partnership. Similar to the substantive participating rights of minority shareholders in a corporate venture, certain rights granted to limited partners may allow the limited partners to effectively participate in significant decisions that are expected to be made in the ordinary course of the limited partnership's business, and the presumption of control of the partnership by the general partners may be overcome.

EITF Issue No. 04-5 provides the following framework:[27] If the limited partners have either (1) the substantive ability to dissolve (liquidate) the limited partnership or otherwise remove the general partners without cause (referred

---

20   SOP 78-9, paragraph 7
21   SOP 78-9, paragraph 7, as amended by FSP SOP 78-9-1
22   SOP 78-9, paragraph 7
23   SOP 78-9, paragraph 6
24   This Section also applies to similar entities, such as limited liability companies with governing provisions that are the functional equivalent of a limited partnership.
25   EITF Issue No. 04-5, paragraph 6
26   SOP 78-9, paragraph 9
27   EITF Issue No. 04-5, paragraph 6

to as "substantive kick-out rights") or (2) substantive participating rights, the general partners do not control the limited partnership.[28]

Substantive Kick-out Rights.   EITF Issue No. 04-5 specifies that for kick-out rights to be substantive, they must have both of the following characteristics:

1. The kick-out rights must be exercisable by a single limited partner or a vote of no more than a simple majority of the limited partners' voting interests held by partners other than the general partners (and entities under common control with the general partners).
2. There cannot be any significant barriers to the exercise of the kick-out right, such as the following:
    a. Conditions that make it unlikely that kick-out rights will be exercisable, such as conditions that limit the timing of exercise of the kick-out right
    b. Financial penalties or operational barriers when liquidating the limited partnership or replacing the general partner
    c. Lack of adequate number of qualified replacement general partners, or lack of adequate compensation to attract qualified replacement

---

EXAMPLES—KICK-OUT RIGHTS[29]

SCENARIO 1

A limited partnership has two limited partners, Able (A) and Benedict (B), and one general partner, Guerand (G), who has no related party relationship to the limited partners. A and B hold equal voting interests. The limited partnership agreement provides that G can be removed by a majority vote of the limited partners.

Is that kick-out right substantive, assuming that no significant barriers to its exercise are present?

Yes, the kick-out right is substantive, as it allows for the removal of G upon a vote of a simple majority voting interest (A and B).

SCENARIO 2

A limited partnership has three limited partners, Able (A), Benedict (B), and Cesar (C), and one general partner, Guerand (G). A, B, and C, which are unrelated to G, hold an equal amount of the limited partners' voting interests. The partnership agreement requires that a vote of two of the limited partners is required to remove G.

Is that kick-out right substantive, assuming that no significant barriers to its exercise are present?

Yes, the kick-out right is substantive, as it allows for the removal of G upon a vote of a simple majority voting interest.

---

28   Paragraph 14 of EITF Issue No. 04-5 provides a list of rights that should be considered protective rights, rather than participating rights. These rights are very similar to the protective rights listed in EITF Issue No. 96-16, which are discussed in Section 6.2.1.2 under "Corporate Venture".

29   Adapted from EITF Issue No. 04-5, footnote 9

  d. Absence of "mechanism" in the partnership agreement or in the laws and regulations by which limited partners holding the rights can call for and conduct a vote to exercise those rights

  e. Inability of limited partners holding the rights to obtain the information necessary to exercise them

Substantive Participating Rights.   EITF Issue No. 04-5 provides that rights of the limited partners, such as the following, should be considered substantive participating rights when determining whether the presumption of control by the general partners is overcome:[30]

- Selecting, terminating, *and* setting the compensation of management responsible for implementing the limited partnership's policies and procedures
- Establishing operating *and* capital decisions of the limited partnership, including budgets, in the ordinary course of business.

The Task Force explains that these rights—illustrative of participating rights—"are participating rights because, in the aggregate, the rights allow the limited partners to *effectively participate in the decisions that occur as part of the ordinary course of the limited partnership's business* and are significant factors in directing and carrying out the activities of the limited partnership. Individual rights, such as the right to veto the termination of management responsible for implementing the limited partnership's policies and procedures (if management is outsourced—via contract with a third party—by the general partners), should be assessed based on the facts and circumstances to determine if they are substantive participating rights in and of themselves."[31]

In evaluating limited partners' rights to determine whether they are substantive participating rights, substantive participation exists when the limited partners have the ability to approve or block actions proposed by the general partners.[32] For rights to be substantive participating rights, it is not necessary that the limited partners have the ability to *initiate* actions.[33]

If it has been determined that the general partners are not in control of a partnership, the rights of the limited partners have to be evaluated to determine whether effectively one of the limited partners controls the partnership by holding over 50% of the total partnership interests, for example. If a limited partner controls the partnership, that limited partner should consolidate the partnership.[34]

---

30   EITF Issue No. 04-5, paragraph 16
31   EITF Issue No. 04-5, paragraph 18
32   Paragraph 19 of EITF Issue No. 04-5 provides factors that should be considered in evaluating whether rights that appear to be participating rights are in effect substantive participating rights.
33   EITF Issue No. 04-5, paragraph 17
34   SOP 78-9, paragraph 10

6.2.2 EQUITY METHOD OF ACCOUNTING Once an investor has determined that consolidation of a venture is not appropriate, the investor needs to analyze whether the equity method of accounting should be used. Most interests in real estate ventures that are not consolidated are accounted for under the equity method.

Accounting Principles Board (APB) Opinion No. 18, *The Equity Method of Accounting for Investments in Common Stock,* provides the primary accounting guidance relating to the equity method of accounting for investments in corporate entities. The equity method is the appropriate method of accounting, if the investment enables the investor to exercise significant influence over the operating or financial policies of the investee. "The investor then has a degree of responsibility for the return on its investment, and it is appropriate to include in the results of operations of the investor its share of the earnings or losses of the investee."[35]

Under the equity method of accounting, an investor initially records its investment in the common stock of an investee at cost and adjusts the carrying amount of the investment to recognize the investor's share of the earnings or losses of the investee after the date of acquisition. Distributions received from an investee reduce the carrying amount of the investment.[36] Intercompany profits and losses are generally eliminated to the extent of the venture partner's interest in the venture, until realized by the investor or investee.[37]

As further discussed in Section 6.2.6 of this Chapter, FASB Statement No. 159, *The Fair Value Option for Financial Assets and Financial Liabilities,* enables venture partners to report at fair value investments that would otherwise be accounted for under the equity method of accounting.[38]

6.2.2.1 Criteria for the Use of the Equity Method APB Opinion No. 18 addresses only investments in common stock of corporations; it does not provide accounting guidance for investments in unincorporated entities. However, investors in unincorporated entities such as partnerships and other unincorporated ventures generally account for their investments using the equity method of accounting by analogy to APB Opinion No. 18.[39] Depending on the legal form of the entity, certain guidelines have been developed that need to be considered when determining whether the use of the equity method of accounting is appropriate (see Exhibit 6.3).

CORPORATION
The equity method of accounting should be followed by an investor whose investment in voting stock gives it the ability to exercise significant influence over the operating and financial policies of an investee. Ability to exercise that influence may be indicated in several ways, such as representation on the board of directors,

---

35   APB 18, paragraph 12
36   APB 18, paragraph 6
37   AIN 1-APB 18
38   See Section 6.2.6 for further discussion.
39   EITF Issue No. 00-1

The following table depicts the thresholds for the use of the equity method of accounting for investments in real estate ventures, assuming consolidation is not appropriate.

Legal Form of Entity	Criteria for Use of Equity Method
Corporation	Significant influence over operating and financial policies of an investee (Presumption: Ownership interest of 20% or more)
General Partnership	All interests
Limited Partnership General Partners Limited Partners	 All interests Interests more than minor (more than 3–5%)
Limited Liability Company Specific Ownership Accounts No Specific Ownership Accounts	 Interests more than minor (more than 3–5%) Significant influence over operating and financial policies of an investee (Presumption: Ownership interest of 20% or more)
Undivided Interests	Treat like partnerships, if elements of joint control Proportionate consolidation permissible, if no joint control

Exhibit 6.3   Table—Use of Equity Method of Accounting

participation in policy-making processes, material transactions between the investor and the investee, interchange of managerial personnel, or technological dependency. The significance of an investor's ownership share in the investee in relation to the concentration of other shareholders is also an important aspect to consider when determining whether the ability to exercise significant influence exists.[40]

If an investor holds 20% or more of the voting stock of an investee, there is a presumption that the investor has the ability to exercise significant influence over the investee.[41] This 20% threshold is based on outstanding securities of the investee that have present voting privileges.[42] Conversely, an investment of less than 20% of the voting stock of an investee leads to a presumption that the investor does not have the ability to exercise significant influence unless such ability can be demonstrated.[43]

Paragraph 4 of FIN 35, *Criteria for Applying the Equity Method of Accounting for Investments in Common Stock,* provides an illustrative list of examples that, if present, trigger the need to evaluate all facts and circumstances relating to the

---

40   APB 18, paragraph 17
41   APB 18, paragraph 17
42   APB 18, paragraph 18
43   APB 18, paragraph 17

investment when determining whether an investor with an investment in common stock of 20% or more does indeed have significant influence:

- The investee challenges the investor's ability to exercise significant influence (e.g., through litigation or complaints to governmental regulatory authorities).
- Investor and investee sign an agreement under which the investor surrenders significant rights as a shareholder.
- Majority ownership of the investee is concentrated among a small group of shareholders who operate the investee without regard to the views of the investor.
- The investor needs or wants more financial information to apply the equity method than is available to the investee's other shareholders (for example, the investor wants quarterly financial information from an investee that publicly reports only annually), tries to obtain that information, and fails.
- The investor tries and fails to obtain representation on the investee's board of directors.

Other-than-common stock investments in corporate ventures are discussed in Section 6.4.1 of this Chapter.

GENERAL PARTNERSHIP

Partners in general partnerships assume joint and several liability. Investments in general partnerships should be accounted for and reported under the equity method if it has been determined that consolidation is not appropriate.[44] For partners in a general partnership, the use of the cost method is not appropriate.[45]

LIMITED PARTNERSHIP

The *general partners* in a limited partnership assume responsibility for the operations of the partnership. Additionally, they have unlimited liability for the obligations of the partnership. For that reason, they generally are the controlling investors, and either consolidate[46] or apply the equity method of accounting.

Limited partners in a limited partnership are generally not in control. Their investments in limited partnerships are accounted for under the equity method of accounting,[47] unless their interest is so minor that they have virtually no influence over the partnership's operating and financial policies;[48] investments of more than 3–5% are generally viewed to be more than minor.[49]

LIMITED LIABILITY COMPANY

Investments in a limited liability company (LLC) that maintains a specific ownership account for each investor should be viewed as being similar to a limited

---

44   See Section 6.2.1 of this Chapter for further discussion.
45   SOP 78-9, paragraph 6
46   See Section 6.2.1 of this Chapter for further discussion.
47   This assumes that consolidation is not appropriate. See Section 6.2.1 of this Chapter for further discussion.
48   SOP 78-9, paragraph 8
49   EITF Topic No. D-46

partnership for purposes of determining whether a noncontrolling interest in an LLC should be accounted for using the cost method or the equity method of accounting.[50] Thus, investments that are more than minor (3–5%) lead to the application of the equity method of accounting. Conversely, if an LLC does not maintain specific ownership accounts for each investor, the guidelines for corporations should be followed: Ownership of 20% or more of the voting stock of a limited liability company leads to the presumption of significant influence, and correspondingly, the equity method of accounting is generally applied.

UNDIVIDED INTERESTS

If real property owned by undivided interests (such as a tenancy-in-common) is subject to *joint control* by the property's owners, the investors should not present their investments by accounting for their *pro rata* share of the assets, liabilities, revenues, and expenses of the venture. A property is subject to joint control if decisions regarding the financing, development, sale, or operations require the approval of two or more of the owners. Most real estate ventures with ownership in the form of undivided interests are subject to some level of joint control. Accordingly, such investments should be presented in the same manner as investments in noncontrolled partnerships. If, however, the approval of two or more of the owners is not required, and each investor is entitled to only its *pro rata* share of income, is responsible for only its *pro rata* share of expenses, and is severally liable only for indebtedness it incurs in connection with its interest in the property, the investment may be presented by recording the undivided interest in the assets, liabilities, revenue, and expenses of the venture.[51]

6.2.2.2 Allocation of Profits and Losses
Venture partners assume different roles and risks in real estate ventures, and profit sharing arrangements of real estate ventures vary widely. Venture agreements may designate different allocations among the investors of the venture's (1) profits and losses, (2) specified costs and expenses, such as depreciation, (3) distributions of cash from operations and refinancings, and (4) distributions of cash proceeds from liquidation.[52]

To determine the investor's share of venture net income or loss, the venture arrangement needs to be analyzed to assess how an increase or decrease in net assets of the venture—determined in accordance with U.S. GAAP—will affect cash payments to the investor over the life of the venture and upon its liquidation. Specified profit and loss allocation ratios should not be used to determine an investor's equity in venture earnings if the allocation of cash distributions and liquidating distributions are determined on some other basis. For example, if pursuant to the provisions of a venture agreement between two investors all depreciation expense is allocated to one investor and all other revenues and expenses are allocated equally to the two

---

50   EITF Issue No. 03-16, paragraph 5
51   SOP 78-9, paragraph 11
52   SOP 78-9, paragraph 25

investors, but irrespective of such allocations, any distributions to investors will be made simultaneously and divided equally between them, there is no substance to the agreed-upon allocation of depreciation expense.[53]

EXAMPLE—ALLOCATION OF INCOME TO INVESTOR

GrandCo. (G) and Central Inc. (C) each hold a 50% partnership interest in partnership GrandCentral (GC). G and C both contribute $10 million to the partnership. The terms of the partnership agreement provide that G is entitled to a preferred return of 10% on its capital. G will not participate in any partnership profits above its return of 10%. In its first year of operations, the partnership earns net income of $3 million.

How much profit should be allocated to G?

Profit in the amount of $1 million should be allocated to G, representing a 10% return on its $10 million investment.

The determination of the amount of income that should be allocated to each investor may pose significant issues in situations in which a venture agreement includes cash distribution or income allocation preferences. For example, a venture arrangement with two investors may provide for cash flow distributions to one investor until its investment plus a certain return on investment is recovered; subsequent cash flows may be distributed to the other investor until that investor's investment is recovered, with any subsequent cash flows being distributed based on a certain predetermined ratio. Other venture agreements may provide for the allocation of a majority of the tax credits and income to one investor in the first few years of a venture, and an allocation of a majority of the income to the other investor in later years.

In complex arrangements, the hypothetical liquidation at book value method (HLBV method, outlined in Section 6.4.6) is useful to help determine how income should be allocated to each investor.

6.2.2.3 Difference between Carrying Amount of Investment and Investor's Share of Underlying Equity   Differences between the carrying amount of an investment in a real estate venture and the investor's equity in the underlying net assets recorded by the venture may arise, for example, from the acquisition of an investment in a venture at a price different from the investor's share of the net assets as recorded on the books of the venture.[54] Such a difference is attributed to the investee's assets and liabilities, based on their estimated fair values at the date of acquisition. Often, the difference between the purchase price for an interest in a real estate venture and the underlying book equity results from the difference between fair

---

53   SOP 78-9, paragraph 25
54   SOP 78-9, paragraph 26

value and carrying amount of real estate held by the investee, and thus that differ-ence is ascribed to the fair value of the real estate owned by the venture.[55]

The difference between the cost of an investment and the amount of the underlying equity in net assets of the investee affects the investor's share of earn-ings or losses of that investee as if the investee were a consolidated subsidiary.[56] For example, if the difference between the cost of the investment and the amount of the underlying equity relates to an office building, that difference will be amor-tized over the remaining useful life of the office building,[57] effectively represent-ing the venture partner's increased depreciation in the office building.

A portion of the difference between the cost of an investment and the amount of underlying equity in net assets of an equity method investee may be recognized as goodwill. Such equity method goodwill is not tested for impairment in accordance with FASB Statement No. 142; rather, equity investments are reviewed for impair-ment in accordance with paragraph 19(h) of APB Opinion No. 18.[58]

6.2.3 *PRO RATA* CONSOLIDATION   Under U.S. GAAP, pro rata consolidation (also referred to as proportionate consolidation) is permitted only in certain lim-ited circumstances as an alternative to the equity method of accounting.

In *pro rata* consolidations, the investor reports its share of the venture's assets, liabilities, revenues, and expenses in its financial statements, rather than applying the equity method of accounting, which requires the reporting of a sin-gle amount in the investor's balance sheet and income statement. For real estate ventures,[59]*pro rata* consolidation is permitted only if there are no elements of joint control, as explained in paragraph 11 of SOP 78-9:

> If real property owned by undivided interests is subject to joint control by the owners, the division believes that investor-venturers should not present their investments by accounting for their pro rata share of the assets, liabilities, rev-enues, and expenses of the ventures. Such property is subject to joint control if decisions regarding the financing, development, sale, or operations require the approval of two or more of the owners. Most real estate ventures with ownership in the form of undivided interests are subject to some level of joint control. Accordingly, the division believes that such investments should be presented in the same manner as investments in noncontrolled partnerships. If, however, the approval of two or more of the owners is not required for deci-sions regarding the financing, development, sale, or operations of real estate owned and each investor is entitled to only its pro rata share of income, is

---

55   SOP 78-9, paragraph 27
56   APB 18, paragraph 19(b); 19(n)
57   This example assumes that there is no difference between the fair value and the carrying value of the land upon which the office building is built.
58   SOP 78-9, paragraph 28
59   That is, for entities subject to SOP 78-9.

responsible to pay only its pro rata share of expenses, and is severally liable only for indebtedness it incurs in connection with its interest in the property, the investment may be presented by recording the undivided interest in the assets, liabilities, revenue, and expenses of the venture.

For entities that are not subject to SOP 78-9, a proportionate gross financial statement presentation of interests in entities is not considered appropriate unless the investee is in either the construction industry or an extractive industry where there is a longstanding practice of its use.[60]

6.2.4 COST METHOD
If consolidation, the equity method of accounting, or *pro rata* consolidation is not appropriate, the investment is accounted for under the cost method.[61] The cost method is used in situations in which the investor has little influence over the operating and financial policies and little involvement in an entity's operations.

Under the cost method, the investor records the investment at cost. Income is recognized only when the investor receives distributions from earnings that have been accumulated by the venture subsequent to the acquisition of the interest by the investor, or upon sale of the venture interest. Any distributions that exceed the investor's share of earnings accumulated since the acquisition of the investor's interest reduce the carrying amount of the investment; they are considered a return of the investor's investment.[62]

6.2.5 CHANGE BETWEEN THE COST AND EQUITY METHOD OF ACCOUNTING
Because of a change in circumstances, such as acquisition or disposition of equity interests in the venture, change in contractual arrangements or legal form of the venture, it may be necessary to change the method of accounting applied by the investor in periods subsequent to the acquisition of the interest in the venture.[63]

CHANGE FROM THE EQUITY METHOD TO THE COST METHOD
At the time that the conditions for the use of the equity method of accounting are no longer met, the equity method is discontinued. The carrying amount of the investment at the date of discontinuance becomes the cost basis of the investment in the venture. Subsequent dividend distributions are accounted for as dividend

---

60   EITF Issue No. 00-1; the existence of joint control does not preclude the application of pro rata consolidation for investees in the construction and extractive industries.

61   FASB Statement No. 159 allows for the reporting of investments at fair value, with certain limited exceptions. See Section 6.2.6 for further discussion.

62   APB 18, paragraph 6(a)

63   APB 18, paragraph 19(l), (m)

income to the extent of the investor's share of earnings for such periods. Any exceeding amounts reduce the carrying amount of the investment.[64]

CHANGE FROM THE COST METHOD TO THE EQUITY METHOD

An investment in an investee that was previously accounted for under the cost method may at a later point in time meet the requirements for use of the equity method. For example, an investor may increase its level of ownership, or a change in circumstances may occur that enables the investor to exercise significant influence over the investee; in that circumstance, a change from the cost method to the equity method is required. A change from the cost to the equity method of accounting entails the retroactive adjustment of the investment account, results of operations for all periods presented, and retained earnings of the investor.[65]

6.2.6 MEASURING INTERESTS IN REAL ESTATE VENTURES AT FAIR VALUE

With the issuance of FASB Statement No. 159, *The Fair Value Option for Financial Assets and Financial Liabilities*,[66] the FASB has given companies a choice of whether to report financial instruments recognized on a company's balance sheet following the historical cost model or to measure them at fair value. Several financial instruments, however, are not eligible for the "fair value option," including:[67]

- An investment in a subsidiary that the company is required to consolidate
- An interest in a variable interest entity that the company is required to consolidate

Investments accounted for under the cost or equity method of accounting, such as interests in real estate ventures that are not consolidated, are generally within the scope of FASB Statement No. 159. Accordingly, companies may elect to measure them at fair value, with changes in fair value reported in earnings.

As a general rule, the fair value option:

- Can be applied on an instrument-by-instrument basis
- Is irrevocable (unless a new election date occurs)
- Is applied only to an entire instrument and not to portions of that instrument[68]

---

64   APB 18, paragraph 19(l)
65   APB 18, para. 19(m)
66   FASB Statement No. 159 is effective as of the beginning of a company's fiscal year that begins after November 15, 2007, which is referred to as "effective date." [FAS 159, paragraph 24]
67   FAS 159, paragraph 8
68   FAS 159, paragraph 5

APPLICATION ON AN INSTRUMENT-BY-INSTRUMENT BASIS—EXCEPTIONS

Exceptions to the general rule that the fair value option is applied on an instrument-by-instrument basis include the following:

- If the fair value option is applied to an investment that would otherwise be accounted for under the equity method of accounting, it must be applied to all of the investor's financial interests in the same entity (equity and debt, including guarantees) that are eligible items.[69]
- If a venture partner makes loans to a venture, such as financing provided during the construction phase of a real estate project, the individual advances lose their identity and become part of a larger loan balance. The fair value option can be applied only to the larger balance and not to each advance individually.[70]

Additionally, the staffs of the SEC and the FASB have indicated that a financial instrument is not eligible for the fair value option under FASB Statement No. 159 if that financial instrument could include a significant compensation component for providing future services; otherwise, the fair value of financial instruments with significant service elements could include profits for services to be provided by the investor in future periods, resulting in revenue recognition before the related services are performed.

The following are two indicators that an equity investment may contain a significant element compensating the investor for future services:

- The investor provides services to the investee, and the investor does not get separately compensated for the services provided (or the investor gets compensated at amounts below market). A disproportionate return on an equity interest relative to other investors could be an indicator that the equity investment includes compensation elements for future services.
- The fair value of the equity interest at inception is greater than the investor's investment, and the investor is expected to provide services to the investee in the future that are more than customary of an investor acting solely as a nonmanagement owner.

A partner may hold both a general partnership interest and a limited partnership interest in the same partnership. If the general partnership interest encompasses a significant service element, it will not be eligible for the fair value option. That does not automatically mean that the partner's limited partnership interest in the same partnership is ineligible for the fair value option also; rather, that evaluation is dependent on the individual facts and circumstances.

---

69   FAS 159, paragraph 12(b)
70   FAS 159, paragraph 12(a)

EXAMPLE—INTEREST IN GENERAL PARTNERSHIP

GrandPark Co. (GP) is a general partner in HousingPartners LP. GP manages the partnership's assets and is entitled to a return on its partnership interest that is disproportionately greater than the return on general partnership interests held by the other general partners. GP acts as asset manager for HousingPartners LP and does not receive a management fee for the asset management services it is required to provide in the future. At inception, GP estimates that the fair value of its investment in HousingPartners LP exceeds the amount of capital contribution. GP does not consolidate Housing Partners LP.

    Can GP elect the fair value option for its partnership interest in HousingPartners LP?

    No. GP's partnership interest in HousingPartners LP entitles GP to a return that encompasses GP's services with respect to managing the partnership's assets. If GP could elect to measure its partnership interest at fair value, the fair value of the partnership interest could include the value of services GP is required to provide to the partnership. Because FASB Statement No. 159 requires that the fair value option be applied to an entire instrument, unless bifurcation is required under other authoritative guidance, GP would not be able to bifurcate the GP interest into an element representing future services and an element representing the portion of the instrument that is "purely" financial.

RECOGNITION OF INTEREST, DIVIDENDS, AND COSTS
FASB Statement No. 159 does not address the methods to be used for recognizing and measuring the amount of interest and dividend income. Origination fees and costs related to items for which the fair value option is elected should be expensed as incurred.[71]

ELECTION DATES SUBSEQUENT TO THE EFFECTIVE DATE
A company may decide at the effective date of FASB Statement No. 159 whether to elect the fair value option for each eligible item, such as an unconsolidated investment in a real estate venture that does not include a service component. Subsequent to the effective date, a company may choose to elect the fair value option for an eligible item only on the date that one of the following occurs:[72]

- The company first recognizes the eligible item.
- The company enters into an eligible firm commitment.
- Financial assets that have been reported at fair value with unrealized gains and losses included in earnings because of specialized accounting principles cease to qualify for that specialized accounting. (An example is a transfer of assets from a subsidiary subject to the AICPA Audit and Accounting Guide, *Investment Companies*, to another entity within the consolidated group not subject to that Guide.)

---

71   FAS 159, paragraphs 3 and A41
72   FAS 159, paragraphs 9 and 10

- The accounting treatment for an investment in another entity changes because:
  - The investment becomes subject to the equity method of accounting
  - The investor ceases to consolidate a subsidiary or variable interest entity but retains an interest
- An event that requires an eligible item to be measured at fair value at the time of the event, but does not require fair value measurement at each reporting date after that, such as a business combination. FASB Statement No. 159 specifically excludes from such "event" the recognition of impairment under lower-of-cost-or-market accounting or other-than-temporary impairment.

6.3 ACCOUNTING FOR TRANSACTIONS WITH A REAL ESTATE VENTURE

In many ventures, multiple contractual relationships exist between a venture and its partners. Transactions between a real estate venture and its venture partners range from the contribution of capital in the form of cash, real estate and services, the sale of properties or intangibles, to providing financing and entering into service contracts.

Transactions between a venture and its investors need to be carefully analyzed to ensure that they are recorded to reflect the substance of the transaction, rather than their legal form. Special consideration needs to be given to the general principle that profits should not be recognized before they are realized in transactions with third parties.

6.3.1 CAPITAL CONTRIBUTIONS

6.3.1.1 Contribution of Cash   If an investor contributes cash to a real estate venture, be it at the time of formation or at a later point in time, the investor records its investment at the amount of cash contributed.[73]

6.3.1.2 Contribution of Real Estate[74]   Generally, an investor that contributes real estate to a real estate venture records its investment in the venture at the investor's carrying amount, regardless of whether the other investors contribute cash, property, or services. If the carrying amount of the real estate that an investor contributes to a venture exceeds its fair value, the investor should recognize a loss (impairment charge); a situation in which an investor obtains a disproportionately small interest in the real estate venture when comparing the carrying amount of the real estate with cash contributed by other investors may indicate that the investor has suffered a loss that should be recognized.[75]

---

73   SOP 78-9, paragraph 29
74   SOP 78-9, paragraph 30
75   SOP 78-9, paragraph 31

If the fair value of the real estate exceeds its carrying amount, the venture partner would generally not record a profit on the contribution of real estate, because a contribution of capital is not the culmination of the earnings process. However, if the contribution of real estate to a noncontrolled venture constitutes in substance a partial sale of the property contributed, profit is recognized by the venture partner in the amount of the difference between the fair value and the carrying amount of the portion considered sold, assuming no profit deferral is required pursuant to the provisions of FASB Statement No. 66, *Accounting for Sales of Real Estate.*

EXAMPLE—CONTRIBUTION OF REAL ESTATE TREATED AS PARTIAL SALE[76]

LandCo. (L) contributes to a real estate joint venture a parcel of land with a fair value of $2 million, and BetterBuild Inc. (B) contributes cash in the amount of $1 million, which is immediately withdrawn by L. Following such contributions and withdrawal, L and B have a 50% interest in the joint venture (the only asset of which is the real estate contributed by L). L is not committed to reinvest the $1 million in the joint venture.

How should L account for the contribution of the land?

The substance of this transaction is a sale by investor L of a one-half interest in the real estate in exchange for cash, with the other half being a capital contribution.

EXAMPLE—CONTRIBUTION OF REAL ESTATE TO VENTURE CONTROLLED
BY CONTRIBUTING INVESTOR

Venture partner LandCo. (L) contributes to a venture a land parcel with a fair value of $1 million, and investor BetterBuild Inc. (B) contributes cash in the amount of $100,000, which is immediately withdrawn by L. Following such contribution and withdrawal, L has a 90% interest in the venture (the only asset of which is the real estate contributed) and controls the venture.

How much profit can L recognize at the time of contribution?

L controls the venture after the contribution of the real estate. L cannot recognize any profit pursuant to paragraph 34 of FASB Statement No. 66, until the profit is realized from transactions with outside parties through sale or operations of the property.

6.3.1.3 Contribution of Services or Intangibles[77]   Investors may contribute services, such as planning and design, or intangibles, such as construction rights. The accounting considerations that apply to real property contributed to a real estate venture also apply to the contribution of services and intangibles.

---

76   Example adapted from SOP 78-9, paragraph 30
77   SOP 78-9, paragraph 32; special rules apply to real estate syndication activities, in which the syndicators receive or retain partnership interests. [SOP 92-1]

Generally, the earnings process has not been culminated, profit recognition is not permissible, and the investor records its contribution at cost. The investor's cost of such services or intangibles should be determined by the investor in the same manner as for an investment in a wholly owned real estate project.

6.3.2 LOANS AND ADVANCES TO A VENTURE[78] The accounting for funds advanced or loaned to a venture depends on the characteristics of the loans or advances, whether they are in substance loans or capital contributions. That determination is facts and circumstances-based. In situations where all investors are required to make loans and advances proportionate to their equity interests, loans and advances are considered capital contributions.[79] The classification of loans and advances on the investor's books as either capital contributions or loans is generally not an issue, because loans and contributions to ventures are usually combined as one line item.

However, the characterization of loans and advances as capital contributions results in the characterization of interest payments received from the venture as dividends; for an investment in a real estate venture that is accounted for under the equity method, dividend distributions reduce the carrying amount of the investment on the investor's books.

Interest income on loans and advances that are not in substance capital contributions are accounted for as follows:

1. *The venture records interest expense.*
   If the venture records the interest as expense, the investor recognizes the interest income as earned. The interest income on the investor's books is offset by its share of the related interest expense on the venture's books.
2. *The venture capitalizes the interest.*
   If the venture capitalizes the interest as part of a real estate project pursuant to the provisions of FASB Statement No. 34, *Capitalization of Interest Cost,* the portion of interest income from loans and advances that relates to the investor's percentage of interest in a venture accounted for under the equity method of accounting should be deferred until the corresponding interest is recognized as expense on the books of the investee. In essence, intercompany interest, which has been capitalized by the investee, is treated like intercompany profits or losses on assets that are on the books of the investor or investee at balance sheet date.

   Notwithstanding the foregoing, the recognition of interest income on the investor's books is not permissible if either or both of the following conditions are present:[80]

---

78   SOP 78-9, paragraphs 33 and 34
79   SOP 78-9, paragraph 33
80   SOP 78-9, paragraph 34

a. *Collectibility of principal or interest is in doubt.* This condition may exist if adequate collateral and other terms normally required by an independent lender are not present.

b. *Reasonable expectation that the other investors will not bear their shares of losses.* This results in uncertainty as to the lender's share of the venture's related interest expense.

6.3.3 SALES OF REAL ESTATE[81] The provisions of FASB Statement No. 66 apply to the recording of real estate sales between a venture and its venture partners and to the recognition of profits relating to such sales. Statement 66 contains stringent requirements that must be met for sale and profit recognition to be appropriate. The following Section includes a brief discussion of the accounting consequences of (1) a sale of real estate by an investor to a venture and (2) a sale of real estate by a venture to one of its investors. Depending on the relationship between venture and investor and the terms of the transaction, sale and/or profit recognition may be precluded. The continuing involvement provisions of Statement 66, which may impact sale or profit recognition, are discussed in detail in Chapter 3.

SALES OF REAL ESTATE BY INVESTOR TO VENTURE
Paragraph 34 of Statement 66 provides for partial or full deferral of profit in a sale of real estate by an investor to an investee, depending on the ownership interests held by the investor:

> If the buyer is not independent of the seller, for example, if the seller holds or acquires an equity interest in the buyer, the seller shall recognize the part of the profit proportionate to the outside interests in the buyer at the date of sale. If the seller controls the buyer, no profit on the sale shall be recognized until it is realized from transactions with outside parties through sale or operations of the property.

Thus, if the seller controls, or is under common control with, the buyer, profit can be recognized only once realized from transactions with third parties and then only proportionate to the third-party interests in the buyer. Paragraph 34 of statement 66 applies even if the seller accounts for its investment in the real estate venture under the cost method of accounting.

Special consideration must be given to support obligations, management contracts and other forms of continuing involvement, which may require a deferral of profit or may preclude sale accounting. For example, if the seller is a general partner in a limited partnership that acquires an interest in the real property and

---

81   SOP 78-9, paragraph 36

the general partner also holds a receivable from the partnership for a significant[82] part of the purchase price, FASB Statement No. 66 requires that the seller account for the transaction as a financing, leasing, or profit-sharing arrangement.[83]

SALE OF REAL ESTATE BY VENTURE TO INVESTOR
Similar to the sale of real estate from an investor to a venture, the sale of real estate from a venture to an investor requires that the portion of the profit relating to the investor purchasing the real estate be deferred until realized from transactions with third parties or through operations.

Paragraph 38 of SOP 78-9 states:

> An investor should not record as income its equity in the venture's profit from a sale of real estate to that investor; the investor's share of such profit should be recorded as a reduction in the carrying amount of the purchased real estate and recognized as income on a pro rata basis as the real estate is depreciated or when it is sold to a third party.

6.3.4 SERVICE ARRANGEMENTS   Services can be a form of capital contribution of a venture partner. Additionally, investor and venture may enter into service arrangements, such as a contract to serve as general contractor for a project, in exchange for the payment of fees.

SERVICES PROVIDED BY INVESTOR TO VENTURE
For an investment accounted for by the equity method, the general concepts relating to the equity method of accounting apply: No interentity profit elimination is necessary if the cost of the services is expensed on the venture's books—for example, cost of administrative services performed by the investor. If the cost of services provided by the investor is capitalized by the venture, the recognition of profit is appropriate to the extent they are attributable to third-party interests in the venture, assuming the following conditions are met:

- The form of the transaction reflects its substance.
- There are no substantial uncertainties regarding the ability of the investor to complete performance or the total cost of services to be rendered.
- It can be expected that the other investors will bear their share of any losses.[84]

---

82   For this purpose, a significant receivable is a receivable in excess of 15% of the maximum first-lien financing that could be obtained from an independent established lending institution for the property. It would include:
- A construction loan made or to be made by the seller to the extent that it exceeds the minimum funding commitment for permanent financing from a third party that the seller will not be liable for
- An all-inclusive or wrap-around receivable held by the seller to the extent that it exceeds prior-lien financing for which the seller has no personal liability
- Other funds provided or to be provided directly or indirectly by the seller to the buyer
- The present value of a land lease when the seller is the lessor (footnote 15). [FAS 66, paragraph 27, footnote 8]
83   FAS 66, paragraph 27
84   SOP 78-9, paragraph 37

The profit relating to the investor's interest is recognized at the time the fees due to the investor are recorded as expense in the books of the venture.

SERVICES PROVIDED BY VENTURE TO INVESTOR
No special consideration is necessary if the cost of services provided by the venture is expensed by the venture partner. If a venture partner that uses the equity method of accounting capitalizes service fees paid to the venture as part of project costs, the investor's share of the venture's profit in the transaction should be recorded as a reduction in the carrying amount of the capitalized cost.[85]

6.3.5 SALE OF INTEREST IN REAL ESTATE VENTURE   Frequently, the primary asset of a real estate venture is real estate. The sale of an investor's interest in a real estate venture that primarily holds real estate is equivalent to the sale of the underlying real estate;[86] the accounting for such sale follows the sale and profit recognition guidelines for real estate,[87] discussed in Chapter 3.

6.4 SPECIAL ACCOUNTING ISSUES RELATING TO THE EQUITY METHOD OF ACCOUNTING

6.4.1 OTHER-THAN-COMMON STOCK INVESTMENTS IN CORPORATE VENTURES   APB Opinion No. 18 is the principal accounting guidance relating to the application of the equity method of accounting to investments in common stock. In 2002, the EITF addressed the issue of whether an investor should apply the equity method of accounting to investments other than in the form of common stock. The Task Force reached the consensus[88] that an investor that has the ability to exercise significant influence over the operating and financial policies of the investee should apply the equity method of accounting only when it has an investment in common stock or *in-substance common stock*. In-substance common stock is an investment in an entity that has risk and reward characteristics that are substantially similar to that entity's common stock.

The presence of any of the following characteristics indicates that the investment is not in-substance common stock:

- *Difference in subordination characteristics.* If an investment has a substantive liquidation preference over common stock, it is not substantially similar to common stock. For example, a liquidation preference in an investee that has little or no subordinated equity from a fair value perspective is

---

85   SOP 78-9, paragraph 38
86   "The provisions of FASB Statement No. 66 do not apply to transactions that involve the following: . . . The sale of the stock or net assets of a subsidiary or a segment of a business if the assets of that subsidiary or that segment, as applicable, contain real estate, unless the transaction is, in substance, the sale of real estate." [FIN 43, paragraph 3(b)]
87   SOP 78-9, paragraph 39; FAS 66, paragraph 101; EITF Issue No. 98-8
88   EITF Issue No. 02-14

nonsubstantive, because, in the event of liquidation, the investment will participate in substantially all of the investee's losses.

- *Difference in risks and rewards of ownership.* If an investment is not expected to participate in the earnings (and losses) and capital appreciation (and depreciation) in a manner that is substantially similar to common stock, the investment is not substantially similar to common stock. The investee paying dividends on its common stock with the investment participating currently in those dividends in a manner that is substantially similar to common stock is an indicator that the investment is substantially similar to common stock. If the investor has the ability to convert the investment into that entity's common stock without any significant restrictions or contingencies that prohibit the investor from participating in the capital appreciation of the investee in a manner that is substantially similar to that entity's common stock, the conversion feature is an indicator that the investment is substantially similar to common stock.
- *Obligation to transfer value.* An investment is not substantially similar to common stock if the investee is expected to transfer substantive value to the investor and the common shareholders do not participate in a similar manner. An example would be a mandatory redemption provision.

In situations in which the determination about whether the investment is substantially similar to common stock cannot be reached based solely on the evaluation of the three characteristics above, the investor needs to analyze whether the future changes in the fair value of the investment are expected to be highly correlated with the changes in the fair value of the common stock. If changes in the fair value of the investment are not expected to be highly correlated with the changes in the fair value of the common stock the investment is not in-substance common stock.

The initial determination of whether an investment is substantially similar to common stock has to be reconsidered if the contractual terms of the investment have changed, if there is a significant change in the capital structure of the investee, or if the investor obtains an additional interest in the investee.

6.4.2 DIFFERENCES BETWEEN ACCOUNTING PRINCIPLES OF INVESTOR AND VENTURE   Real estate ventures may prepare financial statements following tax accounting principles, rather than following U.S. GAAP. Investors accounting for their investment under the equity method of accounting have to evaluate the accounting principles used by the equity method investees and determine whether there are any significant differences between the accounting principles used and U.S. GAAP. If such differences are significant, the financial statements of the investee need to be adjusted before applying the equity method of accounting.[89]

---

89   SOP 78-9, paragraph 24

6.4.3 RECOGNITION OF LOSSES BY THE INVESTOR   Under the equity method, a venture partner's investment in a venture is adjusted every period to reflect the venture partner's share of earnings or losses in the venture. Special consideration has to be given to a situation in which the investee has incurred losses.

6.4.3.1 Investor's Share of Losses in Excess of Its Investment   An investor's share of losses of an investee may equal or exceed the carrying amount of the investment (including any loans and advances made by the investor). As a general rule, the investor should suspend the application of the equity method when the investment (including any loans and advances) is reduced to zero, unless the investor is liable for the obligations of the investee (e.g., as guarantor or general partner) or is otherwise committed to provide additional financial support.[90] An investor without a legal commitment to providing additional financial support to the venture may have

> . . . indicated a commitment, based on considerations such as business reputation, intercompany relationships, or credit standing, to provide additional financial support. Such a commitment might be indicated by previous support provided by the investor or statements by the investor to other investors or third parties of the investor's intention to provide support.[91]

Even if an investor is not liable or otherwise committed to providing additional financial support, the investor should not suspend the equity method of accounting for losses in excess of its investment when the imminent return to profitable operations by the venture appears to be assured. For example, a material nonrecurring loss of an isolated nature, or start-up losses, may reduce an investment below zero though the underlying profitable pattern of an investee is not impaired.[92]

If the equity method of accounting was discontinued due to the investor not having any commitments to provide additional financial support, and the investee reports net income in subsequent periods, the investor resumes applying the equity method only after its share of net income equals the share of losses not recognized during the period the equity method was suspended.[93]

If the equity method of accounting is not discontinued based on the existence of commitments to provide additional financial support, the investor continues to recognize its share of losses in excess of its investment (including loans and advances); that excess is reported as a liability.[94]

---

90   APB 18, paragraph 19(i), SOP 78-9, paragraph 15
91   SOP 78-9, paragraph 15
92   SOP 78-9, paragraph 15, footnote 2
93   APB 18, paragraph 19(i), SOP 78-9, paragraph 17
94   SOP 78-9, paragraph 16

6.4.3.2 Recognition of Losses Relating to Other Investors

ABILITY OF OTHER INVESTORS TO BEAR THEIR SHARE OF LOSSES

When determining the amount of losses to be recognized in an investor's financial statements, the investor has to consider whether the other investors can bear their share of losses or whether the investor should record losses exceeding its own share based on the provisions relating to contingencies in FASB Statement No. 5, *Accounting for Contingencies*. When making that evaluation,

> ... each investor should look primarily to the fair value of the other investors' interests in the venture and the extent to which the venture's debt is nonrecourse in evaluating their ability and willingness to bear their allocable share of losses. . . . However, there may be satisfactory alternative evidence of an ability and willingness of other investors to bear their allocable share of losses. Such evidence might be, for example, that those investors previously made loans or contributions to support cash deficits, possess satisfactory financial standing (as may be evidenced by satisfactory credit ratings), or have provided adequately collateralized guarantees.[95]

   If it is probable that another investor cannot bear its share of losses, the remaining investors record their proportionate share of that investor's losses to the extent they are potentially liable.[96] Nonetheless, the investor that is deemed unable to bear its share of losses continues to record its contractual share of losses unless it is relieved from the obligation to make payment by agreement or as a matter of law. When the venture subsequently reports income, the investors that recorded another investor's losses should record their proportionate share of the venture's net income otherwise allocable to that investor for which they previously recorded losses, until such income equals the excess losses they previously recorded.[97]

LOSSES THAT REDUCE A MINORITY INTEREST BALANCE BELOW ZERO

Losses that reduce a minority interest balance below zero do not result in an asset recorded in the consolidated financial statements for the negative balance in the minority interest account, unless the minority interest has an obligation to "make good those losses." If no such obligation exists, any loss exceeding the minority interest balance is charged against the majority interest.[98] FASB Statement No. 160, *Noncontrolling Interests in Consolidated Financial Statements*,[99] will

---

95   SOP 78-9, paragraph 19
96   In real property jointly owned and operated as undivided interests, for example, an investor would not have to pick up other investors' share of losses if the claims or liens of investor's creditors are limited to investors' respective interests in such property. [SOP 78-9, paragraph 18, footnote 3]
97   SOP 78-9, paragraph 18
98   The majority interest would be credited to the extent of such absorbed losses if the investee were to report income in subsequent periods. [ARB 51, paragraph 15]; EITF Issue No. 94-2 includes a similar concept.
99   FASB Statement No. 160 is effective for fiscal years beginning on or after December 15, 2008. The provisions of that Statement will be applied prospectively as of the beginning of the fiscal year in which FASB Statement No. 160 is initially applied, except for the presentation and disclosure requirements, which will be applied retrospectively.

change the requirement to allocate such excess losses to the majority interest. Under Statement 160, losses attributable to the noncontrolling interest (minority interest) continue to be attributed to the noncontrolling interest, even if that attribution results in a deficit noncontrolling interest balance.[100]

6.4.4 INVESTMENTS IN AN INVESTEE AFTER SUSPENSION OF LOSS RECOGNITION   An investor that has suspended the equity method of accounting because its share of losses exceeded the investor's investment may subsequently make additional investments in the venture. In that situation the question arises as to whether the investor should recognize previously suspended losses up to the amount of the subsequent investment or whether the additional investment does not trigger any loss recognition from prior periods. In EITF Issue No. 02-18, *Accounting for Subsequent Investments in an Investee after Suspension of Equity Method Loss Recognition*, the Task Force reached the consensus that

> . . . if the additional investment, in whole or in part, represents, in substance, the funding of prior losses, the investor should recognize previously suspended losses only up to the amount of the additional investment determined to represent the funding of prior losses.

If the additional funding does not represent the funding of prior losses, loss recognition from prior periods is not appropriate. Judgment is required in determining whether prior years' losses are being funded, and all available information needs to be considered when making that determination. EITF Issue No. 02-18 provides certain factors that need to be evaluated:

- *Whether the additional investment is acquired from a third party.* If the investment is purchased from a third party, it is generally unlikely that prior losses are being funded.
- *Fair value of consideration paid in relation to the value received.* If the fair value of the consideration received is less than the fair value of the consideration paid, there is an indication that prior losses are being funded.
- *Increase in ownership percentage.* Investments made without a corresponding increase in ownership or other interests, or without a *pro rata* equity investment made by all existing investors, indicate that prior losses are being funded.
- *Seniority of the additional investment.* An investment in an instrument that is subordinate to other equity of the investee may indicate that prior losses are being funded.

---

100   FAS 160, paragraph 31

6.4.5 CASH DISTRIBUTIONS IN EXCESS OF INVESTMENT Successful real estate ventures often generate substantial cash flows from the operation of real estate or from the refinancing or sale of appreciated property, which are then distributed to the investors. Under the equity method of accounting, distributions (dividends) received from an equity method investee reduce the investment account.

Any cash distributions received from an equity method investee reduce the investment balance until it reaches zero. Assuming the investor has *no* contractual or legal obligation to reinvest in the investee or to refund the distributions received and no commitment to support the operations of the investee, gain recognition of distributions received in excess of the investment balance may be appropriate.[101] When determining whether contractual or legal obligations exist to refund any distributions, consideration should be given to state laws or obligations that may arise in the case of bankruptcy of the investee.

An issue arises in consolidated financial statements with respect to distributions to minority interest holders in excess of their minority interest balances. Such "excess" distributions are reflected as part of the consolidated net loss attributable to the majority interest, unless (and to the extent that) the minority interest holders have guaranteed the entity's debt or have committed to and are capable of providing additional capital. The author believes that after the effective date of FASB Statement No. 160, distributions in excess of the noncontrolling interest balance (minority interest balance) should be accounted for like losses in excess of the noncontrolling interest balance: Losses attributable to the noncontrolling interest continue to be attributed to the noncontrolling interest, even if that attribution results in a deficit noncontrolling interest balance.

6.4.6 HYPOTHETICAL LIQUIDATION AT BOOK VALUE METHOD Under the HLBV method, an investor determines its share of the earnings or losses of an investee by determining the difference between its "claim on the investee's book value" at the end and beginning of the period. That claim is calculated as the amount that the investor would receive (or be obligated to pay) if the investee were to liquidate all of its assets at recorded amounts determined in accordance with U.S. GAAP and distribute the resulting cash to creditors and investors according to their respective priorities. The difference between the investor's claim on the investee's book value at the end of the period and its claim at the beginning of the period represents the investor's share of the investee's earnings or losses for the period, after taking into consideration any capital contributions or investments

---

101 The AICPA Issues Paper, *Accounting by Investors for Distributions Received in Excess of their Investment in a Joint Venture*, October 8, 1979 (addendum to the July 17, 1979 Issues Paper on Joint Venture Accounting), addresses the issue of excess distributions, but does not reach a conclusion as to the appropriate accounting.

made by the investor during the period and any distributions received by the investor during the period.

The application of the HLBV method was discussed in EITF Issue No. 99-10, *Percentage Used to Determine the Amount of Equity Method Losses*; the Task Force reached a consensus that the HLBV method was an acceptable method for determining the amount of losses to be allocated to an investor using the equity method of accounting in situations where the investor not only owns common stock, but in addition has loans to and investments in other securities of an investee. The application of the HLBV method is further illustrated in the proposed SOP, *Accounting for Investors' Interests in Unconsolidated Real Estate Investments*. That proposed SOP, explains the conceptual difference between the conventional way of applying the equity method of accounting and the HLBV method:[102]

> The conventional way of thinking about the equity method of accounting is income statement oriented. Under the conventional approach, an investor applies its "percentage ownership interest" to an investee's GAAP net income to determine the investor's share of the earnings or losses of the investee. That approach is difficult to use if the investee's capital structure gives different rights and priorities to its owners. In those situations, it is often difficult to describe an investor's interest in an investee simply as a specified percentage. The HLBV way of thinking about the equity method overcomes those difficulties and can be applied to both simple and complex capital structures. It is a balance-sheet oriented approach to the equity method of accounting that is a much more versatile tool.

That proposed SOP suggests the use of the HLBV method as the only appropriate method to follow when applying the equity method. However, that proposed SOP was never issued in final form, and thus, the HLBV method does not replace the conventional income statement–driven approach provided for in APB Opinion No. 18 to determine an investor's share of an investee's income.

Nevertheless, the HLBV is commonly used in situations in which the conventional way to allocate profits and losses of an equity method investee is either not feasible or leads to unreasonable results.

6.4.7 IMPAIRMENT   An investor must recognize a loss in the value of its investment, if the decline is other than temporary. Indicators of a loss in value of the investment include the absence of the investor's ability to recover the carrying amount of the investment or the inability of the investee to sustain an earnings capacity that justifies the carrying amount of the investment. Other investors ceasing

---

102   Proposed SOP, *Accounting for Investors' Interests in Unconsolidated Real Estate Investments*, paragraph 18

to provide support or reducing their financial commitment to the venture may also indicate that a loss in value is other than temporary.[103]

For a real estate venture holding real estate properties under development or used in its operations (such as income-producing properties), complexities arise with respect to the impairment analysis of the real estate: The real estate venture performs a two-step impairment analysis in accordance with FASB Statement No. 144, *Accounting for the Impairment or Disposal of Long-Lived Assets*, as described in Chapter 3. No impairment needs to be recognized by the venture if the carrying amount of the real estate is recoverable on an *undiscounted* cash flow basis. However, the investor in an equity method investee needs to evaluate whether its investment in the venture is impaired pursuant to paragraph 19(h) of APB Opinion No. 18,[104] which is based on a comparison of the investment's *fair value* with the carrying amount of the investment. As a result, an investor may have to recognize an impairment loss on its investment even if the venture did not recognize an impairment loss on its properties.

To the extent the investor has made loans and advances to the investee, the impairment analysis for those loans and advances should be performed following FASB Statement No. 114, *Accounting by Creditors for Impairment of a Loan*, rather than following APB Opinion No. 18.[105] For an investor's loans and advances, the impairment analysis focuses on the collectibility of principal and interest. A loan is considered impaired when, based on current information and events, it is probable[106] that a creditor will be unable to collect all amounts due (including principal and interest) according to the contractual terms of the loan agreement.[107]

OVERVIEW—IMPAIRMENT ANALYSIS FOR EQUITY METHOD INVESTEE		
TYPE OF INVESTMENT	AUTHORITATIVE LITERATURE	CRITERIA
Equity Investment	APB Opinion No. 18; SOP 78-9	FV exceeds investment; decline other than temporary
Loans and Advances	FASB Statement No. 114; SOP 78-9	Collectibility of principal and interest

---

103 APB 18, paragraph 19(h); SOP 78-9, paragraph 20
104 Investments accounted for under the equity method of accounting are scoped out of FASB Statement No. 144. [FAS 144, para. 5]
105 SOP 78-9, paragraph 20
106 The term probable is used in FASB Statement No. 114 consistent with its use in FASB Statement No. 5. It depicts a future event "likely to occur" and does not require virtual certainty. [FAS 114, paragraph 10; FAS 5, paragaraph 84]
107 FAS 114, paragraph 8

6.4.8 INTEREST CAPITALIZATION   Interest incurred during the construction period of a real estate asset is part of that asset's capitalized project cost.[108] Assets qualifying for interest capitalization include assets that are constructed or otherwise produced for a company's own use and assets intended for sale or lease that are constructed or otherwise produced as discrete projects.[109] Qualifying assets also include

> [i]nvestments (equity, loans, and advances) accounted for by the equity method while the investee has activities in progress necessary to commence its planned principal operations provided that the investee's activities include the use of funds to acquire qualifying assets for its operations.[110]

An investor is not permitted to capitalize any interest cost after the date that the investee begins planned principal operations.[111] For a real estate venture, such as a real estate partnership developing a master-planned community, the commencement of planned principal operations—which marks the end of the period during which interest on investments in an equity method investee is capitalized—is generally interpreted as the earlier of (1) completion of construction, at which time the real estate developed is ready for its intended use, or (2) the generation of significant revenues through closings.

EXAMPLE—INVESTMENTS INCLUDED AS QUALIFYING ASSETS[112]

Investors JerryCo. (J) and VictorCo. (V) form a venture (JV) to develop a shopping center in Norwalk, CT, for which construction is completed in December 2006. In 2007, JV commences the development of a shopping center in Westport, CT, which is expected to be completed in February 2008. J and V account for their investments in JV under the equity method of accounting.

Over what period do J's and V's investments in JV qualify for interest capitalization?

J's and V's investments in JV qualify for interest capitalization until the end of the construction period for the shopping center in Norwalk, December 2006. Subsequent to the completion of the shopping center in Norwalk, J's and V's investments in JV no longer qualify for interest capitalization.

The capitalization of interest on the investor's books creates a difference between the investment account on the investor's books and the underlying equity in the net assets of the investee. That difference should be accounted for as if the investee were a consolidated subsidiary;[113] to the extent the difference is associated

---

108   FAS 34, paragraph 6
109   FAS 34, paragraph 9(a) and (b)
110   FAS 34, paragraph 9(c); FAS 58, paragraph 5
111   FAS 34, paragraph 10, FAS 58, paragraph 6
112   Adapted from FASB Status Report, April 27, 1982 Issue
113   APB 18, paragraph 19(b)

EXAMPLE—INTEREST CAPITALIZATION ON FUNDS PROVIDED
TO EQUITY METHOD INVESTEE

Shoreside Community LLC (SC) has recently been established for the purpose of developing Shoreside Community, a master planned community. Palm West LLC (P), a home developer, has made an equity contribution of $2 million to SC, its equity method investee. Additionally, P provides an interest-free loan of $10 million to SC, which is to be used for the development of Shoreside Community. SC is not engaged in any activities besides the development of Shoreside Community and has no revenues, as the development of Shoreside Community has just commenced.

Should P include the equity contributions and the loan as part of its own qualifying assets when determining the amount of interest to be capitalized?

Yes. The investment in SC, which includes both the equity contribution and the loan, constitutes an asset qualifying for interest capitalization on the books of P. SC uses the funds for the development and construction of a real estate project; and SC is not an established real estate joint venture with multiple projects and has not generated any revenues from Shoreside Community.

---

with the estimated useful lives of an investee's assets, amortization over the same period as those assets is appropriate.[114]

6.5 FINANCIAL STATEMENT PRESENTATION AND DISCLOSURE

The presentation and disclosure requirements relating to interests in real estate ventures differ, depending on the accounting method used and the relationships between the parties. Significant presentation and disclosure requirements are summarized below.

FASB Statement No. 57, *Related Party Disclosures*, includes the following disclosure requirements[115] relating to material related party transactions, other than compensation arrangements, expense allowances, and other similar items in the ordinary course of business:

- The nature of the relationship
- For each period for which income statements are presented, a description of the transactions necessary to understand their effect on the financial statements
- For each period for which income statements are presented, the dollar amounts of transactions and the effects of any change in the method of establishing the terms from that used in the preceding period
- Amounts due from or to related parties as of the date of each balance sheet presented and the terms and manner of settlement, if not apparent
- Information required by FASB Statement No. 109, *Accounting for Income Taxes*

---

114   FAS 58, paragraph 23
115   FAS 57, paragraph 2

FASB Statement No. 57 includes a requirement to disclose the nature of an existing control relationship (even if there are no transactions between the investor and the venture) in situations in which the investor and the venture are under common ownership or management control and the operating results or financial position of the investor could be significantly impacted as a result of that existing control relationship.[116]

6.5.1 CONSOLIDATED INVESTMENTS Consolidated financial statements present the results of operations and the financial position of the consolidating investor and the venture essentially as if they were a single company. ARB 51 includes general disclosure requirements relating to the consolidation policy being followed.[117]

For ventures that are variable interest entities, paragraph 23 of FIN 46(R) includes the following disclosure requirements for the investor consolidating the venture, unless that investor also holds a majority voting interest:

- The nature, purpose, size, and activities of the variable interest entity
- The carrying amount and classification of consolidated assets that are collateral for the variable interest entity's obligations
- Lack of recourse if creditors (or beneficial interest holders) of a consolidated variable interest entity have no recourse to the general credit of the primary beneficiary

6.5.2 EQUITY METHOD INVESTEES Under the equity method, an investment in a venture (including any loans and advances) is generally presented in the balance sheet of the investor as a single amount, and the investor's share of earnings or losses from its investment is presented in its income statement as a single amount.[118]

Paragraph 20 of APB Opinion No. 18 provides for certain disclosures relating to investments in common stock accounted for under the equity method. The extent of disclosures to be made by an investor and the determination of whether to combine certain disclosures relating to more than one equity method investee depend on the significance of the investment to the investor's financial position and the results of operations of the investee. Such disclosures include:[119]

- The name of each investee and the percentage of ownership of common stock
- The accounting policies of the investor with respect to investments in common stock

---

116   FAS 57, paragraph 4
117   ARB 51, paragraph 5
118   APB 18, paragraph 11
119   Paragraph 12 of SOP 78-9 refers to the disclosure requirements in paragraph 20 of APB Opinion No. 18.

- The amount and accounting treatment of any difference between the carrying amount of the investment and the amount of underlying equity
- For investments in common stock for which a quoted market price is available, the value of each identified investment based on the quoted market price
- For investments that are in the aggregate material in relation to the financial position or results of operations of an investor, the presentation of summarized information of the assets, liabilities, and results of operations of the investees, either individually or in groups
- Disclosures relating to material effects of possible conversions and contingent issuances of an investee's stock

INTERESTS IN VARIABLE INTEREST ENTITIES

Paragraph 24 of FIN 46(R) requires the following disclosures for investors that hold significant variable interests in variable interest entities:

- The nature of the investor's involvement with the variable interest entity and when that involvement began
- The nature, purpose, size, and activities of the variable interest entity
- The investor's maximum exposure to loss as a result of its involvement with the variable interest entity

STATEMENT OF CASH FLOWS

Real estate ventures often make significant distributions, which may be cash flows from operations or cash flows from the sale or refinancing of real estate properties. FASB Statement No. 95, *statement of cash flows,*[120] requires that a distinction be made between distributions that represent a return *on* investment—which are presented as operating cash flows—and distributions that represent a return *of* investment—which are presented as investing cash flows.[121] The difficulty is determining whether distributions should be considered a return *of* investment or a return *on* investment.

Statement 95 does not prescribe a certain methodology for making that determination. One acceptable method is to analogize to the treatment of dividends received from an investee accounted for under the cost method, as described in paragraph 6(a) of APB Opinion No. 18:

> Dividends received in excess of earnings subsequent to the date of investment are considered a return of investment and are recorded as reductions of cost of the investment.

---

120   Investors in real estate ventures need to follow the guidance in FASB Statement No. 95. [SOP 78-9, paragraph 13]
121   FAS 95, paragraphs 16(b) and 22(b)

When applying that method, an investor compares the distributions it has received from the investee subsequent to the date of its investment to the share of earnings allocated to the investor subsequent to the date of its investment. To the extent that cumulative distributions exceed the investor's cumulative share of earnings, the distributions are classified as investing cash flows. Otherwise, they are considered operating cash flows. The proposed SOP, *Accounting for Investors' Interests in Unconsolidated Real Estate Investments,* also supports the use of that method.[122]

Another acceptable method is to evaluate each individual distribution received to determine whether all or a portion of the distribution clearly relates to a return of investment; examples are distributions from the sale of real estate properties or liquidating dividends.[123]

6.5.3 ITEMS MEASURED AT FAIR VALUE

BALANCE SHEET PRESENTATION

FASB Statement No. 159 sets forth the following requirements with respect to balance sheet presentation of interests measured at fair value following the provisions of that Statement:[124]

> Entities shall report assets and liabilities that are measured at fair value pursuant to the fair value option in this Statement in a manner that separates those reported fair values from the carrying amounts of similar assets and liabilities measured using another measurement attribute. To accomplish that, an entity shall either:
>
> a. Present the aggregate of fair value and non-fair value amounts in the same line item in the statement of financial position and parenthetically disclose the amount measured at fair value included in the aggregate amount
> b. Present two separate line items to display the fair value and non-fair-value carrying amounts.

INCOME STATEMENT PRESENTATION

No requirements have been established by FASB Statement No. 159 regarding income statement presentation.

CASH FLOW STATEMENT PRESENTATION

Paragraph 16 of FASB Statement No. 159 requires that companies classify cash receipts and cash payments related to items measured at fair value according to their nature and purpose pursuant to the provisions in FASB Statement No. 95.

---

122   Proposed SOP, *Accounting for Investors' Interests in Unconsolidated Real Estate Investments,* Summary
123   AICPA Technical Practice Aid, *Presentation on the Statement of Cash Flows of Distributions From Investees with Operating Losses* (TIS Section 1300.18)
124   FAS 159, paragraph 15

DISCLOSURES
Paragraphs 17–22 of FASB Statement No. 159 include extensive disclosure requirements, consistent with the objective that the disclosures should serve to "facilitate
comparisons (a) between entities that choose different measurement attributes for
similar assets and liabilities and (b) between assets and liabilities in the financial
statements of an entity that selects different measurement attributes for similar
assets and liabilities."[125]

Required disclosures include, for example:

- Management's reasons for electing a fair value option for each eligible item
  or group of similar eligible items
- Methods and significant assumptions used to estimate the fair value of
  items for which the fair value option has been elected
- For each line item in the statement of financial position, the amounts of gains
  and losses from fair value changes included in earnings during the period and
  in which line in the income statement those gains and losses are reported
- For investments that would have been accounted for under the equity
  method if the entity had not chosen to apply the fair value option, certain
  disclosures otherwise required for investments in equity method investees

Appendix B of FASB Statement No. 159 provides illustrative fair value
disclosures and suggested forms for presenting disclosure information.

6.6 INTERNATIONAL FINANCIAL REPORTING STANDARDS

Investments in ventures are primarily addressed in three international accounting
standards:

- IAS 27, *Consolidated Financial Statements and Accounting for Investments
  in Subsidiaries*
- IAS 28, *Accounting for Investments in Associates*
- IAS 31, *Interests in Joint Ventures*

No guidance has been issued that relates specifically to investments in real
estate ventures.

IAS 39 allows for a "fair value option" for financial instruments. Like FASB
Statement No. 159, IAS 39 requires that the fair value election:

- Is made at the initial recognition of the financial instrument
- Is irrevocable
- Leads to changes in fair value being recognized in earnings

However, the scope of IAS 39 limits the fair value option to a financial
asset or liability that meets either of the following two conditions:

---

125   FAS 159, paragraph 17

1. It must be classified as held for trading.
2. Upon initial recognition, the entity designates the financial asset or liability as at fair value through profit or loss. Except for embedded derivatives, an entity can use a designation as at fair value only if

. . . doing so results in more relevant information because either

   i. it eliminates or significantly reduces a measurement or recognition inconsistency . . . that would otherwise arise from measuring assets or liabilities or recognising the gains and losses on them on different bases; or
   ii. a group of financial assets, financial liabilities or both is managed and its performance is evaluated on a fair value basis, in accordance with a documented risk management or investment strategy, and information about the group is provided internally on that basis to the entity's key management personnel. . . .[126]

Additionally, the fair value election is not available for investments in equity instruments that do not have a quoted market price in an active market, and whose fair value cannot be reliably measured.[127]

With these requirements, IFRS establishes a hurdle that must be overcome before an investor can make the fair value election for a nonconsolidated investment in a real estate venture. No similar restrictions exist under US-GAAP.

6.6.1 INVESTMENTS IN SUBSIDIARIES   A subsidiary is an entity controlled by another entity, its parent.[128] With limited exceptions,[129] IAS 27 requires that parent companies present consolidated financial statements that include all subsidiaries controlled by the parent.[130] Control, the power to govern the financial and operating policies of an entity, is presumed to exist when the parent owns, directly or indirectly, more than one-half of the voting power of an entity, unless it can be clearly demonstrated that such ownership does not constitute control. Additionally, control is also deemed to exist when the parent owns one-half or less of the voting power of an enterprise when there is at least one of the following:[131]

- Power over more than 50% of the voting rights through an agreement with other investors

---

126 IAS 39, paragraph 9(b)
127 IAS 39, paragraph 9
128 IAS 27, paragraph 4
129 Paragraph 10 of IAS 27 provides that a parent company need not present consolidated financial statements, if all of the following criteria are met: (a) the owners unanimously agree that the parent need not present consolidated financial statements; (b) the parent's debt or equity instruments are not traded in a public market; (3) the parent did not file, nor is it in the process of filing, its financial statements with a regulatory organization for the purpose of issuing securities in a public market; the ultimate or any intermediate parent publishes consolidated financial statements in accordance with IFRS.
130 IAS 27, paragraph 10
131 IAS 27, paragraph 13

- Power to govern the financial and operating policies of the enterprise under a statute or an agreement
- Power to appoint or remove the majority of the members of the board of directors
- Power to cast the majority of votes at meetings of the board of directors, if control of the entity rests with the board

SIC-12, *Consolidation—Special Purpose Entities,* provides guidance relating to the consolidation of special purpose entities (SPEs). As a general principle, an SPE must be consolidated when the substance of the relationship between an entity and the SPE indicates that the SPE is controlled by that entity.[132] In addition to the factors outlined above, which are indicative of control even though an entity may not own more than 50% of the voting power of an entity, SIC-12 provides that the following circumstances may indicate a relationship in which an entity controls an SPE, which would trigger consolidation:[133]

- In substance, the activities of the SPE are being conducted on behalf of the entity according to its specific business needs so that the entity obtains benefits from the SPE's operation.
- In substance, the entity has the decision-making powers to obtain the majority of the benefits of the activities of the SPE or, by setting up an "autopilot" mechanism, the entity has delegated these decision-making powers.
- In substance, the entity has rights to obtain the majority of the benefits of the SPE and therefore may be exposed to risks incident to the activities of the SPE.
- In substance, the entity retains the majority of the residual or ownership risks related to the SPE or its assets to obtain benefits from its activities.

DISCLOSURES

IAS 27 includes the following disclosure requirements:[134]

- Nature of the relationship between parent and subsidiary in situations in which the parent does not own more than half of the voting power
- The reason that ownership of more than 50% of the voting power of an investee does not constitute control
- The reporting date of the financial statements of a subsidiary different from that of the parent, together with a reason for using a different reporting date or period

---

132   SIC-12, paragraph 8
133   SIC-12, paragraphs 9 and 10
134   IAS 27, paragraph 40

- The nature and extent of significant restrictions on the ability of subsidiaries to transfer funds to the parent through cash dividends or the repayment of loans or advances

Under certain circumstances, parent companies do not have to present consolidated financial statements. If these parent companies elect to present separate financial statements, rather than consolidated financial statements, additional disclosure requirements apply.[135]

6.6.2 INTERESTS IN JOINT VENTURES   IAS 31 defines a joint venture as contractual arrangement whereby two or more parties undertake an economic activity that is subject to joint control. Joint control is deemed to exist only when the strategic financial and operating decisions relating to the activity require the unanimous consent of the parties sharing control;[136] no single venturer may be in a position to control the activity unilaterally.[137]

In joint ventures, two or more venturers are bound by a contractual arrangement that establishes joint control.[138] Such contractual arrangement may be evidenced by contracts, minutes of discussions between the venturers, or through by-laws of the joint venture, for example.[139] Activities that have no contractual arrangement to establish joint control are not joint ventures for purposes of IAS 31.[140]

IAS 31 defines three types of joint ventures: Joint ventures with

- Jointly controlled operations
- Jointly controlled assets
- Jointly controlled entities

6.6.2.1 *Jointly Controlled Operations*   With respect to jointly controlled operations, IAS 31 provides the following:[141]

> The operation of some joint ventures involves the use of the assets and other resources of the venturers rather than the establishment of a corporation, partnership or other entity, or a financial structure that is separate from the venturers themselves. Each venturer uses its own property, plant and equipment and carries its own inventories. It also incurs its own expenses and liabilities and raises its own finance, which represent its own obligations. The joint venture activities may be carried out by the venturer's employees alongside the venturer's similar activities. The joint venture agreement usually provides a means by

---

135   IAS 27, paragraphs 10 and 41
136   IAS 31, paragraph 3
137   IAS 31, paragraph 11
138   IAS 31, paragraph 7
139   IAS 31, paragraph 10
140   IAS 31, paragraph 9
141   IAS 31, paragraph 13

which the revenue from the sale of the joint product and any expenses incurred in common are shared among the venturers.

An example of a jointly controlled operation is the combination of operations, resources, and expertise to manufacture, market, and distribute aircrafts. "Different parts of the manufacturing process are carried out by each of the venturers. Each venturer bears its own costs and takes a share of the revenue from the sale of the aircraft, such share being determined in accordance with the contractual arrangement."[142]

For such jointly controlled operations, a venturer recognizes in its financial statements:

- The assets that it controls and the liabilities that it incurs
- The expenses that it incurs and its share of the income that it earns from the sale of goods or services by the joint venture

6.6.2.2 *Jointly Controlled Assets*   Joint ventures may involve the joint control and the joint ownership of one or more assets contributed to or acquired for the purpose of the joint venture. Each venturer may take a share of the output from the assets and each bears an agreed share of the expenses incurred.[143] These joint ventures do not involve the creation of a corporation or other entity that is separate from the venturers; each venturer has control over its share of future economic benefits through its share of the jointly controlled assets.[144]

This type of joint venture is common in the oil, gas, and mineral extraction industries. Paragraph 20 of IAS 31 provides:

> For example, a number of oil production companies may jointly control and operate an oil pipeline. Each venturer uses the pipeline to transport its own product in return for which it bears an agreed proportion of the expenses of operating the pipeline. Another example of a jointly controlled asset is when two entities jointly control a property, each taking a share of the rents received and bearing a share of the expenses.[145]

A joint venturer with interests in jointly controlled assets should recognize in its financial statements its share of the jointly controlled assets, any liabilities that it has incurred, its share of liabilities incurred jointly with the other venturers, any expenses that it has incurred relating to its interest in the joint venture, and any income from the sale or use of its share of the output of the joint venture, together with its share of any expenses incurred by the joint venture.[146]

---

142   IAS 31, paragraph 14
143   IAS 31, paragraph 18
144   IAS 31, paragraph 19
145   IAS 31, paragraph 20
146   IAS 31, paragraph 21

6.6.2.3 Jointly Controlled Entities
The third type of joint venture is a jointly controlled entity. As the name implies, the venturers have joint control over the economic activities of a joint venture, which may be a corporation, partnership, or other entity in which each venturer has an interest. That jointly controlled entity controls the assets of the joint venture, incurs liabilities and expenses, and earns income. The joint venture may enter into contracts in its own name and incur debt to finance its activities. Each venturer is entitled to a share of the profits of the jointly controlled entity.[147]

A venturer in a jointly controlled entity recognizes its interest using proportionate consolidation[148] or the equity method of accounting,[149] unless the venturer is exempted from using proportionate consolidation and equity method to account for its venture interest, which would be the case if one of the following three conditions is met:[150]

1. The interest is classified as held for sale in accordance with IFRS 5, *Non-current Assets Held for Sale and Discontinued Operations.*
2. The exception in paragraph 10 of IAS 27, *Consolidated and Separate Financial Statements,* is applicable, which provides that a parent need not present consolidated financial statements.[151]
3. All of the following apply:
   a. The venturer is a wholly owned subsidiary or is a partially owned subsidiary of another entity, and its owners agree that the venturer need not use proportionate consolidation or the equity method.
   b. The venturer's debt or equity instruments are not traded in a public market.
   c. The venturer did not file, nor is it in the process of filing, its financial statements with a regulatory organization, for the purpose of issuing securities in a public market.
   d. The ultimate or any intermediate parent of the venturer publishes consolidated financial statements in accordance with IFRS.

If a venturer ceases to have joint control over a joint venture (and ceases to have a significant influence in a joint venture, if the equity method is used), the use of the equity method or proportionate consolidation is no longer appropriate and should be discontinued.[152] If the jointly controlled entity becomes a subsidiary of a venturer, the venturer should account for its interest in accordance with IAS 27. Alternatively, a jointly controlled venture may become an associate

---

147   IAS 31, paragraphs 24 and 25
148   Paragraph 40 of IAS 31 provides that proportionate consolidation better reflects the substance and economic reality of a venturer's interest in a jointly controlled entity.
149   IAS 31, paragraphs 30 and 38
150   IAS 31, paragraph 2
151   Section 6.6.1 outlines the criteria that must be met
152   IAS 31, paragraphs 36 and 41

338 Chapter 6 Interests in Real Estate Ventures

of a venturer. From the date on which a jointly controlled entity becomes an associate of a venturer, the venturer should account for its interest in accordance with IAS 28, as outlined in Section 6.6.3.[153]

6.6.2.4 Transactions between a Venturer and a Joint Venture

SALE OR CONTRIBUTION OF ASSETS BY VENTURER

Paragraph 48 of IAS 31[154] provides for partial gain recognition if a venturer sells or contributes assets to the joint venture:

> While the assets are retained by the joint venture, and provided the venturer has transferred the significant risks and rewards of ownership, the venturer shall recognize only that portion of the gain or loss that is attributable to the interests of the other venturers . . . The venturer shall recognize the full amount of any loss when the contribution or sale provides evidence of a reduction in the net realizable value of current assets or an impairment loss.

In a nonmonetary contribution to a joint venture in exchange for an equity interest in the venture, partial gain or loss recognition is not appropriate if any of the following conditions exists:[155]

- The significant risks and rewards of ownership of the contributed nonmonetary assets have not been transferred to the joint venture.
- The gain or loss on the monetary contribution cannot be measured reliably.
- The contribution lacks commercial substance.

SALE OF ASSETS BY VENTURE

When purchasing assets from a venture, the venture partner is not permitted to recognize its share of the profits of the joint venture from the transaction until it resells the assets to an independent third party. Losses need to be recognized immediately if they represent a reduction in the net realizable value of current assets or an impairment loss.[156]

6.6.2.5 Disclosures

If an investor has interests in joint ventures, IAS 27 sets forth certain disclosure requirements in the financial statements of the investor, including the following:[157]

- Separate disclosure of the amount of the following contingent liabilities, unless the probability of loss is remote:
  - Any contingent liabilities that the venturer has incurred relating to its interests in joint ventures

---

153   IAS 31, paragraph 45
154   SIC-13 provides additional guidance relating to the accounting for nonmonetary contributions by venturers.
155   SIC-13, paragraph 5
156   IAS 31, paragraph 49
157   IAS 31, paragraphs 54–57

- • The investor's share of contingent liabilities relating to its interests in joint ventures that have been incurred jointly with other venturers
  - • Its share of the contingent liabilities of the joint ventures, for which it is contingently liable
  - • Contingent liabilities that arise because the venturer is contingently liable for the liabilities of the other venturers of a joint venture
- • Separate disclosure of the aggregate amount of the following commitments with respect to its interests in joint ventures:
  - • Capital commitments with respect to a venturer's interest in joint ventures
  - • Its share of the capital commitments of the joint ventures themselves
- • Disclosure of a listing and description of interests in significant joint ventures and the proportion of ownership interests held in jointly controlled entities[158]
- • Disclosure of the method used (proportionate consolidation or equity method) to recognize its interests in jointly controlled entities

6.6.3 INVESTMENTS IN ASSOCIATES   An associate is an entity, including an unincorporated entity such as a partnership over which the investor has significant influence, that is neither a subsidiary nor an interest in a joint venture.[159] Investments in associates are generally accounted for using the equity method.[160] Like APB Opinion No. 18, an investor holding 20% or more of the voting power of the investee is presumed to exercise significant influence under IFRS.[161] Significant influence by an investor is usually evidenced in one or more of the following ways:[162]

- • Representation on the Board of Directors
- • Participation in policy-making processes, including participation in decisions about dividends or other distributions
- • Material transactions between the investor and the investee
- • Interchange of managerial personnel
- • Provision of essential technical information

---

158   Additional disclosure requirements apply if the investor applies the proportionate consolidation method.
159   IAS 28, paragraph 2
160   Paragraph 13 of IAS 28 provides for an exception if one of the three conditions is present that are outlined in Section 6.6.2.3 of this Chapter. Additionally, IAS 28 does not apply to investments in associates held by venture capital organizations and mutual funds, unit trusts, and similar entities that upon initial recognition are designated as at fair value through profit or loss or are classified as held for trading and accounted for in accordance with IAS 39.
161   IAS 28, paragraph 6
162   IAS 28, paragraph 7

From the date an investor ceases to have significant influence over an associate and the associate does not become a subsidiary, an investor must discontinue the use of the equity method and account for its investment in accordance with IAS 39, *Financial Instruments: Recognition and Measurement.*[163]

DISCLOSURES

IAS 28 requires that an investor disclose in its financial statements information relating to its investments in associates, including the fair value of its interests if there are published price quotations; summarized financial information; the reason for using the equity method of accounting if its investment is less than 20% of the voting power of the investee (or for not using the equity method if its investment is at least 20%); the nature and extent of restrictions on the investee's ability to transfer funds to the investor; any unrecognized share of losses; summarized financial information for associates not accounted for using the equity method; contingent liabilities; and others.

Paragraph 38 of IAS 28 provides for the following reporting requirements if an investor uses the equity method of accounting: "Investments in associates accounted for using the equity method shall be classified as non-current assets. The investor's share of the profit or loss of such associates, and the carrying amount of those investments, shall be separately disclosed. The investor's share of any discontinued operations of such associates shall also be separately disclosed."

6.7 SYNOPSIS OF AUTHORITATIVE LITERATURE

ACCOUNTING RESEARCH BULLETIN NO. 51, *CONSOLIDATED FINANCIAL STATEMENTS*
ARB 51 provides accounting guidance relating to consolidated financial statements, combined financial statements, and parent-company statements. It addresses the purpose of consolidated financial statements; the conditions that, when present, should lead to the preparation of consolidated financial statements; consolidation procedures; the elimination of intercompany investments; and minority interests.

APB OPINION NO. 18, *THE EQUITY METHOD OF ACCOUNTING FOR INVESTMENTS IN COMMON STOCK*
In APB Opinion No. 18, the Accounting Principles Board concludes that the equity method of accounting should be followed by an investor whose investment in common stock gives it the ability to exercise significant influence over operating and financial policies of an investee. Pursuant to the provisions in APB Opinion No. 18, an investment of 20% or more of the voting stock of an investee leads to a presumption that the investor has the ability to exercise significant influence over the investee.

---

163   IAS 28, paragraph 18

FASB STATEMENT NO. 58, *CAPITALIZATION OF INTEREST COST IN FINANCIAL STATEMENTS THAT INCLUDE INVESTMENTS ACCOUNTED FOR BY THE EQUITY METHOD,* AN AMENDMENT OF FASB STATEMENT NO. 34

FASB Statement No. 58 includes investments accounted for by the equity method as qualifying assets of the investor while the investee has activities in progress necessary to commence its planned principal operations, provided that the investee's activities include the use of funds to acquire qualifying assets for its operations.

FASB STATEMENT NO. 94, *CONSOLIDATION OF ALL MAJORITY-OWNED SUBSIDIARIES,* AN AMENDMENT OF ARB NO. 51, WITH RELATED AMENDMENTS OF APB OPINION NO. 18 AND ARB NO. 43, CHAPTER 12

FASB Statement No. 94 amends ARB 51 to require the consolidation of all majority-owned subsidiaries, unless control is temporary or does not rest with the majority owners.

FASB STATEMENT NO. 114, *ACCOUNTING BY CREDITORS FOR IMPAIRMENT OF A LOAN,* AN AMENDMENT OF FASB STATEMENTS NO. 5 AND 15

FASB Statement No. 114 addresses the accounting by creditors for impairment of certain loans. It applies to all loans, uncollateralized as well as collateralized, except for the following:

- Large groups of smaller-balance homogeneous loans that are collectively evaluated for impairment
- Loans that are measured at fair value or at the lower of cost or fair value
- Leases
- Debt securities, as defined in FASB Statement No. 115

It also applies to loans that are restructured in a troubled debt restructuring involving a modification of terms. FASB Statement No. 114 requires that impaired loans be measured based on the present value of expected future cash flows discounted at the loan's effective interest rate or at the loan's observable market price or the fair value of the collateral, if the loan is collateral-dependent.

FASB STATEMENT NO. 118, *ACCOUNTING BY CREDITORS FOR IMPAIRMENTS OF A LOAN—INCOME RECOGNITION AND DISCLOSURES,* AN AMENDMENT OF FASB STATEMENT NO. 114

FASB Statement No. 118 eliminates certain provisions in FASB Statement No. 114 that describe how a creditor should report income on an impaired loan. FASB Statement No. 118 also amends the disclosure requirements in FASB Statement No. 114 to require information about the recorded investment in certain impaired loans and the recognition of interest income related to those impaired loans.

FASB STATEMENT NO. 159, *THE FAIR VALUE OPTION FOR FINANCIAL ASSETS AND FINANCIAL LIABILITIES, INCLUDING AN AMENDMENT OF FASB STATEMENT NO. 115*
FASB Statement No. 159 permits entities to choose to measure many financial instruments, including instruments accounted for under the equity method, and other items at fair value that are not currently required to be measured at fair value. FASB Statement No. 159 also establishes presentation and disclosure requirements relating to items measured at fair value following the provisions of that Statement.

FASB STATEMENT NO. 160, *NONCONTROLLING INTERESTS IN CONSOLIDATED FINANCIAL STATEMENTS, AN AMENDMENT OF ARB NO. 51*
FASB Statement No. 160 amends ARB 51 to establish accounting and reporting standards for the noncontrolling interest (minority interest) in a subsidiary and for the deconsolidation of a subsidiary. It also amends certain of ARB 51's consolidation procedures to make them consistent with the requirements of FASB Statement No. 141(R).

FASB INTERPRETATION NO. 35, *CRITERIA FOR APPLYING THE EQUITY METHOD OF ACCOUNTING FOR INVESTMENTS IN COMMON STOCK, AN INTERPRETATION OF APB OPINION NO. 18*
APB Opinion No. 18 includes a presumption that an investor owning 20% or more of an investee's voting stock exercises significant influence and should use the equity method of accounting. FIN 35 clarifies the application of APB Opinion No. 18: If there is an indication that an investor owning 20% or more of an investee's voting stock is unable to exercise significant influence over the investee's operating and financial policies, all the facts and circumstances related to the investment need to be evaluated to determine whether the presumption of ability to exercise significant influence over the investee is overcome.

FASB INTERPRETATION NO. 46 (REVISED DECEMBER 2003), *CONSOLIDATION OF VARIABLE INTEREST ENTITIES, AN INTERPRETATION OF ARB NO. 51*
FIN 46(R) is an interpretation of ARB 51. It addresses consolidation of variable interest entities. Variable interest entities are entities that have one or more of the following characteristics:

1. Insufficient equity investment at risk
2. Equity investors that lack characteristics of a controlling financial interest
3. Equity investors' voting rights are not proportionate to their economic interests, and substantially all of the activities of the entity involve or are conducted on behalf of an investor with a disproportionately small voting interest

FASB STAFF POSITION SOP 78-9-1, *INTERACTION OF AICPA STATEMENT OF POSITION 78-9 AND EITF ISSUE NO. 04-5*
FSP SOP 78-9-1 amends SOP 78-9 to achieve consistency between SOP 79-8 and EITF Issue No. 04-5. FSP SOP 78-9-1 eliminates the concept of "important rights" and replaces it with "substantive participating rights" and "kick-out rights."

EITF Issue No. 84-39, *Transfers of Monetary and Nonmonetary Assets among Individuals and Entities under Common Control*

Deemed no longer technically helpful.

EITF Issue No. 86-21, *Application of the AICPA Notice to Practitioners regarding Acquisition, Development, and Construction Arrangements to Acquisition of an Operating Property*

Issues.   Loans granted to acquire operating properties may grant the lender a right to participate in expected residual profit from the sale or refinancing of the property.

The issues are:

1. Does the third Notice, which deals with acquisition, development, and construction financing, apply to the acquisition of operating properties?
2. If so, how should the guidance be applied?

Consensus/Status

1. The Task Force reached a consensus that the third Notice should be considered in accounting for shared appreciation mortgages, loans on operating real estate, and real estate ADC arrangements entered into by enterprises other than financial institutions.
2. The Task Force reached a consensus that the discussion of expected residual profit contained in paragraphs 3–5 of the third Notice should be consulted to determine the nature of the expected residual profit.

EITF Issue No. 89-7, *Exchange of Assets or Interest in a Subsidiary for a Noncontrolling Equity Interest in a New Entity*

Issue.   An enterprise transfers its ownership of an asset or its ownership interest in a subsidiary to a newly created entity in exchange for an ownership interest in that entity. Subsequent to the transfer, the enterprise does not control the entity.

The issues are:

1. Should the enterprise record a gain at the date of transfer?
2. If a gain should be recorded, how should it be determined?

Consensus/Status.   Codified in EITF Issue No. 01-2.

EITF Issue No. 94-2, *Treatment of Minority Interests in Certain Real Estate Investment Trusts*

Issue.   In a typical Umbrella Partnership Real Estate Investment Trust (UPREIT) transaction, an operating partnership is formed by a sponsor. The sponsor contributes real estate properties and related debt to the operating partnership in exchange for a limited partnership interest in the operating partnership. Typically, the contributed assets and liabilities are accounted for by the operating partnership at the sponsor's historical cost.

How, and at what amount, should the sponsor's interest in the operating partnership be reported in the REIT's consolidated financial statements?

Consensus/Status.   The Task Force reached a consensus that the sponsor's interest in the operating partnership should be reported as a minority interest in the REIT's consolidated financial statements. The net equity of the operating partnership (after the contributions of the sponsor and the REIT), multiplied by the sponsor's ownership percentage in the operating partnership, represents the amount to be initially reported as the minority interest in the REIT's consolidated financial statements. If the net equity of the operating partnership is less than zero, then the initial minority interest is zero unless there is an obligation of the minority interest to make good its share of those losses. If the minority interest's share of a current-year loss of the REIT would cause the minority interest balance to be less than zero, the minority interest balance should be reported as zero unless there is an obligation of the minority interest to make good those losses. Any excess losses attributable to the minority interest balance should be charged against the majority interest.

NULLIFIED BY FASB STATEMENT NO. 160. EITF ISSUE NO. 95-7, *IMPLEMENTATION ISSUES RELATED TO THE TREATMENT OF MINORITY INTERESTS IN CERTAIN REAL ESTATE INVESTMENT TRUSTS*

Issue.   In UPREIT structures, the sponsor generally has the right to redeem its minority interest in the operating partnership for a price equal to the market value of the REIT's stock. If the sponsor exercises its redemption right, the REIT can acquire the sponsor's interest for cash or REIT stock, or it can cause the operating partnership to acquire the sponsor's interest for cash.

The issues are:

1. How should the operating partnership's income (losses) and distributions be allocated between the minority and majority interests in the REIT's consolidated financial statements if the minority interest balance at formation of the REIT is less than zero based on the minority interest's proportionate share of the operating partnership's net deficit?
2. Should the interim period allocation of the operating partnership's income (losses) and distributions be based on discrete interim period results, year-to-date results, or expected results for the entire year?
3. How should the REIT account for any subsequent acquisitions of the sponsor's minority interest in the operating partnership for either cash or shares of the REIT?

Consensus/Status

1. While the minority interest balance is negative, the minority interest charge in the REIT's consolidated income statements should be the greater of:

    a. The minority interest holder's share of the operating partnership's earnings for the year

    b. The amount of distributions to the minority interest holder

2. No consensus was reached on Issue 2.

3. The REIT should account for any subsequent acquisitions of the sponsor's minority interest in the operating partnership for cash in a manner consistent with the accounting for the formation of the REIT. Subsequent acquisitions of the sponsor's minority interest in the operating partnership in exchange for REIT shares should be recorded at the book value of the minority interest acquired.

NULLIFIED BY FASB STATEMENT NO. 160. EITF ISSUE NO. 96-16, *INVESTOR'S ACCOUNTING FOR AN INVESTEE WHEN THE INVESTOR HAS A MAJORITY OF THE VOTING INTEREST BUT THE MINORITY SHAREHOLDER OR SHAREHOLDERS HAVE CERTAIN APPROVAL OR VETO RIGHTS*

Issue.   What minority rights held by the minority shareholder should overcome the presumption of FASB Statement No. 94 that all majority-owned investees should be consolidated?

Consensus/Status.   The assessment of whether the rights of a minority shareholder should overcome the presumption of consolidation by the investor with a majority voting interest in its investee is a matter of judgment that depends on the facts and circumstances. It should be based on whether the minority rights provide for the minority shareholder to effectively participate in significant decisions that would be expected to be made in the ordinary course of business. Effective participation means the ability to block significant decisions proposed by the investor with a majority voting interest. The consensus includes guidelines for the determination of whether minority rights should be considered protective rights or substantive participating rights.

EITF ISSUE NO. 98-6, *INVESTOR'S ACCOUNTING FOR AN INVESTMENT IN A LIMITED PARTNERSHIP WHEN THE INVESTOR IS THE SOLE GENERAL PARTNER AND THE LIMITED PARTNERS HAVE CERTAIN APPROVAL OR VETO RIGHTS*

Issue.   What rights held by the limited partners preclude consolidation in circumstances in which the sole general partner would consolidate the limited partnership in accordance with generally accepted accounting principles, absent the existence of the rights held by the limited partners?

Consensus/Status.   No consensus was reached. The Task Force did not object to a concept proposed by the working group: A partnership agreement that provides for the removal of the general partner by a reasonable vote of the limited partners, without cause, and without the limited partners or partnership incurring a significant penalty, indicates that the sole general partner does not control the limited partnership.

EITF Issue No. 98-8, *Accounting for Transfers of Investments That Are in Substance Real Estate*

Issue.   The criteria for sales recognition under FASB Statement No. 125[164] are substantially different from the criteria for sales recognition under FASB Statement No. 66. The issue is whether the sale or transfer of an investment in the form of a financial asset that is in substance real estate should be evaluated using the criteria provided in FASB Statement No. 125 or those provided in FASB Statement No. 66.

Consensus/Status.   The Task Force reached a consensus that the sale or transfer of an investment in the form of a financial asset that is in substance real estate should be accounted for in accordance with FASB Statement No. 66.

Transfers of acquisition, development, and construction loans (ADC loans) that are in substance real estate investments under EITF Issue No. 84-4, *Acquisition, Development, and Construction Loans*, are subject to this consensus. A marketable investment in a REIT that is accounted for in accordance with FASB Statement No. 115 would not be considered an investment that is in substance real estate.

EITF Issue No. 98-13, *Accounting by an Equity Method Investor for Investee Losses When the Investor Has Loans to and Investments in Other Securities of the Investee*

Issue.   Investors that own common or other voting stock in an entity may also own debt securities or preferred stock, or they may have extended loans to the investee. For an investor accounting for its investment under the equity method of accounting, how should the equity method loss pickup from the application of APB Opinion No. 18 (when the carrying amount of the common stock has been reduced to zero) interact with the applicable literature relating to investments in the other securities of the investee (either FASB Statement No. 114 or FASB Statement No. 115)?

Consensus/Status.   In situations where (1) an investor is not required to advance additional funds to the investee, and (2) previous losses have reduced the common stock investment account to zero, the investor should continue to report its share of equity method losses in its statement of operations to the extent of and as an adjustment to the adjusted basis of the other investments in the investee. The order in which those equity method losses should be applied to the other

---

164   FASB Statement No. 125 has been superseded by FASB Statement No. 140. Paragraph 4 of FASB Statement No. 140 provides that transfers of ownership interests that are in substance the sale of real estate are outside the scope of FASB Statement No. 140. Therefore, these transfers should follow the guidance in FASB Statement No. 66. As a result, this Issue is affirmed by the issuance of FASB Statement No. 140.

investments should follow the seniority of the other investments (that is, priority in liquidation). For each period, the adjusted basis of the other investments should be adjusted for the equity method losses, and the investor should apply FASB Statements No. 114 and 115 to the other investments, as applicable.

EITF Issue No. 99-10, Percentage Used to Determine the Amount of Equity Method Losses

Issue. An investor may own common stock and "other investments" in an investee. How should equity method losses be measured and recognized by the investor, if previous losses have reduced the common stock investment account to zero and the investor is not required to advance additional funds to the investee?

Consensus/Status. The Task Force reached a consensus that an investor should not recognize equity method losses based solely on the percentage of investee common stock held by the investor. The Task Force did not reach a consensus as to whether an investor should recognize equity method losses based on (1) the ownership level of the particular investee security or loan/advance held by the investor to which the equity method losses are being applied or (2) the change in the investor's claim on the investee's book value. The Task Force observed that both approaches may be acceptable. Exhibits 99-10 A and B provide an example and journal entries for the approaches (1) and (2). An entity should use a single entity-wide approach to determine the amount of its equity method losses when previous losses have reduced the common stock investment account to zero, and the selected policy should be disclosed in the footnotes to the financial statements.

EITF Issue No. 00-1, Investor Balance Sheet and Income Statement Display under the Equity Method for Investments in Certain Partnerships and Other Ventures

Issue. Paragraph 19(c) of APB Opinion No. 18, which addresses investments in common stock of corporations, requires investments accounted for by the equity method to be displayed as a single amount in the investor's balance sheet and the investor's share of the investee's earnings or losses to be displayed as a single amount in the investor's income statement. Are there circumstances in which proportionate gross presentation is appropriate under the equity method of accounting for an investment in unincorporated legal entities, such as partnerships and other unincorporated ventures?

Consensus/Status. The Task Force reached a consensus that a proportionate gross financial statement presentation is not appropriate for an investment in an unincorporated legal entity accounted for by the equity method of accounting, unless the investee is in either the construction industry or an extractive industry where there is a longstanding practice of its use.

EITF Issue No. 02-14, *Whether an Investor Should Apply the Equity Method of Accounting to Investments Other Than Common Stock*

Issues. The issues are:

1. Should an investor apply the equity method of accounting to investments other than common stock?
2. If the equity method should be applied to investments other than common stock, how should the equity method of accounting be applied to those investments?
3. Should investments other than common stock that have a "readily determinable fair value" under paragraph 3 of FASB Statement No. 115 be accounted for in accordance with FASB Statement No. 115?

Consensus/Status. The Task Force reached a consensus on Issue 1 that an investor that has the ability to exercise significant influence over the operating and financial policies of the investee should apply the equity method of accounting only when it has an investment in common stock or in-substance common stock. In-substance common stock is an investment in an entity that has risk and reward characteristics that are substantially similar to that entity's common stock. EITF Issue No. 02-14 outlines certain characteristics that an investor should consider when determining whether an investment in an entity is substantially similar to an investment in that entity's common stock.

No consensus was reached on Issues 2 and 3.

EITF Issue No. 02-18, *Accounting for Subsequent Investments in an Investee after Suspension of Equity Method Loss Recognition*

Issues. The issues are:

1. Should an investor that has suspended equity method loss recognition (in accordance with paragraph 19(i) of APB Opinion No. 18 and EITF Issue No. 98-13) recognize any previously suspended losses when accounting for a subsequent investment in that investee?
2. If it is determined in Issue 1 that the additional investment represents the funding of prior losses, should all previously suspended losses be recognized, or should the previously suspended losses be recognized only for the portion of the investment determined to represent the funding of prior losses?

Consensus/Status. The Task Force reached consensuses on Issues 1 and 2 that if the additional investment represents in substance the funding of prior losses, the investor should recognize previously suspended losses only up to the amount of the additional investment determined to represent the funding of prior losses. EITF Issue No. 02-18 sets forth certain factors to consider when making that determination.

EITF Issue No. 03-16, *Accounting for Investments in Limited Liability Companies*

Issue.   Should an LLC be viewed as similar to a corporation or similar to a partnership for purposes of determining whether a noncontrolling investment in an LLC should be accounted for using the cost method or the equity method?

Consensus/Status.[165]   An investment in an LLC that maintains a "specific ownership account" for each investor—similar to a partnership capital account structure—should be viewed as similar to an investment in a limited partnership for purposes of determining whether a noncontrolling investment in an LLC should be accounted for using the cost method or the equity method. The provisions of SOP 78-9 and the guidance provided by the SEC staff in Topic No. D-46 would also apply to those LLCs.

EITF Issue No. 04-5, *Investor's Accounting for an Investment in a Limited Partnership When the Investor Is the Sole General Partner and the Limited Partners Have Certain Rights*

Issue.[166]   When does a sole general partner (or the general partners as a group) control a limited partnership or similar entity when the limited partners have certain rights?

Consensus/Status.   The Task Force reached a consensus that the general partners in a limited partnership should determine whether they control a limited partnership: General partners in a limited partnership are presumed to control that limited partnership, regardless of the extent of the general partners' ownership interest in the limited partnership. The general partners do not control the limited partnership if the limited partners have either (1) the substantive ability to dissolve (liquidate) the limited partnership or otherwise remove the general partners without cause, or (2) substantive participating rights. EITF Issue No. 04-5 provides guidance on each of these concepts.

EITF Topic No. D-46, *Accounting for Limited Partnership Investments*

The SEC staff's position is that investments in all limited partnerships should be accounted for pursuant to paragraph 8 of SOP No. 78-9. That guidance requires the use of the equity method unless the investor's interest "is so minor that the limited partner may have virtually no influence over partnership operating and financial policies." The SEC staff understands that practice generally has viewed investments of more than 3–5% to be more than minor.

---

165   The scope of this consensus excludes investments in LLCs that are required to be accounted for as debt securities pursuant to paragraph 14 of FASB Statement No. 140.

166   The scope of this Issue is limited to limited partnerships or similar entities that are not variable interest entities under FIN 46(R).

EITF TOPIC NO. D-68, *ACCOUNTING BY AN EQUITY METHOD INVESTOR FOR INVESTEE LOSSES WHEN THE INVESTOR HAS LOANS TO AND INVESTMENTS IN OTHER SECURITIES OF AN INVESTEE*

The FASB staff has been asked to interpret the guidance in APB Opinion No. 18 for an investor's accounting when more than one type of interest is held. Should an investor that owns common (or other voting) stock and also (1) owns debt securities, (2) owns preferred stock, or (3) has extended loans to the investee continue to provide for operating losses of the investee when the investor's investment in common (or other voting) stock has been reduced to zero?

Guidance has since been provided by EITF Issue No. 98-13.

EITF TOPIC NO. D-84, *ACCOUNTING FOR SUBSEQUENT INVESTMENTS IN AN INVESTEE AFTER SUSPENSION OF EQUITY METHOD LOSS RECOGNITION WHEN AN INVESTOR INCREASES ITS OWNERSHIP INTEREST FROM SIGNIFICANT INFLUENCE TO CONTROL THROUGH A MARKET PURCHASE OF VOTING SECURITIES*

The SEC staff addressed a fact pattern in which a subsequent investment was made in an equity method investee after suspension of equity method loss recognition in accordance with APB Opinion No. 18. The issue arises as to how an investor should account for a subsequent investment in an investee after the suspension of equity method losses has occurred. The SEC staff believes that in the circumstances in which an investor increases its ownership interest from one of significant influence to one of control through a purchase of additional voting securities in the market, and where no commitment or obligation to provide financial support existed prior to obtaining control, the acquisition should follow step acquisition accounting. Recognition of a "loss on purchase" or a restatement of prior-period financial statements is not appropriate.

AICPA STATEMENT OF POSITION NO. 78-9, *ACCOUNTING FOR INVESTMENTS IN REAL ESTATE VENTURES*

SOP 78-9 provides guidance on how to account for investments in real estate ventures. The SOP addresses the applicability of the equity method of accounting to interests in real estate ventures, common issues in the application of the equity method of accounting, and the accounting by the investor for transactions with a real estate venture.

AICPA STATEMENT OF POSITION NO. 92-1, *ACCOUNTING FOR REAL ESTATE SYNDICATION INCOME*

SOP 92-1 provides guidance for the recognition of income from real estate syndication activities. Syndication activities are efforts to directly or indirectly sponsor the formation of entities that acquire interests in real estate by raising funds from investors. The investors receive ownership interests or other financial interests in the sponsored entities.

AICPA Proposed Statement of Position, *Accounting for Investors' Interests in Unconsolidated Real Estate Investments*

The proposed SOP provides guidance on accounting for investors' interests in unconsolidated real estate investments. It explains the application of the hypothetical liquidation at book value method (HLBV method). Among the issues addressed are the allocation of income to the individual investors, the treatment of losses attributable to other investors and of losses in excess of an investor's basis, the accounting for excess distributions, the adequacy of disclosures, and cash flow presentation.

AICPA Accounting Interpretation 1, *The Equity Method of Accounting for Investments in Common Stock*, of APB Opinion No. 18

Question.   In applying the equity method of accounting, intercompany profits or losses on assets still remaining with an investor or investee are eliminated. Should all of the intercompany profit or loss be eliminated or only that portion related to the investor's common stock interest in the investee?

Interpretation.   Assuming the investor does not exercise control (e.g., through guarantees of indebtedness, extension of credit, or other special arrangements), it would be appropriate for the investor to eliminate intercompany profit in relation to the investor's common stock interest in the investee. The percentage of intercompany profit to be eliminated would be the same regardless of whether the transaction is "downstream" (i.e., a sale by the investor to the investee) or "upstream" (i.e., a sale by the investee to the investor).

AICPA Accounting Interpretation 2, *The Equity Method of Accounting for Investments in Common Stock*, of APB Opinion No. 18

Question.   Do the provisions of APB Opinion No. 18 apply to investments in partnerships and unincorporated joint ventures?

Interpretation.   APB Opinion No. 18 applies only to investments in common stock of corporations. However, many of the provisions of the APB Opinion No. 18 are appropriate in accounting for investments in unincorporated entities (e.g., partnerships and unincorporated joint ventures) such as the elimination of intercompany profits and losses.

AICPA Technical Practice Aid (TIS Section 1300.18), *Presentation on the Statement of Cash Flows of Distributions from Investees With Operating Losses*

Inquiry.   An entity accounts for an interest in a limited partnership under the equity method. The partnership had operating losses during the year, but made distributions to its investors. Would that distribution be classified on the investor's statement of cash flows as cash inflows from investing activities or as cash inflows from operating activities?

Reply. Distributions to investors from investees should be presumed to be returns on investments and be classified by the investors as cash inflows from operating activities. That presumption can be overcome based on the specific facts and circumstances. For example, if the partnership sells assets, the distribution to investors of the proceeds of that sale would be considered a return of investment and be classified by the investor as cash inflows from investing activities.

AICPA Technical Practice Aid (TIS Section 2220.14), Effect of Unrecorded Equity in Losses on Additional Investment

Inquiry. Company A holds 40% of Company B and does not guarantee the debt of Company B. Subsequent to the investment made by A, B incurred large operating losses and A ceased to record equity in B's losses after its investment in B was reduced to zero. A few years later, A purchased an additional 5% interest in B. Should Company A offset the amount of this additional investment by the unrecorded equity in losses of Company B?

Reply. No. Company A's additional investment would not be offset by the unrecorded equity in Company B's losses.

AICPA Technical Practice Aid (TIS Section 2200.15), Accounting for Distribution from Joint Venture

Inquiry. A corporation invests in a real estate joint venture and accounts for it under the equity method. The joint venture is a corporation and is not controlled by the corporate investor. As a result of losses incurred by the joint venture, the investment account on the corporation's books has declined to zero. The joint venture pays the corporation a cash distribution. How should the corporation account for this distribution?

Reply. APB Opinion No. 18 states that the investor ordinarily shall discontinue applying the equity method when the investment is reduced to zero and shall not provide for additional losses unless the investor has guaranteed obligations of the investee or is otherwise committed to provide financial support for the investee. In this situation, the corporate investor in the joint venture should account for the cash distributions received as income if the distribution is not refundable by agreement or by law and the investor is not liable for the obligations of the joint venture and is not otherwise committed to provide financial support to the joint venture.

AICPA Issues Paper, Joint Venture Accounting (July 17, 1979)

That AICPA Issues Paper identifies and addresses a wide variety of issues arising in (1) the accounting and reporting of investments in joint ventures and (2) the accounting by joint venture entities.

International Accounting Standard 27, Consolidated and Separate Financial Statements

IAS 27 provides guidance for the preparation and presentation of consolidated financial statements for entities under the control of a parent, and for the accounting for investments in subsidiaries, jointly controlled entities and associates when an entity prepares separate, rather than consolidated, financial statements.

INTERNATIONAL ACCOUNTING STANDARD 28, *INVESTMENTS IN ASSOCIATES*

IAS 28 sets forth accounting, reporting, and disclosure requirements for investments in associates. Associates are entities, including unincorporated entities such as partnerships, over which the investor has significant influence and that are neither a subsidiary nor an interest in a joint venture. IAS 28 does not apply to investments in associates held by (1) venture capital organizations or (2) mutual funds, unit trusts, and similar entities that upon initial recognition are designated as at fair value through profit or loss or are classified as held for trading and accounted for in accordance with IAS 39.

INTERNATIONAL ACCOUNTING STANDARD 31, *INTERESTS IN JOINT VENTURES*

IAS 31 provides accounting guidance for interests in joint ventures. IAS 31 does not apply to investments in jointly controlled entities held by (1) venture capital organizations or (2) mutual funds, unit trusts, and similar entities that upon initial recognition are designated as at fair value through profit or loss or are classified as held for trading and accounted for in accordance with IAS 39.

SIC INTERPRETATION 12, *CONSOLIDATION—SPECIAL PURPOSE ENTITIES*

SIC-12 requires that an SPE be consolidated when the substance of the relationship between an entity and the SPE indicates that the SPE is controlled by the entity. SIC-12 describes circumstances indicative of control.

SIC INTERPRETATION 13, *JOINTLY CONTROLLED ENTITIES—NON-MONETARY CONTRIBUTIONS BY VENTURERS*

SIC-13 deals with the venturer's accounting for nonmonetary contributions to a jointly controlled entity in exchange for an equity interest in the jointly controlled entity that is accounted for using either the equity method or proportionate consolidation.

TIME-SHARING TRANSACTIONS

7.1 OVERVIEW

Real estate time-sharing is a concept based on the sharing of vacation properties between different owners. Purchasers of vacation intervals receive the right to use a vacation home, typically a condominium, for a specified number of years, or in perpetuity. In its plain-vanilla form, a purchaser buys into a vacation property in intervals of weeks and obtains the right to occupy the interval purchased during the same week each year.

Typically, ownership of a time-sharing unit is divided into 50- or 51-week interval interests, with one or two weeks reserved for maintenance. Accordingly, each real estate time-sharing unit would have 50 or 51 owners. Exhibit 7.1 depicts a time-share property with seven units; each unit is divided into 51 intervals.

In addition to the purchase price, the buyer is also responsible for an annual fee to cover the management, maintenance, and operations of the resort, which generally provides a variety of amenities, such as parks, swimming pools, playgrounds, tennis courts, and golf courses.

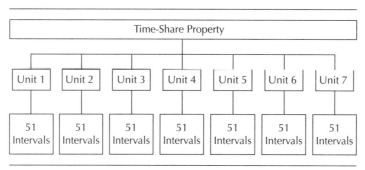

EXHIBIT 7.1   TIME-SHARE PROPERTY WITH UNITS AND INTERVALS

Customer demand for flexible arrangements prompted time-share companies to introduce floating weeks,[1] exchange programs, and points-based systems.[2] Exchange networks, such as Resort Condominium International (RCI) and Interval International (II) were created in the 1970s to facilitate this exchange. Owners of vacation intervals in an exchange network-affiliated resort can exchange their weekly interval for a week at another resort affiliated with the same network. Similarly, some developers of time-share properties maintain exchange programs that allow for an exchange of weekly intervals between different resorts of that developer.

The time-sharing concept was first developed in Europe in the 1960s, and was introduced to the United States in the 1970s. The depressed real estate market in the mid-1970s induced hotel and condominium developers to convert hotels and condominium projects into time-share properties in an effort to generate additional revenues. In its infancy, the time-sharing industry had a reputation of selling inferior vacation properties to an uninformed public, often using aggressive sales tactics. This perception started to change in the mid-1980s, when reputable hospitality companies entered the time-sharing market to participate in the relatively high margins in this industry.

As time-sharing grew in popularity, the American Resort Development Association (ARDA), the industry association of time-share companies, developed standards of conduct, and federal and state regulation increased. The development of industry standards, increased legislation, and monitoring has resulted in higher quality properties and better consumer information, which has raised consumer confidence and has contributed to the continued demand for time-share properties.

The accounting did not keep pace with the developments in the time-sharing industry:

When the Financial Accounting Standards Board (FASB) issued FASB Statement No. 66, *Accounting for Sales of Real Estate*, in 1982, the time-sharing

---

1   In a floating system, the owner can purchase an interval within a particular season, but not a specific week.
2   Under a points-based system, the customer obtains vacation credit each year that may be redeemed at different resorts.

industry received little attention. The sale of time-sharing intervals was treated like the sale of condominiums, and the unique risks of the industry were not addressed. These risks include:

- A high default rate on sales, which are generally seller-financed
- Substantial marketing and sales expenses, largely incurred in periods before a sale takes place

Wide diversity in practice developed in the industry, as time-share companies adapted the sale and profit recognition principles provided in FASB Statement No. 66 to the sale of time-sharing intervals; and as they interpreted the provisions relating to cost deferral in FASB Statement No. 67, *Accounting for Costs and Initial Rental Operations of Real Estate Projects*.

The steady growth of the time-sharing industry, the multitude of new structures, and the observed diversity in industry practice prompted the American Institute of Certified Public Accountants (AICPA) to form a Task Force under the direction of the AICPA Accounting Standards Executive Committee (AcSEC) with the mandate to develop a comprehensive accounting model for the time-sharing industry. In December 2004, the AICPA issued SOP 04-2, *Accounting for Time-Sharing Transactions*. Many unique aspects of accounting for time-sharing transactions, such as the application of the relative sales value method, the determination of the allowance for uncollectibles, the treatment of incentives, and the deferral of marketing and sales expenses, are also addressed by the SOP.

7.2 TYPES OF TIME-SHARING ARRANGEMENTS

Time-sharing arrangements can be categorized into one of three basic types (see Exhibit 7.2):

1. Structures in which deed passes to the buyer
2. Right-to-use structures
3. Hybrid structures

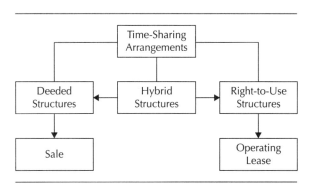

EXHIBIT 7.2   TIME-SHARING ARRANGEMENTS

DEEDED STRUCTURES

In deeded structures, the purchaser of a time-sharing interval assumes the risk of property ownership and is responsible for any liabilities that arise from the property; the seller relinquishes the usual risks and rewards of ownership and transfers title to the purchaser of the time-sharing interval. To qualify for sale recognition under FASB Statement No. 66, title transfer must be nonreversionary; that is, property ownership may not revert back to the time-share seller. A contract-for-deed arrangement, under which the deed to a time-sharing interval will be transferred at a future point in time when the purchaser has paid a specified portion (or all) of the sales price of the time-sharing interval, also meets the transfer of title requirement.[3]

Various types of time sharing-arrangements fall within the group of "deeded structures:"

- *Interval Ownership*. The time-share buyer is deeded a specific unit for a specific week. For example, the buyer is deeded the right to use Unit 1A for the first week in July each year.
- *Undivided Interest*. An undivided interest is a tenant-in-common interest in a specific unit or in the entire vacation property. The interest holder is then assigned a specific week.
- *Floating Time*. A deed is recorded, with the time-share owner not being entitled to a specific week, but to any week within a certain season. Reservation systems are used to manage owners' requests for a specific unit and week.

Throughout this Chapter, the term "sale of time-sharing interval" is used to denote a sale of any type of ownership in time-share properties, including interval ownership, undivided interest, and floating time arrangement.

RIGHT-TO-USE STRUCTURES

In right-to-use structures, ownership of the vacation property remains with the developer; the purchaser of a vacation interval acquires the right to use the unit for a specified number of years.[4] This type of structure is similar to a lease. Accordingly, a time-share seller does not record a sale, but treats the arrangement like an operating lease.

HYBRID STRUCTURES

Hybrid structures include features of both a sale and a right-to-use arrangement. A sale of a vacation ownership interest in a hybrid structure is accounted for as a lease or sale, depending on whether the developer relinquishes the usual risks and rewards of ownership in the real estate. The floating time concept discussed above

---

3   SOP 04-2, paragraph 13
4   Right-to-use structures may also be set up as floating unit/floating week arrangements.

may be implemented in the form of point systems or vacation clubs, enabling the owner to exchange a week in the purchased resort for a week in another resort.

The accounting treatment of more complex time-sharing structures, such as special purpose entities, points-based systems, and vacation clubs, should follow the sale and profit recognition criteria of the deeded structures or right-to-use structures discussed previously, depending on their characteristics.

Hybrid arrangements frequently encountered include:

- *Special Purpose Entities (SPEs).* Special-purpose entities may be used to facilitate the sale of vacation properties in countries that place restrictions on the ownership of real estate by foreign nationals, or for other reasons. The time-share seller establishes a special purpose entity, typically in the legal form of a corporation or trust, and transfers the vacation property to the SPE in exchange for all of the shares/beneficial interests in the SPE. The time-share seller then sells the shares/beneficial interests in the SPE to buyers of time-sharing intervals. If the developer relinquishes the usual risks and rewards of ownership in the vacation property, profit is recognized at the time the shares/beneficial interests are sold to purchasers of the time-sharing intervals. Generally, the accounting for the sale of interests in a time-share SPE is consistent with the accounting for the sale of interests in other real estate entities.[5]

- *Term for Years Arrangements.* Under a "term for years" arrangement, the purchaser of the time-sharing interval has the right to use the interval for a certain number of years, for example, 40 years. If the vacation property reverts to a substantive party unrelated to the time-share seller at the end of that term, the time-share seller has relinquished all risks and rewards of ownership; the transaction is treated like a sale of a time-sharing interval.

7.3 ACCOUNTING FOR THE SALE OF TIME-SHARING INTERVALS

The accounting for the sale of time-sharing intervals follows the guidance for other than retail land sales in FASB Statement No. 66, discussed in Chapter 3.[6] In general, a prerequisite for the recording of a real estate sale is that a sale transaction is consummated,[7] which requires that: (1) the parties are bound by the terms

---

5   Paragraph 56 of SOP 04-2 provides the following exception: ". . . an SPE should be viewed as an entity lacking economic substance and established solely for the purpose of facilitating sales if (a) the SPE structure is legally required by the applicable jurisdiction(s) to sell time-sharing intervals to the nonresident customers that the developer-seller wishes to sell to (for example, for purposes of being able to sell intervals to United States citizens in a country in which citizens of other countries are not allowed to own real estate) and (b) the SPE has no assets, other than the time-sharing intervals, and the SPE has no debt. In those circumstances, the seller should show on its balance sheet as time-sharing inventory the interests in the SPE not yet sold to end users."

6   FAS 66, paragraph 37

7   FAS 66, paragraphs 6 and 20

of a contract, (2) all consideration is exchanged and (3) any permanent financing for which the seller is responsible is arranged.[8] For a sale that is consummated and recorded, the time-share seller needs to determine the appropriate profit recognition method in accordance with the provisions of FASB Statement No. 66.

Paragraph 9 of AICPA Statement of Position (SOP) 04-2 states, in part: "This SOP provides guidance to illustrate the application of the provisions of FASB Statement No. 66 to the specific terms typically encountered in time-sharing transactions. This SOP also establishes standards for accounting issues not addressed in FASB Statement No. 66."

7.3.1 APPLICATION OF THE ACCRUAL AND PERCENTAGE-OF-COMPLETION METHODS   The accrual method provides for immediate recognition of profit. Paragraphs 3 and 4 of FASB Statement No. 66 provide, in part:

> Profit shall be recognized in full when real estate is sold, provided (a) the profit is determinable, that is, the collectibility of the sales price is reasonably assured or the amount that will not be collectible can be estimated, and (b) the earnings process is virtually complete, that is, the seller is not obligated to perform significant activities after the sale to earn the profit. . . . Collectibility of the sales price is demonstrated by the buyer's commitment to pay, which in turn is supported by substantial initial and continuing investments that give the buyer a stake in the property sufficient that the risk of loss through default motivates the buyer to honor its obligation to the seller. Collectibility shall also be assessed by considering factors such as the credit standing of the buyer, age and location of the property, and adequacy of cash flow from the property.

Determining whether the buyer's financial commitment is adequate is often a critical factor in evaluating whether the accrual method—or percentage-of-completion method for properties that have not been completed—is appropriate.

7.3.1.1 *Financial Commitment of the Buyer*   A buyer's commitment is measured as the percentage of a buyer's down payment and subsequent principal payments, referred to as initial and continuing investments, in relation to the sales value of the time-sharing interval purchased.[9]

FORMULA—CALCULATION OF BUYER'S FINANCIAL COMMITMENT IN PERCENT

$$\text{Financial Commitment} = \frac{\text{Initial and Continuing Investments}}{\text{Sales Value of Time-Sharing Interval}}$$

---

8   Paragraph 6 of FASB Statement No. 66 states that all conditions precedent to closing must have been met, which would include a certificate of occupancy. However, paragraph 20 of FASB Statement No. 66 provides an exception to this requirement for buildings that require longer construction periods, such as condominiums, which also applies to time-sharing properties.

9   FAS 66, paragraphs 7–12

Paragraph 54 of FASB Statement No. 66, which specifies different minimum percentages for a buyer's initial investment depending on the specific property type, does not address time-share properties. For real estate time-share sales, time-share sellers have used a threshold of 10%, by analogy to minimum percentage requirements for condominiums used as secondary residences.[10]

DETERMINATION OF THE SALES VALUE

As in the sale of other real estate properties, the stated sales price for the time-sharing interval may have to be adjusted when computing the sales value of the interval.[11] Paragraph 7 of FASB Statement No. 66 provides as a general concept that payments made by a buyer that are in substance additional sales proceeds to the seller are to be added to the stated sales price; and that the present value of services that the seller performs without compensation (or the net present value of the services in excess of compensation), as well any discounts to reduce the buyer's note receivable to present value, are to be subtracted from the stated sales price to arrive at sales value.

SOP 04-2 specifically addresses how (1) programs to accelerate the collection of receivables, (2) fees charged to buyers, and (3) incentives impact the calculation of sales value.

Programs to Accelerate the Collection of Receivables.[12]   Time-share sellers may use programs to accelerate the collection of receivables or include contract provisions that encourage prepayment with a reduction of payments as inducement for prepayment. If a seller offers such programs to buyers at the time of sale or has established a practice of offering such programs subsequent to the sale, the seller should incorporate the estimated reduction of payments into the determination of sales value.

Fees Charged to Buyers.[13]   Time-share sellers may charge fees to a buyer in addition to the stated sales price of a time-sharing interval. The accounting for fees charged to a time-share buyer depends on the nature of the fees:

- *Fees related to financing.* Fees related to financing, such as loan origination fees, are accounted for in accordance with FASB Statement No. 91, *Accounting for Nonrefundable Fees and Costs Associated with Originating or Acquiring Loans and Initial Direct Costs of Leases.*
- *Pass-through fees.* Pass-through fees are fees that the seller charges to the buyer to pay to a third party, such as a municipality or taxing authority.

---

10   Paragraph 54 of FASB Statement No. 66 allows for an analogy to other types of properties, if the property sold is not specifically addressed.
11   See Chapter 3 for a more detailed discussion of items that require an adjustment of the stated sales price.
12   SOP 04-2, paragraph 22
13   SOP 04-2, paragraph 21

Pass-through fees are not added to the sales value. and payments made by buyers for pass-through fees are not part of his/her initial or continuing investment on the time-sharing interval.

- *Other fees*. Fees charged to a buyer other than fees related to financing and pass-through fees constitute additional sales proceeds; they are added to the stated sales price of the time-sharing interval.

EXAMPLE—FEES CHARGED TO BUYERS

Soleil Inc. (S), a time-share seller, sells a time-sharing interval to Benedict (B) for a stated purchase price of $10,000. In addition to the purchase price, S charges $30 loan origination fees and $70 administrative fees, which will cover recording tax and stamp tax to be paid to a municipality ($20), title costs ($40) to be paid to an affiliate of S, as well as S's internal administrative expenses. B makes a down payment of $1,000 on the interval and pays for the loan origination and administrative fees.

How will the fees charged to B affect the sales value of the time-sharing interval and the amount of B's initial and continuing investments?

- The $30 loan origination fee does not impact sales value or the buyer's initial and continuing investments. Loan origination fees are deferred and recognized over the life of the loan as an adjustment to interest income in accordance with FASB Statement No. 91.
- The administrative fee includes $20 of taxes (pass-through fees) to be paid to a municipality. That amount is not included in sales value or the amount of the buyer's initial and continuing investments. The fact that the $20 are included in the administrative fees, rather than stated separately, does not impact the accounting treatment.
- The remainder of the administrative fee ($50) is added to the stated sales price when calculating the sales value of the interval, as that amount is being paid to cover costs incurred by the seller and its affiliates. Similarly, the payment of the $50 is included in the amount of the buyer's initial investment.

Incentives.[14]   Time-share sellers typically offer incentives to buyers, such as airline vouchers or the payment of owners association fees for the first year after the purchase of a time-sharing interval. When calculating the sales value of a time-sharing interval, the stated sales price of the time-sharing interval is reduced by the excess of the fair value of these incentives over any stated compensation. The buyer's down payment is first applied to the incentive; it is not applied *pro rata* to the sale of the time-sharing interval and the incentive.[15]

---

14   SOP 04-2, paragraphs 24–27
15   Special rules apply for incentives conditioned on future performance, as explained in Section 7.3.1.1 under "Incentives Conditioned on Sufficient Future Performance."

EXAMPLE—OWNERS ASSOCIATION FEES PAID BY SELLER
FOR FIRST YEAR AFTER PURCHASE

Benedict (B) purchases a time-sharing interval for a stated sales price of $10,000. The time-share seller agrees to pay the first year of owners association fees (OA fees) for B's interval (fair value of $500). B makes a down payment of $1,000. The seller has determined that 10% initial investment is sufficient for the application of the accrual method. All other criteria for profit recognition under the full accrual method are met.

Is the down payment sufficient to use the accrual method of accounting?

Stated Sales Price of Interval	$10,000
Less: Fair Value of OA Fees	($ 500)
Sales Value of Interval	$ 9,500
Required Down Payment (10%)	$ 950
Down Payment Received from B	$ 1,000
Less: Portion of Down Payment to be Applied to OA Fees	($ 500)
Down Payment Applied to Interval	$ 500

The down payment is not sufficient to recognize profit on the sale of the time-sharing interval under the accrual method of accounting. The payment of OA fees by the time-share seller represents an incentive[16] provided to the buyer that needs to be considered when computing sales value and down payment applied to the interval.

Incentives Conditioned on Sufficient Future Performance. A time-share seller may commit to providing a buyer with an incentive *after* the buyer has fulfilled its contractual obligations for a certain period of time. In that case, the time-share seller needs to determine whether the sum of the down payment and future payments (principal and interest) to be received from the buyer until the time the buyer becomes entitled to the incentive satisfies the initial investment criterion of FASB Statement No. 66 *and* is sufficient to cover the fair value of the incentive (plus any interest on the unpaid portion of the incentive).

The SOP explains the allocation of a buyer's payments to the interval and the incentive conditioned on future performance as follows:[17]

> For accounting purposes, the seller allocates cash received as if there were two separate notes (with the same interest rate)—one for the purchase of the interval (with a term of the note the buyer signs) and one for the other products or services (with a term ending on the date the buyer can use them). AcSEC believes that this approach represents a systematic and rational allocation of the cash received between the interval and other products and services.

The application of that guidance is best demonstrated in an example.

---

16   Section 7.4.2 further explains the accounting treatment for incentives, differentiating between cash incentives and noncash incentives.

17   SOP 04-2, paragraph A14

EXAMPLE—OWNERS ASSOCIATION FEES PAID BY SELLER FOR SECOND YEAR AFTER PURCHASE[18]

Assume the same fact pattern as above, with one exception: The seller is offering to pay the buyer's *second* year of owners association fees if the buyer remains current on his monthly payments of $175 for one year.

Is the down payment sufficient for the use of the accrual method of accounting?

Excess of OA Fees over Future Payments:

Fair Value of OA Fees	$ 500
Future Payments[19]	($2,100)
Excess of OA Fees over Future Payments	$ 0
Sales Value of Interval	$9,500
Required Down Payment	$ 950
Down Payment Received from Buyer	$1,000
Less: Portion of Down Payment to be Applied to OA Fees	($ 0)
Down Payment Applied to Interval	$1,000

The down payment is sufficient to recognize profit under the accrual method of accounting. Since the payments the buyer is required to make before being entitled to the waiver of the OA fees exceed the fair value of the OA fees, the down payment made by the buyer can be applied in full to the time-sharing interval.

A different conclusion is reached in the following example:

EXAMPLE—INCENTIVE WITH INSUFFICIENT FUTURE PERFORMANCE[20]

Assume the same fact pattern as above, with one exception: Instead of paying the buyer's OA fees, the seller is offering to the buyer amusement park tickets with a fair value of $500 if the buyer remains current on his monthly payments ($175) for the next two months.

Is the down payment sufficient for profit recognition under the accrual method of accounting?

Excess of Incentive over Future Payments:

Fair Value of Incentive	$ 500
Future Payments[21]	($ 350)
Excess of Fair Value of Incentive over Future Payments	$ 150
Sales Value of Interval	$9,500
Required Down Payment	$ 950
Down Payment Received from Buyer	$1,000
Less: Portion of Down Payment to be Applied to Incentive	($ 150)
Down Payment Applied to Interval	$ 850

---

18   This example ignores any interest considerations.
19   To be entitled to a "waiver" of the second year owners association fees, the buyer has to make 12 monthly payments: 12 × $175 = $2,100.
20   This example ignores any interest considerations.
21   To be entitled to the amusement part tickets, the buyer has to make two monthly payments: 12 × $175 = $350.

The down payment is not sufficient to recognize profit under the accrual method of accounting, since it is less than 10% of the sales value of the interval ($950). The payments the buyer is required to make before being entitled to the amusement park tickets are less than the fair value of the tickets; as such, the down payment made by the buyer needs to be allocated to the amusement park tickets ($150) and the interval ($850). The buyer's first two monthly payments will be allocated in full to the amusement park tickets. After the third payment, the buyer's investment is adequate for the recognition of profit under the accrual method of accounting, as the cumulative payments in excess of the value of the amusement park tickets exceed 10% of sales value of the interval ($850 plus $175).

CONTINUING INVESTMENT

In addition to the initial investment requirement outlined earlier in this Section, FASB Statement No. 66 also contains continuing investment requirements that must be met for the accrual method of accounting to be appropriate. Specifically, paragraph 12 of Statement 66 requires that the buyer be contractually required to:

> . . . pay each year on its total debt for the purchase price of the property an amount at least equal to the level annual payment that would be needed to pay that debt and interest on the unpaid balance over no more than . . . the customary amortization term of a first mortgage loan by an independent lending institution for other real estate.

In a typical sale of a time-sharing interval, any portion of the purchase price not paid for in cash is financed by the time-share seller over a period of five to ten years. Due to this relatively short time frame, meeting the continuing investment requirement generally does not present an issue.

The following two circumstances deserve special consideration, however:

1. *Time-share property not completed at time of purchase.* If the time-share property is not completed at the time of purchase, the continuing investment requirement should be applied from the time the seller recognizes the sale and starts applying the percentage-of-completion method, rather than from the time the property is deeded to the buyer, by analogy to Emerging Issues Task Force (EITF) Issue No. 06-8, *Applicability of the Assessment of a Buyer's Continuing Investment under FASB Statement No. 66 for Sales of Condominiums.*

2. *Incentives conditioned on sufficient future performance.* As outlined above, an incentive conditioned on the buyer's future performance requires the allocation of the buyer's payments so that the incentive is paid for in full at the time the buyer becomes entitled to it. If the initial investment is adequate, the application of the accrual method of accounting is considered appropriate, even if the buyer's future payments are allocated solely to the incentive until the incentive (plus any interest on the unpaid portion of the incentive) is paid for in full, rather than being allocated to the interval.

When deliberating that issue, AcSEC concluded that the buyer's continuing performance on the contract did provide sufficient assurance of the buyer's commitment to fulfill its obligations.[22]

7.3.1.2 Determining a Project's Percentage of Completion

If a time-sharing project has not been completed—including improvements, facilities, and amenities—the percentage-of-completion method of accounting is used, assuming certain criteria in paragraph 37 of Statement 66 are met; otherwise, the deposit method is appropriate.

The percentage of project completion is determined by measuring the relationship of costs already incurred to the sum of the costs already incurred and future costs expected to be incurred (often referred to as cost-to-cost method).[23] Sales and marketing costs, which constitute a relatively large portion of the total cost of a time-sharing project, are excluded from the percentage-of-completion calculation.[24]

7.3.1.3 Application of the Relative Sales Value Method

The provisions of Statement 66 are generally applied to the sale of real estate on a transaction-by-transaction basis. However, for time-sharing sales, cost of sales is recognized based on a pool of costs and expected sales from a project,[25] rather than on a transaction-by-transaction basis. The relative sales value method, which is similar to a gross profit method, is used to determine cost of sales in conjunction with a sale. Under the relative sales value method, cost of sales is calculated by applying a cost-of-sales percentage to total estimated time-sharing revenue. "The estimate of total revenue (actual to-date plus expected future revenue) should incorporate factors such as incurred or estimated uncollectibles, changes in sales prices or sales mix, repossession of intervals that the seller may or may not be able to resell, effects of upgrade programs, and past or expected sales incentives to sell slow-moving inventory units."[26]

FORMULA—CALCULATION OF COST OF SALES FOR THE PERIOD

$$\text{Period Cost of Sales} = \text{Period Sales} \times \frac{\text{Estimated Total Project Cost}^{27}}{\text{Estimated Total Project Sales}}$$

---

22   SOP 04-2, paragraph A14
23   SOP 04-2, paragraph B3
24   SOP 04-2, paragraph 12
25   If a project is divided into several phases, the relative sales value method is based on the individual phase, rather than the project as a whole. [SOP 04-2, paragraph 40]
26   SOP 04-2, paragraph 41
27   If a project is divided into phases: Cost of sales is determined based on sales and costs relating to each individual phase, rather than the project as a whole.

EXAMPLE—RELATIVE SALES VALUE METHOD[28]

Time-share company Soleil Inc. (S) has completed Phase 1 of its luxury resort in West Palm Beach. S expects to sell the time-sharing intervals for $10 million. S estimates that approximately 10% of the buyers will default, and that the recovered intervals will be recovered and resold for a total of $950,000.

OTHER RELEVANT DATA

Initial down payment (nonrefundable)	10%
Buyers' forfeiture on defaulted notes	100% of cash paid
Inventory cost	$ 2,500,000
Sales for Year 1	$ 5,025,000

S has determined that the accrual method of accounting is appropriate. What are the journal entries to record sales and corresponding cost of sales in Year 1?

EXPECTED REVENUES FROM PHASE 1

Estimated sales from intervals (original sales)	$10,000,000
Additional sales from recovered intervals	$ 950,000
Total sales	$10,950,000
Estimated uncollectible notes	($ 985,500)[29]
Estimated net sales from Phase 1	$ 9,964,500

COST OF SALES PERCENTAGE

Total project cost of Phase 1	$ 2,500,000
Net sales from Phase 1	$ 9,964,500
Cost of sales percentage	25.08906%

JOURNAL ENTRIES YEAR 1

Notes Receivable	$ 4,522,500	
Cash	$ 502,500	
Sales		$5,025,000
Estimated Uncollectible Sales (Sales Contra)	$ 452,250[30]	
Allowance for Uncollectibles		$ 452,250
Cost of Sales	$1,147,260[31]	
Inventory		$1,147,260

---

28 Adapted from SOP 04-2, Appendix B, Example 1
29 Calculated as:

Sales:	$10,950,000
Less: Down payment	$ 1,095,000
	$ 9,855,000
10% default rate	$ 985,500

30 Calculated as:

Sales Year 1	$ 5,025,000
Less: Down payment	$ 502,500
	$ 4,522,500
10% default rate	$ 452,250

31 Calculated as:

Sales Year 1	$ 5,025,000
Less: Uncollectibles	$ 452,250
	$ 4,572,750
COS-Percentage (25.08906%)	$ 1,147,260

EXAMPLE—IMPLEMENTATION OF A CHANGE IN ESTIMATE

Continuing the previous example: If time-share seller Soleil Inc. at the end of Year 2 estimates that the default rate for the project phase will approximate 13% rather than 10%, as originally anticipated, an adjustment would have to be recorded.

EXPECTED REVENUES FROM PHASE 1

Estimated sales from intervals (original sales)	$10,000,000
Additional sales from recovered intervals	$ 950,000
Total sales	$10,950,000
Estimated uncollectibles	($ 1,281,150)[32]
Estimated net sales from Phase 1	$ 9,668,850

COST OF SALES PERCENTAGE

Total project cost of Phase 1	$ 2,500,000
Net sales from Phase 1	$ 9,668,850
Cost of sales percentage:	25.585622%

JOURNAL ENTRIES TO ADJUST UNCOLLECTIBLES AND INVENTORY FROM YEAR 1 SALES TO THE REVISED ESTIMATES:

Estimated Uncollectible Sales (Sales Contra)	$135,675	
Allowance for Uncollectibles		$135,675[33]
Inventory	$12,007[34]	
Cost of Sales		$ 12,007

EFFECTS OF CHANGES IN ESTIMATE

Cost estimates may need to be adjusted during the construction period to reflect price changes or changes in the design of the project or its amenities. Similarly, estimates of revenues may change as a result of changed market conditions. A time-share seller should review its estimates for revenues and project costs at least quarterly and record any adjustments arising from such changes in estimates[35] through an adjustment in the

---

32	Calculated as:	
	Sales	$10,950,000
	Less: Down payment	$ 1,095,000
		$ 9,855,000
	13% default rate	$ 1,281,150
33	Calculated as:	
	Allowance Year 1 (previously recorded)	$ 452,250
	Allowance Year 1 (per revised estimate)	$ 587,925
	Adjustment to be recorded:	($ 135,675)
34	Calculated as:	
	Sales Year 1	$ 5,025,000
	Less: Uncollectibles (revised)	$ 587,925
		$ 4,437,075
	COS-Percentage (rev.) 25.58622%	$ 1,135,253
	Cost of Sales (originally recorded)	$ 1,147,260
		$ 12,007
35	SOP 04-2, paragraph 41	

current period, similar to the cumulative catch-up method for the construction industry described in paragraph 83 of SOP 81-1, *Accounting for Performance of Construction-Type and Certain Production-Type Contracts*,[36] rather than on a prospective basis. Under the cumulative catch-up method, any changes in estimate are fully absorbed in the period of change so that the balance sheet at the end of the period of change and the accounting in subsequent periods reflect the revised estimates.[37]

7.3.2 ACCOUNTING FOR COSTS TO SELL TIME-SHARING INTERVALS Costs to sell time-sharing intervals are largely incurred for a project or phase as a whole, rather than in connection with individual sales transactions. The costs are allocated to a specific sale transaction based on the ratio of the relative fair value of the interval sold to the fair value of the project or phase. Industry practice has been diverse as it relates to the treatment of costs to sell time-sharing intervals; before the issuance of SOP 04-2, companies in the time-sharing industry frequently deferred certain marketing and sales costs, such as costs to generate leads or to tour vacation resorts, until profit on the sale of an interval was recognized.

Paragraph 44 of SOP 04-2 provides as a general rule that costs to sell are to be expensed, unless they specifically qualify for deferral. A deferral of costs— until sale and related profit is recognized—is only appropriate if the costs meet one of the following criteria:[38]

- The costs are reasonably expected to be recovered from the sale of the time-sharing intervals or from incidental operations, and they are incurred for either of the following:
  - Tangible assets that are used directly throughout the selling period to aid in the sales of the time-sharing intervals, such as the costs of model units and their furnishings, sales equipment, and semipermanent signs
  - Services that have been performed to obtain regulatory approval of sales, such as the costs of preparing and filing of prospectuses
- Other costs incurred to sell time-sharing intervals are deferred until profit from a sale transaction is recognized, if the costs meet all of the following criteria:[39]
  - They are reasonably expected to be recovered from the sale of the time-sharing intervals.
  - They are directly associated with the sales transactions.
  - They are incremental; that is, the costs would not have been incurred by the seller had a particular sale transaction not occurred.

---

36 For retail land sales, any changes in cost and revenue estimates are accounted for prospectively. [FAS 66, paragraph 76]
37 SOP 04-2, paragraph 41; SOP 81-1, paragraph 83
38 SOP 04-2, paragraph 45
39 SOP 04-2, paragraph 46

Costs that meet these criteria for deferral include sales commissions and payroll and payroll benefit–related costs of sales personnel for time spent directly on *successful* sales efforts. They are charged to expense in the period in which the related profit is recognized. If a sales contract is canceled, the related unrecoverable deferred selling costs are charged to expense in the period of cancellation.[40]

ADDITIONAL LIMITATIONS ON COST DEFERRAL

The SOP places additional limitations on cost deferral, if the deposit or cost recovery method of accounting is used:[41]

- Under the *deposit method* of accounting, deferred selling costs are limited to the nonrefundable portion of the deposits received by the seller.[42] This limitation is intended to eliminate the risk of not recovering deferred selling costs in the event of a buyer default.
- Under the *cost recovery method* of accounting, all selling costs are expensed because of uncertainties regarding the recoverability of deferred selling costs.

Paragraph 48 of SOP 04-2 reiterates that all other costs that do not satisfy the criteria for cost deferral have to be expensed as incurred, including "all costs incurred to induce potential buyers to take sales tours (for example, the costs of telemarketing call centers); all costs incurred for unsuccessful sales transactions; and all sales overhead such as on-site and off-site sales office rent, utilities, maintenance, and telephone expenses."[43] Direct incremental costs of the tour itself are expensed in the period the tour takes place.[44]

7.4 SPECIAL ACCOUNTING ISSUES

7.4.1 UNCOLLECTIBILITY OF RECEIVABLES

In a typical time-share sale, a large portion of the sales price is seller-financed, and collectibility of the sales price is a major concern for time-share sellers. Delinquency and default rates of receivables from time-share sales vary significantly, depending on the customer group, the location and desirability of the project, the quality of credit checks performed by the time-share seller, and other factors, such as the general state of the economy.

As a general rule, Statement 66 provides: "Profit shall be recognized in full when real estate is sold, provided (a) the profit is determinable, that is, the collectibility of the sales price is reasonably assured or the amount that will not be

---

40   SOP 04-2, paragraph 47
41   SOP 04-2, paragraph A40
42   SOP 04-2, paragraph 46
43   For advertising costs incurred, the guidance in SOP 93-7, *Reporting on Advertising Costs,* should be followed. [SOP 04-2, paragraph 48]
44   SOP 04-2, paragraph 48

EXAMPLE—ANALYSIS OF ALLOWANCE FOR UNCOLLECTIBLES[45]

Time-share seller Soleil Inc. (S) sells time-sharing intervals in a project in West Palm Beach, Florida. The project is similar to S's previously sold vacation property in Palm Coast, Florida, which enables S to use the historical data of that prior project to estimate uncollectibles for the West Palm Beach project. Prior experience shows that over the lifetime of the project, S should expect a 12% default rate.

S is calculating the allowance for uncollectibles to be recorded at the end of FY 2007, as outlined in the following table.

YEAR	2007 SALES		2006 SALES		2005 SALES		2004 SALES		PRIOR YEARS' SALES	
Sales—$[46]	10,000		20,000		40,000		60,000		60,000	
Defaults	$	%	$	%	$	%	$	%	$	%
Year of Sale	230	2.3	460	2.3	720	1.8	1,140	1.9	1,320	2.2
1 Year after Sale			660[47]	3.3	1,440	3.6	1,860	3.1	1,980	3.3
2 Years after Sale					720	1.8	1,140	1.9	1,020	1.7
3 Years after Sale							660	1.1	900	1.5
4+ Years after Sale[48]	—	—	—	—	—	—	—	—	1,080	1.8
Defaults to Date	230	2.3	1,120	5.6	2,880	7.2	4,800	8.0	6,300	10.5
Expected Defaults	1,200[49]	12.0	2,400	12.0	4,800	12.0	7,200	12.0	7,200	12.0
Allowance Needed	970[50]	9.7	1,280	6.4	1,920	4.8	2,400	4.0	900	1.5

In FY 2007, S records an allowance for uncollectibles of $7,470.[51] In subsequent years, S continues to monitor the defaults on its sales by year. The use of historical data enables S to identify and analyze any deviation in default rates from default rates experienced historically and to adjust the allowance percentage accordingly.[52]

---

45 Adapted from SOP 04-2, Appendix D
46 Sales, net of down payments.
47 $660 is the amount of defaults that occurred in 2007 relating to 2006 sales.
48 For simplicity, earlier years have been combined.
49 Time-share seller S expects a 12% default rate relating to its FY 2007 sales ($10,000): $1,200.
50 The amount of $970, which represents the allowance for uncollectibles relating to FY 2007 sales to be recorded as of December 31, 2007, is calculated as follows:

Sales FY 2007:	$10,000
Expected uncollectibles (12%):	$ 1,200
Less defaults in FY 2007:	$ 230
Expected defaults in future periods:	$ 970

51 Calculated as follows:

Allowance relating to FY 2007 sales:	$ 970
Allowance relating to FY 2006 sales:	$ 1,280
Allowance relating to FY 2005 sales:	$ 1,920
Allowance relating to FY 2004 sales:	$ 2,400
Allowance relating to earlier years' sales:	$ 900
Total allowance needed:	$ 7,470

52 See SOP 04-2, Appendix D, for more detailed analyses and financial statement disclosures relating to uncollectibles.

collectible can be estimated. . . ."[53] Unless a time-share seller is able to estimate the default rate based on historical data, the use of the accrual method of accounting is not appropriate. When estimating default rates for a new project, time-share sellers may use their prior experience with projects that have the same characteristics as the new project. Industry experience cannot be substituted for a company's own experience, due to the wide fluctuations in default rates; a company new to the time-sharing industry with no historical data may have to use the installment or cost recovery method during the first few years of a project, due to its inability to estimate uncollectibles.

A time-share seller that uses the accrual or percentage-of-completion method of accounting must estimate uncollectible amounts and reduce time-sharing revenue by the amounts that are estimated to be uncollectible. Subsequent to the sale, a time-share seller is required to evaluate the adequacy of the allowance for uncollectibles at each reporting period, and at least quarterly. Any subsequent adjustments to the allowance are recorded through a contra-revenue account (estimated uncollectibles), rather than through bad debt expense.[54]

The time-share seller must compute the allowance for uncollectibles "based on consideration of uncollectibles by year of sale, as well as the aging of notes receivable and factors such as the location of time-sharing units, contract terms, collection experience, economic conditions, and other qualitative factors as appropriate in the circumstances."[55] Time-share companies predominantly use a method to track uncollectible amounts of time-share revenues by year of sale, often referred to as "static pool analysis." That method is not dissimilar to the way insurance companies monitor their losses in determining the appropriate amount of loss reserves.

TROUBLED DEBT RESTRUCTURING

The restructuring of debt is considered a troubled debt restructuring if a creditor for economic or other reasons related to the debtor's financial difficulties grants a concession to the debtor that it would not otherwise consider.[56] Note receivable modifications, deferments of payments, or downgrades of time-sharing intervals constitute forms of troubled debt restructuring that should be accounted for in accordance with FASB Statement No. 114, *Accounting by Creditors for Impairment of a Loan*. Paragraph 34 of SOP 04-2 explains the accounting consequences:

> Any reductions in the recorded investment in a note receivable resulting from the application of FASB Statement No. 114 should be charged against the allowance for uncollectibles, because the estimated losses were recorded against revenue at the time the time-share sale was recognized or were recorded subsequently against revenue as a change in estimate. Incremental, direct costs

53   FAS 66, paragraph 3
54   SOP 04-2, paragraph 36
55   SOP 04-2, paragraph 37
56   FAS 15, paragraph 2

associated with uncollectibility, such as costs of collection programs, should be charged to expense as incurred.

7.4.2 INCENTIVES AND INDUCEMENTS   In the time-sharing industry, it is common to provide buyers with incentives, such as airline or amusement park tickets, when they purchase time-sharing intervals. The SOP defines *incentives* as products or services that are provided to a buyer either free of charge or below their fair value. The SOP differentiates between incentives and inducements. *Inducements* are products or services provided to *potential* buyers regardless of whether a sale occurs. They are included in a time-share seller's selling expenses. (See Exhibit 7.3.)

The sales price of a time-sharing interval is reduced by the fair value of an incentive. Section 7.3.1.1 discusses the impact of an incentive on the calculation of sales value and the allocation of the buyer's payments to the interval and the incentive. The accounting for incentives is based on EITF Issue No. 01-9, *Accounting for Consideration Given by a Vendor to a Customer (Including a Reseller of the Vendor's Products)*. That EITF differentiates based on the classification of the incentive as either cash or noncash. In EITF Issue No. 01-9, the Task Force reached a consensus that

cash consideration . . . given by a vendor to a customer is presumed to be a reduction of the selling prices of the vendor's products or services and, therefore, should be characterized as a reduction of revenue when recognized in the vendor's income statement. . . . If the consideration consists of a "free" product or service . . . the cost of the consideration should be characterized as an expense (as opposed to a reduction of revenue) when recognized in the vendor's income statement. That is, the "free" item is a deliverable in the exchange transaction and not a refund or rebate of a portion of the amount charged to the customer.[57]

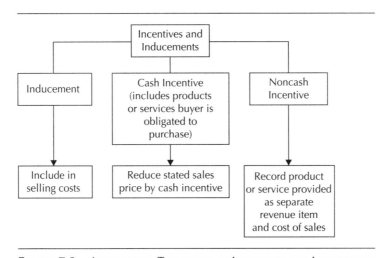

EXHIBIT 7.3   ACCOUNTING TREATMENT OF INCENTIVES AND INDUCEMENTS

---

57   EITF Issue No. 01-9, paragraphs 9 and 10

CASH INCENTIVES

SOP 04-2 provides that a cash incentive is either (1) cash or (2) a product or service provided to a buyer for less than its fair value that the purchaser would otherwise be required to purchase, such as the seller's payment of a buyer's owners association fees.[58] Providing a product or service to the buyer that the buyer is otherwise required to pay for is equivalent to the seller reimbursing the buyer for that product or service. AcSEC therefore determined it was appropriate to treat such products or services like a cash incentive.[59]

Both, the stated sales price of a time-sharing interval and the seller's cost of providing the product or service are reduced by the fair value of products or services that are deemed to be cash incentives.[60]

NONCASH INCENTIVES

A noncash incentive is a product or service provided to a buyer free of charge or for less than its fair value that the buyer is *not* required to purchase in conjunction with the purchase of a vacation interval. For example, the payment of the buyer's membership fees in an exchange program for one year is a noncash incentive if the buyer is not *required* to purchase the membership in the exchange program. Noncash incentives (products or services) are accounted for by analogy to paragraphs 7(b) and 31 of FASB Statement No. 66: The product or service provided to the buyer is recorded as a separate revenue item with associated costs of sales.

7.4.3 INCIDENTAL OPERATIONS   The time period that time-sharing intervals are held and available for sale is referred to as holding period. Time-share companies typically rent unsold intervals to recover some of their operating costs, or they offer prospective buyers a stay in a vacation resort, which generates significant "traffic" for a new time-share property and serves as a marketing tool.

During development and holding periods, time-share properties are accounted for as inventory and are not depreciated,[61] and rental and other revenue-producing activities are accounted for as incidental operations:

- Incremental revenues from incidental operations in excess of incremental costs of incidental operations are accounted for as a reduction of inventory costs. Incremental costs of operations during holding periods are costs associated with holding unsold intervals; they include maintenance fees and subsidies to owners associations. If a time-share property is expected

---

58   SOP 04-2, paragraph 18
59   SOP 04-2, paragraph A10
60   SOP 04-2, paragraph 18
61   SOP 04-2, paragraph 51

to create excess revenues during the development or holding period, such excess should not be factored into the calculation of project revenue for purposes of applying the relative sales value method.[62]

- Incremental costs in excess of incremental revenue are charged to expense as incurred.[63]

Direct incremental costs incurred to rent units during holding periods are deferred until the rental takes place to the extent their recovery from the rental of units is reasonably expected. At the time the rental takes place, the costs are either charged to expense (if incremental costs exceed incremental revenues) or recorded as reduction of inventory costs (if incremental revenues exceed incremental costs).[64]

7.4.4 UPGRADE AND RELOAD TRANSACTIONS[65]   Subsequent to the purchase, a satisfied buyer of a time-sharing interval may enter into a contractual agreement with the time-share seller to trade his or her time-sharing interval for a larger or more luxurious one (a so-called upgrade), or the buyer may purchase a second interval (a second week of usage), referred to as a reload. The guidance provided in Statement 66 is applied to determine the appropriate accounting for upgrade and reload transactions.

UPGRADE TRANSACTION

In an upgrade transaction, buyer and seller agree that the interval purchased be exchanged for a more expensive one. AcSEC did not consider upgrade transactions to be obligations to repurchase,[66] because "both buyer and seller must agree to an upgrade transaction. Neither has a unilateral right to compel the other."[67] Rather, AcSEC considered an upgrade transaction a modification and continuation of the original sale transaction. The buyer's initial and continuing investments from the original interval and any down payment received on the upgrade interval are combined and compared to the sales value of the upgrade interval when evaluating whether the buyer's financial commitment is adequate for the application of the accrual method of accounting.

---

62   The relative sales value method is "[a] method of allocating inventory cost and determining cost of sales in conjunction with a time-sharing sale. Cost of sales is calculated as a percentage of net sales by applying a cost-of-sales percentage, determined as the ratio of total estimated inventory cost (including costs to complete, if any) to total estimated time-sharing revenue to be collected from sales of the inventory. The inventory balance reported in the balance sheet is considered to be a pool of costs that will be charged against future revenue." [SOP 04-2, Glossary]

63   SOP 04-2, paragraph 50

64   SOP 04-2, paragraph 52

65   SOP 04-2, paragraphs 28 and 29

66   If the terms of a real estate transaction allow the buyer to compel the seller to repurchase the real estate sold, sale accounting is not appropriate. [FAS 66, paragraph 26]

67   SOP 04-2, Appendix C

EXAMPLE—UPGRADE

In January 2007, Benedict (B) purchases a time-sharing interval at a stated sales price of $10,000 and makes a down payment of $1,000, with the remainder being financed by the seller. The stated sales price is equal to the sales value of the interval. The note is deemed to be collectible. In January 2009, buyer and seller enter into an upgrade arrangement, under which the buyer will upgrade to a more luxurious interval with a sales value of $15,000. The buyer does not make any additional down payment when entering into the upgrade transaction. In the years 2007 and 2008, B has made principal payments of $2,000 on his note for the interval originally purchased. The seller has determined that 10% initial investment is sufficient for the application of the accrual method.

At the time of the upgrade transaction, is the buyer's investment adequate for the use of the accrual method?

Sales Value of Upgrade Interval:	$15,000
Required Down Payment Percentage:	10%
Required Initial Investment for Upgrade Interval:	$ 1,500

Payments Included when evaluating the Adequacy of Buyer's Financial Commitment.

Down Payment on Original Interval:	$ 1,000
Principal Payment on Note:	$ 2,000
	$ 3,000

The buyer's investment is adequate for the use of the accrual method of accounting, since the buyer's down payment on the original interval purchased and the subsequent principal payments on the note exceed the minimum investment requirement of 10% on the upgrade interval.

RELOAD TRANSACTION

A reload transaction is the purchase of an additional interval, which is considered a transaction separate from the purchase of the original interval. Therefore, the seller should not include the buyer's initial and continuing investments from the original time-sharing interval toward the measurement of the buyer's commitment for the second interval.[68]

7.4.5 SELLER SUPPORT OF OPERATIONS   Owners of time-sharing intervals are responsible for paying the costs of owning and managing their intervals, such as property taxes, repairs, and maintenance, and reservation systems. Generally, a time-share developer establishes a nonprofit organization that acts as owners association, manages the day-to-day operations of the vacation property, and collects owners association fees. During the early stages of project sellout, a large percentage of the time-sharing intervals is still owned by the developer. Rather than paying owners association fees for the unsold intervals, the developer may

---

68   In a points-based time-sharing transaction, the purchase of additional points is considered a reload transaction. [SOP 04-2, Glossary]

subsidize the owners association to cover operating deficits. These seller subsidies generally diminish as additional time-sharing intervals are sold. Payments by the seller of dues or maintenance fees, as well as any amounts paid to subsidize losses of the owners association, are charged to expense as incurred, except when accounted for as incidental operations.[69]

Subsidies that extend beyond sell-out periods or that do not diminish during the sell-out period raise the question whether the seller has transferred substantially all the risks and rewards of ownership of the time-sharing intervals sold, that is, whether sale recognition is appropriate.[70]

7.4.6 DIVISION OF PROJECT INTO PHASES[71] Similar to other real estate projects that are completed over several years, time-share developers often divide projects into phases to allow for proper cost allocation. If a project is divided into phases, the relative sales value method is based on the individual phase, rather than the project as a whole. For a variety of reasons, a time-share developer may decide to change the phases of a time-share project in subsequent periods.

Such change is accounted for on a retrospective basis as a change in accounting principle pursuant to the provisions of FASB Statement No. 154, *Accounting Changes and Error Corrections*. Retrospective application requires that the financial statements for each individual prior period presented be adjusted to reflect the period-specific effects of applying the new accounting principle.[72]

7.5 FINANCIAL STATEMENT PRESENTATION AND DISCLOSURE[73]

A time-share developer should disclose its policies with respect to the criteria established for assessing a buyer's commitment and the collectibility of the sales price.[74]

SOP 04-2 requires the following disclosures relating to receivables from time-share sales:

- Gross notes receivable from time-share sales, a deduction for the allowance for uncollectibles and a deduction from notes receivable for any profit deferred under FASB Statement No. 66
- Maturities of notes receivable for each of the five years following the date of the financial statements and in the aggregate for all years thereafter
- The weighted average and range of stated interest rates of notes receivable
- A roll-forward of the allowance for uncollectibles (the balance of the allowance at the beginning and end of each period, additions associated

---

69   SOP 04-2, paragraph 59; see Section 7.4.3 of this Chapter for a discussion of incidental operations.
70   SOP 04-2, Appendix C, Section titled "Seller Support of Operations"
71   SOP 04-2, paragraph 15
72   FAS 154, paragraph 7
73   SOP 04-2, paragraphs 63 and 64
74   FAS 66, paragraphs 5(b) and 37(d); SOP 04-2, paragraph 64(e)

with current period sales, direct write-offs charged against the allowance, and changes in estimate associated with prior period sales)

- A roll-forward of the allowance for uncollectibles for receivables sold with recourse

For time-share projects that have not been completed, a time-share developer should disclose the estimated costs to complete improvements and amenities.

If the financial statements include a change in accounting estimate (for example, relating to the application of the relative sales value method or the percentage-of-completion method[75]) or a change in accounting principle (such as a change relating to the delineation of the project into phases), the financial statements should include the disclosures required by FASB Statement No. 154.

7.6 SYNOPSIS OF AUTHORITATIVE LITERATURE

FASB STATEMENT NO. 66, *ACCOUNTING FOR SALES OF REAL ESTATE*
Outline provided in Chapter 3.

FASB STATEMENT NO. 67, *ACCOUNTING FOR COSTS AND INITIAL RENTAL OPERATIONS OF REAL ESTATE PROJECTS*
Outline provided in Chapter 1.

AICPA STATEMENT OF POSITION 04-2, ACCOUNTING FOR REAL ESTATE TIME-SHARING TRANSACTIONS
SOP 04-2 provides guidance on the accounting by a seller for real estate time-sharing transactions. A time-share seller should apply the relative sales value method to determine the appropriate amounts of revenues and cost of sales to be recorded. The method of profit recognition follows the provisions in FASB Statement No. 66. The issues addressed by SOP 04-2 include accounting for uncollectibility of receivables, the treatment of marketing and selling costs, accounting for incentives, and operations during holding periods.

---

75   SOP 04-2, paragraph 41

RETAIL LAND SALES

8.1 OVERVIEW

Sales of real estate can be categorized into retail land sales and sales of real estate other than retail land sales. The accounting for sales of real estate other than retail land sales is explained in Chapter 3. Retail land sales are lot sales on a volume basis to retail customers, as opposed to homebuilders. Sales of real estate other than retail land sales include the sale of land (not classified as retail land sales) and buildings (commercial developments, office buildings, shopping centers, homes, etc.). Wholesale or bulk sales of land and retail sales from projects comprising a small number of lots also fall within the category of sales of real estate other than retail land sales.[1]

Retail land sales companies typically acquire large tracts of unimproved land for subdivision into lots;[2] they develop master plans and commit to construct or construct improvements (roads, utilities) and amenities (golf courses, lakes) to make the lots more attractive. These lots are sold to retail customers through intensive marketing programs and may be purchased with relatively small down payments; often, the down payment is less than 10% of the purchase price, and it may be as low as 1%.

---

1   AICPA Industry Accounting Guide, *Accounting for Retail Land Sales*, paragraph 8
2   Frequently, retail land sales companies are not separate legal entities, but divisions of land development companies. Throughout this chapter, the term "retail land sales companies" also includes divisions of land development companies.

The balance of the purchase price is typically financed directly with the retail land sales company, rather than a financial institution, and paid over several years. Under the terms of a typical contract, the buyer may discontinue payments at any time. If payments are discontinued after the contractually specified refund period, the buyer loses his/her interest in the lot and all payments made, and the retail land sales company repossesses the land for resale. The financing of retail land sales usually involves no credit investigation or personal credit obligation, and the seller cannot require performance or seek deficiency judgments by operation of law or contract.[3]

In the 1960s and early 1970s, the financial reporting of retail land sales companies was widely criticized as being too aggressive. The allegations included premature profit recognition, inadequate provisions for costs to be incurred after the sale, and distortion of revenues through inclusion of interest in sales revenues.

As a result of the perceived abuses, the American Institute of Certified Public Accountants (AICPA) established the Committee on Land Development Companies, which performed a review of the industry's methods of operation and accounting and reporting. In 1973, the Industry Accounting Guide, *Accounting for Retail Land Sales,* was issued as a result of that Committee's review. That Accounting Guide established criteria for the timing of revenue recognition, as well as appropriate methods for profit recognition. The recognition of a sale is deferred until certain conditions are met that indicate that (1) the customer is serious about fulfilling its contractual obligations, and (2) the retail land sales company is capable of fulfilling its obligations under the contract.[4] The Financial Accounting Standards Board (FASB) extracted the specialized accounting and reporting practices from that Industry Accounting Guide and incorporated them in the retail land sales section of FASB Statement No. 66, *Accounting for Sales of Real Estate.*

In the present environment it is rare that a sale of land meets the definition of a retail land sale; most land sales fall in the category of—and are accounted for as—*other than retail land sales*, discussed in Chapter 3.

8.2 ACCOUNTING FOR RETAIL LAND SALES

Similar to the accounting guidance governing sales of real estate other than retail land sales, the accounting for revenue and profit recognition for retail land sales is very rule-driven and contains bright-line tests. Since these bright lines are frequently *minimum* requirements that must be met for the recording of a sale or for the use of a certain profit recognition method, even a minor violation of these thresholds may cause accounting consequences; the concept of materiality is not applied in these circumstances.

The flowchart in Exhibit 8.1 graphically depicts the revenue and profit recognition provisions for retail land sales.

---

3   AICPA Industry Accounting Guide, *Accounting for Retail Land Sales*, paragraph 5
4   AICPA Industry Accounting Guide, *Accounting for Retail Land Sales*, paragraph 15

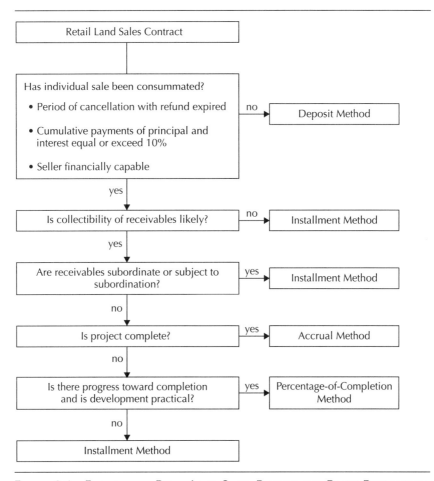

EXHIBIT 8.1   FLOWCHART—RETAIL LAND SALES: REVENUE AND PROFIT RECOGNITION

8.2.1 REVENUE RECOGNITION   The characteristics of sales in the retail land sales industry—small down payment, unenforceability of the sales contract, customer refunds within established cancellation periods—were drivers for the development of specialized revenue recognition criteria. Retail land sales are recognized upon consummation of a sale.[5] A sale is considered consummated when the following three criteria are met:[6]

1. The period of cancellation with refund has expired, and the buyer has made the down payment and each required subsequent payment until the period of cancellation with refund has expired. That period is the longer of the periods required by local law, established by the seller's policy or specified in the contract.

---

5   FAS 66, paragraph 44
6   FAS 66, paragraph 44, footnote 18; FAS 66, paragraph 47

2. Cumulative payments of principal and interest equal or exceed 10% of the contract sales price.

3. The seller is financially capable of funding the planned improvements in the project when required and of completing agreed-upon land improvements and off-site facilities. That capability may be indicated by the seller's equity capitalization, its borrowing capacity, or its positive cash flow from operations.

If a retail land sales transaction does not meet these three criteria, it is accounted for under the deposit method.[7] Under the deposit method, the seller continues to report the property and related debt on its balance sheet and discloses the fact that the property and related debt are subject to a sales contract. Payments received from the buyer are reported as deposits on the contract.[8] Portions of cash received that are designated by the contract as interest are recognized as income when the retail land sales transaction is recorded as a sale.[9] The treatment of costs incurred to sell depends on the character of the costs; they are accounted for in accordance with the provisions in FASB Statement No. 67, *Accounting for Costs and Initial Rental Operations of Real Estate Projects.*[10]

8.2.2 PROFIT RECOGNITION   One distinct difference between the profit recognition provisions for sales of real estate other than retail land sales and the provisions relating to retail land sales is that for retail land sales, one method of profit recognition is applied to all consummated sales transactions within a project.[11]

When determining the appropriate accounting method, a company needs to take into consideration the company's collection experience with the retail land sales project; a company's own experience cannot be substituted with industry experience. However, a company's experience with prior projects may be used to evaluate a new project, if the prior projects had predominantly the same characteristics as the new project.[12]

FASB Statement No. 66 allows for three different methods of profit recognition for retail land sales:

- Accrual Method

---

7   FAS 66, paragraph 48
8   FAS 66, paragraphs 65–67
9   FAS 66, paragraph 66
10   Paragraphs 17–19 in FASB Statement No. 67 distinguish between three categories of costs incurred to sell real estate projects:
    (1) Costs incurred to sell real estate projects are capitalized if they are reasonably expected to be recovered from the sale of the project or from incidental operations and are incurred for tangible assets that are used directly throughout the selling period to aid in the sale of the project or for services that have been performed to obtain regulatory approval.
    (2) Other costs incurred to sell are accounted for as prepaid costs if they are directly associated with and their recovery is reasonably expected from sales.
    (3) All other costs incurred to sell are expensed as incurred.
11   FAS 66, paragraph 44
12   AICPA Industry Accounting Guide, *Accounting for Retail Land Sales*, paragraph 19

- Percentage-of-Completion Method
- Installment Method

8.2.2.1 Accrual Method   The accrual method provides for the immediate recognition of all of the profit relating to consummated sales transactions of a project that has been completed, if certain criteria are met. Specifically, paragraph 45 of FASB Statement No. 66 states that the accrual method of accounting is applied to transactions that meet all of the following three criteria:

1. The seller must have fulfilled its obligations to complete improvements of lots sold or to construct amenities or other facilities relating to the lots sold.[13]
2. Receivables are collectible. A down payment of at least 20% is an acceptable indication of collectibility. Alternatively, collection experience for the project must indicate that at least 90% of the contracts in the project that are in force six months after the criteria for sale recognition have been met will be collected in full.[14]

   The seller's collection experience with prior projects may be used for the purpose of assessing collectibility of the receivables, if the prior projects:

   a. Had predominantly the same characteristics (type of land, environment, type of customer, contract terms, sales methods) as the new project and
   b. Had a sufficiently long collection period to indicate the percentage of current sales of the new project that will be collected to maturity.
3. The seller's receivables are not subordinated to new loans on the property.[15] However, the subordination of individual lot buyers' receivables to new home construction loans is permissible if the collection experience on those contracts is the same as on contracts not subordinated.

COLLECTIBILITY OF RECEIVABLES
When evaluating the collectibility of receivables from current sales using historical data, companies need to consider paragraph 71 of FASB Statement No. 66, which provides very specific guidance:

> The historical data is selected from a representative sample of receivables that reflect the latest available collection data and cover an adequate period of time. The receivables in the sample are considered uncollectible . . . if payments due are unpaid at the end of the sample period selected for the following delinquency periods:

Percent of Contract Price Paid	Delinquency Period
Less than 25 percent	90 days
25 percent but less than 50 percent	120 days
50 percent and over	150 days

---

13   FAS 66, paragraph 45(e)
14   FAS 66, paragraph 45(c)
15   FAS 66, paragraph 45(d)

Longer delinquency periods may be used if the recent experience of the seller has been better or if there is recourse to the buyer personally and the buyer is financially capable of making the payments required under the contract.[16]

DETERMINATION OF AMOUNT OF REVENUE TO BE RECORDED

When applying the accrual method of accounting, the stated sales price is generally payable over several years. Payments due from the buyer in future periods need to be discounted to reflect present value. The receivable on the seller's books should approximate the amount at which the receivable could be sold to a third party at the date of the sales contract without recourse to the seller.[17] The discount rate may differ from the interest rate stated in the contract; it should reflect:

> . . . the rate which would have resulted if an independent borrower and an independent lender had negotiated a similar transaction under comparable terms and conditions with the option to pay the cash price upon purchase or to give a note for the amount of the purchase which bears the prevailing rate of interest to maturity.[18]

However, the rate should not be lower than the rate stated in the sales contract.[19] In periods subsequent to the sale, that discount is recognized as interest income, rather than revenue.

If a seller uses or intends to use programs that encourage prepayment by reducing the principal amount of the note receivable, the profit recognized at the date of sale is reduced to allow for expected amounts of such discounts.[20]

8.2.2.2 Percentage-of-Completion Method

The percentage-of-completion method is applied to a project for which the seller has not completed its development or

FORMULA FOR COMPUTING NET SALES

Sales Prices per Contracts
Less: Estimated Uncollectibles
Less: Discount to Reflect Present Value
Less: Reduction for Prepayment Programs
Net Sales

---

16   FAS 66, paragraph 71
17   FAS 66, paragraph 70(a)
18   APB Opinion No. 21, paragraph 13
19   FAS 66, paragraphs 70(a)
20   FAS 66, paragraph 72

EXAMPLE—APPLICATION OF THE ACCRUAL METHOD[21]

In Year 1, SceniCo., a retail land sales company, enters into retail land sales contracts totaling sales prices of $1 million, and receives 10% nonrefundable down payments ($100,000). The stated interest rate is 6%; the appropriate discount rate is 12%. The receivables balance is payable over a 10-year period. It is estimated that 20% of the contracts will ultimately not be collected in full.

SceniCo. has determined that the application of the accrual method is appropriate, and has made the following present value calculation (in thousands):[22]

YEAR	ANNUAL COLLECTIONS	PRINCIPAL	INTEREST	PRESENT VALUE AT 12%
2	104	62	42	97
3	104	66	38	87
4	104	70	34	77
5	104	75	29	68
6	104	79	25	60
7	104	84	20	53
8	104	89	15	47
9	104	95	9	43
10	104	100	4	38
	936	720	216	570

What amount of revenue should SceniCo. record in Year 1 relating to these sales contracts?

Revenues to be recognized for the sales made in Year 1 are calculated as follows:

Gross sales per contracts (stated interest rate of 6%)	$1,000,000
Less: Estimated uncollectible principal amount	(180,000)[23]
Less: Discount to reflect 12% interest rate	
Collections of principal projected for Years 2 through 10	720,000
Present value of future payments at 12%[24]	570,000
Discount to reflect interest rate of 12%	(150,000)
Revenue to be recognized in Year 1	670,000[25]

Revenues are recognized net of sales that are expected to be cancelled in future periods. Therefore, the retail land sales company recognizes revenues of $670,000 in Year 1.

---

21   Adapted from FASB Statement No. 66, paragraph 91, Exhibit I
22   Adapted from FASB Statement No. 66, paragraph 92, Schedule A; the computation assumes no interest for Year 1.
23   The amount of $180,000 is derived at as follows: 20% of the contracts will not be collected in full ($200,000). The sales contracts require a 10% down payment. Thus, payments of $20,000 related to the contracts that will not be collected in full have already been made by the customers through down payments.
24   FAS 66, paragraph 92
25   Alternatively, the amount of $670,000 can be calculated as: $100,000 down payment plus $570,000 present value of future payments.

construction obligations and the seller's obligations are significant in relation to total costs,[26] with all other requirements for the application of the accrual method of accounting being met. Estimates of the costs to complete and the progress toward completion must be reasonably dependable. Further, there should be no indication of significant delays, such as the inability to obtain permits, contractors, or equipment.[27]

The percentage-of-completion method can only be applied if the seller has already started with the construction of the improvements or amenities the seller is obligated to complete. For the percentage-of-completion method to be appropriate, paragraph 46 of FASB Statement No. 66 requires that:

- *The development of the project is practical.* There must be a reasonable expectation that the land can be developed for the purposes represented and that the properties will be useful for those purposes at the end of the normal payment period. For example, legal restrictions, including environmental restrictions, should not be expected to seriously impact development. The construction of improvements, such as access roads, water supply, and sewage treatment or removal, must be feasible within a reasonable time period.[28]
- *There has been progress on improvements.* The project's improvements must have progressed beyond preliminary stages, and there must be indications that the work will be completed according to plan. Some indications of progress are:
  - Expenditure of funds on the proposed improvements
  - Commencement of work on the improvements
  - Existence of engineering plans and work commitments relating to lots sold
  - Completion of access roads and amenities, such as golf courses, clubs, and swimming pools[29]

The amount of revenue to be recognized under the percentage of completion method is determined by multiplying the contract prices—discounted to reflect present value if the contract provides for seller financing at a rate below market—by the percentage of contract completion. The percentage of contract completion is measured by applying the cost-to-cost method, which requires measuring the relationship of costs already incurred to the total estimated costs incurred and to be incurred.[30] Such costs include land cost, interest, and project carrying costs, as well as selling costs directly associated with a project.[31] Cost estimates are based on costs expected to be incurred in the construction

---

26   FAS 66, paragraph 73
27   FAS 66, paragraph 46
28   FAS 66, paragraph 46(f)
29   FAS 66, paragraph 46(e)
30   FAS 66, paragraph 73
31   FAS 66, paragraph 74

industry locally.[32] Additionally, any unrecoverable costs of off-site improvements, utilities, and amenities need to be provided for. When determining the amount of unrecoverable costs, "estimates of amounts to be recovered from the future sale of the improvements, utilities and amenities are discounted to present value as of the date the net unrecoverable costs are recognized."[33]

EXAMPLE—APPLICATION OF THE PERCENTAGE-OF-COMPLETION METHOD[34]

This example continues the scenario presented in Section 8.2.2.1 relating to the accrual method of accounting. The difference in this example is that SceniCo. is required to construct improvements after the sale, which are significant when compared to total costs. Therefore, the percentage-of-completion method, rather than the accrual method is appropriate.

Future Improvement Costs Relating to the Sales of $800,000[35] in Year 1:	$ 120,000
Land Cost (applicable to sales contracts of $800,000):	$ 60,000
Selling Expenses Incurred at the Time of Sale:	$ 300,000
How much revenue must SceniCo. defer at the time of sale?	
Costs to be Incurred in Future Periods:	$ 120,000
Total Costs Applicable to Sales Contracts of $800,000:	
Land Costs	$ 60,000
Selling Expenses in Year 1	$ 300,000
Costs to be Incurred in Future Periods	$ 120,000
Total Costs	$ 480,000
Percentage of Completion	75%
Percentage of Revenue to be Deferred:	25%
Amount of Revenue to be Deferred:	
Gross sales:	$1,000,000
Less: Cancellations/Uncollectibles	$ (200,000)
Less: Discount[36]	$ (150,000)
Basis for Calculating Deferral of Revenues	$ 650,000
Deferral of 25%	$ 162,500

SceniCo. must defer $162,500 in revenue, because the costs relating to that revenue have not yet been incurred.

---

32 FAS 66, paragraph 75(a)
33 FAS 66, paragraph 75(b)
34 Adapted from FASB Statement No. 66, paragraph 91, Exhibit I
35 $1,000,000 stated sales prices less estimated cancellations of $200,000
36 Discount is determined as: Collections of principal projected in Years 2 through 10 ($720,000) less present value of receivable at 12% ($570,000); see example under the accrual method of accounting.

CHANGES IN ESTIMATES[37]

Since the costs actually incurred to complete a project, and the revenues to be realized from a project generally differ from their original estimates, the percentage-of-completion calculation must be reviewed throughout the project, at least annually. Generally, the changes are accounted for prospectively in current and future periods, because they arise from changes in estimates. No cumulative adjustment is made to retroactively apply such revised percentage-of-completion calculations to prior years' sales, except in the following circumstance: If a loss is expected to be incurred relating to prior sales, the total amount of the loss needs to be recognized, once the loss is probable and can be estimated, in accordance with paragraph 8 of FASB Statement No. 5, *Accounting for Contingencies*. Additionally, when a loss is expected to be realized from executed sales contracts, a retail land sales company is also required to evaluate whether a loss needs to be recorded on land and improvements not yet sold.

8.2.2.3 Installment Method   Unless the conditions for the use of the accrual method (if the project is complete) or the percentage-of-completion method (if the seller has not fulfilled all of its obligations) are met for the entire project, the installment method is applied to all sales that have been consummated.[38] The installment method is frequently the appropriate method for recording retail land sales transactions, because the collectibility criterion required under both the accrual and the percentage-of-completion methods is not met.[39]

Most defaults of retail land sales contracts occur within the first few years after the purchase contract is signed, because the buyer's investment in the lots increases with the periodic payments required under the contract. After a buyer has made a substantial investment in the lot, the buyer is less likely to default on his/her obligations. If a project has a high default rate, the percentage of contracts that are likely to be uncollectible remains high as long as the company continues to make new sales.

Under the installment method, a company reports the entire contract price as sales and records the corresponding cost of sales and selling expenses (incurred and to be incurred). The difference between the recorded revenues and costs is deferred profit. This deferred profit is recognized as cash is received by the seller. Each payment is apportioned between cost and profit. The apportionment is in the same ratio as total cost and total profit bear to reported sales.[40]

In contrast to the accrual and percentage-of-completion methods, the installment method does not require discounting the sales price of the lot to reflect present value if the stated interest rate is less than an appropriate interest rate,[41] and interest income may be recorded at the rate stated in the contract when received.

---

37   FAS 66, paragraph 76
38   FAS 66, paragraph 44
39   FAS 66, paragraphs 45(c) and 46(b)
40   FAS 66, paragraph 56
41   FAS 66, paragraph 57

EXAMPLE—APPLICATION OF THE INSTALLMENT METHOD

This example illustrates the application of the installment method to the fact pattern outlined under Section 8.2.2.1, with the following difference: The default rate cannot be estimated due to a lack of the seller's prior experience.

In Year 1, SceniCo., a retail land sales company, enters into retail land sales contracts totaling $1 million sales prices, and receives 10% down payment ($100,000). The sales are consummated. The balance is payable over a 10-year period, bearing interest at 6%. The appropriate discount rate for the receivable balance has been determined to be 12%. The seller has no further obligations under the contract. As of the end of Year 1, no defaults have occurred. Cost of sales relating to the sales contracts amounts to $225,000.

How should SceniCo. account for these sales?

Since collectibility cannot be estimated, the installment method has to be used. SceniCo.'s policy is to record the contractually agreed-upon sales prices as sales, rather than reducing the receivable to its present value using a discount rate of 12%.

The amounts recorded are determined as follows:

Revenues:	$1,000,000
Cost of Sales Attributable to Gross Sales Contracts:	$ 225,000[42]
Selling Costs in Year 1:	$ 300,000
Profit from the Sale of the Lots:	$ 475,000
Gross Profit Percentage:	47.5%
Cash Received:	$ 100,000
Percent of Cash Received as Compared to Revenues:	10%
Percent of Profit to be Recognized:	10%
Amount of Profit to be Recognized:	$ 47,500
Amount of Profit to be Deferred:	$ 427,500

Journal Entries:

Cash	$ 100,000	
Receivables	$ 900,000	
Revenues		$1,000,000
Cost of Sales	$ 225,000	
Inventories		$ 225,000
Profit Deferred (income statement)	$ 427,500	
Profit Deferred (contra receivables)		$ 427,500

The accounting for a repossession of the lots upon customer default is outlined in Section 8.3.2.

---

42   Cost of sales is computed based on gross sales, rather than net sales. This is different from the computation of cost of sales under the accrual method.

8.3 SPECIAL ACCOUNTING ISSUES

8.3.1 CHANGE FROM THE INSTALLMENT TO THE PERCENTAGE-OF-COMPLETION METHOD   Once the conditions for the use of the percentage-of-completion method[43] are met for the entire project, the retail land sales company changes its profit recognition method for the whole project for current and prior years' sales.[44] The effect is accounted for as a change in accounting estimate.[45]

In the period of change, the retail land sales company calculates the income it would have recognized had it applied the percentage-of-completion method for all prior sales in the project. This amount is compared to the income the retail land sales company has recognized using the installment method of accounting. This difference is presented within the revenue-section of the income statement as "Income resulting from change from installment to percentage-of-completion method."[46] The retail land sales company credits to income the amount of profit not yet recognized less (1) a valuation reserve for receivables, (2) a discount to reduce receivable balances to present value at the date of change to the percentage-of-completion method (using appropriate interest rates at the time of the original sales), if applicable, and (3) a liability (also discounted) for remaining future performance. The change results in a "catch-up" credit to income in the year of change equal to the additional profit that would have been reported under the percentage-of-completion method for periods prior to the change to the percentage-of-completion method.[47]

8.3.2 ACCOUNTING FOR REPOSSESSED LAND   Similar to repossessed time-sharing intervals in the time-sharing industry, discussed in Chapter 7, repossessed lots cannot be distinguished from lots that have never been sold. This distinguishes such repossessions in the retail land sales industry from repossessions of other products, such as consumer goods. Because the repossessed land is no different than land never sold, the repossessed land is recorded at the company's "original" cost. In reselling the land, the retail land sales company incurs similar advertising, promotion, and commission charges as it does for land sold for the first time, and it accounts for such costs as it would in an original sale.

The accounting for repossessed land, that is, the accounting for defaulted contracts, depends on the accounting method used for the project:

USE OF INSTALLMENT METHOD
Under the installment method, sales and receivables are recorded gross, without considering expected defaults. Estimated total costs of land and future development

---

43   Or accrual method, if the project is complete

44   FAS 66, paragraph 44; paragraph 49 of FASB Statement No. 66 indicates that the change from the installment method to the percentage-of-completion method is not mandatory.

45   FAS 66, paragraph 49

46   FAS 66, paragraph 97

47   FAS 66, paragraph 49

are charged to cost of sales. Any resulting profit is recognized into income as cash payments are received from the customer. Upon default, the receivables are removed from the books, and deferred profit is reduced as it relates to these receivables. Land and improvement costs are recovered as the retail land sales company repossesses the land. Any difference is recognized as income or results in a loss if the selling costs have not been fully recovered.

EXAMPLE—CUSTOMER DEFAULT UNDER THE INSTALLMENT METHOD[48]

This example continues the scenario outlined in Section 8.2.2.3.

In Year 1, SceniCo., a retail land sales company, enters into retail land sales contracts totaling $1 million sales price and receives 10% down payment ($100,000). The sales are consummated. The balance is payable over a 10-year period. The stated interest rate is 6%; the appropriate discount rate for the receivables balance has been determined to be 12%. Different from the scenario outlined in Section 8.2.2.3, sales contracts totaling $200,000 are cancelled in Year 1. SceniCo. has recorded sales of $1 million in Year 1.

How should SceniCo. account for the repossessed land and any unrecovered selling costs?

Contracts Cancelled in Year 1	$200,000
Customer Deposits (10%)	$(20,000)
Unpaid Balance	$180,000
Cost Recovered:	
Land at Cost	$ 45,000
Less: Profit at 47.5% of $180	$ 85,500
Unrecovered Selling Cost (Loss)	$ 49,500

Journal Entry upon Customer Default and Recovery of the Land:

Inventories	$ 45,000	
Loss on Cancellations	$ 49,500	
Deferred Profit (contra receivables)	$ 85,500	
Receivables		$180,000

USE OF PERCENTAGE-OF-COMPLETION OR ACCRUAL METHOD

Under both the percentage-of-completion and accrual methods of accounting, sales are recorded net of expected uncollectibles; correspondingly, cost of sales is also recorded based on sales, net of uncollectibles. As long as the actual customer defaults occur as expected by the company, no journal entries are necessary,

48   Adapted from FASB Statement No. 66, paragraph 96

because sales for these defaulted contracts were never recorded; for accounting purposes, the land was never removed from the company's inventory.

If the default experience differs from the defaults originally estimated, an adjustment to sales/cost of sales needs to be recorded to reflect that change.

8.4 FINANCIAL STATEMENT PRESENTATION AND DISCLOSURE

FINANCIAL STATEMENT PRESENTATION—INSTALLMENT METHOD

When using the installment method, sales, the gross profit that has not yet been recognized, and the total cost of the sale (cost of sale, selling expenses, and loss on cancellations, if any) are presented in the income statement or disclosed in the footnotes. Revenue and cost of sales (or gross profit) are presented as separate items on the income statement or disclosed in the footnotes when profit is recognized.[49]

DISCLOSURES

Paragraph 50 of FASB Statement No. 66 requires the following five disclosures for entities that engage in retail land sales transactions:

1. Maturities of accounts receivable for each of the five years following the date of the financial statements
2. Delinquent accounts receivable and the methods for determining delinquency
3. The weighted average and range of stated interest rates of receivables
4. Estimated total costs and estimated dates of expenditures for improvements for major areas from which sales are being made over each of the five years following the date of the financial statements
5. Recorded obligations for improvements

8.5 SYNOPSIS OF ACCOUNTING LITERATURE

FASB STATEMENT NO. 66, ACCOUNTING FOR SALES OF REAL ESTATE

An outline of FASB Statement No. 66 is provided in Chapter 3.

The AICPA Industry Accounting Guide, *Accounting for Retail Land Sales*, set forth specialized accounting principles to be applied to retail land sales. These accounting principles have been extracted and included in FASB Statement No. 66, *Accounting for Sales of Real Estate*.

---

49   FAS 66, paragraph 59

GLOSSARY

Acquisition, Development, or Construction Arrangement (ADC Arrangement). Lending arrangements in which a lender participates in the expected residual profit of a real estate project. Expected residual profit is the amount of profit (often called equity kicker), above a reasonable amount of interest and fees.[1]

ADC Arrangement. See *Acquisition, Development, or Construction Arrangement.*

Adjusted Funds from Operations (AFFO).[2] A measure of a real estate company's cash flows generated by operations. AFFO is calculated by adjusting Funds from Operations (FFO) by (1) normalized recurring property expenditures that are capitalized by the real estate company and then amortized, such as new carpeting and tenant improvement allowances, and by (2) the impact of "straight-lining" of rents.

Air Rights. The right to air space above real property. Air rights are rights that can be sold or leased.

Amenities. Features that enhance the attractiveness or value of a real estate property. Examples of amenities include golf courses, clubhouses, swimming pools, tennis courts, indoor recreational facilities, and parking facilities.[3]

Antispeculation Clause. A clause included in a land sale agreement that requires the buyer to develop the land in a specific manner or within a stated period of time. If the buyer fails to comply with the provisions of the sales contract, the seller has the right to reacquire the property.[4]

Asset Retirement. The other-than-temporary removal of a long-lived asset from service, which includes its sale, abandonment, or disposal in some other manner.[5]

Asset Retirement Cost. See *Asset Retirement Obligation.*

Asset Retirement Obligation. An obligation associated with the retirement of a tangible long-lived asset. The term asset retirement cost refers to the amount capitalized that increases the carrying amount of the long-lived asset when a liability for an asset retirement obligation is recognized.[6]

Bargain Purchase Option. A provision allowing the lessee, at its option, to purchase the leased property for a price sufficiently lower than the expected fair value of the property at the date the option becomes exercisable that exercise of the option appears, at the inception of the lease, to be reasonably assured.[7]

Bargain Renewal Option. A provision allowing the lessee, at its option, to renew the lease for a rental sufficiently lower than the fair rental of the property at the date the option becomes

---

1   AICPA's Third Notice to Practitioners on ADC Arrangements (Exhibit I in AICPA Practice Bulletin 1)
2   AFFO may be defined differently by different companies.
3   FAS 67, Glossary; SOP 04-2, Glossary
4   EITF Issue No. 86-6
5   FAS 143, paragraph A6
6   FAS 143, paragraph 1, footnote 1
7   FAS 13, paragraph 5

exercisable that exercise of the option appears, at the inception of the lease, to be reasonably assured.[8]

Blind Pool or Partially Blind Pool Partnerships. Partnerships in which investment units are sold before some or all of the properties to be acquired are identified.[9]

Bona Fide. In good faith; without fraud.

Build-to-Suit Lease. A transaction in which a lessee is involved in constructing an asset that will be owned by the owner-lessor. Build-to-suit leases are often structured as synthetic leases.

CAD. See *Cash Available for Distribution.*

CAM. See *Common Area Maintenance Costs.*

Capitalization Rate (Cap Rate). The capitalization rate for a property is determined by dividing the property's net operating income by its purchase price. Higher cap rates indicate higher returns and greater perceived risk.

Carried Interest. The North American Securities Administrators' Association, Inc. (NASAA) defines a carried interest in the "Real Estate Programs" section of its Statements of Policy as an equity interest (other than a "promotional interest") that participates in all allocations and distributions and for which full consideration is neither paid nor to be paid. A syndication in which the syndicator receives a carried interest is a "no load" offering.[10]

Carrying Costs. Costs incurred by a property owner (such as interest, insurance, and property taxes) to hold or "carry" the property.

Cash Available for Distribution (CAD).[11] A measure of an entity's ability to generate cash and to distribute dividends to its shareholders. CAD, also referred to as funds available for distribution (FAD), is derived by subtracting nonrecurring expenditures from AFFO.

Cash Flow Mortgage. A mortgage under which the payments to the lender are limited to cash flow generated by rental income from the property. The mortgage does not have a stated interest rate.

Certificate of Occupancy. A certificate issued by a local governmental body stating that the building is in a condition to be occupied.

Closing. The act of transferring ownership of a property (legal title) from seller to buyer.

Collateral. Property pledged as security, generally for a loan.

Common Area Maintenance Costs (CAM). Amounts charged to tenants for expenses to maintain common areas.

Common Areas. Areas of a property used by all property owners or tenants, such as the parking lot of a shopping center, recreational areas in a condominium development, or hallways and stairs of an apartment building.

Common Costs. Costs that relate to two or more units (or phases) within a real estate project.[12]

Conditional Asset Retirement Obligation. A legal obligation to perform an asset retirement activity in which the timing and (or) method of settlement are conditional on a future event that may or may not be within the control of the entity.[13]

---

8   FAS 13, paragraph 5
9   SOP 92-1, paragraph 6
10   SOP 92-1, footnote 1
11   Different definitions of CAD exist.
12   Adapted from FASB Statement No. 67, Glossary
13   FIN 47, paragraph 3

Condominium. Ownership of a divided interest in a multiunit structure, combined with joint ownership of common areas. Each individual owner may sell or encumber his/her own unit.

Contingent Rentals. The increases or decreases in lease payments that result from changes occurring subsequent to the inception of the lease in the factors (other than the passage of time) on which lease payments are based.[14]

Continuing Investment. Amounts paid by the buyer (subsequent to the initial investment) on debt related to the purchase of real estate.

Continuing Involvement. A seller's involvement with a property after it is sold that results in retention of risks or rewards of ownership.[15]

Contract-for-Deed. A purchase contract by which the seller agrees to convey title to the purchaser at some future point, when the purchaser has paid a specified portion of the purchase price. The transfer of title may not be dependent on other factors or contingencies.[16]

Contribution-Leaseback. The contribution of real estate to an entity in exchange for an equity interest in that entity, with the transferor entering into a lease arrangement for the contributed property.

Corporate Joint Venture. A corporation owned and operated by a small group of businesses (the "joint venturers") as a separate and specific business or project for the mutual benefit of the members of the group. A government may also be a member of the group. The purpose of a corporate joint venture frequently is to share risks and rewards in developing a new market, product, or technology; to combine complementary technological knowledge; or to pool resources in developing production or other facilities. A corporate joint venture also usually provides an arrangement under which each joint venturer may participate, directly or indirectly, in the overall management of the joint venture. Joint venturers thus have an interest or relationship other than as passive investors. An entity that is a subsidiary of one of the "joint venturers" is not a corporate joint venture. The ownership of a corporate joint venture seldom changes, and its stock is usually not traded publicly. A minority public ownership, however, does not preclude a corporation from being a corporate joint venture.[17]

Cost Recovery Method. A method of recognizing profit from the sale of real estate. Under the cost recovery method, no profit is recognized until cash payments by the buyer, including principal and interest on debt due to the seller and on existing debt assumed by the buyer, exceed the seller's cost of the property sold. The receivable less profits not recognized should not exceed what the value of the depreciated property would have been if the property had not been sold.[18]

Costs Incurred to Rent Real Estate Projects. Examples of such costs include costs of model units and their furnishings, rental facilities, semipermanent signs, rental brochures, advertising, "grand openings," and rental overhead, including rental salaries.[19]

Costs Incurred to Sell Real Estate Projects. Examples of such costs include costs of model units and their furnishings, sales facilities, sales brochures, legal fees for the preparation of prospectuses, semipermanent signs, advertising, "grand openings," and sales overhead including sales salaries.[20]

---

14   FAS 13, paragraph 5(n)
15   FAS 66, paragraph 18
16   SOP 04-2, Glossary
17   APB 18, paragraph 3
18   FAS 66, paragraph 62
19   FAS 67, Glossary
20   FAS 67, Glossary

Debt Service. The sum of principal and interest payments on a loan or other borrowing.

Deed. Written document that conveys title to real property.

Deed Restriction. Clause in a deed that limits the use of real property.

Deferment. The postponement of some or all of a debtor's payment obligations.[21]

Deposit Method. Under the deposit method, no sale is recognized. The seller does not recognize any profit, does not record notes receivable, and continues to report in its financial statements the property and the related existing debt, even if the debt has been assumed by the buyer. Cash received from the buyer is reported as a deposit on the contract.[22]

Downgrade. A transaction under which, as a result of credit concerns, the holder of a time-sharing interval returns the interval to the seller in exchange for a lower-valued interval (and a corresponding reduction in contractual payment obligation). The determination of whether the value is lower is based on a comparison of the sales value of the new interval with the original sales value of the original interval.[23]

DownREIT. A DownREIT's structure is similar to the structure of an UPREIT, but the REIT owns and operates real properties in a DownREIT, rather than holding partnership interests in a partnership that owns and operates the properties.

Easement. A right to use the land of a third party for a specific purpose.

Economic Life of Leased Property. The remaining period during which the property is expected to be economically usable by one or more users, with normal repairs and maintenance, for the purpose for which it was intended at the inception of the lease, without limitation by the lease term.[24]

Economic Penalty in a Lease. See penalty in a lease.

Eminent Domain. The right of a government or governmental entity to acquire property for necessary public use by condemnation. The owner is generally fairly compensated.

Encumbrance. Any third-party right to or interest in land that negatively impacts its value. Encumbrances include outstanding mortgage balances, unpaid taxes, easements, and deed restrictions.

Equity REIT. A REIT that owns, or has an equity interest in, rental real estate, as opposed to a Mortgage REIT, which makes or holds loans or debt securities secured by real estate collateral. See *Real Estate Investment Trust*.

Estimated Residual Value of Leased Property. The estimated fair value of the leased property at the end of the lease term.[25]

Exchange (or Exchange Transaction). Reciprocal transfer between an enterprise and another entity that results in the enterprise's acquiring assets or services or satisfying liabilities by surrendering other assets or services or incurring other obligations.[26]

Executory Costs. Certain costs that are incurred in connection with leased property, such as insurance, maintenance, and taxes. Executory costs are excluded from minimum lease payments.[27]

---

21   SOP 04-2, Glossary
22   FAS 66, paragraph 66
23   SOP 04-2, Glossary
24   FAS 13, paragraph 5(g)
25   FAS 13, paragraph 5(h)
26   APB 29, paragraph 3(c)
27   FAS 13, paragraph 5(j)

FAD. See *Funds Available for Distribution.*

Fair Value of Leased Property. The price that would be received to sell the property in an orderly transaction between market participants at the measurement date. Market participants are buyers and sellers that are independent of the reporting entity, that is, they are not related parties at the measurement date.[28]

Fee Simple. The absolute right of ownership to real property.

FFO. See *Funds from Operations.*

First Mortgage. A first mortgage (also referred to as senior mortgage) is a mortgage that has priority over all other mortgages. In the case of foreclosure, the first mortgage is satisfied before other mortgages.

Fiscal Funding Clause. A clause commonly found in a lease agreement in which the lessee is a governmental unit. A fiscal funding clause generally provides that the lease is cancelable if the legislature or other funding authority does not appropriate the funds necessary for the governmental unit to fulfill its obligations under the lease agreement.[29]

Fixture. An item of personal property attached to real property. A fixture becomes part of the real property.

Flip Transactions. Transactions in which syndicators acquire ownership interests and resell them to the partnerships shortly thereafter.[30]

Foreclosure. The process by which a lender sells property securing a loan in order to repay the loan in the event of the debtor's default.

Full Accrual Method. The full accrual method (also referred to as accrual method) provides for profit recognition on the sale of real estate in full, once certain specified criteria in FASB Statement No. 66 are met.

Funds Available for Distribution (FAD). See *Cash Available for Distribution.*

Funds from Operations (FFO). Net income (determined in accordance with U.S. GAAP), adjusted for gains or losses from the sales of real property and real estate depreciation.

General Partnership. A general partnership is an entity formed by agreement between two or more parties to operate a business venture in which the owners of the entity (general partners) are jointly and severally liable for the obligations of the entity.[31]

GPM. See *Graduated Payment Mortgage.*

Graduated Payment Mortgage (GPM). A flexible-payment mortgage where the payments increase for a specified period of time and then level off.

Gross Leasable Area (GLA). The total amount of leasable space in a real estate property. See *Net Leasable Area.*

Ground Lease. A rental agreement for the use of land.

Holding Costs. See *Carrying Costs.*

Hybrid REIT. A REIT that combines the investment strategies of both an Equity REIT and a Mortgage REIT. See *Real Estate Investment Trust.*

---

28   FAS 13, paragraph 5
29   FTB 79-10, paragraph 2
30   SOP 92-1, paragraph 6
31   AICPA Issues Paper, *Joint Venture Accounting*, Definition of Terms

Incentive. A product or service that the seller of a time-sharing interval provides to the buyer for stated compensation (often, for no compensation) that is less than the fair value of that product or service. See also *Inducement.*[32]

Incidental Operations. Revenue-producing activities engaged in during the holding or development period to reduce the cost of developing the property for its intended use, as distinguished from activities designed to generate a profit or a return from the use of the property.[33]

Incremental Borrowing Rate. See *Lessee's Incremental Borrowing Rate.*

Incremental Costs of Incidental Operations. Costs that would not be incurred except in relation to the conduct of incidental operations. Interest, taxes, insurance, security, and similar costs that would be incurred during the development of a real estate project regardless of whether incidental operations were conducted are not incremental costs.[34]

Incremental Revenues from Incidental Operations. Revenues that would not be produced except in the relation to the conduct of incidental operations.[35]

Indirect Project Costs. Costs incurred after the acquisition of real estate property, such as construction administration (for example, the costs associated with a field office at a project site and the administrative personnel that staff the office), legal fees, and various office costs, that clearly relate to projects under development or construction. Examples of office costs that may be considered indirect project costs are cost accounting, design, and other departments providing services that are clearly related to real estate projects.[36]

Inducement. A product or service that a time-share seller provides to a potential buyer for stated compensation (often, no compensation) that is less than the fair value of the product or service. The differences between an inducement and an incentive are the condition for receipt and the timing of the offer. An inducement is offered to potential buyers regardless of whether a consummated sale occurs, whereas an incentive is typically offered at the point of sale and is provided only to buyers of time-sharing intervals.[37]

Initial Direct Costs. Initial direct costs are costs incurred by the lessor that are (1) costs to originate a lease incurred in transactions with independent third parties that (a) result directly from and are essential to acquire that lease and (b) would not have been incurred had that leasing transaction not occurred and (2) certain costs directly related to specified activities performed by the lessor for that lease.[38]

Initial Investment. Consideration paid by the buyer at the time a sale is recognized, pursuant to FASB Statement No. 66. Included in a buyer's initial investment are only: (a) cash paid as down payment, (b) the buyer's notes supported by irrevocable letters of credit from an independent established lending institution, (c) payments by the buyer to third parties to reduce existing indebtedness on the property, and (d) other amounts paid by the buyer that are part of the sales value.[39]

---

32   SOP 04-2, Glossary
33   FAS 67, Glossary
34   FAS 67, Glossary
35   FAS 67, Glossary
36   FAS 67, Glossary
37   SOP 04-2, Glossary
38   FAS 13, paragraph 5(m)
39   FAS 66, paragraph 9

Installment Method. A method of recognizing profit on the sale of real estate. The installment method apportions each cash receipt and principal payment by the buyer on debt assumed between cost recovered and profit. The apportionment is in the same ratio as total cost and total profit bear to the sales value.[40]

Insured Mortgage. See *Mortgage Insurance.*

Investment Property. Property (land, or a building, or part of a building, or both) held (by the owner or by the lessee under a finance lease) to earn rentals or for capital appreciation or both, rather than for:

- Use in the production or supply of goods or services or for administrative purposes
- Sale in the ordinary course of business[41]

Integral Equipment. See *Property Improvements and Integral Equipment.*

Interest-only Mortgage. A loan under which the principal amount borrowed is paid back in one balloon payment at the time of the maturity of the loan. During the time the loan is outstanding, the borrower is obligated to make only interest payments on the amount borrowed.

Interest Rate Implicit in the Lease. The discount rate that, when applied to (1) the minimum lease payments, excluding that portion of the payments representing executory costs to be paid by the lessor, together with any profit thereon, and (2) the unguaranteed residual value accruing to the benefit of the lessor, causes the aggregate present value at the beginning of the lease term to be equal to the fair value of the leased property to the lessor at the inception of the lease, minus any investment tax credit retained by the lessor and expected to be realized by the lessor.[42]

Interval (Time-Sharing Interval). The specific period (generally, a specific week) during the year that a time-sharing unit is specified by agreement to be available for occupancy by a particular party.[43]

Joint Control. Joint control is used to describe a situation in which the major decisions relating to an entity require the approval of all of the owners.[44]

Joint Tenancy. Undivided interest in property that passes to the surviving joint tenant upon death of one of the joint tenants.

Joint Venture. An arrangement whereby two or more parties (the venturers) jointly control a specific business undertaking and contribute resources towards its accomplishment. The life of the joint venture is limited to that of the undertaking, which may be of short- or long-term duration depending on the circumstances. A distinctive feature of a joint venture is that the relationship between the venturers is governed by an agreement (usually in writing) which establishes joint control. Decisions in all areas essential to the accomplishment of a joint venture require the consent of the venturers, as provided by the agreement; none of the individual venturers is in a position to unilaterally control the venture. This feature of joint control distinguishes investments in joint ventures from investments in other enterprises where control of decisions is related to the proportion of voting interest held.[45]

---

40   FAS 66, paragraph 56
41   IAS 40, paragraph 5
42   FAS 13, paragraph 5(k)
43   SOP 04-2, Glossary
44   AICPA Issues Paper, *Joint Venture Accounting*, Definition of Terms
45   Canadian Institute of Chartered Accountants (CICA) Handbook, Section 3055; AICPA Issues Paper, *Joint Venture Accounting*, Definition of Terms

Junior Mortgage. Mortgage of lesser priority than another mortgage that is already recorded.

Key Money. Money paid to an existing tenant who assigns a lease to a new tenant where the rent is below market. In some parts of the world, it is used synonymously with security deposits.

Lease. An agreement conveying the right to use property, plant, or equipment (land and/or depreciable assets), usually for a stated period of time.[46]

Lease Commencement. Lease commencement marks the beginning of the lease term.

Lease Inception. The date of the lease agreement or commitment, if earlier. For purposes of this definition, a commitment should be in writing, signed by the parties in interest to the transaction, and should specifically set forth the principal provisions of the transaction. If any of the principal provisions are yet to be negotiated, such a preliminary agreement or commitment does not qualify for purposes of this definition.[47]

Lease Term. The fixed noncancelable term of the lease plus all periods covered by bargain renewal options; all periods for which failure to renew the lease imposes a penalty on the lessee in such amount that a renewal appears, at the inception of the lease, to be reasonably assured; all periods covered by ordinary renewal options during which a guarantee by the lessee of the lessor's debt directly or indirectly related to the leased property is expected to be in effect or a loan from the lessee to the lessor directly or indirectly related to the leased property is expected to be outstanding; all periods covered by ordinary renewal options preceding the date as of which a bargain purchase option is exercisable; and all periods representing renewals or extensions of the lease at the lessor's option. However, in no case does the lease term extend beyond the date a bargain purchase option becomes exercisable. A lease that is cancelable only upon the occurrence of some remote contingency, only with the permission of the lessor, only if the lessee enters into a new lease with the same lessor, or only if the lessee incurs a penalty in such amount that continuation of the lease appears, at inception, reasonably assured shall be considered "noncancelable" for purposes of this definition.[48]

Leaseback. An arrangement whereby the seller of a property leases all or part of the same property back from the buyer.

Leasehold Improvement. Improvements or personal property attached to leased real property, which generally become part of the real estate. Cabinets, light fixtures, and carpets are examples of leasehold improvements.

Lessee. A lessee is the party to a lease that has the right to use leased property.

Lessee's Incremental Borrowing Rate. The rate that, at the inception of the lease, the lessee would have incurred to borrow over a similar term the funds necessary to purchase the leased asset.[49]

Lessor. A lessor is the party to a lease that grants the right to use leased property.

Leveraged Lease. A leveraged lease is a direct financing lease that meets certain criteria. It involves at least three parties: a lessee, a long-term creditor, and a lessor. The financing, which provides the lessor with substantial "leverage" in the transaction, is nonrecourse as to the general credit of the lessor. The lessor's net investment declines during the early years once the investment has been completed and rises during the later years of the lease before its final elimination.[50]

Like-Kind Exchange. An exchange of real property for other real property that meets the criteria of Section 1031 of the Internal Revenue Code.

---

46   FAS 13, paragraph 1
47   FAS 13, paragraph 5(b)
48   FAS 13, paragraph 5(f)
49   FAS 13, paragraph 5(l)
50   FAS 13, paragraph 42

Limited Partnership. An entity formed by agreement by two or more parties to operate a business venture in which one or more of the parties are general partners and have unlimited liability for the obligations of the entity and one or more parties are limited partners whose liability for the obligations of the entity is limited to their investment.[51]

Master Limited Partnership (MLP). Partnership in which interests are publicly traded. Most MLPs are formed from assets in existing businesses. Typically, the general partner of the MLP is affiliated with the existing business.[52]

Mineral Rights. Mineral rights are legal rights to explore, extract, and retain at least a portion of the benefits from mineral deposits.[53]

Minimum Lease Payments (from the standpoint of the lessee). The payments that the lessee is obligated to make or can be required to make in connection with the leased property. A guarantee by the lessee of the lessor's debt and the lessee's obligation to pay (apart from the rental payments) executory costs such as insurance, maintenance, and taxes in connection with the leased property are excluded. If the lease contains a bargain purchase option, only the minimum rental payments over the lease term and the payments called for by the bargain purchase option are included in the minimum lease payments.

Minimum lease payments include:

- The minimum rental payments called over the lease term
- Any guarantee by the lessee of the residual value at the expiration of the lease term, whether or not payment of the guarantee constitutes a purchase of the leased property
- Any payment that the lessee must make or can be required to make upon failure to renew or extend the lease at the expiration of the lease term, whether or not the payment would constitute a purchase of the leased property[54]

Minimum Lease Payments (from the standpoint of the lessor). Minimum lease payments (from the standpoint of the lessor) equal the minimum lease payments from the standpoint of the lessee, plus any guarantee of residual value or of rental payments beyond the lease term by a third party unrelated to either the lessee or the lessor, provided the third party is financially capable of discharging the obligations that may arise from the guarantee.[55]

Money-over-Money Lease Transaction. A money-over-money lease transaction exists when an enterprise manufactures or purchases an asset, leases the asset to a lessee, and obtains nonrecourse financing in excess of the asset's cost using the leased asset and the future lease rentals as collateral.[56]

Monetary Assets and Liabilities. Monetary assets and liabilities are assets and liabilities with amounts that are fixed in terms of units of currency by contract or otherwise. Examples are short- or long-term accounts and notes receivable in cash, and short- or long-term accounts and notes payable in cash.[57]

Mortgage. A pledge of real estate as security for the repayment of a loan.

Mortgage Insurance. Insurance obtained, generally purchased by a borrower, that will indemnify the lender in case of foreclosure.

---

51 AICPA Issues Paper, *Joint Venture Accounting*, Definition of Terms
52 EITF Issue No. 87-21
53 EITF Issue No. 04-2, paragraph 5
54 FAS 13, paragraph 5(j)
55 FAS 13, paragraph 5(j)
56 FTB 88-1
57 APB 29, paragraph 3(a)

Mortgage REIT. A REIT that makes or holds loans or debt securities that are secured by real estate collateral. See *Real Estate Investment Trust*.

Mortgage Release Price. A specified amount that has to be paid to a lender to get real property, such as a parcel of land, released from a lien.

Mortgagee. A lender that receives a pledge of real estate as security for the repayment of a loan.

Mortgagor. A borrower that pledges real estate to secure a loan or assure performance of an obligation.

NAREIT. The National Association of Real Estate Investment Trusts, the REIT industry's trade association.

Negative Amortization. Occurs when monthly payments are not large enough to pay all of the interest due on a loan. The unpaid interest is added to the unpaid principal balance of the loan.

Net Leasable Area. Leasable area that excludes common areas (including space for heating, cooling, and maintenance equipment of a building).

Net Lease. A lease whereby the tenant pays certain operating expenses. The types of operating expenses to be paid by the tenant are agreed upon between landlord and tenant. See also *Triple Net Lease*.

No Load Offering. See *Carried Interest*.

Nominal Interest Rate. Rate of interest stated in a loan agreement.

Nonmonetary Assets and Liabilities. Assets and liabilities other than monetary ones. Examples include inventories; investments in common stocks; property, plant and equipment; and liabilities for rent collected in advance.[58]

Nonreciprocal Transfer. Transfer of assets or services in one direction, either from an enterprise to its owners (whether or not in exchange for their ownership interests) or another entity, or from owners or another entity to the enterprise. An entity's reacquisition of its outstanding stock is an example of a nonreciprocal transfer.[59]

Nonrecourse Debt. Debt that does not grant the lender recourse against the borrower or any assets of the borrower other than the property pledged as collateral.

Nonrecourse Financing. Lending or borrowing activities in which the creditor does not have general recourse to the debtor but rather has recourse only to the property used for collateral in the transaction or other specific property.[60]

Note. See *Promissory Note*.

Operating Segments. Components of an enterprise about which separate financial information is available that is evaluated regularly by the chief operating decision maker in deciding how to allocate resources and in assessing performance.[61]

Organization Costs. Costs of setting up and organizing a new entity.[62]

Participating Mortgage. A mortgage loan that allows the lender to participate in the appreciation of the market value of the mortgaged real estate project, its results of operations, or both.[63]

---

58   APB 29, paragraph 3(b)
59   APB 29, paragraph 3(d)
60   FAS 98, Glossary
61   FAS 131, Summary
62   SOP 98-5, paragraph 5
63   SOP 97-1, paragraph 5

Penalty in a Lease. Any requirement that is imposed or can be imposed on the lessee by the lease agreement or by factors outside the lease agreement to disburse cash, incur or assume a liability, perform services, surrender or transfer an asset or rights to an asset, or otherwise forego an economic benefit or suffer an economic detriment.[64]

Percentage-of-Completion Method. A method of recognizing sale and profit on real estate sales if the seller has not completed improvements or facilities relating to the sold property that are significant in relation to total costs. The amount of revenue recognized is measured by the relationship of costs already incurred to total estimated costs to be incurred. The portion of revenue related to costs not yet incurred is recognized as the costs are incurred.[65]

Personal Property. All property other than real property.

Phase. A parcel of land on which units are to be constructed concurrently.[66]

Points (in Time-Sharing Transactions). Purchased vacation credits that a buyer may redeem for occupancy at various sites. The number of points redeemed depends on such factors as unit type and size, site location, and season.[67]

Preacquisition Costs. Costs related to a property that are incurred for the express purpose of, but prior to, obtaining that property. Examples of preacquisition costs may be costs of surveying, zoning or traffic studies, or payments to obtain an option on the property.[68]

Project Costs. Costs clearly associated with the acquisition, development, and construction of a real estate project.[69]

Project Financing Arrangement. The financing of a major capital project in which the lender looks principally to the cash flows and earnings of the project as the source of funds for repayment and to the assets of the project as collateral for the loan. The general credit of the project entity is usually not a significant factor, either because the entity is a corporation without other assets or because the financing is without direct recourse to the owner(s) of the entity.[70]

Promissory Note. A written unsecured note promising to pay a specified amount of money on demand, transferable to a third party. Also referred to as *Note*.

Property Improvements and Integral Equipment. Any physical structure or equipment attached to the real estate that cannot be removed and used separately without incurring significant cost.[71]

Proportionate or *Pro Rata* Consolidation. Proportionate or *pro rata* consolidation is a method of accounting for investments in which the investor's proportionate interest in the assets, liabilities, revenues, and expenses of the investee are combined with each item of the corresponding elements of the investor's financial statements without distinguishing the amounts.[72]

Quitclaim Deed. A deed conveying title to real property by which the grantor transfers whatever interest it had without any warranties, guarantees, or obligations.

---

64   FAS 13, paragraph 5(o)
65   FAS 66, paragraph 73
66   FAS 67, Glossary
67   SOP 04-2, Glossary
68   FAS 67, Glossary
69   FAS 67, Glossary
70   FAS 47, paragraph 23
71   FIN 43, paragraph 2
72   AICPA Issues Paper, *Joint Venture Accounting*, Definition of Terms

Real Estate. For purposes of FASB Statement No. 66, real estate encompasses land and land with property improvements or integral equipment.

Real Estate Investment Trust (REIT). A company that meets certain requirements established by the Internal Revenue Code. No federal income tax is paid by the REIT on distributed net income. See *Equity REIT* and *Mortgage REIT*.

Recourse Loan. A loan that grants the lender recourse against the general credit of the borrower in addition to any collateral.

Reduced Profit Method. A method of recognizing profit on the sale of real estate that may be used when the buyer's initial continuing investment does not meet the requirements in FASB Statement No. 66.[73]

Refinancing. Obtaining a new loan and paying off an existing loan.

Refund Period. The period of time after the real estate sales contract has been executed during which the buyer may cancel the contract and be entitled to the refund of all consideration paid.[74]

REIT. See *Real Estate Investment Trust.*

Relative Fair Value before Construction. The fair value of each land parcel in a real estate project in relation to the fair value of the other parcels in the project, exclusive of value added by on-site development and construction activities.[75]

Release Provision. An agreement between lender and borrower that upon the payment of a specific sum of money, a real estate property, such as a parcel of land, will be released from a lien. See *Mortgage Release Price*.

Relative Sales Value Method. A method of allocating inventory cost and determining cost of sales relating to real estate sales.[76]

Reload. A time-sharing transaction whereby a customer obtains a second time-sharing interval from the same seller but does not relinquish the right to the first—for example, obtaining an interval or additional points.[77]

Rescission. Statutory right of the buyer to cancel a sales contract within a certain defined time period and obtain a return of all consideration paid to the seller. See also *Refund Period*.[78]

Residual Value of Leased Property. The fair value of the leased property at the end of the lease term.[79]

Retail Land Sales. Retail land sales are sales of lots that are subdivisions of large tracts of land on a volume basis. They are characterized by down payments so small that local financial institutions would not loan money on the property at market rates or purchase the buyer's note for the remaining purchase price without a substantial discount.[80]

Right of First Refusal. A right to purchase property on the same terms and conditions that a third party has offered to the seller.

Sale-Leaseback. An arrangement in which the owner sells a property and leases the property (or part of the property) back from the buyer.

---

73   FAS 66, paragraph 23
74   SOP 04-2, Glossary
75   FAS 67, Glossary
76   FAS 67, paragraph 11(b)
77   SOP 04-2, Glossary
78   SOP 04-2, Glossary
79   FAS 13, paragraph 5(h)
80   FAS 66, paragraph 100

Sale-Leaseback Accounting. A method of accounting for a sale-leaseback transaction in which the seller-lessee records the sale, removes all property and related liabilities from its balance sheet, recognizes gain or loss from the sale, and classifies the leaseback in accordance with FASB Statement No. 13.[81]

Sales Value. Sales value of real estate sold is determined by adding to the stated sales price payments (which are, in substance, additional sales proceeds) and subtracting from the stated sales price a discount to reduce the receivable to its present value, and by the net present value of services that the seller commits to perform without compensation or by the net present value of the services in excess of the compensation that will be received.[82]

Securities Placement Fees. See *Syndication Fees.*

Senior Mortgage. See *First Mortgage.*

Specific Performance. A legal action in which a court rules that a party to a contract must perform under the terms of the contract.

Start-Up Costs. One-time activities related to opening a new facility, introducing a new product or service, conducting business in a new territory, conducting business with a new class of customer or beneficiary, initiating a process in an existing facility, or commencing a new operation. Start-up activities include activities related to organizing a new entity.[83]

Syndication Activities. Efforts to directly or indirectly sponsor the formation of entities that acquire interests in real estate by raising funds from investors. As consideration for their investments, the investors receive ownership or other financial interests in the sponsored entities. All general partners in syndicated partnerships are deemed to perform syndication activities.[84]

Syndication (or Securities-Placement) Fees. Compensation, including commissions and reimbursement of expenses, for selling debt or equity interests in partnerships. Such fees are generally paid in cash, notes, or partnership interests.[85]

Syndicators. Entities that perform real estate syndication activities, regardless of whether their primary business is related to real estate.[86]

Synthetic Lease. A synthetic lease is a hybrid financing arrangement that has characteristics of both lease financing and traditional debt financing. A synthetic lease is a leasing transaction that is structured to meet the operating lease tests of FASB Statement No. 13, while being treated as a financing for tax purposes. This structure results in the lessee achieving off-balance sheet treatment for financial accounting purposes, while retaining the tax benefits of ownership.

Take-or-Pay Contract. An agreement between a purchaser and a seller that provides for the purchaser to pay specified amounts periodically in return for products or services. The purchaser must make specified minimum payments, even if it does not take delivery of the contracted products or services.[87]

Tenancy-in-Common. An ownership of real estate by two or more parties, each of which has an undivided interest without the right of survivorship. Upon the death of one of the owners, the ownership share of the decedent is passed to the party or parties designated in the decedent's will.

---

81   FAS 98, Glossary
82   FAS 66, paragraph 7
83   SOP 98-5, paragraph 5
84   SOP 92-1, paragraph 6
85   SOP 92-1, paragraph 6
86   SOP 92-1, paragraph 3
87   FAS 47, paragraph 23

Throughput Contract. An agreement between a shipper (processor) and the owner of a transportation facility (such as an oil or natural gas pipeline or a ship) or a manufacturing facility that provides for the shipper (processor) to pay specified amounts periodically in return for the transportation (processing) of a product. The shipper (processor) is obligated to provide specified minimum quantities to be transported (processed) in each period and is required to make cash payments even if it does not provide the contracted quantities.[88]

Time-Sharing. An arrangement in which a seller sells or conveys the right to occupy a dwelling unit for specified periods in the future. Forms of time-sharing arrangements include, but are not limited to, fixed and floating time, interval ownership, undivided interests, points programs, vacation clubs, right-to-use arrangements such as tenancy-for-years arrangements, and arrangements involving special-purpose entities (SPEs).[89]

Time-Sharing Interest. See *Interval*.[90]

Triple Net Lease. A type of lease that requires the tenant to pay its *pro rata* share of all recurring maintenance and operating costs of the property, such as utilities, property taxes, and insurance. The landlord receives a net rent payment.

Umbrella Partnership Real Estate Investment Trust (UPREIT). Partners of existing real estate partnerships and a REIT become partners in a partnership (the Operating Partnership) that holds the real estate properties. The partners of the existing partnerships contribute properties to the Operating Partnership in exchange for equity interests ("Units") in the Operating Partnership, and the REIT contributes cash. The REIT typically is the general partner and majority owner of the Operating Partnership. See *Real Estate Investment Trust*.

Undivided Interest. An ownership right to property that is shared among co-owners, with no one co-owner having exclusive rights to any portion of the property.

Unguaranteed Residual Value. The estimated residual value of the leased property, exclusive of any portion guaranteed by the lessee or by a third party unrelated to the lessor.[91]

Unincorporated Joint Venture. An unincorporated joint venture is an unincorporated entity having the characteristics ascribed to a joint venture entity.[92]

Upgrade. A time-sharing transaction whereby a customer relinquishes the right to a currently held time-sharing interval and obtains a higher-priced time-sharing interval from the same seller.[93]

Vacation Club (Affinity Program). A time-sharing arrangement whereby a buyer receives the right to use accommodations at all resorts belonging to the club. Membership may include a priority reservation right to the member's home resort. Other typical attributes include finite term of membership; use of points to obtain accommodations or other benefits; the privilege of being able to use different kinds of lodging, such as time-sharing units, condominiums, hotels, and campgrounds; the privilege of being able to exchange one's yearly interval for cruises, hotel stays, airline tickets, or car rentals; and benefits other than lodging, such as travel services, hotel discounts, golf packages, or health club memberships.[94]

Warranty Deed. A deed conveying title to a property with a warranty of clear marketable title.

---

88   FAS 47, paragraph 23
89   SOP 04-2, Glossary
90   SOP 04-2, Glossary
91   FAS 13, paragraph 5(i)
92   AICPA Issues Paper, *Joint Venture Accounting*, Definition of Terms
93   SOP 04-2, Glossary
94   SOP 04-2, Glossary

Wrap-Around Mortgage. A mortgage that includes in its balance an underlying mortgage. Rather than having distinct and separate first and second mortgages, a wrap-around mortgage includes both the first and the second mortgage.

Wrap Lease Transaction. A wrap lease transaction exists in the following situation: An enterprise purchases an asset, leases the asset to a lessee, obtains nonrecourse financing using the lease rentals or the lease rentals and the leased asset as collateral, sells the asset subject to the lease and the nonrecourse debt to a third-party investor, and leases the asset back while remaining the substantive principal lessor under the original lease.[95]

---

95 FTB 88-1; EITF Issue No. 87-7

INDEX

A